T0279915

THE ZELENSKY EFFECT

NEW PERSPECTIVES ON EASTERN EUROPE AND EURASIA

The states of Eastern Europe and Eurasia are once again at the centre of global attention, particularly following Russia's 2022 full-scale invasion of Ukraine. But media coverage can only do so much in providing the necessary context to make sense of fast-moving developments. The books in this series provide original, engaging and timely perspectives on Eastern Europe and Eurasia for a general readership. Written by experts on—and from—these states, the books in the series cover an eclectic range of cutting-edge topics relating to politics, history, culture, economics and society. The series is originated by Hurst, with titles co-published or distributed in North America by Oxford University Press, New York.

Series editor: Dr Ben Noble—Associate Professor of Russian Politics at University College London and Associate Fellow at Chatham House

OLGA ONUCH
HENRY E. HALE

The Zelensky Effect

Oxford University Press is a department of the University of Oxford. It furthers the University's objective of excellence in research, scholarship, and education by publishing worldwide.

Oxford New York
Auckland Cape Town Dar es Salaam Hong Kong Karachi
Kuala Lumpur Madrid Melbourne Mexico City Nairobi
New Delhi Shanghai Taipei Toronto

With offices in
Argentina Austria Brazil Chile Czech Republic France Greece
Guatemala Hungary Italy Japan Poland Portugal Singapore
South Korea Switzerland Thailand Turkey Ukraine Vietnam

Published in the United States of America by
Oxford University Press
198 Madison Avenue, New York, NY 10016

Library of Congress Cataloging-in-Publication Data is available
Olga Onuch and Henry E. Hale.
The Zelensky Effect.
ISBN: 9780197684511

Printed in the United Kingdom on acid-free paper
by Bell and Bain Ltd, Glasgow

CONTENTS

ACKNOWLEDGMENTS

It has long been a cliché to say that writing a book requires the backing of a whole village, and by now it is even clichéd to observe that this particular cliché happens to be true. Far be it from us to let the village go un-thanked just because it has become clichéd. In our case, the "village" includes not only individuals but a robust set of scholarly networks, institutions, and, most importantly, a country.

The country is, of course, Ukraine. We thank all ordinary Ukrainians for inspiring our research for decades. Your strong sense of civic duty and identity, as well as your constant willingness to mobilize en masse when your lives and futures are at stake, lie at the heart of the nation that gave birth to and nurtured the man at the center of our story, Volodymyr Zelensky. But while our book bears his name, it is more fundamentally about his country, about the people who made the man and co-produced the leadership that he has shown in the dark days since February 2022, when Russia launched its full-scale invasion. This means *all Ukrainians*. You have fought for Ukrainian democracy and sovereignty for decades and you continue that fight today. And to those Ukrainians currently living under occupation, your resilience and sense of civic duty are awe-inspiring—Kherson is Ukraine, Donetsk is Ukraine, Luhansk is Ukraine, Zaporizhzhya is Ukraine, and Crimea is Ukraine!

Among the individuals in our village, we would first single out our families: Miles, Mirka, Yuri, Isabelle, and, yes, even Yara, Blanche, and Stella. All put up with burdens neither of us had intended to impose on them during the writing of this book. Without their unconditional love and understanding, as well as the insights they have shared as we discussed our project in progress with them, there would be no book. Many dear friends have also listened to us ramble on about our research, and the fascinating (to us, at least!) conversations that followed have often given us pause and helped us improve our analysis. We mention in particular Olesya, Taras, Irka, Marta, Yuliya, and Sasha. With our own friends and, in Olga's case, family in harm's way, we also give special thanks to others who provided support through some of the hardest periods of 2022, including Carol, Sorana, Laurence, Jen, Katie, Anna, Maria, Miriam, Evrim, Jane, Orest, Vitalik, and Zsofi—they all know how they helped and we thank them.

On the professional side, we would begin by thanking Irina, Katya, and Anna for their outstanding research assistance. To our dear colleagues who discussed the book with us, read related papers, provided feedback on associated presentations, checked our analyses, provided us useful leads or other information, and/or have been understanding when we have been distracted from other joint projects, we are extremely grateful. While not all may agree with everything we have argued, we would name here Volodymyr Kulyk, Gwendolyn Sasse, David Doyle, Mark Beissinger, Graeme Robertson, Grigore Pop-Eleches, Bryn Rosenfeld, Jane Green, Javier Pérez-Sandoval, Tymofiy Brik, Irina Soboleva, Tanya Lokot, Emily Channell-Justice, Tamara Martsenyuk, Erik Wibbels, Ernesto Calvo, Joshua Tucker, Lucan Way, Samuel Green, Tomila Lankina, Oxana Shevel, Maria Popova, Emma Mateo, Nadiya Kravets, and Timothy Colton. We also express our gratitude to the numerous insiders and other interlocutors who have shared their insights about Ukraine with us this year and long before—without them we would not know much that we do today.

Certain scholarly networks and projects have also been invaluable forums for the development of our ideas. Immensely important has been the MOBILISE project "family," including country principal investigators and co-investigators David Doyle, Evelyn Ersanilli, Gwendolyn Sasse, Sorana Toma, and Jacquelien Van Stekelenburg, as well as postdoctoral researchers Javier Pérez-Sandoval, Anna Glew, Felipe Gonzalez-Santos, Sébastien Michiels, and Piotr Goldstein, and PhD students and PhD research assistants Astrid Bodini, Kostyantyn Fedorenko, Emma Mateo, Ana Martinez, Alex Josid, Alina Nychyk, Cressida Arkwright, and Kateryna Marina. Exchanges through PONARS Eurasia have also been especially important, with special thanks going to all who participated in its March 2022 round-the-clock *Ukrainathon*, which featured an early presentation of our Zelensky Effect idea and generated crucially important feedback. Special mention also goes out to our co-investigators in two projects from which we draw data, the Identities and Borders in Flux (IBIF) Ukraine project (Kulyk and Sasse) and the Ukrainian Crisis Elections Panel Survey (UCEPS) project (Colton and Kravets).

Funding that contributed directly to this book has come from many sources, including: the Open Research Area, which funded the MOBILISE project (www.mobiliseproject.com) with Grant Ref ESRC ES/S015213/1; the British Academy, which funded the IBiF Ukraine Project with grant IC4/100280; the U.S. National Science Foundation, which funded the UCEPS project under grant SES-1445194; the George Washington University, through PONARS Eurasia and the Petrach Program on Ukraine at the Elliott School of International Affairs' Institute for European, Russian, and Eurasian Studies (IERES, directed by Marlene Laruelle); the Harvard Ukrainian Research Institute

(HURI); ZOiS; the Ukraine Research Fund; and the OUP John Fell Fund.

We additionally thank and acknowledge the long list of entities that have made publicly available data we have used in our project (ESS, Rating Group, DIF, PEW, SMaPP Lab, Polity, V-Dem, World Bank, and Freedom House, among many others). Here we are particularly indebted to our longtime partners in Kyiv at the Kyiv International Institute of Sociology (KIIS). We have been working with KIIS for many years, and this is because Nataliya Kharchenko, Volodymyr Paniotto, and their whole team epitomize professionalism and scientific rigor. They have collaborated with us on the framing, phrasing, and structure of our surveys and have shared their own data with us to allow us to cover more in this book than we otherwise could have. Eugene Ilenko and Nataliya replied to countless e-mails when bombs were falling in Kyiv. We will never forget their bravery and we want the world to know of their deep commitment to science and knowledge. None of our research would have been possible without this particular partnership. May we be able to keep working together for years to come!

Naturally, we are also deeply grateful to our primary editors—Michael Dwyer and David McBride—for believing in the project, for prodding us to produce it in a timely way, for carefully guiding us through the publication process, and for providing all kinds of input that has improved the book along the way together with their outstanding teams. Warm thanks also go to Ben Noble for including our book in the new series he is curating. We also express our appreciation to three anonymous reviewers for their feedback, which also helped us produce the best book we could within the time frame available. Of course, here we should make clear that the views expressed in our book are ours alone, not those of any other individual or institution or funder, and that we alone bear responsibility for any shortcomings.

Finally, to our friends and family currently in Ukraine—Olesyu, Alevtyno, Olyu, Volodymyre, Tymofiyu, Natliyu, Serhiyu, Vadyme, Yuliye, Olezhe, Oleksandre, Mykhayile, Andriyu, Bohdane—may you stay safe and may you stay strong. We dedicate this book to you. *Vse Bude Ukrayina! Ukrayina Peremozhe! Heroyam Slava!*

NOTE ON TRANSLITERATION

Throughout this book we follow the BGN/PCGN 1965 System—used by the UK and US governments and the United Nations—for the transliteration/romanization of names and places from the original Ukrainian (and, for some sources, Russian). We make two sets of exceptions to this rule. First, for readability, we drop ' and " in Ukrainian words that appear in the main text. Second, we adopt globally popularized spellings that deviate from this pattern in two instances: "Kyiv" and "Zelensky." In going with "Kyiv," we adopt common usage and the Ukrainian state's preferred spelling. According to the BGN/PCGN 1965 System, Volodymyr Zelensky's surname should be spelled "Zelens'kyy," and his own spelling would render it "Zelenskyy," but at the urging of our publishers we defer to dominant worldwide English-language usage and go with "Zelensky."

BGN/PCGN 1965 System

The United States Board on Geographic Names (BGN) and the Permanent Committee on Geographical Names for British Official Use (PCGN) system:

Ukrainian	*Romanisation*	*Ukrainian*	*Romanisation*
А	a	Н	n

Б	b	О	o
В	v	П	p
Г	h	Р	r
Ґ	g	С	s
Д	d	Т	t
Е	e	У	u
Є	ye/je	Ф	f
Ж	zh	Х	kh
З	z	Ц	Ts
И	y	Ч	Ch
І	i	Ш	Sh
Ї	yi/ji	Щ	Shch
Й	y/j	Ю	yu/ju
К	k	Я	ya/ja
Л	l	Ь	’
М	m	’	”

N.B.: The character sequences зг, кг, сг, тс, and цг may be romanised **z-h**, **k-h**, **s-h**, **t-s**, and **ts-h**.

Ukrainian poet Lina Kostenko celebrates her birthday on March 19. I sincerely congratulate you. On behalf of all Ukrainians I will remind you of her words today: There is no need to think meagerly…

—Volodymyr Zelensky, reciting Lina Kostenko, 20 March 2022[1]

Citizens of Ukraine. What do we hear today? It's not just rocket explosions, battles, the roar of aircraft. It is the sound of a new Iron Curtain lowering and closing Russia away from the civilized world. Our national task is to make this curtain pass not through our Ukrainian territory, but at the home of Russians. The Ukrainian army, our border guards, police, and special services stopped the enemy's attacks. In the language of conflict, this can be called an operational pause....

... What can Ukrainians do? Help the national defense. Join the ranks of the Armed Forces of Ukraine and territorial defense units. Any citizen with combat experience will now be useful. It is up to you and all of us whether the enemy will be able to advance further into the territory of our independent state. Please help the volunteer community and the medical system, for example by donating blood. Politicians and community leaders—help people, ensure normal life on the ground as much as possible. Everyone should take care of their loved ones and take care of those neighbors or acquaintances who need it. The duty of journalists, an important duty, is to defend democracy and freedom in Ukraine.

I spoke today with many leaders—the United Kingdom, Turkey, France, Germany, the EU, the United States, Sweden, Romania, Poland, Austria, and others. If you, dear European leaders, dear world leaders, leaders of the free world, do not help us today, then tomorrow the war will knock on your door. Glory to the Armed Forces of Ukraine! Glory to Ukraine!

—Volodymyr Zelensky, 24 February 2022[2]

1

GLOBAL HERO

A few ticks of the clock past 2 am in the Ukrainian capital Kyiv, Russia issues a NOTAM, military speak for "notice to airmen." This one is unusual. It warns all civilian flights to leave Ukrainian airspace. Within seconds, international flights change their routes to avoid Ukraine, and a few private flights that had just taken off have to return to the tarmac. A US Air Force reconnaissance flight makes its way out of the country's airspace. Ukraine's own airborne surveillance still circles along the northern and eastern borders. The radar screen is now empty. It is 24 February 2022.

To those in the know, these flight path changes signaled something very grave. Russia had begun a full-scale invasion of Ukraine. If President Volodymyr Zelensky was indeed asleep as some have reported, this was surely when his team woke him up. We doubt he actually slept, at least very well. Because on the 23rd, he tried to call Vladimir Putin, and the Russian president refused even to pick up the phone. Ukraine's fate already seemed clear.

Attempting to speak to the Russian population over Putin's head, Zelensky immediately issued a last-ditch appeal in Russian.

This was, after all, his native tongue, the language he used most often in his private and business life before becoming president. He had even worked for six years in Russia and had a certain measure of fame there, so he knew its people well and many knew him.[3] He hoped they might understand:

> You have been told this flame will bring liberation to Ukraine's people. But the Ukrainian people are free. They remember their own past and will build their own future. They build, they do not destroy, as they themselves have told you day after day on television. The Ukraine in your news and the Ukraine of real life are two entirely different places, and the difference is that the latter is real ... Who will suffer the most from this? People. Who does not want this more than anyone? People. Who can prevent this? People ... I know that they will not show this appeal of mine on Russian television. But the citizens of Russia must see it. They must know the truth. And the truth is that this needs to stop, before it is too late. And if the Russian leadership does not want to sit down at the table with us for the sake of peace, then, perhaps, they will sit down at the table with you ... Do Russians want war? I would very much like to answer this question. But the answer depends only on you, the citizens of the Russian Federation.[4]

It was to no avail. The invasion was here, and many ordinary Russians were going to support it in rather large numbers. Zelensky knew what these first events meant. What had previously been unimaginable to many ordinary Ukrainians was about to become a tragic reality. A peaceful European country was being militarily assaulted by its neighbor, and thousands would now die. To those of us watching from abroad, especially those with the deepest personal connections, the big questions were sometimes small ones. Should Olga, one of this book's authors watching from her Manchester flat, wake up her friend Olesya in Kyiv or her Aunt Olya in Lviv to tell them Russia was about to bomb Ukraine, or should she give them a few more minutes of sleep, knowing they would wake up to this nightmare soon enough? In these wee hours of 24 February, Zelensky must also have thought about his wife, Olena, his children, his friends, parents, none of who would be going into the war room with him.

Just past 3:50 am, reports come in that Russian forces have crossed the Crimean checkpoint into Ukraine's southern Kherson oblast (province). At 4:50, Russia releases a prerecorded video. Vladimir Putin is wearing the same tie, shirt, and suit as he did in a video released on 21 February, so we know both videos were part of a planned build-up to the assault. The Russian president did not want to call it the all-out invasion that it was, instead announcing only a "special military operation" in Ukraine. Putin, who has been waging a hot military war with Ukraine over Crimea and parts of the Donetsk and Luhansk oblasts since 2014, had now given the order to bring war to the whole of the country. At 5 am, Russian missiles begin to rain down from east to west, north to south. "Elite" Russian paratroopers try to land in major army bases and airports in key cities. Ground troops made up mostly of very young and inexperienced men from highly impoverished Russian regions, with aging trucks and tanks, start to cross the Russian or Belarusian border into Ukraine's Chernihiv, Kharkiv, Kherson, Kyiv, Sumy, and Zhytomyr oblasts, as well as Ukrainian-controlled Donetsk and Luhansk oblasts.

By now, not only Zelensky but also his family and Ukraine's main political actors know that Russia has invaded. Many are taken to safe locations around Ukraine, sometimes personally taking up arms to protect themselves.

* * *

In the following pages, we explain Ukraine's resistance as a story of both nation and leader. We emphasize what can happen when a president works creatively and consistently to shore up what social scientists call "civic national identity," an inclusive version of who belongs to the nation, and links it to democratic, pro-European, and liberal values. This is not simply Zelensky's doing. In deeper historical perspective, which we address in Chapters 2–4, he himself is a product of a Ukrainian culture steeped in the same sense of civic national belonging and duty that he advocates, advances, and now symbolizes. Herein lies Ukraine's and Ukrainians' success in the fight of their lives. It is also the formula behind what we call the Zelensky Effect.[5]

Ukrainians rise and resist

The whole of Ukraine woke up that morning much like Zelenksy's own family did, either by nearby blasts in their home cities or by frantic calls from loved ones. The experience was nearly identical for all ordinary Ukrainians, our own friends and relatives there included. Even having long known, like Zelensky, that this day could come, they were shocked, overwhelmed with an understandable fear. Yet, they were also suddenly, instantly prepared, ready to fight back and defend what was theirs. In Kyiv, a mother puts her bleary-eyed teenage daughter on a train to the western part of the country for safety—but she stays behind with her husband. They will defend their country, she says, fighting back tears on the phone. A businessman packs his young family into a car to flee Kyiv. His wife and kids drive off, but he turns around, walks to a nearby office, and enlists in the territorial defense. A family of four in Kharkiv rushes to a basement with their beloved dog Shashlik. There, they meet all of their neighbors. Everyone is stoic. They watch video footage intently as villagers in their own home region and in Kherson try to block invading Russian tanks with their bare hands, shouting in Russian "Shame!" and "Go home, we don't need you here!" Like countless other Ukrainians, Onuch's own relatives, in the city of Lviv, opened up their home to strangers fleeing from other parts of the country.

The Ukrainian army also rose to the occasion. With many battalions already secretly in place, the fighters respond to the invasion with precision and speed. They turn out to be far better prepared and more resolute than anyone seemed to expect. On strategic Snake Island in the Black Sea, a small group of Ukrainian soldiers received a demand to surrender from the flagship of Russia's storied Black Sea Fleet, the *Moskva*. In 2014, many Ukrainian units had given in upon receiving such a demand. This time, though, their response was different, captured in a famous audio recording: "Russian ship, go fuck yourself!" This act of bravery in the face of Russia's deadly response is so emblematic of the Ukrainian spirit that it is now immortalized in Internet memes, pop songs, and even a postage stamp. It quickly became clear that Ukrainian citizens—be they military or civilian, Russian- or Ukrainian-speaking, Orthodox or non-Orthodox, western or eastern—were strongly united against the Russian assault, with only a handful of exceptions. They were united in this fight, and even though Zelensky's job approval ratings had declined prior to 2022, suddenly all were fully behind their president. He and they were to defend their country together.

Made of the same stuff as these ordinary Ukrainians, Zelensky famously rejected American offers to evacuate him. Reports emerged that he had even scolded the Americans for suggesting it, uttering the now-legendary words "I need ammunition, not a ride." While some doubts have emerged as to whether he actually said it, what is important is that the line resonated deeply and was adopted by Ukrainians and international media alike.[6]

Zelensky's decision to stand with his country rather than flee is especially remarkable since he was widely believed to have personally been a strategic target of the Russian operation, which aimed to supplant what it called Kyiv's "nazi junta" with Kremlin collaborators. As reputed target number one, with his family being numbers two through four, it is believed he survived from three to more than a dozen assassination attempts.[7] Moreover, Western intelligence, including that of the United States and the UK, believed Kyiv would likely fall within days and told this to Zelensky. Some reports had it that this might happen in seventy-two hours. But to the surprise of many, Zelensky remained in place, demonstrating through personal courage that he had faith in the military, its leadership, and most importantly Ukraine's citizens.

He continued to manage operations and record speeches to his people. Still on 24 February, Zelensky issued a new video from his undisclosed location responding to Putin. The message was that Joe Biden had just called, and "the West is with us." Another announcement declared martial law. Soon, men ages eighteen to sixty would not be able to leave the country. He would make such a recording every day as the war developed, sometimes more than one per day. In Chapter 7, we will analyze over 140 of his appeals in some detail. But in these first twenty-four hours, he set the theme that continued to underlie his message throughout the next months of war. The theme was not new. In fact, it repeats ideas central to the seventy speeches he had given since his election and that had their roots much earlier, not only in his campaign but also in the political satire he had been performing for more than a decade.

The theme was simple. He rallied citizens at home and allies abroad by reminding all of us that Ukrainians are a diverse yet united and dignified nation, a people with a long cultural history and strong sense of civic duty, a factor to which he had long appealed. In their own way, each citizen can, will, and does help the war effort. He stressed that Ukrainians—unlike their enemy—are democrats with European values. He appealed to these values not only among Ukrainians but also among EU members when they stalled on sanctions or military aid.

In his trademark green T-shirt, with phone often in hand, Zelensky made use of social media platforms that are familiar to many ordinary citizens and are where most people spend much of their time. Crucially, this is no longer just the young. The nonagenarian Ukrainian dissident poetess Lina Kostenko, for example, is a regular Facebook user. As in his 2019 election campaign, Zelensky's direct line to the citizenry allowed him and his team to bypass any repackaging of his message and create a powerful, personal connection with many ordinary Ukrainians, augmenting the sense of earnestness he conveyed.

Stardom at home and abroad

Before Russia's 2022 invasion became a reality, hardly anyone would have predicted Zelensky would soon become an international superstar, not to mention an avatar of heroism and bravery. After bringing his country together with a record-breaking landslide win in 2019, his public support had steadily declined to the point that disapproval had come to outweigh approval. Some objective realities explain why. COVID-19 was still ravaging public health, the economy was still struggling, and war was raging in the east of the country. In the West, publics knew very little about Zelensky at all, except perhaps as a curiosity, a "comedian" becoming president. In the United States and much of the world, he became best known for his unwitting embroilment in the impeachment trial of American President Donald Trump, who had tried to pressure the Ukrainian president into announcing a political prosecution by threatening to withhold the military aid Zelensky was urgently requesting.

With the start of the war, all this changed. In Ukraine, his approval ratings skyrocketed to an astounding 93 percent, according to polling by the Rating Group.[8] In the rest of the world, media coverage of his leadership now emphasized themes of bravery and even personal charisma. Western media portrayals of ordinary people changed in the same way. Whereas the country had previously wound up in the international news when some form of corruption scandal would arise, or when a revolution occurred, now ordinary Ukrainians were depicted as courageous, fearless, brave, inspiring, and stoic—that is, as ordinary heroes in tragic and extraordinary times. We have documented that Zelensky gained 5,197,000 new Twitter followers between 24 February and 24 March 2022 (up from just 8,628 followers on 7 May 2019 and 398,000 on 1 February 2022).[9] And thanks to our friends at the Social Media and Political Participation (SMaPP) Lab at NYU who produced some data we discuss in greater detail in Chapter 7, we know that his tweets began being retweeted at a much higher rate while mentions of him shot up to the millions. He was becoming the most talked about figure in the world, even more so than the TV stars and sports figures who tend to dominate attention on social media. Zelensky and his media-savvy team supported all these messages by churning out a steady stream of posts, clips, and memes with high potential to go viral across all social media platforms. As anyone present on TikTok or Instagram knows, this team "understood the assignment." The message got out and was extremely effective: Ukrainians will fight, and its leaders are strong and united. Fortunately for Ukraine, subsequent events tended to validate these claims.

Realizing his ability to rally world audiences, Zelensky began giving inspirational speeches around the globe. He hoped ordinary citizens would pressure their governments to sacrifice more for Ukraine and realize that Ukraine's fight against Russia was the front line of a war against authoritarian governments' ability to spread their own tyranny at will. The degree to which Ukraine's cause has resonated with ordinary people in the West is impressive. It is perhaps the only issue that strongly unites both Republicans and Democrats in the United States and Labour and Conservatives in the UK, with blue-and-yellow Ukrainian flags flying in the front yards of ordinary houses in the reddest of red states and the bluest of blue states in the US, and from north to south in the British Isles—not to mention across Canada, the EU, and beyond. Surely this grassroots support is one reason why the West has shown more resolve than many thought possible prior to the invasion in sanctioning Russia and arming Ukraine.

Resistance Ukrainian style

Ukraine truly stunned the world in rebuffing what had previously seemed like a Russian military juggernaut. UK and US intelligence briefings kept having to use phrases like "it is unlikely that Russia has met its day one/first seventy-two hour/first week/first month military objectives." Instead of being overrun within seventy-two hours, Ukraine won the battle for Kyiv, driving Russian forces into retreat and thereby ensuring Ukraine's continued existence as an independent state.

Perhaps paradoxically, part of Zelensky's leadership success lay in knowing when not to impose his personal leadership on other Ukrainians. Crucially, but not often recognized in adulating media coverage, the president actually took a step back when it came to making military decisions. While as military commander in chief he had the right to issue specific orders, to direct events on the battlefield much like Putin is reported to do, Zelensky instead let Ukraine's generals and battlefield commanders make the decisions they needed to. Zelensky's willingness to trust his commanders resonated well with important military reforms that had been initiated by his predecessor, Petro Poroshenko, and that he himself had deepened: decentralizing military decision-making so that commanders on the ground could alter tactics quickly in response to rapidly changing conditions. This reform also set Ukraine apart from Russia, which retained the more centralized control typical of the former Soviet military. We suspect history will also confirm that this display of faith in Ukraine's top brass increased army morale, another dimension of the Zelensky Effect.

Outside the military, Ukrainians supported the war effort in other ways. One was simply managing to keep doing their jobs in the face of Russia's best efforts to disrupt them, keeping Ukrainian life going and livelihoods afloat. Bus drivers showed up to work, shop clerks opened their doors when they were able. Others intervened directly against the invaders. In cities and villages that were in the direct path of invasion or otherwise came under occupation, we know that elderly people put their own bodies in the way of tanks, that locals took down signs to confuse Russian convoys, that farmers stole Russian military vehicles. Ordinary folk in Donetsk, Kherson, Mykolayiv, and Zaporizhzhya came out to protest occupation when it arrived, and as the *Data for Ukraine* project demonstrates daily, these people continue to resist even as we write.[10] They hang posters and paint graffiti across towns and cities in Kherson and Zaporizhzhya regions and target Russian night patrols.

To assess the extent of such everyday resistance by ordinary Ukrainians, we conducted a survey with a nationally representative sample of the population in May and July 2022. We found that nearly 2 percent said they had taken up arms, 3 percent were participating in civilian resistance, 6 percent were volunteering in the territorial defense, 32 percent were helping in different civil society organizations and grassroots activities, and a whopping 60 percent were giving their own funds to defend their country.[11] Our favorite examples of everyday Ukrainian civilian resistance include making a hearty soup and walking it over to the local army barracks, helping local elderly farmers with their land cultivation, and milking young goats to provide the army with fresh nourishment. These were all impressive displays of what social scientists would call Ukraine's previously underappreciated "social capital."[12] We return to these data in Chapter 7.

Zelensky knew that he had this "44-million army" at his disposal. And the actual Ukrainian army felt the whole population's support personally when they received the fresh local milk and soup. Everyone was defending their state in the only ways they knew how.

By the end of March, under Zelensky's presidency, with his people united and behind him, Ukraine was victorious in the battle for Kyiv, sending the Russian army retreating north to Belarus. This early victory ensured Ukraine's survival as a state and paved the way for further Russian retreats from the eastern cities of Kharkiv and Sumy. The Russian army was forced to completely restructure its invasion plan. Within a month, the Kremlin decided to shift its military focus to Ukraine's east, where its forces did begin making some small territorial gains. Ukraine's biggest loss was arguably the strategically important port city of Mariupol in Donetsk oblast, where Ukrainian forces held out for weeks and nearly to the last man in the bowels of the city's fabled Azovstal steel factory. Russia had tried to take this city in 2014–15 but had been thwarted by fierce local resistance.

Among the major victories in the first months of war was a geopolitical and economic one: Ukraine finally achieved EU candidate status, a widely shared national dream that had started to become official in 1994, twenty-eight years earlier, when parliament declared Ukraine's EU-bound intentions and President Leonid Kuchma signed the EU–Ukraine Partnership and Cooperation Agreement. Our survey data show that by 22 February 2022, 69 percent of the population wanted Ukraine to join the EU.[13] This was also an important victory for Zelensky as a leader, as he had made Ukraine joining the EU a major talking point on his road to becoming president. Even before he announced his candidacy for president, EU aspirations were a central feature of his character's aims on the *Servant of the People* TV show, where he played a fictional president named Vasyl Holoborodko. In fact, we find evidence that he actively led many citizens to this position. Our statistical analysis, further discussed in later chapters, shows that people who voted for his party and who were from his native southeast were 18 percentage points more likely than others to shift to a more pro-EU integration position after he won the presidency in 2019.

Surprise

Different elements of this story proved surprising to different sets of observers. The reasons for this are both situational and systemic. We highlight five situational reasons. First, most in the West and many who opposed Zelensky in 2019 were preoccupied with his political inexperience prior to winning the presidency, frequently using terms like "novice," "neophyte," and even "pretend president."[14] True, he was new to electoral politics as of 2019: he was a comedian, and even called himself a "clown" on occasion—in his trademark ironic tone.[15] As we will argue in Chapters 6–7, too much has been made of his being inexperienced and a former comedian. In fact, we show, he learned rather quickly on the job and was having a surprisingly successful first term as president by Ukrainian standards before Russia's full-on invasion, including passing some key reform policies. Moreover, he may have been new to electoral politics, but he was not new to politics in general, having been a businessman and high-level executive (general producer of the country's most watched television network) who had made a small fortune out of relatively nuanced political satire and media management.

Second, the 2019 election campaigns were rather divisive, leaving their residue on how people saw the resulting winner. The "25-percenters", as many of those 24.4 percent who voted for the incumbent Poroshenko in the May 2019 run-off election came frequently to call themselves, had accused him of being a puppet in Russia's revanchist plot.[16] Poroshenko even hosted a television marathon dedicated to this notion on his own television channels in the run-up to the parliamentary elections in July 2019. All this left Ukrainian society rather divided, if not outright polarized, between the so-called 25-percenters and everyone else. Their discourse at times seemed to separate the country into "true patriots" (or "conscious Ukrainians") and, on the other hand, *homo sovieticus*, people of a Soviet mindset regarded as generally apathetic and sometimes derogatively called *sovoks*. This discursive polarization made it seem to many outsiders in London, DC, Ottawa, Brussels, and Moscow that Zelensky was not a secure political leader—especially when his job approval ratings declined substantially during the COVID-19 pandemic. His credentials were thus sometimes questioned by 25-percenters and other critics even as Russia was on the eve of invading, as in the case of Olga Rudenko's op-ed "The Comedian-Turned-President Is Seriously in Over His Head" that appeared in the *New York Times* on 21 February 2022.[17]

Third, as noted above, Zelensky was best known in the West as the weaker and naïve victim of US President Trump's attempted bullying just weeks into his presidency in the scandal surrounding Trump's impeachment.[18] This would not be a good look for any president, and while he did not wind up giving Trump what he wanted, it did not exactly make him look like a leader who commanded international respect.

To this end, and fourth, the Kremlin used this opportunity to belittle the new president. It is clear the Kremlin did not expect much from Zelensky and assumed that he and his team would be weak and easy to manipulate.[19] Russian Foreign Minister Sergey

Lavrov famously called Zelensky "an unstable and dependent man, directly dependent on his American curators," and "not capable of anything."[20] Putin rarely if ever mentions Zelensky directly but has made clear that he does not see him as an equal. So ingrained was Putin's low opinion of Ukraine's president that even the day after the all-out invasion began, he openly called on the Ukrainian military to "take power into your own hands" and overthrow Zelensky.[21] This Kremlin narrative would be influential where Russian media dominate, though it had clear potential to backfire elsewhere.

Fifth and finally, back home in Ukraine, the president's polls had gone from record-breaking highs just after his 2019 election to steadily declining over the course of 2020 and remained lower throughout 2021 (see Figure 1.1). Going into the invasion, our polling found that only about a third of the Ukrainian population approved of his performance in office. That said, this decline in popularity is a typical phenomenon in Ukraine, and Zelensky's experience with it seemed to follow the trends of almost every previous Ukrainian president. Moreover, he was doing better than his predecessors at the same point in their presidencies, and he had arguably had more crises to deal with. Nonetheless, for many, this created a sense of "here we go again," a feeling that inevitable failure was coming.

Along with these situational reasons, we also see several systemic reasons why people as of 2022 did not expect much from Zelensky and Ukrainians. For one thing, Ukrainian politics follows a certain logic, a logic of "patronalism," that is common throughout much of the world. This term focuses on the importance of networks of actual personal acquaintance in society, networks that tend to have a hierarchical character in that people at the top are well positioned to mobilize people below them for favors, though people at lower levels also typically turn to their "patrons" for help as well. "Patronalism," then, refers to societies in which people organize their political or material pursuits primarily through these personal connections rather than through impersonal institutions with protection by a rule of law. People rely primarily on these connections (including connections developed through personal material exchange or threats) because they believe that everyone else does, that this is simply, if unfortunately, the way things get done. Many of Zelensky's performances over the years are in fact all about exposing (and ridiculing) patronalism as a feature of society and politics, about how even people who might prefer to be honest succumb to pressures to accept or pay a bribe because they are simply resigned to the idea that this is how things work.[22]

One feature of such systems is that the main competitors for power are not simply "parties" or "movements" but extended power networks typically headed by the rich and powerful who frequently use parties and movements for their own ends, be they material, political, or ideological. In highly "patronalistic" polities like Ukraine, things are frequently not what they seem. Parties often claim to be ideological, but instead act more like extensions of their patrons' interests. In Ukraine's case, a central political role has been played by its biggest businesspeople, colloquially called "oligarchs," who fight their political battles through their networks extending from political parties to the media and even the courts. As Zelensky's performances themselves satirize, these oligarchs frequently create new parties seeking to capture shifts that they discern in the public mood, which over time badly erodes the public trust in parties and politics more generally, generating considerable cynicism.[23] In this context, as we will show in Chapters 4–5, observers could be forgiven for thinking that Zelensky's rise was just another "oligarch project," one of the kind that Zelensky himself had skewered for years in his comedy.

Patronal politics frequently comes with high levels of corruption, and Ukraine is no exception to this pattern. Transparency

International (see Figure 1.2) has long placed Ukraine in the bottom quarter of the most corrupt countries in the world, and political scientist Erik Herron has shown that corruption has essentially become normalized there.[24] This does not exclude the possibility of democracy. As Hale has argued elsewhere, for example, Ukraine's 2010 election, judged free and fair by international observers, was nevertheless "a corrupt competition for the hearts, minds, and pocketbooks of voters." But that is the key—in countries like Ukraine, the corrupt entities have to compete for voter support, and the votes are generally counted honestly, ultimately letting voters have their say. In this sense, "Ukraine's path, though highly imperfect, may still be the best near-term democratic option for high-corruption, low-rule-of-law states."[25] Nonetheless, it would be the systemic corruption that, some thought, might make Ukraine weak and vulnerable to Russian aggression. Not least because local state actors could be bought and sold with ease, as they were accustomed to doing business this way. This is, of course, a mistake. For one thing, patronal politics can be a highly effective way of mobilizing people to get things done. For another, people have their limits: while they may be willing to strike corrupt deals to better their lot among their compatriots, this does not mean they will sell out their country for Putin and rule from Moscow. And because patronalism is usually unpopular, there is always a latent public reward for politicians who can convince people of their sincerity.

Second, in the immediate aftermath of its transition from communism, Ukraine was widely seen as having a weak civil society. Several studies by Onuch have shown this is a misconception, one leaving a lasting impact on the lens through which observers have understood ordinary Ukrainians' political engagement.[26] Over the decades, Ukraine did not shake this reputation, though with its citizens organizing multiple moments of mass mobilization, Ukrainians instead gained a reputation as a "protest nation," one able to deliver multiple "revolutionary moments" but never a truly transformative democratic breakthrough.[27] These moments of mass mobilization were frequently seen as "critical junctures," a term coined by political scientists for moments when politics as usual is disrupted and countries at least have the possibility of changing their long-run trajectories, even though Ukrainians usually wound up disappointed.[28] What many observers have missed, though, is that between those moments of mass mobilization there was a growing nationwide pattern of civic engagement in Ukraine, a pattern involving a mutually reinforcing relationship between ordinary citizens' everyday acts of contention and their sense of national identity.[29]

A third systemic reason why Ukraine's 2022 response came as a surprise to some centered on the widespread notion that Ukraine is deeply divided between two halves, sometimes even to the point of claiming there are "two Ukraines."[30] Geographically, these two Ukraines are divided between "West" and "East," one half more ethnically and linguistically Ukrainian, the other with a larger ethnic Russian and Russophone (Russian-speaking) population.[31] One side is more pro-European, the other wants to maintain closer ties to Russia. And the two sides are always, the story goes, voting for different candidates. Indeed, in Ukraine's presidential elections of 2004 and 2010, the electoral line seemed to cut the country in half. Foreign observers, in particular, sometimes thought these aspects were so fully entrenched in Ukrainian society that they took them for granted. They thus repeatedly expected little of the divided Ukrainians and their leaders. But while divided at times electorally, Ukraine is not politically polarized into two halves, either ethnically, linguistically, culturally, or electorally.[32] In fact, our nearly decade-long research on identity and public dispositions in Ukraine shows that although there are relatively small poles at each extreme, there is a big middle ground, and the median voter[33] represents a large coalitional majority. And bread-and-butter issues (economic evaluations, experiences, expectations, and prospects) are more and more often the key dividing lines among ordinary voters—something that Zelensky's campaign spoke to directly and Poroshenko's sidestepped in 2019.

Fourth, and relatedly, there remained lingering doubts in the West (especially among UK, US, German, and French policymakers, but less so among Ukraine experts) about the commitment of southeastern Ukrainians specifically to the idea of Ukraine as an independent state. Their attachment to this independent state was thought to be tepid at best, and at worst rooted in deep local identities like attachment to the Donbas.[34] This impression appears to have come from incorrectly extrapolating certain findings reported in a large volume of studies of Ukrainian politics, society, and identity. These findings show that larger shares of ordinary citizens in these territories—namely Odesa, Mykolayiv, Kherson, Dnipropetrovsk, Donetsk, Luhansk, and Kharkiv oblasts—than in others supported not only stronger ties with Russia but also greater integration with Russia and even Kremlin-sponsored ideas like a "Russian World" uniting all who speak Russian with Moscow.[35] As we show throughout this book, it does not follow that such attitudes mean people actually desire Russian rule and will not stand up for their state.[36] And more generally, the identity politics of Ukraine's southeastern populations is far from simple. It involves a robust civic attachment to Ukraine that nevertheless goes along with a strong sense of economic vulnerability that is linked both to relations with Russia and to distributional politics within Ukraine. Locals frequently saw these issues in particular as putting a premium on having "one of our own people" in charge in Kyiv, even if this "our person" was far from ideal.

Lastly, some expressed concerns that remnants of Soviet generations past remained embedded in Ukraine's security services and army apparatus. It is established fact that the 2014 events in Crimea and then later in Donetsk and Luhansk could not have happened without some local security service and army collaboration. Even if collaborators were a small minority—even if they were singular individuals—their presence and possible ties to Russian secret services again created a systemic weakness, making Ukraine vulnerable. This fear was given credence by UK and US intelligence when they revealed that individuals representatives of the Ukrainian secret services, opposition parties, and various state agencies were involved in Russian plotting of a coup to depose Zelensky in February 2022.[37]

Taken together, these situational and systemic factors would push many observers and policymakers—including in Russia as in the West—to the wrong calculus about the likelihood that Zelensky would prove to be an effective wartime leader, that Ukraine's east and south would fall quickly, that corruption and Soviet-era allegiances would mean Kyiv would be vulnerable to enemies from within, and, finally, that Ukrainian divisions could even come to the surface to further escalate tensions between ethnic and linguistic groups in the country.

As for why this did not happen, our explanation is encapsulated in the idea of the Zelensky Effect.

Our argument

To understand the actions of ordinary Ukrainians and their leader in 2022, it is vital to understand what Zelensky represents. First and foremost, we will show, Zelensky embodies civic Ukrainian national identity. And as a Russian-speaker of Jewish heritage from the country's industrial southeastern heartland, few were better positioned than him to understand how "The Divide" in Ukraine is a kind of myth, based on a dichotomous rendering of certain statistics that obscures the middle ground into which he tapped. Having come of age after Ukraine became an independent state, he is like many people in Ukraine's southeast who spoke Russian and might have been derided as *sovoks* but became more politically engaged and patriotic in their daily lives. They rejected the idea there was one way of being a "good patriotic Ukrainian." Seeing direct benefits from European integration and democratic consolidation, they were also very frustrated by the lack of progress on this path and their people's continued poverty.

We find three clusters of political science concepts helpful in understanding these dynamics. We introduce each of them now, as they frame the central argument and analysis in our book.

Civic national identity and democratic civic duty

Civic national identity means that people identify strongly with their country not because it represents any specific ethnic, linguistic, or religious group but because it represents an inclusive vision of the citizenry as a whole.[38] Strong national identification means they see the nation as important for their life chances, the set of opportunities they have and will have long into the future to pursue what they define as a good life.[39] As goes Ukraine, so go the fortunes of all citizens within it—at least to some degree.[40] This notion of all Ukrainians being in the same boat can be quite powerful, in particular fostering a sense that each member of the nation has a duty to the others, a sense of national duty. And because the duty is to all citizens, not any ethnolinguistic group, it is a sense of civic duty. Everyone in the nation has a duty, at a minimum, to be a "good citizen."

Each country has its own sense of what it means to be a good citizen. Those who focus on it have in mind something much more than flag-waving, which scholars have called demonstrative or symbolic patriotism.[41] Perhaps the most basic civic duty is simply to engage in the politics of their state, to do what one can to help it improve the lot of fellow citizens.[42] Not widely recognized, but as we show in Chapter 2, Ukraine's versions of civic identity and duty build on a long history of civic activism. This includes several key moments of mass mobilization, not only in recent years but also pre-dating its independence. And because of its long history as a battleground for would-be conquerors, Ukrainian civic national identity is also tied tightly to a quest for liberation from them, its quest for independence. Since World War II, the threat has come primarily from Moscow.

Social scientists have documented that civic national identity has been on the rise since Ukraine gained independence in 1991.[43] Our Kyiv-based friend and sometimes co-author Volodymyr Kulyk has made some of the strongest contributions here. Most recently, he has shown that over the last two decades, Ukrainian citizens' attachment to the state has dramatically strengthened across ethnolinguistic divides.[44] This has gone along with what he calls a "shedding of Russianness" in Ukraine since 2014. This means that when given opportunities to identify themselves to others, Ukrainians have become more and more reluctant to identify with categories linking them to Russia, in particular Russian nationality. People whose parents once held Soviet passports categorizing them as "Russian" but who were born in Ukraine, for example, might now consider themselves simply Ukrainian by nationality.[45] Prior work by Onuch has also shown that joining the massive Orange Revolution and Euromaidan mass mobilizations was powerfully linked to having strong senses of civic national identity and democratic duty.[46] As we will show later in this volume, this sense of civic duty continued to grow after the Euromaidan and during Zelensky's presidency (see Figures 1.3 and 1.4).

Rally effects

In politics, "rallying around the flag" (or simply "rallying") occurs when people set aside their prior political differences to back a national leader in the face of a crisis, resulting in a surge in that leader's mass support.[47] Typically, the crisis is an international conflict, though rallying can also occur in the face of other threats to the nation. For years, social scientists mainly debated whether these surges resulted mostly from rising senses of patriotism sparked by the crisis or instead from media and politicians refraining from criticizing the leader during the crisis.[48] More recently, however, researchers have come to see rallying as a much more complicated phenomenon. For one thing, as Hale has documented in the case of Russia, rallying can sometimes be insincere: people may not actually approve of what the leader is doing in the crisis but refrain from saying so because they do not want to appear unpatriotic.[49] Others may simply be going with the flow, supporting the leader just because they see other people doing so, perhaps figuring that so many others must be right or perhaps simply wanting to be part of a powerful collective experience.[50]

We build on this new direction in the study of rallying, showing how many people can come to support a leader for a wide variety of reasons. In particular, we join a strand of this research emphasizing the importance of national identity in underpinning such rallying.[51] Drawing on extensive public opinion research and other evidence, our analysis shows how the surge of support for Zelensky tapped into the civic Ukrainian identity we have been discussing, but that identity had this effect for a complex array of reasons that could vary from individual to individual. The 25-percenters, we argue, have had a particularly complicated relationship with Zelensky even as they rally strongly to his leadership in war.

Generational effects

This brings us to the third social science concept we invoke here, that of generational differences in political behavior. We do not delve here into the rich array of studies on why some generations appear to behave differently from previous ones, debates that consider the influence of everything from age itself to the particular experiences of different cohorts to the development of new ideas and forms of consciousness.[52] What many of these theories have in common is what interests us here: the idea that socialization occurring at a particularly important time in one's childhood or young adulthood can have long-term implications for how people engage the political world throughout their lives.[53]

In particular, we argue that there is an important sense in which Zelensky represents not simply his country or his home region but a set of perspectives and attitudes common to many people we call the "Independence Generation." The Independence Generation consists of those Ukrainians who came of age politically in an independent Ukraine. Now in their late thirties and forties, they were born under communism (between 1975 and 1985—or thereabouts), and although children at the time of Ukrainian independence, they have personal memories of it. They were old enough to understand what was happening at the time and its significance but were too young to engage in the changes and transition in any meaningful manner. They also—and crucially—share vivid personal memories of the mayhem and crises of the 1990s that followed.

We center our analysis of Zelensky's upbringing and coming of age on this idea. We argue that it is first and foremost the Independence Generation, more than the younger ones, that came to form the backbone of Ukraine's sense of civic national identity and sense of democratic civic duty as we see it playing out across Ukraine today.

The Zelensky Effect

Perhaps paradoxically, therefore, Volodymyr Zelensky is a Ukrainian everyperson in a way few others could or, crucially, dared to be. We write "dared" because at the same time that he laid out a patriotic and Europe-oriented vision for Ukraine, he did not shy away from his Russian language (even if he switched to Ukrainian for official duties), did not apologize for his southeastern Ukrainianess, did not paper over his proclivity for *sovok* jokes. Instead, he embraced, embodied, and most importantly of all affirmed the Ukrainianness of the country's vast majority. This was a civic Ukrainianess, coming with a proud sense of state attachment and civic duty. It was a vision in which elites and oligarchs were not the only ones to blame for the country's corruption, and in which not all problems could be blamed on Russia's bloody aggression, but in which ordinary people also had to bear a measure of responsibility when they did not engage, did not live up to their civic national duty. This could be a difficult message to hear, but it caught on under his leadership.

Ultimately, we argue that all this made Zelensky a particularly dangerous leader for Putin and his narrative that Ukraine was an artificial state captured by a "nazi junta" propped up by American force. A Russophone from the southeast of the country, and of Jewish origins no less, Zelensky was just the kind of person that Russian forces thought would not really care enough about the Ukrainian idea to fight and die for it. So, when Ukrainians rose up en masse, symbolized by their president, it undercut the Kremlin's story like nothing else could have done. Sadly, Putin and his minions realized all this too late, if they have yet realized it at all. Ukraine's train had long ago left the Russian imperial station, and there was no turning back.

Roadmap for the book

We structure this book around several critical junctures in Ukraine's history as experienced by Zelensky and the Independence Generation. Chapters 2 and 3 examine the aftermath of two such junctures, the USSR's 1991 collapse and the 2003 Orange Revolution, in the process covering Zelensky's childhood and early adulthood. Here the book addresses the rise of civic national identity and the pervasiveness of patronalism in Ukraine and makes clear that some Ukrainians rallied to the Ukrainian state's cause sooner than others. In Chapter 3 in particular, we cover the rise of Zelensky's career—from university student studying law with hopes of being a diplomat to producer of the most watched Ukrainian network and famous actor with a media empire of his own to president. Chapter 4 then takes us from the next critical juncture, the 2013–14 Euromaidan mass mobilization and the first stage of Russia's invasion, through the Poroshenko presidency to the eve of Ukraine's 2019 presidential election campaign. Here we learn how someone playing a president on TV became a leading contender for the real thing. In Chapters 5 and 6, we explore what arguably became another critical juncture in Ukraine's history, Zelensky's election and presidency. Chapter 5 focuses on his electoral campaign and his innovative—and probably completely unique—strategy of running as a "virtual incumbent." In Chapter 6, we examine Zelensky's presidency prior to 24 February 2022, while Chapter 7 assesses his wartime leadership. Here we analyze in detail the content of his speeches and the dispositions of Ukrainian citizens to understand the current context as best as we can. Finally, in Chapter 8, we look to the future. Throughout, we provide a nuanced analysis of the content of Zelensky's *Kvartal 95* concert performances and *Servant of the People* television series, which wind up yielding considerable insight into the Zelensky Effect at the core of our account.

* * *

The sources we draw on to answer these questions and address these themes are numerous, and for those who are interested, we provide full details about methodologies employed, data analyzed, and analyses cited in an online appendix at www.zelensky-effect.com. Here we lay out the four broad types of data and sources we used and how we analyzed them.

First, we employed extensive qualitative data and conducted detailed discourse and content analysis of the following: Kvartal 95 skits and songs (in original language); *Servant of the People* television series transcripts (in original language as well as translations); all available (at the time of writing) transcripts of President Zelensky's official speeches in both Ukrainian and English translations; all Ukrainian presidents' inaugural addresses (in original Ukrainian and English translation); key war speeches by Vladimir Putin, his letter from July 2021, and interviews/press conferences where he mentions Zelensky; the top ten pages of articles mentioning Zelensky during the 2019 electoral campaign and separately during all of 2019 using the Google news search function (covering all English-language articles that appear in the first ten pages of the search); the 2019 presidential debate and electoral campaign documentation; and his and First Lady Olena Zelenska's Instagram and Twitter posts, as well as Facebook content. To analyze some of these data, we employ NVivo software.

Second, we conducted descriptive quantitative analyses using data from the Central Electoral Commission, Ukrainian State Statistics/Census, World Bank, Transparency International, Polity, V-Dem, Freedom House, the Television Industry Committee (TIC), SMaPP Lab Data (Twitter open API), and

Data for Ukraine. To analyze some of these data, we employed GIS software GeoDa in order to map the data geospatially.

Third, we conducted quantitative descriptive and regression analyses employing nationally representative data from eleven surveys comprising data from four projects that we lead: EuroMaidan Protest Participant Survey (EPPS, 2013/14), Ukraine Crisis Election Panel Survey (UCEPS, 2014), MOBILISE Project (2019–22), and Identities and Borders in Flux: Ukraine (IBIF, 2020–1). In addition to these nationally representative survey data, we also utilize secondary survey data from the European Social Survey, Kyiv International Institute for Sociology (KIIS), the Razumkov Center, and Rating Group. We are particularly grateful for the help provided by our colleagues from KIIS: Nataliya Kharchenko, Volodymyr Paniotto, and Eugene Ilenko, who have been extremely helpful in providing extra data to us from the KIIS omnibus survey series.

We conducted limited but in our view key interviews with individuals close to or in the administration, business contacts, and journalists who have followed Zelensky's career (and are part of the Independence Generation). We also engaged many of our regular informants and colleagues on whom we have relied for our research in Ukraine for many years. We spoke to interlocutors under Chatham House Rules, which involve anonymity. As this is a wartime context, we feel this is not only appropriate but also warranted under our obligations to ensure our informants' safety.

We also accessed hundreds of secondary articles, scholarly works, and documents that we cite as and when appropriate.

Finally, we also use our own personal experiences, interactions, and field notes. We hope that these personal reflections and field-based experiences provide extra color and nuance to the data we rely on in the book. We love data, but we hope we struck the right mix of detailed empirical analysis and more personal reflection that come together following years of research on identity, mobilization, and the Zelensky Effect in Ukraine, and many months of preparation for writing this particular book.

We recommend our readers listen to “Dopomozhe ZSU” (“The Army Will Help”)
By Chiko, Qutoshi
Found on the “Top Songs Ukraine” Playlist on Spotify
https://open.spotify.com/track/5mGns7qagKDzP4L2YC5ea2

Javelin on the maximum
Orcs will get what they should
I left on a tractor
And returned with some tanks
Don't ask where I got them
I will not return them
Better take them in to the field
And donate them to the ARMY

—Authors' own translation

I will remind you of her words today:
"Immortality is still here ..."

—Volodymyr Zelensky, reciting Lina Kostenko, 20 March 2022[1]

Glory to the Armed Forces of Ukraine!

Men and women, our defenders!

You are brilliantly defending the country from one of the most powerful countries in the world.

Today Russia attacked the entire territory of our state. And today our defenders have done a lot.

They defended almost the entire territory of Ukraine, which suffered direct blows. They regain the one that the enemy managed to occupy. For example, Hostomel near Kyiv. This gives more confidence to the capital …

… But now the fate of the country depends entirely on our army, on our heroes, our security forces, all our defenders. And on our people, your wisdom and the great support of all friends of our country.

Glory to Ukraine!

—Volodymyr Zelensky, Wartime Speech, 24 February 2022[2]

Mathematics is valued as a science. That's all very fine. But history, as you said, is dog shit? Then we wonder why our politicians make the same mistakes when they enter the halls of power? Because they're great mathematicians! All they know is to divide and subtract. That's all! . . . I tell you this as a teacher of history.

—Vasyl Holoborodko, *Servant of the People*, Season 1, Episode 1[3]

2

THE INDEPENDENCE GENERATION

Who was Zelensky before he became the Zelensky we see today? This question is central, because our argument is not that the man made the country, but that the country made the man. The key to understanding Volodymyr Zelensky, including his motivations and his successes and failures, can be found first and foremost by looking at what it was like for ordinary people in newly independent Ukraine, the setting for his childhood and early adulthood. This was a time when politics and economics were a kind of free-for-all for the country's emergent patronal political networks, a period when more senior generations found creative ways to convert privileged Soviet-era positions into profit and power, creating a new post-Soviet reality. But while the well connected were realizing unprecedented opportunity and upward mobility, ordinary Ukrainians struggled just to make ends meet. This generational experience of the 1990s and 2000s shaped Zelensky profoundly, yielding the repertoire of cultural references and insights that facilitated his ability to connect with audiences through his satire and, later, his political activities and wartime leadership.

This is the experience of Ukraine's Independence Generation. At the time we are writing this, members of this generation are in their late thirties and forties, bear a living memory of childhood life under communism, and well recall the long queues and empty shelves. They also likely recall 1986. This year would stand out not for Gorbachev's announcement of *glasnost* (opening) and *perestroika* (restructuring). Instead, this was the year of the deadly nuclear disaster at a plant in Chornobyl (known more widely by the Russian name Chernobyl), just 90 kilometers north of Kyiv in Ukraine. When the danger finally became known, parents took their children to the mountains or the sea to flee the fallout. Onuch was one such child in Poland who was taken to the mountains and given iodine; some of her friends from Kyiv and other cities in Ukraine were not so lucky. A few years later, children living in big cities may have witnessed firsthand Ukraine's university student movement for independence, protests organized by the grassroots nationalist movement *Rukh* ("the movement"), and then what later became called the Revolution on the Granite, a moment of mass mobilization spanning several months in 1990–1.[4] The workers' strikes that shook the country in the final days of communist rule surely made an impression as well, as would have the "Human Chain" uniting Ukrainians east to west during the same period.[5] This generation is also old enough to have been consciously aware of the independence referendum on 1 December 1991, when 84 percent of Ukrainian voters came together to register a 92 percent vote in favor of independence from the USSR. They generally know that all of Ukraine's regions voted in favor, even the Crimean peninsula, which Russia later annexed. This is a moment Ukrainians frequently pause to remember, as did Zelensky when marking Ukraine's Independence Day in 2021:

> Fellow citizens!
>
> On this holiday, we must remember thanks to whom we can be here. These are our defenders of Ukraine. Defenders of our independence. Heroes who gave their lives for it!

Let's honor their bright memory with a moment of silence!

[A moment of silence]

They died for the future of our children and grandchildren.

We are sure that they will definitely celebrate the 130th anniversary of Ukraine's independence and the thousandth anniversary of our state's independence here.

To do this, let's remember the past, act today, think about the future.

—Volodymyr Zelensky, thirtieth anniversary of Ukrainian independence, 24 August 2021[6]

Onuch, now a child in Toronto whose family had fled Communist Poland, remembers the announcement of the referendum results perfectly. Her family called relatives back home—not easily done in 1991—with Baba Melania and Dido Yaroslav overwhelmed by tears of joy. Onuch was then dressed up in a yellow and blue hat, scarf, and gloves and taken to a square in the city center to celebrate. In Lviv by the Taras Shevchenko statue, in Kyiv on the Maidan, and in other gathering places in Warsaw and Toronto, her relatives stood in the cold and sang the national anthem: "Still, Ukraine's glory and it's freedom has not yet died, Fate will still smile on us brother Ukrainians." Those living in Ukraine—like Sasha from Odesa, Antonina from Dnipro, Yuliya or Mykola from Kharkiv, Olesya or Yaryna from Lviv, Oleg or Nastya from Kyiv, Oleksiy or Maxim from Donetsk, and Vasyl or Nadiya from Ternopil—also remember this moment of national unity.[7] Some Russophone, some ethnically Russian, but from east to west, they all remember. Some might only remember their family discussing the occasion at the dinner table, but they remember it. Now, they are all, like Zelensky, in their forties or late thirties and leading Ukraine's resistance to Russia's invasion.

Zelensky, who grew up in the "Kvartal 95" (Block 95) neighborhood in the city of Kryvyy Rih in the highly industrialized

Dnipropetrovsk oblast, was to turn fourteen the following month, January 1992. He surely has a vivid memory of the day and the events that followed. Over 90 percent of his home region, which Putin now claims consists primarily of misguided Russians, voted for independence. In his first Independence Day celebrations as president, Zelensky said:

> Today, an entire generation, born in independent Ukraine, has already formed. For them, this is a normal state of affairs. It can't be different for them. And that's wonderful. Because this generation is our mental foothold. Foothold for freedom, democracy, and development. They think differently, they think in a modern way, which means that Ukraine will only move forward.
>
> However, we should not forget that independence did not appear by magic. The active struggle for it began over 100 years ago. It lasted in times of the Soviet Union. Mykola Rudenko, Vasyl Stus, Petro Hryhorenko, Vyacheslav Chornovil, Levko Lukyanenko, participants of the Revolution on Granite. This is an incomplete list of those who fought for independence. Sometimes at the cost of one's freedom, and sometimes at the cost of one's life. For the sake of this one day, 24 August 1991. And this day was inevitable. Because, as Levko Lukyanenko said, the desire for independence is embedded in our genetic code.
>
> —Volodymyr Zelensky, thirtieth anniversary of Ukrainian independence, 24 August 2021[8]

A tradition of dissidence and satire

Zelensky was born in Kryvyy Rih on 25 January 1978, an only child of Oleksandr and Rymma Zelensky, both engineers. One of his grandfathers was Symon Zelensky, a colonel in the Soviet Army and the only member of his family to have survived the Holocaust. Kryvyy Rih, which means "Crooked Horn" in Ukrainian, is the largest city in the region and was a major industrial hub for mining and metallurgy. In 1978, things were slowly collapsing, as in the whole of the USSR,[9] and Ukraine was experiencing one of its worst periods of economic decline. The informal economy, sometimes known as the black market, was the only way to obtain even basic goods.

The year of Zelensky's birth also stood out for extreme levels of political repression. This is because it came just after one of the most vibrant periods of civic activism in Soviet-era Ukraine. The 1956 post-Stalin cultural thaw marked the emergence of a new underground civic Ukrainian activism. The most famous of activists were the so-called "sixtiers" (*shistdesyatnyky*) and included writers, poets, literary critics, and human rights activists. Many were members of the Club of Creative Youth (*Klub Tvorchoyi Molodi*), something that will be important to our story later on, as it appeared around the same time as did the Club of the Funny and Inventive (*Klub Vesyolykh i Nakhodchivykh*, or KVN) in Moscow.[10]

The sixtiers in Ukraine were most famous for their *samvydav* (Ukrainian for *samizdat* or self-published works). Central to this notoriety was a brand of political satire that skewered the experienced realities of communist-era society—which the Communist Party preferred to keep otherwise hidden. In Ukraine, this satire directed its fire at Russian imperial tendencies within the Soviet system, which was supposedly internationalist rather than ethnocentric. Not all dissidents opposed communism per se. Some were in fact themselves ideologically communists but were against how the socialist rhetoric of equality was being used to impose russification upon Ukrainians and more generally to subjugate Ukraine.

Importantly, these Soviet-era dissidents with an acumen for satire hailed from across the whole of the Ukrainian Soviet Socialist Republic, as Ukraine was officially called at the time. Many were not ethnically Ukrainian or even native Ukrainian-speakers, though most wrote in Ukrainian and defended the language in the same breath as their defense of workers' rights. Their texts lambasted authoritarian oppression and included calls for the protection of civic and human rights. Ivan Dzyuba, for example, was born in Donetsk oblast, did not speak Ukrainian until he taught himself in adulthood, and ultimately penned one of the most famous critiques of Russian chauvinism. He was even so bold as to deliver it himself to Party officials. Lina Kostenko also belongs to this tradition. A poetess from the western Ukrainian city of Lviv, family lore has it that she rejected many offers of marriage that would have enabled her to leave the USSR. Instead, she decided to stay and do her civic duty as a Ukrainian, articulating her political critique in verse. Perhaps the most famous of the group was Vyacheslav Chornovil, from Cherkasy oblast in central Ukraine. He co-founded the most influential *samvydav* publication of the era, the anonymous newsletter *Ukrayinskyy Vistnyk* (Ukrainian bulletin, 1970–3)[11] and was a key member of the Helsinki Group—a dissident organization founded to monitor the USSR's compliance with the human rights obligations it had taken on in the 1975 Helsinki Accords—and also led the nationalist movement *Rukh*.[12]

Dissident mobilization in Ukraine peaked in 1965–9 and again in 1976. Zelensky was born during the repressive wave following one such peak. Although casual observers of Ukraine might expect the mobilization and repression to be concentrated in western or even central Ukraine, this was not the case in the 1970s. The number of political arrests in the east was roughly equal to that in the west.[13] The Ukrainian Helsinki Group, a beacon of civic and human rights activism established in 1976, included a founding committee whose home oblasts read like a map of modern Ukraine (see Figure 2.1): Ivan Kandyba from Lviv, Levko Lukyanenko from Chernihiv, Mykola Matusevych from Kyiv, Mykola Rudenko from Donetsk,

Myroslav Marynovych from Lviv, Nadiya Svitlychna from Luhansk, Nina Karavanska from Odesa, Oksana Meshko from Poltava, Oleksa Tykhyy from Donetsk, Oles Berdnyk from Kherson, Petro Hryhorenko from Zaporizhzhya. Their import and influence is so great that decades later many of them were mentioned by Zelensky in his first Independence Day speech as president—as we noted earlier.

So threatened was the Soviet government by this pan-Ukrainian group of activists monitoring its Helsinki Accord compliance that in less than two years, all founding members had either gone into exile or been arrested and handed seven to ten years in prison.[14] By the time Zelensky was five, out of thirty-seven members, twenty-two were in prison and eleven in exile.[15] Not until 1986, when Gorbachev launched *glasnost* and *perestroika* in the wake of the Chornobyl nuclear disaster, were Ukraine's dissidents released from prisons and camps. When they were released, they wasted no time, quickly organizing to push for more reform than Gorbachev was offering and ramping up a long drive for Ukrainian independence. By this time, Zelensky was back in Ukraine after having moved to Mongolia with his family in 1981 for a four-year stint where his father worked as an engineer. In one interview prior to his election, he recalled returning home to industrial Kryvyy Rih in 1985: "I still remember! I returned to Ukraine, to the motherland."[16]

It is important to note that Ukrainian cultural dissidents like Dzyuba, Karavansk, Rudenko, Lukyanenko, and Chornovil strongly supported industrial workers and often wrote about major labor strikes that occurred in Ukraine. Crucially, labor strikes were more prominent in the southeast of the country. In fact, Zelensky's native Dnipropetrovsk oblast was often an epicenter. Of the five largest strikes in 1960–80, three took place there.[17] Aside from strikes, other forms of mass resistance were not unheard of. In 1963, in Zelensky's hometown of Kryvyy Rih, a large protest broke out following a food price hike. The result was one of the most infamous riots in Ukraine. The Kremlin ultimately sent troops in from Moscow to repress the crowd, fearing local militia were not capable or could side with the local protesters.[18] Zelensky's parents undoubtedly remembered this event.

We must be careful not to trace a direct line between this local history and Zelensky's later behavior, but it would be equally naïve to assume that it made no impression on him at all. Zelensky himself claims it did. As president, he frequently mentioned the plight of dissidents and used their words in his speeches to give his messages more weight. For example, he invoked Dzyuba's and Kostenko's words in (respectively) speeches criticizing Russian military escalation in the Donbas on 23 February 2022 and blasting national political actors who were engaging in treason on 20 March.[19] Simply put, in analyzing Zelensky's speeches and skits, as well as the dialogue of the characters he played, one sees a clear pattern of repeatedly referencing cultural dissidents from Ukraine's past and linking them to Ukraine's independence.[20]

More broadly, Ukraine has a long history of civic activism, one that was among the strongest if not the strongest in the USSR.[21] Crucially, the southeast of the country was at the heart of much of this late anti-Soviet contention. Civil resistance was never just a Kyiv-and-western-Ukrainian phenomenon. In the television show that helped make Zelensky famous, *Servant of the People*, the history-teacher-turned-president he played would repeatedly stress how important it is for his students to know their country, to know Ukrainian history. It is tempting to speculate that even the name Vasyl Petrovych Holoborodko (that of the fictional character played by Zelensky) is a nod to Vasyl Ivanovych Holoborodko, a famous Ukrainian poet from the eastern Ukrainian oblast of Luhansk.

The dissident poet Holoborodko was kicked out of university in neighboring Donetsk in 1967 for distributing Dzyuba's forbidden text *Internationalization or Russification?* among its students, and his book of poetry was banned due to his refusal to work with the KGB and only published in 1986. The show's producers and the poet himself, however, say this is a coincidence (Holoborodko being a common name) and the poet has expressed distaste for the program's low-brow humor.[22] Either way, while Zelensky is making history now, his actions themselves build upon a much longer history that has made him who he is and Ukraine what it is today.

Zelensky's home Dnipropetrovsk oblast was certainly not all about dissidence and protest, of course. In fact, with its capital being a closed city where rockets and other sensitive products were designed and manufactured, the region was also the center of major political and criminal networks that emerged in the 1980s and then flourished in the 1990s. Ukraine's second president, Leonid Kuchma, rose out of this milieu, and a striking number of Ukrainian "oligarchs" and future politicians got their start by exploiting the connections they had to Soviet resources there.[23] These include such major figures as Yuliya Tymoshenko, Ihor Kolomoyskyy, Victor Pinchuk, and Serhiy Tihipko, many of whom attended the Dnipropetrovsk Metallurgical Institute.[24] This industrial heartland was a particularly tough place to grow up.

> ... *Have a simple teacher live like a president, and a president live like a teacher!*
>
> —Vasyl Holoborodko, *Servant of the People*, Season 1, Episode 1

Growing up in the Wild East

What did it mean to grow up as part of the Independence Generation in 1990s Ukraine? The period immediately after the

USSR's demise was extremely difficult for ordinary Ukrainians. While Ukraine's territorial sovereignty was a source of national pride, everyday life was marred by uncertainty, conflict, and poverty. The country was poor, poorer than expected, as widespread hopes that Ukraine would quickly rise to Western European levels once Communist exploitation ended were quickly dashed.

Leonid Kravchuk, the erstwhile Communist Party ideologist and former chairman of Ukraine's Supreme Soviet who had become the independent country's first president, had his work cut out for him. The unplanned rupturing of an economy deliberately organized to be dependent on Moscow resulted in chaos. There was little money in the new nation's coffers, and Russia's own economy had become embroiled in galloping inflation and instability, spilling over into Ukraine because the ruble initially remained currency in Ukraine. We conducted a content analysis of Kravchuk's inauguration speech, and as we see from the frequency word cloud in Figure 2.2, in which larger print reflects more frequent mention, the top two issues of priority for Kravchuk were foreign and economic policy, each mentioned twelve times and in the top four words used in the speech as a whole, signifying their import to him. But he would not be as successful in either as he might have hoped.

For ordinary Ukrainians, it became even harder to buy things in stores than it had been in Soviet days. Queues remained long, and people simply did not have money when items were available. Basic goods like toilet paper were in short supply. When we traveled to Kyiv or Lviv, we brought our own. Unemployment skyrocketed from essentially zero to 12 percent by 1999, consumer product inflation reached record highs of 4,784.9 percent by 1993 (declining to 376.7 percent by 1995) (see Figure 2.3), and poverty (measured by the World Bank as a headcount ratio living off only $3.20, 2011 Purchasing Power Parity (PPP)) nearly doubled from 11 percent in 1992 to 19 percent of the population by 1995.[25] Economic decline had many knock-on effects, one of which was the rise of criminal gangs and mafia, which in turn resulted in homicides going up from 5 to 10 per 100,000 between 1990 and 1995.[26] The Ukraine of the 1990s had winners and losers, and most ordinary Ukrainians were decidedly economic losers as of 1995.[27]

With industrial decline and rising unemployment came a new wave of labor strikes across the whole of southeastern Ukraine. Most famously, in 1998 Donbas miners went on strike and marched on Kyiv.[28] They gained support from a broad swath of Ukrainian society following a *Berkut* (special police forces) crackdown in Luhansk and the self-immolation of local miner Oleksandr Mykhalevych.[29] In our research, we have often heard ordinary citizens recall the march on Kyiv as a moment of national unity. The reason is that the Donetsk and Luhansk miners were already widely seen as heroes—many of them had risked their own lives to fight and contain the Chornobyl disaster in 1986. They had also held solidarity strikes with dissidents in the 1960s and 1970s and students in 1991, and thus occupied a particular space in the collective understanding of the national myth. If we flash forward to 2017, Zelensky's Kryvyy Rih witnessed yet another episode of labor unrest at three major enterprises (an iron ore plant, an iron ore mine, and ArcelorMittal Kryvyy Rih, Ukraine's largest steel company).[30] One wonders whether this might have helped nudge him to seek the presidency two years later. We will discuss the episode later, but the Donbas miners also played a key role in the ending to the *Servant of the People* series that was broadcast during the 2019 campaign.

> *Do you think it's acceptable to eat sandwiches with red caviar in Parliament's cafeteria for 12 hryvnyas, when a senior citizen collects pennies … to buy a carton of milk?*
>
> —Vasyl Holoborodko, *Servant of the People*, Season 1, Episode 7

An unsurprising outcome of the economic turmoil was mass emigration. In the first decade of independence, the total population of Ukraine declined by 2.7 million, from 51.8 to 49.1 million.[31] This pattern continued over the decades, and before 24 February 2022 it was estimated that just 43.8 million people resided in the country (see Figure 2.6 on population growth). In Kryvyy Rih, a city hit hard by the uncertainties of transition, the population declined from 705,537 to 673,462 in those early years (see Figure 2.8). By the time Zelensky was elected to the presidency in 2019, the city's population was but 623,894.[32] Working abroad was often a necessity (see Figure 2.5 on unemployment). Zelensky's own father Oleksandr continued to work in Mongolia as an engineer until he returned to Kryvyy Rih National University in 1992, where he was a professor for many years.[33] While "professor" is an impressive title, academia was just as impoverished as the rest of the country. So, while it did position Zelensky in a highly educated milieu, he was just as vulnerable to the country's economic problems as were millions of other Ukrainians (see Figures 2.4 on HIV infections and 2.7 on GDP per capita).

> *Let's imagine an average Ukrainian family that gathers at one table in the evening. Is it happy? No. First, because there are empty chairs at this table.*
>
> *The first chair belongs to the one who is currently defending the country in the east.*
>
> *And for thousands of Ukrainian families, this chair will remain empty forever …*
>
> *The second chair is a wage earner. Yes, he regularly sends money to his family. But is this enough for happiness? His wife, his parents, his child, himself?*
>
> *He himself is a university graduate who picks apples?! And in the fight against poverty, he loses his own dignity.*
>
> *Look at our Ukrainian language: what are the two big differences—poverty (bidnist) and dignity (hidnist). One letter, but what a difference.*

There is a second reason why this family is unhappy. Because those who stayed at the table want to leave it. The first category is grandparents. They receive a meager pension and feel simply useless. They worked for many years and now they could travel the world, as it is in other countries. What do they have in return? A journey from an abandoned polyclinic to an expensive pharmacy.

—Volodymyr Zelensky, 13 September 2019 (authors' translation)[34]

While President Kravchuk struggled to keep the country afloat, he was often perceived as focusing too much on establishing the new country's foreign relations and not paying enough attention to the bread-and-butter issues that were now of more immediate concern to voters (this pattern of behavior would be repeated by several future presidents). He traveled the world opening up embassy after embassy but failed to make headway on economic reforms or building up the rule of law. After a movement to try to recall the president gained steam, the Ukrainian parliament—the Verkhovna Rada or just Rada for short—called early parliamentary elections for March 1994 and early presidential elections to follow in June.

In the 1994 elections, Kravchuk was challenged by his own prime minister, Leonid Kuchma, a "red director" who had previously run the Soviet Union's largest missile factory in Dnipropetrovsk. Both men were deeply embedded in former Communist Party networks. But Kuchma gave the appearance of being a capable reformer with technocratic knowhow. Moreover, Kravchuk played a particularly bad hand. Attempting to cover up his policy failures by playing the ethnic card so as to try to win just over half the country, he criticized Kuchma for being a Russophone representing the country's east and its interests, implying he might just sell Ukraine back to the Russians. But Kuchma, born in central Chernihiv oblast and later having attended the prestigious Dnipropetrovsk National University, replied to his opponent in perfect Ukrainian and said he would be a president for all Ukrainians. He admonished voters not to fall for Kravchuk's attempts at dividing the country to save his career. In the end, Kravchuk lost in a 10 July 1994 runoff to Kuchma, who won 52.3 percent of the vote.[35]

This first election in democratic Ukraine should have come to signify what was arguably most important: Ukraine had accomplished its first peaceful transfer of power through elections. Instead, however, the narrative became one of Ukrainian "East" versus Ukrainian "West," Ukrainophone versus Russophone. The "divided Ukraine" narrative was cast. Many would reach for it in the future as a tool for winning votes or manipulating the electorate to shore up constituencies by scaring them into thinking their rights might be taken away.

But while the discourse was polarizing, closer examination of the electoral map shows less a bimodal divide and more of a spectrum, with a large middle that was nearly evenly split between the candidates. As Figure 2.9 shows, only in the far eastern (darkest) and far western (white) regions did we see one side overwhelming the other. Donbas in the east and Halychyna (Galicia) in the west would become the two constituencies that would be pitted against each other for the next quarter century—in fact, lasting up until Zelenksy's groundbreaking campaign in 2019, which we discuss in another chapter. And as we will see, Zelensky repeatedly criticized such attempts to divide Ukrainians politically.

> *And the language you speak does not matter at all. Leave those primeval mottos behind. Stop dividing the country along east, west, south-north lines. We are one country, we are all Ukrainians. But if we want to remain one country, we have to learn to live as humans, to have at least respect for each other.*
>
> —Vasyl Holoborodko, *Servant of the People*, Season 3, Episode 3

Once elected, Kuchma continued to pursue a Euro-Atlantic course for Ukraine. One move, though, would later give rise to considerable speculation about what might have been. Kuchma's government ultimately succumbed to strong Western pressure and signed what became known as the 5 December 1994 Budapest Memorandum with the United States, United Kingdom, and Russia. In it, Ukraine committed to being a non-nuclear state, and in return the other signatories guaranteed Ukraine's security. Unfortunately for Ukraine, this was not a treaty that came with concrete obligations on the part of the United States or the UK to intervene militarily to defend it. At the time, though, this was not particularly controversial. The need for nuclear weapons seemed remote. From most people's perspective, the government would do better plowing its money into helping improve people's lives. Few imagined that in late 2022, Russian President Vladimir Putin would outwardly threaten the use of nuclear arms and American President Joe Biden would, addressing the UN but speaking to the Russians, say: "Don't do it."

As ordinary Ukrainians were living through the tribulations of the early 1990s, local criminal networks were colluding with political ones and creating opportunities for local political and economic barons to arise. Kryvyy Rih, an industrial city with a hardshell exterior, was no exception. When describing the town of his childhood, Zelensky called it a "gangster city."[36] It was in this context that his parents, because he liked piano, signed him up for Greco-Roman wrestling and weightlifting to toughen him up.[37] And as a teenager, Zelensky, like many of his generation, personally saw the rise of localized crime turned oligarchy through a reliance on personal connections that is typical of patronal politics.

> *Secondly, I am grateful to all the critics of the law. Your remarks are valuable: you have been working with oligarchs for many years, either for oligarchs or under oligarchs, and therefore, you clearly understand all the shortcomings of the law, being, as they say, deep in the material.*
>
> —Volodymyr Zelensky, 4 June 2021[38]

The rise of the oligarchs[39]

The 1990s also marked a period of wild privatization. Privatization was the process of taking state property—almost everything in the communist economy—and putting it into private hands to form the basis of a market economy. But who should become the new private owners? Typically for countries where patronalism is the norm, the answer revolved around personal connections.[40] Individuals with familial ties or other connections to Communist Party networks, or who had access to hidden resources through the black market or criminal and mafia-like endeavors, began deploying them to accumulate the newly available private wealth that the government was now shedding.

This period saw the private takeover of all major gas, oil, metallurgy, coal, and other heavy industry assets in Ukraine, as well as the agribusiness and banking sectors. It was then that key players, still rather young but a generation older than Zelensky, began their rise to prominence in Ukraine's political economy. Zelensky's Dnipropetrovsk was a hotbed of this activity. For instance Tymoshenko, whose father-in-law was a senior Dnipropetrovsk Communist Party official, was part of a so-called "discotech mafia" that brought bootleg Western music and video cassettes to her formerly closed city. She soon shifted to the lucrative energy industry, acquiring the monicker "gas princess" before eventually becoming prime minister and one of Ukraine's most resilient politicians.[41] Kolomoyskyy, eventual owner of the TV channel that aired Zelensky's TV shows, also came from Dnipropetrovsk, where he worked with the region's former Communist Youth League chief (the future big businessman Tihipko) to create what became Pryvat Bank, one of Ukraine's biggest, while in his twenties.[42] Pinchuk founded the energy business Interpipe at age thirty.

Similar processes were going on in other regions with major industrial assets across Ukraine. Next door to Dnipropetrovsk,

Donetsk oblast was also teeming with embryonic oligarchs. There, Rinat Akhmetov began his coal-and-gas empire under the umbrella of his System Capital Management. Some attribute his economic rise to reported organized crime links, though he has vigorously denied this.[53] Regardless, he would soon gain the reputation as the most powerful figure in what some called the "Donetsk clan."[44] In Kyiv, future president and Zelensky rival Petro Poroshenko would get his start at age twenty-seven building up a chocolate empire by trading and supplying coco beans to the still-Soviet chocolate industry in 1991. Poroshenko, Kolomoyskyy, Akhmetov, and others soon added major media assets to their portfolios. Such were the origin stories of the cast of characters widely known today as Ukraine's powerful, behind-the-scenes "oligarchs," figures that would become a source of so much of the popular outrage that Zelensky tapped into when he ran for president.

Political competition started to revolve as much around competing oligarch interests (often called political "clans") as around issues and ideas. This soon extended to elections, which might be described as fierce competitions between rival political machines for voters, battling it out through the media they controlled and the voters they could more directly mobilize through workplace pressure or personalized incentives.[45] This theme was ever present in Zelenksy's political satire, as we find in our content analysis of skits put on by his Kvartal 95 comedy troupe and episodes of his *Servant of the People* series. In fact, the opening scene of the TV series is a dialogue between three such oligarchs filmed from behind while looking out over Kyiv's Independence Square, cocktails in hand but their faces obscured. They negotiate how they will collectively manage Ukraine's upcoming presidential election:

> Oligarch 1: Friends, we didn't gather here for the scenic view.
>
> Oligarch 2: Gentlemen, aren't you tired of pointlessly wasting money? First, we spend millions to bring our candidates to the political forefront, and then we spend twice as much to ruin our competitors.

Oligarch 1: Those are the rules. You want to install your own president? Then back him.

Oligarch 2: Let us be honest with each other for once.[46]

The would-be oligarchs' competition for property and power played out on city streets with weapons far cruder than the mass media. The most violent episodes involved criminal networks that some believed were connected to the rise of some of Ukraine's oligarchs. They were not hidden, occurring in plain sight and daylight. Onuch recalls entering a restaurant where two men were dining with their guns on the table. By the 2000s, the suits got sleeker, but few traveled without their personal bodyguards and always in their armored cars. In certain central Kyiv restaurants, it could be difficult to get seats for a business lunch because the "businessmen" present needed an entire second separate table for their entourage of bodyguards. All while ordinary Ukrainians could find it hard even to make ends meet and were frequently expected to pay bribes to access medical care or education.

So public and so egregious was the behavior of these elites that they almost seemed to be mocking the rest of the population. Dodging luxury cars could be a form of exercise. Yelling at them might provoke the flash of a gun. Every Ukrainian has a story of a policeman stopping their car on the highway for a bribe, just like what happened to the father of Zelensky's fictive president in the first season of *Servant of the People*. Apartments and apartment-building basements could be appropriated by corrupt means and sold off. The basement of the apartment building where Onuch's family lived was sold off like this, meaning that when air-raid sirens sounded in 2022, the building's residents could not shelter there. Seemingly every family had tales to tell of neighbors who had built something illegally or relatives or friends being paid in envelopes.

This is how the Independence Generation grew up. One of Zelensky's biggest strengths throughout his performance career has been in portraying this aspect of social life, connecting with the ordinary people who experienced it, calling it out—all of which resonated deeply with ordinary Ukrainians. Indeed, when his lead character unexpectedly becomes president in the first season of *Servant of the People*, his own family immediately seizes the opportunity to take bribes or promise favors until he makes clear to them that he will not honor any promises they make on his behalf. In one of Holoborodko's monologues (Season 1, Episode 15), he describes how a typical, good little Ukrainian is transformed as they grow up into a "*khokhol*," a derogatory term for Ukrainians. It all starts in maternity hospital itself, where something needs to be given under the table to the doctor. Then as he grows up, he sees his parents giving bribes, littering, and not paying taxes. The child comes to accept this as simply how things are. "We ourselves are guilty, people like you, people like me," the fictive president admonishes. The real-life Zelensky's inaugural address as president hit on similar themes, reminding Ukrainians that being European is a state of mind and a set of values, and that they each must play a role in not succumbing to corrupt systems.[47]

The Independence Generation comes of age

Not only did the Independence Generation have to live through economic turmoil and the wildest forms of patronal politics; they were growing up very differently from their parents. And their experience also differed greatly from those who had been in their twenties and thirties at the time of independence, the cohort that grew up when the black market and Communist Party hierarchies still reigned supreme.

Most importantly, their formative years were spent in a culturally more liberal society that openly allowed and even encouraged things Ukrainian as opposed to Soviet. Music, film, television shows, and books that had been banned in the 1980s were now available on seemingly every street corner, at least in bootleg form, including books on Ukrainian history and culture. This generation also completed most of their education after the 1989 language law was passed that made Ukrainian the primary language for all instruction in Ukraine. While measures remained in place to provide education in other languages, students after 1989 received more Ukrainian-language instruction than previous generations. The study of Ukrainian itself became obligatory for all children in primary and secondary school. And while in higher education it was possible to take all of one's other courses in Russian, it was still a requirement to study the Ukrainian language. Higher education entrance exams were also to be conducted in Ukrainian. Thus, all those who still had at least three to ten years of primary or secondary school instruction to go in 1989 received a substantial level of Ukrainian-language instruction even if they lived in cities where Russian was widely spoken like Kyiv, Odesa, Dnipropetrovsk (now Dnipro), or Kryvyy Rih.

Furthermore, in 1996, Kuchma championed a new constitution, and one of the changes was to enshrine Ukrainian as the only official state language in Ukraine. The new basic law ensured that Ukrainian was used "in all spheres of social life," though it also guaranteed the development, use, and protection of Russian and other minority languages.[48] This of course did not change the realities of everyday language use for many in the country who still consumed Russian-language media and spoke daily in Russian yet were able to use Ukrainian in all formal settings. But the country became essentially bilingual.

This bilingualism is consistently on display in Zelensky's political satire, including the *Servant of the People* series. For the most part, President Holoborodko, even when he is in the classroom as a history teacher, uses Russian. But in certain contexts, his character shifts pointedly to Ukrainian. The same can be said for all the other main characters in the series. Sometimes they speak in Ukrainian, sometimes in Russian. This is true even of the nationalist characters. In many scenes, as in real daily life in central and southeastern Ukraine, conversations take place in both languages. It is important to note, however, that in most of western Ukraine, one would almost never hear Russian. Overall, at least in formal settings, in the 1990s almost everyone switched to Ukrainian, and for the Independence Generation this was easier than for the generation that came before them, whose childhood education coincided with a period of forced russification.

> *This is why we are strong together.*
>
> *Why we, so different, from east and west, Ukrainian-speaking and Russian-speaking, must be one family.*
>
> *Because Ukraine unites us. Because we all tell it: "You are my only one!"*
>
> *Because we all defend it.*
>
> —Volodymyr Zelensky, 24 August 2021[49]

Emergent civic national identity

Political scientists Oxana Shevel, Volodymyr Kulyk, and Lowell Barrington have shown that what it meant to declare oneself as belonging to the Ukrainian nation changed after Ukraine became independent, a phenomenon that was to shape the Independence Generation more than its predecessors.[50] Most importantly, Ukrainian national identity took on more of a civic quality. That is, declaring oneself Ukrainian by nationality became less about ancestry and ethnicity and more about attachment to the newly independent state. Even in the first years of independence, and even accounting for the fact that the population decreased by as much as 1 percent annually according to the 1989 and 2001 censuses, we can already see a pattern that Kulyk has called the "shedding of Russianness," which includes a rise in self-identification as a Ukrainian by nationality. Figure 2.10 depicts the percentage point change in the share of residents in each region self-identifying as Ukrainian by nationality. As can be seen, all regions except Crimea experienced an increase in the percentage of citizens calling themselves Ukrainian. Interestingly, the largest increases (of 6–10 percentage points) were in the southeastern and central oblasts. And, again, these increases cannot be explained by population shifts alone; the western region of Vinnytsya experienced the largest population shift, and Kyiv actually saw its population grow.

This emergent civic national identity also took on increasingly European associations in culture and values. For the Independence Generation, it was common to see Western Europe as a potential destination for themselves (to visit, attend school, or work) and for their country (in becoming more "normal," as respondents in our focus groups and interviews have repeatedly highlighted). This was particularly true regarding the European Union, born around the same time Ukraine broke from the USSR.[51] And while this generation had presidents and prime ministers from both east and west during their early years, all of these leaders articulated the idea that Ukraine was EU-bound. Ukraine made a declaration that it would like to join the EU as early as 1993, and by 1994 it had signed an EU–Ukraine Partnership and Cooperation Agreement.

Kuchma, dismaying Kremlin leaders who had thought he might take Ukraine back to Russia's fold, kept up and even accelerated Ukraine's European orientation. In 1997, the first EU–Ukraine summit took place in Kyiv, and Kuchma announced publicly that Ukraine was keen to sign an association agreement with the EU by 2004 to meet all EU membership requirements by 2011 at the latest.[52] There would be eight EU–Ukraine summits by July 2004, though Ukraine received no commitment from the Europeans that Ukraine could ever actually achieve candidate status. The question of NATO was much more controversial, consistently with minority support. But Ukraine's general aspiration to EU status was something like a consensus among Ukraine's governing elites while the Independence Generation was on the rise.[53]

The Zelensky origin story

Zelensky appears to have been a good student as a teenager. When he was sixteen, he and another female student won a Test of English as a Foreign Language (TOEFL) competition in Dnipropetrovsk, the prize for which was a full scholarship to study in Israel. His father, he reports, would not allow it.[54]

While prior to the presidency he was known primarily as a comedian and secondarily as a writer and producer, his interest in affairs of state extends back to his childhood. At sixteen, his biggest interest was in fact international relations, and his dream was to become a diplomat. It was to this end that he studied in a specialized English school. When the time came, he considered applying to the two elite international relations schools potentially available to him then, the Russian Foreign Ministry's MGIMO (Moscow State Institute of International Relations) and the newer Kyiv Institute of International Relations (KIMV). KIMV, he reports, was a real possibility. But at a time when admissions to elite institutions frequently required strong connections or bribes, Zelensky reports that he ultimately decided against the top schools and instead went to his hometown institution, Kryvyy Rih National University, in 1997. This was also the university at which his father was a professor, though in cybernetics rather than international relations. To hear Zelensky tell it, when he decided to go there for his higher education, his father immediately embarked on a new multi-year stint in Mongolia to avoid any appearance that he might be helping his son at university.[55]

As an undergraduate, the future president followed up on his interest in foreign relations and studied international economics and law, where he concentrated on legal science.[56] He recalled in an interview that his first exam was on English, and the second addressed the theory of the state and law.[57] His interest in high politics was thus not something that emerged out of the blue later. And his training in economics, state governance, and law would surely inform his biting political satire and his later diagnoses of Ukraine's political problems.[58] In 2000, Zelensky received his degree in law.

An extracurricular activity, however, soon took over his university experience and later his career. In 1994, when he was seventeen, Zelensky (with friend Denys Manzhosov) found his calling in the Soviet-era phenomenon known as KVN, the *Klub Vesyolykh i Nakhodchivykh*. KVN was not simply a performer's club but also an international competition in which teams at different levels would be judged for the quality of their skits, which typically involved both song and dance, and their ability to answer questions cleverly.

Zelensky initially joined a local youth team, Young Kryvyy Rih. His performance earned good reviews, and he soon received an invitation to join the Zaporizhzhya–Kryvyy Rih-Transit team, becoming its dance director and writer in 1995. Others in this group would later become core members of Zelensky's Kvartal 95 Studio team, including Manzhosov, Yuriy Krapov, Oleksandr Pikalov, and Olena Kravets. The latter three would also make up the core of fictive President Holoborodko's cabinet in the *Servant of the People* series.[59] This was a tight group. They all grew up and went to school together. And while they eventually shared tremendous success, in the 1990s they were just a bunch of ordinary but clever children of the Independence Generation trying to catch a break. Zelensky later recalled how difficult it was for them to pursue their dreams in the context of the turbulent 1990s. In 1999, when the first McDonald's opened in Kryvyy Rih, Kravets went to work there. Referring to her salary, Zelensky exclaimed: "100 bucks—you can't even imagine how much this is for Kryvyy Rih!"[60] Also at this time, he began working with the Shefir brothers, later co-creators of the *Servant of People* show. Serhiy Shefir would go on to join Zelensky's presidential team as a principal advisor and First Assistant to the President of Ukraine, a post he holds to the day.

The people who constituted this group separated from the Transit KVN team in 1997 and created the now-famous "Kvartal 95" troupe, named after the neighborhood in Kryvyy Rih where Zelensky had grown up. Translated as "Block 95," this rather generic and most unglamorous name already hinted at the seams of humor and social commentary it would mine for decades, themes relevant to millions of other ordinary people living in such ordinary residential blocks. At age nineteen, Zelensky was not only an actor but also the captain of the troupe and lead author of most of the team's skits.

In this way, as Ukraine's oligarchs-to-be were miraculously becoming millionaires, chocolate barons, gas princesses, and bank owners in their twenties and thirties, Zelensky as a teenager was leaving his political ambitions behind (temporarily, as it turns out) to build a team and apply his creative talents in the cultural and entertainment sector. From 1999 to 2003, Kvartal 95 performed in the highest KVN league, headquartered in Moscow. Many of his team members lived in Moscow at this time and toured the entire post-Soviet region. They were the only team from Ukraine, and it was especially unusual for there to be a team in this league from hardscrabble Kryvyy Rih. Zelensky proudly describes people being stunned that such a team could beat the Muscovites. His success led to an invitation to leave Kvartal for a job as editor at the central KVN organization, but Zelensky refused, citing his loyalty to his friends and his distaste for Moscow life. After this, the Kvartal group returned to Ukraine and soon began work on what would soon become their signature show, the "Evening Kvartal" (*Vechernyy Kvartal*) series of concerts.[61]

> *Why didn't I like Moscow, even though I lived and worked there for six years? Because you can knock and yet, the door will not be opened. And not just to some neighbor—it's in general, in everything. It's about life.*
>
> —Volodymyr Zelensky, interview with Dmytro Hordon in 2018[62]

Some in Ukraine, especially his later political opponents, deride Zelensky for his long involvement in the "Russian" and "Soviet-style" KVN. What they rarely mention is the show's associations with movements for democracy and change in the USSR to which we alluded above. First launched in 1961 during the post-Stalinist cultural thaw as *An Evening of Funny Questions*, it was taken off the air by Soviet censors in 1971.[63] Live satirical comedy and sketch shows were considered anti-Soviet. The revived version of the show, the one that initially attracted Zelensky, started up only in 1986 with the advent of Gorbachev's *perestroika* and *glasnost* policies.[64] The show thus waxed and waned with the Soviet dissident movement, blossoming during its height before falling victim to repression until 1986, though of course the dissidents suffered a much worse fate than the show's original producers and performers. This is not to say that the show (and hence Zelensky) had no relationship to the spread of Russian cultural influence and russification in Ukraine. But it complicates simplistic accounts of Zelensky's professional beginnings that smear him with ties to Russia.

Elections, polarization, and revolution

The heads of Ukraine's burgeoning patronal networks knew all too well that if they wanted to secure the wealth they had already acquired, not to mention gaining more in the future, they needed influence over politics, if not outright control. This seldom meant entering politics directly themselves, although some like Tymoshenko did take that path. The majority strategy was to get others whom they could trust into key political posts. Trust could come from their own friendship or familial networks, though a good substitute involved forging new ties by effectively "buying" promising candidates for office.

One interesting feature of Ukrainian politics in the 1990s and 2000s is that while the campaigning and voter mobilization could be highly corrupt, the actual counting was often relatively honest—competing networks were usually strong enough to keep each other from controlling election commissions nationwide. To elect their preferred candidates, therefore, it was not enough to pay for their campaigns and lend them their local political machines. Citizens could be reached in still other ways. Most importantly, they watched television and, to a lesser extent, read newspapers and listened to radio (soon enough, they would also use the Internet).

This was a concern for the oligarchs. The 1990s and 2000s saw an explosive rise in independent journalism, with outlets like *Chas*, the American-funded *Radio Svoboda* ("Liberty"), *Post Postup*, and *Ukrayinska Pravda* leading the way. Assassinating journalists was a poor way to manipulate such media. The 2000 murder of the critical investigative journalist Heorhiy Gongadze, founder of *Ukrayinska Pravda*, only strengthened his publication's determination to fiercely expose high-level corruption.

Most major oligarchs thus started to acquire mass media assets that they could use to get their messaging out to the electorate. Over time, Rinat Akhmetov acquired the Ukrayina Channel. Dmytro Firtash bought Inter TV. Kolomoyskyy became owner of 1+1. Not all of these acquisitions were reputed to have been friendly takeovers. Rather than obtain an existing television channel, Poroshenko set up a new one, Channel 5, gradually building up an audience for it. This new wave of wealthy media owners came mainly from Ukraine's southeast or from Kyiv. Later in the 2000s, though, western Ukrainians also got into the act. For instance, Arseniy Yatsenyuk, who was to become prime minister in 2014, bought shares in *Espreso* TV, and Lviv Mayor Andriy Sadovyy's family owned Channel 24.[65]

This was the beginning of what Andrew Wilson has famously called "virtual politics" in Ukraine.[66] Not only were former communists and their kin suddenly dressing up as democrats and businesspeople but information could now be manufactured on the media they controlled, ballots could be delivered through coercion, and a wide range of other tactics could be deployed to divert votes from undesired candidates and push them to the favored ones. Deadly force could be deployed as a last resort if the stakes were high enough. For instance, some believe that the car accident that killed former dissident and likely presidential candidate Chornovil in March 1999 was not accidental. While this has not been proven, and Kuchma has denied any involvement, Chornovil's death did clear the way for Kuchma to win his second term in October of that same year by taking massive majorities in the west of the country that Chornovil might have siphoned away from him. It also facilitated a runoff that pitted Kuchma against Communist Party of Ukraine leader Petro Symonenko, who matched up particularly poorly in a head-to-head contest against Kuchma in Ukraine's west, where Symonenko was loathed and Kuchma was at least given credit for pursuing a European orientation for Ukraine (see Figure 2.11).

The result was a major shift in Kuchma's apparent "ethnic" base of support. As Figure 2.12 illustrates, Kuchma's backers in 1994 came mainly from regions that had the most people who identified as Russian by nationality, since his opponent, Kravchuk, had raised questions about his connections to Russia and appealed on themes most attractive to central and western Ukrainians. The 1999 election produced the opposite: a correlation between Kuchma's support and the share of Ukrainians (not Russians) in a given region. Looking beyond the 1994 and 1999 comparison, the figure also shows something else: that the correlation between nationality and voting in Ukrainian presidential elections became much more pronounced in the next (2004) election. Just like the patterns that came before it, this one also proved to be a product of deliberate strategies by Ukraine's political elites to polarize the country along ethnolinguistic or regional lines in hopes of improving otherwise dubious electoral prospects, as we discuss in Chapter 3.

The period after the 1999 election marked even further backsliding into the most nefarious version of competitive patronal politics. Political machines grew further entrenched in Ukraine's regions, and many localities became almost exclusively dependent on particular local bosses. It was quite common for election promises to include buying individuals basic goods (even caskets) in return for their votes. Ukraine's emerging situation made such tactics viable. As the country's oligarchs accumulated extreme wealth, for whom buying a casket was as trivial as could be, ordinary people were so poor that they worried they would not be able to afford funerals for themselves or their relatives.

Lucan Way calls this brand of freewheeling politics "pluralism by default," where political competition existed not because of any strong democratic norms but simply because no one political-economic force was strong enough to conquer the others.[67] Kuchma invested considerable effort into gaining such strength by using the presidential administration to coordinate oligarchs' power around his own. He was implicitly offering them a deal: recognize his ultimate authority, and help politically where needed, and they would be able to keep their gains and expand their influence. Competition between the power networks would be permitted, but only so long as it did not infringe on his own interests. Such efforts gave rise to the concept of "the blackmail state," whereby a leader (here Kuchma) actually encourages corruption among his officials, variously in coordination or competition with oligarchs, so that he can document it and thereby always have "dirt" on them, making them easier to control.[68] The irony is that one of his own underlings, his bodyguard, also turned the recorder on when Kuchma himself appeared to be directing this process.

> *And now I want to address not those who stayed with Ukraine and in Ukraine, but those who left it at the most crucial moment. Your strength is not in your money and planes, but in the civic position you can show. Return to your people and the country due to which you got your factories and wealth. Today, everyone passes a real test for a citizen of Ukraine. Pass it with dignity. Let everyone understand for whom Ukraine is really the Homeland, and for whom it is just a platform for money making.*
>
> —Volodymyr Zelensky, 14 February 2022[69]

But it wasn't all a losing game for the masses. If we go back to the civic-centered mission of the dissidents of the 1970s and 1980s, we see that they did not disappear in 1991. In fact, they became the guardians of Ukrainian democracy, even if some were more preoccupied with nation-building than state-building (among a few, these two missions were fused). And still in school, many of Ukraine's Independence Generation would come to spearhead this battle for what being Ukrainian would mean.

At the center of this battle was the activism of journalists like Gongadze, who had been reporting on corruption involving Kuchma and many connected to him. The manner of his demise was gruesome. In 2000, he went missing and was later found beheaded. Just the announcement of these facts had been enough to mobilize activists. But soon the tapes made by Kuchma's bodyguard were leaked and released by the activist website *Maidan Inform* and seemed to implicate Kuchma directly. In the wake of this revelation, the old guard of former dissidents and the new generation of activists from across the country united against *Kuchmizm* (a term used to mean endemic corruption, repression, and control of the media). In 2000 and 2001, they staged several large protests. Together, these events made up the "Ukraine without Kuchma" protest wave.[70] While unsuccessful in bringing Kuchma down, and criticized by then-Prime Minister and future president Viktor Yushchenko for being made up of hooligans and terrorists, it brought a large number of Independence Generation activists onto the streets for the first time. The largest protests took place in Kyiv and Lviv, though there were some smaller isolated actions across the country in Kharkiv in the east and in Odesa in the south. Dnipro and Kryvyy Rih were relatively quiet, not least because former "rocket city red director" Kuchma was seen as having strong ties to the region. But it did resonate among some youth, and as Onuch has found in her research, the years until 2004 represented a major renaissance of Ukrainian activism.[71] What was new is that this time the Independence Generation assumed the driver's seat.

Zelensky was living mostly in Moscow with his Kvartal 95 partners during this time, returning to Ukraine with his team only in 2003. Upon their return, they signed a contract with the Ukrainian television Channel 1+1, co-owned at the time by Oleksandr Rodnyanskyy. The channel was one of the leading media outlets in Ukraine, with hugely popular shows. At the same time, it was one of many channels known for accepting the Kuchma team's political directives on how the news should be reported, the infamous *temnyky*. It would not be until the Orange Revolution in 2004 that its journalists would break rank and start reporting honestly. In fact, in the lead-up to the 2004

Figure A. Sticker made by yellow Pora depicting that 1+1 is lying to its audiences

presidential elections, young activists whom Onuch interviewed extensively and who were coordinating a major youth movement had actually designed a protest sticker specifically criticizing 1+1 (among other major TV channels), saying "they are lying" (see fig. 2.13).[72] This channel, then, was an odd choice of pre-2004 business partnership for a young man who in 2018 had said "parents are great, important people for me, especially before the appearance of my family—wife and children. They gave me a fundamental thing—upbringing, a painful sense of the world, a painful sense of lies and untruths."[73]

Kvartal 95 was about to begin its journey into comedy, entertainment, and political satire. Zelensky was soon going to become a household name. Ukraine was about to be plunged into its first major crisis since independence. Perhaps, just like millions of other Ukrainians who were about to have their eyes opened by the massive (and unusual) electoral fraud that was planned by Kuchma and his chosen successor's (Viktor Yanukovych's) political teams, Zelensky was about to be awakened as to how extensively his new employer and Ukraine's political elite were in fact lying to ordinary Ukrainians.

Orange is the color of revolution

In preparation for the 2004 presidential elections, the unpopular Kuchma did not seek reelection. This was at first seen as a major success in Ukraine's democratic transition. But instead, as a succession strategy, Kuchma reversed Ukraine's Euro-Atlantic course and attempted to hand over the reins to Yanukovych, ending Ukraine's pursuit of NATO and attempting to usher in the highly undemocratic Party of Regions machine with its Donetsk oblast base. They planned to do this by using the now flourishing Party of Regions patronal networks and their controlled media to manufacture the desired electoral result. What they got instead was large-scale opposition from political elites, Independence Generation youth activists, and, as it turned out, millions of ordinary people.

There were four problems with their plan. First, they seemed to forget that Kuchma was highly unpopular. Second, they

Figure B. Sticker made by yellow Pora: It Is Time to Act

Figure C. Sticker made by black Pora: Kuchma is For Yanukovych ... And you? Part of their anti-Kuchmism campaign

кучма за януковича. а ти?

didn't count on Yushchenko, Kuchma's former prime minister, becoming so popular with ordinary Ukrainians. This should not have been such a surprise; a bloc he had put together had done very well in parliamentary elections just two years prior. Third, they did not expect that their political opponents would enter into formal and informal agreements on building a united electoral coalition, nor that this coalition would not fall apart under strain. Fourth, they did not count on activists and youth social movements planning for exactly this possibility for over three years, recruiting more members, and training the next generation of youth.[74]

The two youth social movements that got the most attention were both named *Pora*, which means "it is time," one becoming known as yellow Pora and the other black Pora because of certain themes in their symbolism. The first had stronger ties to Kyiv and Kharkiv activist networks and the Yushchenko campaign. The second, whose actions predated the first, was more closely connected to western Ukrainian and former dissident Kyiv activist networks.[75] These were, though, as Onuch has found in her research, just two of over twenty such youth and university student social movements set up across the country. They were all collaborating, together keeping tallies on lies told in the mass media and then tracking electoral fraud when it occurred.[76] Rival elites that had once been part of Kuchma's coalition, including Poroshenko (Party of Regions) and Yushchenko (prime minister), defected in a cascading fashion to the burgeoning opposition, with the latter becoming the favorite to win. Poroshenko's defection, most notably, gave the opposition a television channel, Channel 5, that would report on it favorably.

But Yanukovych and Kuchma persevered, trying every way they could to gin up votes for themselves and harm their opponents. Yushchenko was even poisoned with dioxin at a staged meeting, an attempt to remove Kuchma's rival, perhaps with

Russian help, that left him weakened and his face disfigured. When regime machinations failed to produce enough votes, the Kuchma regime resorted to blatant fraud. Since election results in the past had mostly been counted honestly, this attempt at falsification was shocking to most of the country. Journalists and activists easily exposed many of the regime's vote-manufacturing attempts with cameras. Techniques included busing factory workers to cast ballots, threatening workers and their families with unemployment or violence, paying people for votes, setting up carousel voting, threatening election staff, stealing whole ballot boxes and replacing them with preprinted and pre-filled-in votes, changing the vote numbers on protocols, and even using disappearing ink in the west of the country to depreciate the vote in places where their political machine could not reach.[77]

The result was a mass explosion onto the streets after the 21 November 2004 runoff, with protesters adopting the color orange as a symbol of their cause. Onuch's extensive research on protesters' motivations shows that people felt their universal rights were being infringed upon in such a way that they had no choice but to stand up for them, that their dignity as human beings was being taken away.[78] On 22 November, students and activists from across the country descended onto Kyiv's main square, *Maidan Nezalezhnosti* (Independence Square). This was the first major turning point largely engineered by the Independence Generation, convincing their family and neighbors to join them wherever they were, be it Kyiv, Lviv, Odesa, Simferopol, Donetsk, or elsewhere. And they did. With the Kuchma coalition crumbling under the pressure, the falsified election result was overturned. The runoff was re-run in December. Yushchenko won.

The victory came at a price for the orange coalition, however. As a condition for allowing the repeat runoff, Kuchma and Yanukovych forced Yushchenko to accept constitutional amendments that substantially weakened the presidency he would inherit. The new constitution was of a kind Hale has described as a "divided-executive constitution," one in which executive power is separated and roughly balanced between a directly elected president and a prime minister who is beholden primarily to parliament, meaning that the president now had much less control over the prime minister.[79] Yushchenko became president and his Orange Revolution partner Tymoshenko became prime minister, and so began a rivalry that came to color the half decade to follow—as will be discussed in Chapter 3. Even though both had been key figures in Kuchma's team prior to defecting to the opposition, hope and optimism reigned supreme in Ukraine. The people had risen up to oust what they believed was a corrupt regime and now had new leaders from a younger generation promising to turn the country around.

The country and its citizens, though, were left more divided. This increased sense of division did not involve any clean break down the middle (see Figure 2.13). Instead, the 2004 elections and mass mobilization that followed accentuated differences between two very distant island and largely localized constituencies: Halychyna (Galicia) in the west and the Donbas in the east. This is a divide that was to be nurtured and exploited multiple times over the ensuing years—at times by well-meaning patriots and at other times by those who wanted political advantage or even to destabilize Ukraine and spark separatist sentiment.

Was Zelensky Orange or Blue?

The Orange Revolution was a major political awakening for other cultural figures of Zelensky's generation. For example, Svyatoslav Vakarchuk, a musician and lead singer of the very popular rock band *Okean Elzy* and son of a major political player in Lviv, said: "Today, I forgot that I am a musician ... Now I can bring more benefit not as a musician, but as a public figure."[80] Many others followed suit. Several of the older activist leaders also found themselves either entering into political party blocs or in a few cases setting up their own parties, such as a "Pora" party. In most cases, they were eaten up by the system, or worse, corrupted by it. It is thus important to note that some in the Independence Generation rallied to public activism much sooner than did Zelensky. Doing more than Zelensky had done in 2004, it is understandable that they might be skeptical of his political rise fifteen years later.

Perhaps the Orange Revolution's biggest impact of all is that the Independence Generation learned that people power was real. They came to understand first-hand that they could, at a minimum, get rid of specific leaders whom they considered bad for the country. While Chapter 3 will discuss how disillusionment would soon follow, people nevertheless had gained experience in mobilizing that could be applied, and improved, to effect change. With the revolution behind them, members of the Independence Generation were now in their twenties, setting up family, careers, taking out loans for flats and cars, often in euros and dollars, leaving them vulnerable to economic downturns that would soon follow across all of Europe. But this was a generation on the rise.

We recommend our readers listen to "Vona" By Taras Chubay & Plach Yaremiyi
Found on the "Ukraine Top 100" Playlist on Spotify, a playlist by Vova Zavadskyy

https://open.spotify.com/track/1qDqswcqJ7QxtbVlDv5P6W

And soon autumn will come,
And we will all flee
To Russified cities!
But she, only she,
Will sit sad,
She will drink—not get drunk,
From cheap wine

—Authors' own translation[81]

I will remind you of her words today:
"Someone blow away in the wind, like a grain"

—Volodymyr Zelensky, reciting Lina Kostenko, 20 March 2022[1]

This is not just Russia's invasion in Ukraine, this is the beginning of the war against Europe.

...

… *When bombs fall in Kyiv, this happens in Europe, not only in Ukraine.*

...

Glory to Ukraine!

—Volodymyr Zelensky, wartime speech, 25 February 2022[2]

3

ORANGE IS THE NEW CORRUPTION

As of early 2005, the Orange Revolution was a major source of inspiration and pride for many in the Independence Generation, proof that people power could set Ukraine on track to a bright future. The world also took note, with observers holding the mass mobilization up as a shining example of hope for global democracy. If you were in your twenties in Ukraine at the time, you could not help but be excited about what the apparent "democratic breakthrough" would bring.

Yet in the context of Ukraine's patronal politics, the Orange Revolution meant something even more fundamental. After a decade of everybody seemingly being resigned to Ukraine's corrupt reality, the revolution appeared to show that people could behave in an entirely different way. This is a common outcome of revolutions in highly patronalistic countries. Examples outside Ukraine include Georgia's 2003 Rose Revolution and Armenia's 2018 Velvet Revolution. It is awe-inspiring to see so many people out on the streets calling for democracy, transparent government, and change more generally. The feeling prevails that not only the leadership but society itself has completely changed, shedding its reliance on cronyism and coercion and transforming itself into a consolidated community where progressive, democratic ideas and a public spirit dominate. People frequently recall experiencing euphoria. In Ukraine's case, a critical mass of its citizens had finally lived up to their civic duty after accepting the old regime's machinations for too long. They were standing up to protect the electoral process at the heart of their young democracy. "Together they are many, they will not be defeated," rang the popular hip-hop song that became a second anthem of the Orange Revolution.

These high hopes soon crashed hard against the realities of Ukrainian politics. Several warning signs pointed in this direction. For one thing, the "new" leaders were mostly establishment politicians. While the Independence Generation had provided much of the revolution's horsepower, the usual suspects had kept control of the reins. The resulting president, Viktor Yushchenko, had been Kuchma's prime minister, and the resulting prime minister, Yuliya Tymoshenko, was the reputed "gas princess" who had also been part of the Kuchma team. These were hardly fresh faces. For another, not all the country was swept up in the euphoria. In fact, the strategy for getting President Kuchma's prime minister Viktor Yanukovych elected was predicated on polarizing the country, forcing a contest that would become about southeast versus west and center. Yushchenko would oblige, especially after his election win, pursuing a symbolic cultural agenda as material conditions in the country stagnated or deteriorated. The Orange joy, then, did not extend to those who had backed the "blues," represented by the Donetsk-based Yanukovych. Although the revolution certainly had its supporters in the southeast, it was not the nationally unifying event it had seemed to many in the rest of the country. Zelensky himself was typical of many from the southeast in that he did not oppose the revolution but was not actively involved in it either. He even reports that his parents, natives of southeastern Kryvyy Rih, had always voted for the blue side in elections.[3] Yanukovych soon tapped into such sentiments when intense in-fighting between the Tymoshenko and Yushchenko networks, using many of the same sorts of methods that Kuchma had used, opened up space for him to mount a stunning political comeback for the blues.

The Independence Generation's first personal experience with mass mobilization, then, turned out to be a disappointment, and their frustration mounted under the Yanukovych presidency of 2010–14. Zelensky's career, however, not only survived but thrived. Yanukovych provided him with an endless source of comedy material, and his repression never extended to the Kvartal 95 troupe, which continued to mercilessly poke fun at the increasingly repressive president. At the same time, however, Zelensky switched to a TV channel (Inter) known for its friendly coverage of the regime and became its general producer, which meant that he now oversaw the production of the channel's politically biased news output. Yet by the time Yanukovych started to threaten the country's European orientation in 2013, Zelensky's Independence Generation had the wherewithal to stop it, hoping the result would not be disappointment once again. This is the story told in the present chapter.

Orange euphoria

The Orange Revolution mass mobilization was remarkably peaceful and had a joyous, festival-like atmosphere. As one activist leader said in an interview, it seemed like a "discotech." To be in Kyiv, Lviv, or any big city in the center and west of Ukraine at the time was to witness popular opposition on a daily basis. As Onuch has explained elsewhere, while activists are in the business of protest, ordinary citizens generally avoid engaging in extra-institutional politics.[4] According to MOBILISE project data,[5] for example, in a "normal" non-crisis setting, about 3–5 percent of the Ukrainian population say they have participated in a demonstration over a national issue. According to Ukrainian Crisis Election Panel Survey (UCEPS) data,[6] in the context of a mass mobilization, only 10 percent of the population reported that they had participated in the protests. Ordinary citizens, much like the characters depicted in *Servant of the People*, may or may not vote, may or may not pay their taxes, and are generally disengaged from politics. But in those rare moments of mass mobilization, it is ordinary people who are moved by their civic duty to join in, and to do so en masse.[7]

In November 2004, of course, not everyone could take part in the physical protests on regular working days, as they had work or caring duties, and thus, some of the the largest public gatherings took place mainly on weekends and evenings. Nonetheless, ordinary Ukrainians found other ways to make their discontent known and engage in civic activism in the days in between. Before the orange Yushchenko flags and yellow Pora flags were printed and distributed, people used what they had on hand to join in however they could. Some would wear an orange hat or scarf; others would sport an orange handkerchief or tie an orange ribbon or piece of yarn to their clothing, bag, or basket; and still others might simply hold a piece of orange paper on the bus or in the subway. Any signal would do. Stores placed their collection of orange items by the front entrance, and suddenly the streets of Kyiv teemed with orange jumpers. For example, after work, Onuch's father brought an actual orange, an object considered a luxury in the Soviet era, something children would get as a treat for Christmas. Carrying it in his hands from the Podil neighborhood where he worked to Kyiv's main public space, its Independence Square (often called simply "the Maidan," short for *Maidan Nezalezhnosti*), he found he was not the only one to have had the same idea. Dozens of people were there holding the same summer fruit—in sub-zero temperatures in the dead of winter.

The protests were not confined to Kyiv, and hence it would be a mistake to view them as a phenomenon of western Ukraine and Kyiv, even if some western Ukrainians believed they had been the heart and soul of the protests, implicitly if not explicitly downplaying the roles of eastern Ukrainians. For instance, a famous activist originally from Lviv told Onuch with more than a hint of irony that while it was true that Kyiv rose up, these Kyivans attended schools number X–Y in Lviv.[8] This echoed related sentiments that it was they, the western Ukrainians, who were struggling for democracy on behalf of the rest of Ukraine.

However, in her research on the Orange Revolution, Onuch has met with people who played leading roles in the mobilization from across Ukraine, including not only Kyiv but Sumy, Odesa, Kharkiv, and even Crimea. Some did not even speak Ukrainian.[9] Even in 2004, the protesters were a diverse group. They shared a common goal and common grievance but differed in many other ways. To unite the crowd, activists would lead the protesters in song. While not all traditional songs are known equally across Ukraine, two were able to unite the protesters regardless of the language they spoke or where they grew up: the national anthem and *Chervona Ruta*, a popular Ukrainian love song. That year's EuroVision Song Contest winner, "Wild Dances" by Ruslana, also united the square and was played repeatedly on all radio stations. Singing these songs was a way to make everyone feel at ease, to build a collective identity, a sense that "we are one." Nevertheless, there was still a sense that the goals of the Orange Revolution were not aimed at the entire country.

The protesters' experiences differed along regional lines in other ways too. For one thing, activists in the southeast faced much more brutal repression as it was easier to target protest leaders there—not simply because there were fewer of them but also because the southeast tended to have the strongest regional and local political machines.[10] In this region, protesters identified more than did others with Soviet-era dissidents who had hailed from Donetsk, Kharkiv, or Odesa. Yellow Pora activist leaders who grew up in these parts of the country often mentioned this in interviews. They saw themselves as being connected to the same purpose. As Onuch wrote in her book *Mapping Mass Mobilization*, one Kharkiv-based leader saw their activities in 2004 as the continuation of the Ukrainian civic liberation movement that had begun before independence and that they intended to continue until Ukraine was a fully consolidated democratic member of the European Union. In Kharkiv, Odesa, and even Simferopol, activists organized their own marches and set up smaller tent cities.[11] In Donetsk, young activists in their twenties also tried to set up a tent city but were repressed.[12] Dnipropetrovsk and Kryvyy Rih also hosted some smaller protest events, but activists were more likely to be followed and arrested. In the southeast of the country, therefore, a passerby was much more likely to encounter blue than orange when surveying the local political situation on the streets. Some of the political elite capitalized on this, using these regional differences to ramp up discourses of national division.

Media and politicians came to speak more and more in terms of these divisive lines. Ukraine was now, at least in these accounts, a country of the blues and the oranges. The elite discourse of the blues was more centered on regional identity and Soviet history, while the oranges talked more about liberalism, Europe, democracy, and Ukrainian national identity and language. The broader debate revolved around what sort of national identity Ukraine would adopt: a democratic one championing civic and European values, or one in which machine politics, repression, and the infringement of civic rights was the norm—typically defended as producing competent management and stability.

While millions did side with the minority blues in the end, the Orange Revolution brought many converts to a more democratic orientation. Among the converts were employees of the 1+1 channel for which Zelensky and his team then worked. Live on the air, its journalists shocked viewers by declaring that they could no longer lie to the people of Ukraine and then announcing they were resigning.

Power to the people or to the elites?

Despite people power being on full display, an elite deal was key to the outcome of the Orange Revolution. As his allies were defecting to the Maidan, including generals refusing orders to clear the square, Kuchma moved to seek a compromise before it was too late.[13] He already had lines of communication, having been in regular touch with the orange team during the crisis. Foreign actors, including Poland's president at the time, Aleksander Kwaśniewski, also played a key role in negotiating a deal.[14]

What is most important about this is not the contents of the deal, but simply the fact that there was an elite deal. The people power of the Orange Revolution was real, authentic, and indigenous. Detailed process tracing of the mobilization by Onuch shows that most of the funds came from small and medium businesses in Ukraine rather than foreign actors, as some have asserted.[15] But the reason it stayed peaceful and ended so quickly in a rerun election was because at the center of the resolution were negotiations among elites, a roundtable, a managed exit of the old authorities, and numerous concessions.

The chief concession was the constitutional change we mentioned earlier. In exchange for Yanukovych backing down, Kuchma got Yushchenko to accept a constitutional reform that the outgoing president had sought for a couple of years but had failed to pass through parliament. This change would create a divided-executive constitution, one in which executive branch powers are divided up between a directly elected president and a prime minister who is beholden to the parliament rather than the president. Such constitutions typically constitute important democratic progress since they significantly complicate the ability of future presidents to consolidate their power and take the country in a more authoritarian direction: one center of executive power always has an incentive to stymie the other's power grabs.[16] Presidents like Kuchma typically initiate such reforms when they think they will lose a presidency, so they try to weaken that institution for their successors, and this clearly appeared to be Kuchma's plan.[17] The reform also gave Yanukovych's Party of Regions two chances to regain a foothold in national politics rather than one, since it could now aspire not only to the presidency (which appeared lost) but also to the office of prime minister. To many orange supporters, then, this was not a welcome change, even though most paid little attention to it, focusing more on Yushchenko's victory and the tasks that now lay ahead.

> *Those who use money to buy power for cash are used to making a profit out of this acquisition. Who said that? Aristotle. The phrase is more than 2000 years old, and we are still reluctant to study history.*
>
> —University history teacher from year 2044 in a prosperous Ukraine in *Servant of the People*, Season 3, Episode 3

These sorts of machinations are a frequent theme in Zelensky's *Servant of the People* series. Many watching the series think that because it started in 2015, the central figures and events are all post-Euromaidan references. But the series could just as easily be about the post-Orange Revolution period. At its heart lie the backroom deals, unlikely coalitions, infighting, and political repression that made the 2004–13 period so incredibly unstable. One key scene comes immediately to mind. In the third season, the (fictional) president at the time, Dmytro Surikov, is hosting all the political party leaders one by one in his office. He has a fancy "Kyiv-style" cake on his table. As he is making offers of ministries and policy remits to his competitors, they are warned that their cut is (for example) 40 percent and his 60 percent of any profits made. Each time, he demonstratively cuts the cake and offers them a slice. The symbolism here is on the nose—but while the account is of course oversimplified, in general this is how much of politics was done before and after the Orange Revolution. And it would not take long for the Independence Generation to see this first-hand.

Anyone entering politics at this time, such as the famed singer Svyatoslav Vakarchuk and journalist Andriy Shevchenko, who were about to observe this wheeling and dealing up close, could be forgiven for concluding that true revolutionaries and reformers did not stand much of a chance. And anyone setting up a business in Ukraine, like young Zelensky was, would also have to be prepared for people from one politician's side or another coming to them for bribes, protection offers, or simply their business.

Orange chaos

One of the most important effects of a divided-executive constitution like the one adopted in Ukraine after the Orange Revolution is to sustain division among the elites. Each power network has an incentive to check the others, resulting in what Hale and others have called "patronal democracy," fierce competition among rival political machines for voters' hearts and minds—and pocketbooks.[18] In Ukraine's case, the new constitution was not accompanied by new elites. Very few new faces and reformers made it into parliament, let alone key posts.[19] In an interview, Ukrainian journalist Nataliya Gumenyuk explained that members of the Independence Generation were still young and lacked the experience necessary to hold their own against the country's major power brokers. What she said was most puzzling to her, though, is why it was taking so long for the generation that came before them—the likes of Yushchenko, Tymoshenko, and Poroshenko—to abandon their ways of doing business and politics.

> *Journalist: How did you acquire your business? You've been a civil servant since 2001.*
>
> *President Surikov: I have repeatedly argued that combining businesses and politics is inadmissible.*
>
> *Journalist: But you still mysteriously own it. Your … shops are next to each metro station.*
>
> —Journalist to Surikov, *Servant of the People*, Season 3, Episode 3

Indeed, Yushchenko had a strong reputation as a reformer but was not truly a new-style politician. As well as having been Kuchma's prime minister, he had also derided the "Ukraine without Kuchma" protesters as hooligans. In order to defeat Kuchma in 2004, Yushchenko had made a broad range of alliances with members of the old elite. In *Servant of the People*, electoral machinations are shown forcing different candidates to leave the race, their oligarchic backers having struck a backroom deal. Similarly, in the lead-up to 2004, several potentially very popular candidates gave their backing to Yushchenko, such as Tymoshenko.

While many saw this broad and inclusive opposition coalition as necessary to defeat the old regime,[20] what it meant for the post-revolutionary era was that all these elite backers now wanted to cash in. For this reason, Yushchenko felt he had to concede coalition places to established politicians like Oleksandr Moroz, Volodymyr Lytvyn, Tymoshenko, and Poroshenko, as well as to right-wing and nationalist party leaders. Rather than bring in a new team of dedicated reformers like Mikheil Saakashvili had done in Georgia following the Rose Revolution, the post-Orange

Revolution coalition was a broad conglomeration of old elites who each had to be given spoils and who each had different visions of what needed to be done, including who should dominate and where resources should be distributed.[21]

The biggest battle for post-revolutionary government positions was between the Yushchenko and Tymoshenko factions and the two politicians themselves. Yushchenko's decision to appoint Tymoshenko as prime minister was itself the denouement of an elite deal. Tymoshenko had been a top presidential contender in her own right but had sacrificed her own ambitions for the sake of opposition unity under Yushchenko against Yanukovych, with the understanding that in return she would get the number-two post. Poroshenko also had to be given a key post, not least because his television channel, Channel 5, had played a key role during the mobilization. The result of all these concessions was that there could be no bold, immediate reform strokes à la Saakashvili.[22] This also helps explain why Yushchenko began focusing more on issues involving ethnonational and cultural myths, history, and language. He had to carve out an image for himself and what he represented, and studies in different contexts have shown that governments that are unable to win support through progressive redistribution or other major reforms often focus on identity-related issues.[23]

While the new divided-executive constitution was not to come fully into effect until the scheduled 2006 parliamentary elections, it undermined the perception that the president was (or would become) all-powerful, leading to something like a free-for-all battle among politicians and the political machines they controlled. Most prominently, the president and the prime minister each tried to consolidate power for themselves and their own networks through these two institutions. But none had the strength to dominate because the prime minister could check the president and vice versa.

This led to a cycle of battles. In the first round, it was Yushchenko versus Tymoshenko. This ended when Yushchenko dismissed Tymoshenko in September 2005, using the presidential power to dismiss the prime minister that would expire when the new constitution came fully into force with elections scheduled for a few months later. The 2006 parliamentary elections, though, brought Yanukovych to the prime ministership after Yushchenko's party was unwilling to make the political compromises necessary to build a coalition. This set up round two, which pitted a now-Prime Minister Yanukovych against President Yushchenko, with Tymoshenko (mostly) aligning with the latter. The Yushchenko-Tymoshenko tandem managed to topple the rising power of Yanukovych by forcing early elections in 2007, which they and their allies won, returning Tymoshenko to the prime ministership. This led to round three, which again featured Yushchenko versus Tymoshenko, with Yanukovych playing the the opportunist, exploiting the battle at the top as he gathered strength for a new presidential run. These battles played out through politicized courts and efforts to seize control of them, rumored attempts to buy off parliamentary deputies, standoffs in the streets, and media biased to the different players.[24] The overall result was a sense in the country of constant in-fighting and uncertainty, not to mention an unsettled feeling that in the months and years after the protests few reforms were being implemented that could secure the protest's broader aims.

The media lapped up the drama and could not help but further add fuel to the fire with their sensationalistic reporting. The different media outlets—which were typically loyal to, or entirely controlled by, oligarchs—presented their own candidates' opponents in a negative light. This was specifically the case when it came to coverage of Tymoshenko, who was the target of highly direct, personal, and often sexist attacks. Watching seasons 1 and 2 of the *Servant of the People* series with this history in mind, it is hard to be sure where the creative license begins and reality ends.

At the same time, it seemed, at least to ordinary citizens, that the politicians were not only fighting incessantly but also that they were more preoccupied with their global image, and personal power, than with reforms. Like Kravchuk had done, Yushchenko went on a world tour. Allies saw it as useful cultural diplomacy, though many others interpreted it as a lack of focus on the most pressing domestic issues. Tymoshenko and her team did a better job at capitalizing on her revolutionary image by prioritizing a look steeped in ethnic and cultural Ukrainian symbols, not least her famous hairstyle of a long braid wrapped around the top of her head—typical of Ukrainian women in villages in the nineteenth century and strongly associated with the famous Ukrainian poetess who wrote under the pseudonym Lesya Ukrayinka. Tymoshenko started to appear on the covers of magazines around the globe and ultimately became the more recognized of the two. As all this was happening, however, a key window for reform was missed. To ordinary Ukrainians, it often seemed politicians were more concerned with co-opting the revolutionary spirit and image than they were with meeting its goals, like qualifying for EU accession.

Gas wars

While this was a time when Ukraine's pro-EU accession stance was further clarified, Ukrainians increasingly came to sense that Russia might go to extremes to prevent Ukraine's joining the EU and, especially, NATO. To make matters worse for Yushchenko and Tymoshenko, Putin and the Kremlin were beginning to punish Ukraine for its revolutionary "misadventures" and for ratcheting up its EU and NATO membership aspirations in public discourse. One tool that Russia began to mobilize more assertively during this period was its "energy weapon," triggering the so-called gas wars. Related gas wars have continued through the time of this writing, in 2022, and involve the whole of the European continent and beyond.[25]

In March 2005, a conflict erupted over the transit of gas through Ukraine, with Russia accusing Ukraine of keeping more gas than it paid for. By January 2006, Russia had cut off all gas supplies going through Ukraine. A quick agreement was reached, and gas transit was restored. Then, in October 2007, the issue of gas debts arose, with Russia claiming Ukraine's debts were higher than Ukraine was prepared to pay. Tensions continued in 2008 with a reduction in gas supply in Ukraine and across the region. In 2009 and the period leading up to the presidential elections in 2010, tensions resurfaced, and this time Ukraine was accused of not buying enough gas. The whole episode was to serve as a reminder and warning to the EU that: (a) its member states are dependent on Russian gas; (b) that Russia has the upper hand in this relationship; and (c) that Ukraine cannot be trusted as a transit state in the supply of Russian gas to the rest of Europe.[26]

The August 2008 Russo-Georgian War

It was also during this period that Russia began asserting its grievances more generally, with perhaps the loudest early signal being Putin's warning to the West in a speech to the 2007 Munich Conference on Security Policy. Within a year, a complex series of events, including exchanges of mortar fire between Georgian and South Ossetian forces, led Georgian President Mikheil Saakashvili to attempt militarily to reclaim the breakaway ethnic minority territory. The conflict's roots were complicated, as South Ossetians had claimed independence from Tbilisi ever since Georgian nationalist forces had tried to eliminate their autonomy in the early 1990s. Almost from the beginning, Moscow had exploited the situation to sow division in Georgia and weaken its NATO prospects, including by militarily propping up the separatists there and encouraging South Ossetians to obtain Russian passports.[27] Moscow had also made no secret of its loathing of Saakashvili, who had cast Russia as Georgia's primary enemy for such behavior and boldly declared the country's intention to join both NATO and the EU. When Saakashvili's forces tried to restore Georgian control over its internationally recognized territory in August 2008, Russia used the opportunity to send its troops well beyond South Ossetia and deep into Georgian territory. While Russian forces soon pulled back to South Ossetia, Moscow announced its recognition of the breakaway region's independence (a step hardly any other country followed). Importantly, this took place at the height of the ongoing gas wars in Ukraine and with global attention diverted by the Beijing Olympics.[28]

In Kyiv, there was little doubt what had just happened: a clear pre-planned Russian military operation that had intentionally provoked Saakashvili as a pretext for invading and expanding its influence. Onuch recalls sitting with policymakers and journalists in a Kyiv bar a few steps from some TV studios on the eve of the war when someone received a call about what was happening in Georgia. As the news was conveyed, the whole group immediately interpreted the events as being not just about Georgia. Instead, it was about the Kremlin punishing countries that had embarked on reforms and were pursuing a Euro-Atlantic course, and it was only a matter of time before Putin's Kremlin would go further and somehow attack Ukraine. One journalist even joked that it was a "good thing ours haven't been able to do the reforms because they are so busy fighting each other."

The backdrop to this particular conversation was a sushi-cum-karaoke bar, where in the corner a group of forty- to fifty-year-old "businessmen" in shiny striped suits surrounded by young Ukrainian women were hashing out deals while getting drunk off *horilka* (the Ukrainian word for vodka) and singing *popsa* (pop songs) from the 1990s mixed in with some Soviet-era tracks. Among the Independence Generation crowd there that night, sitting just a few tables away from this "old guard," the overwhelming feeling was that things were not getting better and instead actually getting worse.

It was a scene and a feeling of the type frequently exploited for laughs in Zelensky's *Vechernyy Kvartal* skit show, yet for most in their late twenties and early thirties, who like Zelensky also wanted to make a name for themselves and find success, it was not all that funny. In the back of everyone's mind was the April 2008 Bucharest NATO summit at which Germany and France had made it clear they would not support discussions of Georgia and Ukraine joining NATO any time soon,[29] and at which Putin made his infamous hot mic comment to US President George Bush that Ukraine is not "a real state."[30] Many wondered: Would Ukraine be next? The promise made by NATO at the same summit that Georgia and Ukraine would one day become members seemed remote enough to be meaningless.

Am I dead?

As a politician you are. As an anatomical unit, you're still throbbing on.

—Holoborodko and Chuyko, former prime minster,
Servant of the People, Season 3, Episode 1

The Orange fall from grace

These factors all came together to delegitimize the post-revolutionary politicians in Ukraine. The hopes of the Orange Revolution seemed to be dashed, and this was reflected in the mood of ordinary Ukrainians. By 2008, Yushchenko's approval rating had fallen to 10 percent. According to KIIS, in February 2009 nearly 70 percent of Ukrainians believed Yushchenko should leave the presidency, and as many as 56 percent thought he should be impeached.[31] As early as April 2008, the Razumkov Center's polling for the next presidential election had Yushchenko at 13 percent—while Tymoshenko was at 24 percent and Yanukovych at 20 percent. By December of the same year, Yushchenko's approval rating was as low as 4.5 percent, with the other two coming in at 16 and 20 percent respectively.[32] This placed Yushchenko in sixth place overall. On 17 January 2010, when the first round of the presidential elections was held, Yushchenko received only 5.45 percent of the vote and fifth place.[33] It was a humiliating defeat for a sitting president—there seemed to be no incumbent advantage to speak of.

> *They come, steal and leave. Then successors come and steal some more. Kings for a day.*
>
> —Dream conversation of Herodotus with Plutarch, *Servant of the People*, Season 1, Episode 2

Our analysis of a variety of indicators that measure the state and quality of liberal democracy in countries around the globe suggests that Ukraine was at least initially moving in a democratic direction. According to Freedom House's Freedom in the World index, Ukraine had become fully "free" owing to its vibrant political competition starting in 2005, a status that only the Baltic countries had previously achieved among the post-Soviet states.[34] Freedom House's separate "Nations in Transit" report also noted some improvements between 2004 and 2008, specifically in the media sector and in electoral processes (see Figure 3.1).[35] But by 2008 all the indicators had returned to their 2003 levels or worse. Specifically, corruption and judicial independence both showed significant backsliding, which continued after Yanukovych was elected in 2010. Judicial corruption is also a frequent theme in Kvartal 95 skits and the *Servant of the People* series. In the show's first season, the only honest person the new president can find to fill an important judicial post is a half-crazy and monkish former Orthodox priest, who is later shown in Episode 13 singing his verdict as if it were a religious chant. As Peter Solomon and Maria Popova note, the 2000s saw the Ukrainian judiciary at the center of major corruption scandals.[36]

What kind of social order do they have?
A democracy. Well … They call it a democracy.

—Dream conversation of Herodotus with Plutarch,
Servant of the People, Season 1, Episode 2

The third, and no less important, is to restore citizens' faith in justice by overcoming years of corruption, thanks to political will and the creation of independent law enforcement, anti-corruption, and judicial bodies.

—Volodymyr Zelensky, 13 September 2019[37]

Yet another indicator of the quality of democracy in a state is a country's "Polity2" score, which ranges from the least democratic -10 to the most democratic 10. Ukraine's score went up one point in 2006–11, rising from 6 to 7 (see Figure 3.2).[38] Ukraine also improved in different measures of democracy prepared by the Varieties of Democracy project (V-Dem) (See Figure 3.3.). This being said, these scores are notably problematic because they reflect common perceptions of experts, who are often biased in very specific ways.[39] Notably, the way ordinary people perceive the democracy they live in might be even more indicative of backsliding or at least of perceptions of it.

Surveys asking about people's actual levels of satisfaction with democracy are better positioned to capture this aspect of a country's democratic development. And, as we can see from data collected by the European Social Survey (Figure 3.4), ordinary Ukrainians' perception of and satisfaction with democracy remained extremely low throughout this period. Seventy-seven percent of Ukrainians were more likely to choose 5 or less when asked how satisfied they were with democracy in Ukraine on a scale of 0 to 10, where 10 denotes the most satisfied position and 0 the least. In fact, between 2004 and 2012 the lowest mean score was registered in 2008 (2.86), with the highest coming in 2004 (4.03) before dropping immediately after the Yushchenko and Tymoshenko teams took control of the government. Neither the Orange Revolution on its own nor those politicians who rose on its wave were able to make Ukrainians feel like they were living in a noticeably more democratic country.

It was during this period that Kvartal 95 began to make political satire central to their endeavor, famously lampooning the infighting between Yushchenko and Tymoshenko, often poking fun at their love–hate relationship. Tymoshenko's dealings with Putin in the negotiations over gas supplies were also a frequent target. As we have already noted, Yushchenko's and Tymoshenko's battles and relationship were also alluded to in *Servant of the People*, where the character Zhanna Borysenko is a clear reference to Tymoshenko.

It is no surprise that ordinary Ukrainians felt this way. Theirs was a patronal democracy, a corrupt democracy.[40] Much like in Seasons 1 and 2 of *Servant of the People*, political competition at the time involved competing patronal power networks exposing each other's corruption and creating a sense among most observers and ordinary people that corruption was worse than under Kuchma, where reports of it were often squelched. According to Transparency International's score assessing levels of governance, political and economic corruption in Ukraine were very high, making the country the second most corrupt in Europe after Russia.

– *Do the people live a poor life?*

– *Well. They lead the world in oil production.*

– *Olive oil?*

– *Sunflower oil.*

– *...I see.*
– *The world's third largest grain producer.*
– *That's right.*
– *They also make airplanes, combine harvesters, machines...*
– *Cars?*
– *Not really...*
– *Tractors!*
– *Right, tractors. That's good...*
– *So, what needs changing? They've got paradise.*
– *But the country is facing default.*
– *How is that possible? Where's all the wealth going, then?*
– *Into people's pockets.*

—Dream conversation of Herodotus with Plutarch
with interruptions from a sleeping Holoborodko,
Servant of the People, Season 1, Episode 2

Living off loans

On top of the pervasive corruption, the political elite was unable to implement the types of reforms that would improve the economic situation in Ukraine, which remained very poor, even compared to its neighbors in the east and west (except Moldova). There were, though, some improvements. For one, foreign direct investment and foreign aid increases brought a measure of economic stability. GDP per capita also increased—more than doubling over this period (Figure 3.6). But life expectancy was still very low, at around sixty-eight. Thus, the Independence Generation was entering middle age in a country where its members could barely get started, let alone get settled financially and professionally, by the time the end of their expected lifespan would start to near. And while the percentage of Ukrainians living on $3.20 a day declined sharply from 6 to less than 1 percent, the proportion of people living below 50 percent of the median income initially rose from 6.8 to 8.5 percent before falling to 6 percent by 2008 and again to 4.6 percent by 2013 (see Figure 3.7 on poverty).

> *A citizen who hired you for work saves their hard-earned money for two years to spend one week at a low-grade resort when you fly to Goa every month on their dime.*
>
> —Holoborodko, *Servant of the People*, Season 1, Episode 6

> *... He took out a loan to buy a microwave oven and makes monthly payments of 74 hryvnyas.*
>
> —A report on Holoborodko to the oligarchs, *Servant of the People*, Season 1, Episode 2

Most ordinary people, especially those from the Independence Generation trying to start out in life, began to take out loans in order to live—a long-running theme in the *Servant of the People* series. In fact, newly elected fictional president Holoborodko has an outstanding loan for a microwave he bought and against which he makes monthly installments of 74 hryvnyas (or $10 in 2004 prices). His parents also buy televisions and other household items on quotas—credit oftentimes pegged to international currencies. Although not uncommon in places like Argentina with extremely unstable economies, few middle-class West Europeans could understand buying a microwave or radio on credit instalments, as these items are typically affordable to those in the middle-income bracket. In the UK a low-end microwave can be bought for 45 pounds—easily affordable for a history teacher. Thus, the 2000s in Ukraine were characterized not only by political instability, but also by the squeezing of the middle class. Zelenksy's Kvartal 95 troupe made frequent quips about the indebtedness of ordinary citizens and how keeping up with the Joneses often meant getting further into debt. Those in their twenties and thirties also began buying flats and taking out loans in euros and dollars. And when the price of the hryvnya fell from 7 to 11 per dollar, they were suddenly near doubly indebted.

With an inflation rate of 9–25 percent (Figure 3.9), this situation did not improve for ordinary citizens. Food became increasingly unaffordable, with families choosing whether to purchase more expensive meat products or forgo meat altogether. When talking in an interview about his childhood, Zelensky noted that his father worked extra hard so that he and his friends from the block would always have meat to eat when they came over to his home. This is simply how ordinary Ukrainians thought about things—you either had to work extra hours and help feed your child's friends or you had to cut back.[41] To make matters worse, unemployment also hovered at 6.3 to 9.06 percent (Figure 3.8). And stabilization in unemployment came largely from out-migration, with a mass exodus of Ukrainians seeking to find work abroad.

But we also share a common pain. Each of us has died in the Donbas …

And each of us is a refugee …

And each of us is a migrant worker—the one who couldn't find himself at home, but has found income in a foreign country, and the one who is struggling with poverty, is forced to lose his own dignity.

But we will overcome all of this! Because each of us is a Ukrainian.

We are all Ukrainians: there are no bigger or lesser, or correct or incorrect Ukrainians. From Uzhhorod to Luhansk, from Chernihiv to Simferopol, in Lviv, Kharkiv, Donetsk, Dnipro and Odesa—we are Ukrainians. And we have to be one. After all, only then we are strong …

… I appeal to all Ukrainians on the planet!

… To all who are ready to build a new, strong, and successful Ukraine, I will gladly grant Ukrainian citizenship. You must come to Ukraine not to visit, but to return home. We are waiting for you. There is no need to bring souvenirs from abroad, but please, bring your knowledge, experience, and values …

—Volodymyr Zelensky, 20 May 2019, inauguration speech[42]

And you, the education minister? I trust you're okay? Where do your children study? Abroad?

—Holoborodko, *Servant of the People*, Season 1, Episode 5

Flight not fight

Between 2003 and 2013, Ukraine's population declined from 47.8 to 45.4 million (see Figure 3.10). It is estimated that nearly 2 million people left the country to find work elsewhere. According to research from the MOBILISE project, the most common countries people migrated to were Russia, Poland, Italy, and Spain, with immigration to the latter three being more tricky as it required visas, resulting in many Ukrainians working in the informal economy with few protections and often in extremely vulnerable positions.[43] It is hard not to think of the work of Albert O. Hirschman,[44] who wrote that in times of political and economic crisis ordinary citizens have two choices: to stay and fight and voice their discontent, or to flee—and in the 2000s many Ukrainians chose the latter route after seeing that even a revolution could not bring the change they so badly needed.

When abroad, Ukrainians began sending personal financial remittances to their families back home. These personal remittances in part kept the country running and by 2013 accounted for 5.07 percent of the country's GDP, an increase from 2.9 percent in 2003 (see Figure 3.11). As Ukraine found itself on the list of poorer economic countries, it also received higher rates of overseas development assistance per capita, although many claimed that this money never made it to ordinary people—another theme in Kvartal 95 skits and the *Servant of the People* series.

Episode 14 in Season 1, for example, unravels the multi-layered corruption involved in roadworks. Fictional president Holoborodko realizes leaders at every level—from the minister down to the local councilor and even to the workers themselves—all take a piece of the funding, making the price of needed infrastructural improvements more expensive at each level they go up. In the end, only a very small fraction of the allocated funds ever go to the actual work and materials involved. The politician tasked with the job ends up buying a house abroad, a boat, and cars for their family. Yet at the very bottom level the ordinary workers also steal, which is also a running theme in Kvartal 95's performances and *Servant of the People* as well as in Zelensky's messages to ordinary citizens. In this case, the forewoman explains that they steal the concrete and sand so they can sell it at the local market. Why? Because they have not been paid for several months and have to buy food for their families. And these ordinary workers can barely afford to buy food because the price of basic goods is constantly going up. This hits a nerve with many Ukrainians because they instantly recognize it as an authentically and sadly Ukrainian scene. It is no surprise then that millions of Ukrainians fled abroad to find work during this period, trying to find ways to pay for basic items or to simply make careers for themselves.

Things would get so bad for the orange leaders that people would eventually elect Yanukovych president in a democratic election in 2010.

Orange demise, Yanukovych's rise

With the orange politicians registering record low approval ratings, a seemingly chaotic political context, and fears that Russia would place further pressure on Ukraine, a significant portion of voters who had elected Yushchenko five years earlier or may even have protested decided either to abstain in the 2010 presidential election or place their bets with the Orange Revolution's villain—Viktor Yanukovych. At the core of Yanukovych's revival was not only deep disillusionment with the orange team, but a concerted effort to revive the former prime minister's image in order to project an air of normalcy, to convey that electing him president would bring a return to a familiar form of stability. The Party of Regions and its leading figure (Yanukovych) was finally shedding some of its Soviet image. The suits got sharper, the hair less helmet-like, and the speeches focused on a united Ukraine that would be European but non-aligned. In fact, signing an association agreement with the EU was part of his electoral campaign. But his message was not pro-NATO, the alliance being still unpopular among large segments of the Ukrainian population. The campaign's tone was positive, even optimistic, with the candidate recast as a kind of gruff but loving uncle who in fact had people's best interests at heart.[45] Among the architects of the party's makeover was the American political consultant Paul Manafort, who we now know was working with some Ukrainians, Russians, and Republicans—often with ties to the Kremlin and even criminal networks in Russia.[46]

In the end, a quite democratic election produced victory for an authoritarian movement. With Yushchenko not even making the runoff, the second round pitted Yanukovych against Tymoshenko. Procedurally, everything went without a hitch. Election commissions seemed more professionalized, any issues were quickly resolved, and the voting was generally free and fair, as the Organization for Security and Co-operation in Europe (OSCE) and other observation missions confirmed.[47]

Grandfather: Yes. At least I did [vote] while somebody didn't even care to vote.

Granddaughter: Why choose between a thief and bribe-taker? I'm a patriot, my future is in this country.

Mother: You may stay in this country for good, patriot. The plane won't wait.

Grandfather: … Go on, fly to your Poland, you patriot. But whine, whine from there that we elect the wrong guys.

Granddaughter: When there's someone worth electing I'll creep back in on all fours.

—Exchange between Holoborodko's father, niece, and sister, *Servant of the People*, Season 3, Episode 1

Yushchenko had concentrated mostly on attacking Tymoshenko, even refusing to endorse her over Yanukovych in the runoff. Political scientists suggest that such politics is what led 4.36 percent of voters to vote "against all" (a ballot option in Ukraine); in large urban centers like Kyiv and Lviv, the figure was 8 percent.[48] The electorate was indeed divided: even in the run-off, neither Yanukovych nor Tymoshenko won over 50 percent of the vote, receiving 48.95 percent and 45.47 percent respectively, with about 1 million votes separating the two.[49] The 4.36 percent voting "against all" was notably larger than the 3.48 percent margin separating the two candidates (see Figure 3.12 on Yanukovych's vote share). It is likely that Yushchenko's attacks on Tymoshenko cost her the presidency. This was of course a particularly sore point, as Tymoshenko had rallied behind Yushchenko in 2004 and was later imprisoned by Yanukovych. Yet just as quickly as he was elected, Yanukovych had proved a disappointment, just like his predecessors and immediate successor.

Where does it say that servants should live better than their masters?
Or maybe you're simply confused and serve another master? Instead of serving the people, you're the lackeys of oligarchs.

—Holoborodko, *Servant of the People*, Season 1, Episode 6

Another disappointment

Throughout this period, Russia continued to place pressure on Ukraine and the wider region. And almost immediately after his election, Yanukovych's team and the Party of Regions schemed to seize control of the parliament. They changed the constitution to make it more presidential, augmenting his power. As can be seen from the figures above, the 2010–13 period can only be described as one of steady, creeping democratic backsliding. Tymoshenko's imprisonment was a cause of particular concern among international observers and Ukrainian NGOs. But this was only one of many politically motivated cases: the whole of the judiciary became even further compromised and corrupt, with bribes being paid to rule in favor of connected individuals. In some ways, it felt like a return to the days of the 1990s but worse because Yanukovych relied heavily on a very small inner circle, and he was not a masterful manager like Kuchma. There were multiple infamous cases of family members of Party of Regions' deputies and local bosses driving drunk and even hitting pedestrians but receiving no sentences for their actions.

Taking all this together, it is no surprise that in 2012, according to the European Social Survey, 83.12 percent of Ukrainians agreed or strongly agreed that "the courts protect the rich and powerful over ordinary people." And the mean response on a scale of 0–10 reflecting how much Ukrainians trusted the legal system fell from an already low 3.9 to 1.9.

> *And remember well: in this country the law is the same [one] for all. And this "one" is me!*
>
> —Fictional President Surikov, *Servant of the People*, Season 3, Episode 1

Civic national identity in question

Yanukovych presided over two major policy changes touching on Ukrainian national identity. First, Yanukovych again sought to capitalize on the divisions over language in Ukraine, pushing through a new law on minority languages and implementing swift changes to the educational curriculum, including changes to textbooks that downplayed the Orange Revolution or even left it out altogether. This would again increase tensions between the island constituencies in the Donbas to the east and in Halychyna to the west. Still, for most Ukrainians in the middle of the country, this issue was not a priority.

Second, Yanukovych, who campaigned on closer ties to the EU, increasingly embraced and became more politically dependent on Russia, slowly turning his back on the EU and the pending free trade and association agreements he and his team had been negotiating. This reversal would indeed raise alarm bells among a wider cross-section of Ukrainian society, as many were eagerly awaiting closer ties with the EU and the visa-free travel that had been promised to them. Ukrainians still hoped that their country would become a "normal European country," as so many had told Onuch in over forty focus groups she conducted among Ukrainians between 2005 and 2020[50] and interlocutors had told Hale regularly as far back as the Kravchuk era.[51] That is what Europe represented to many Ukrainians, as well as the chance for a "normal," stable, and secure life. As Gumenyuk told us in an interview, for the Independence Generation specifically, "Europe for them was not about the opposition to Soviet Union. It was a place of comfortable life, of civilization ... Europe was about the quality of life ... and maybe democracy in the general terms."

Independence Generation in the 2000s

The first decade of the twenty-first century was a period of huge disappointment for Zelensky and others of his generation, not to mention the large majority of older Ukrainians who had also hoped for something better and remained oriented to Europe more than Russia. When listening to Kvartal 95 songs or watching the *Servant of the People* series, it is impossible to avoid the sense that Ukraine is a society and a culture based on frustration.

They, the politicians, always lie, cheat, and steal, and we, the people, do everything we can just to get by. But that also involves implicitly buying into the system, paying bribes and trying to use what contacts one has to get ahead. The Ukraine of the 2000s was a country entrenched in systemic corruption and informal patron-client relationships. Since no-one could rely on the state, they had to rely on a parallel system. Although there were big fish (the so-called oligarchs) who were particularly corrupt, the sea was also filled with many small fish that participated in the corruption at work, in the hospital, and at school. There was a sense that everyone was part of the problem, and whatever hope had been born in 2004 or 1991 seemed to be fading away. Indeed, the sense of "everybody does it" is the self-fulfilling prophecy at the heart of corrupt practices in patronalistic societies like Ukraine's.[52] This, indeed, was the main point of the story we discussed in the previous chapter told by President Holoborodko in Season 1, Episode 15, about how the transition from innocent Ukrainian baby to corruption-enabling adult begins with petty gifts to doctors at the maternity hospital itself.

Several key works studying youth in Ukraine and other younger post-communist generations have shown that those who had still been children in 1991 were turning away from politics, disenchanted by all these developments.[53] The presidential election of 2010 was the first election in which Ukrainians born in 1991 would be eligible to vote, and thus, their first election was one where there was little choice: all the candidates had risen to prominence in the late communist period and the turbulent 1990s, and the two in the final runoff had ties to major oligarchic clans. And of course, there was Yushchenko, a former "revolutionary" president who did not want to leave despite his paltry polling numbers. Unsurprisingly, youth turnout in the elections was lower, and their support for democracy had declined.[54] Moreover, for this generation, the elite discourse about ethnolinguistic divides made little sense, as they had grown up in a free and liberated Ukraine.

It is a surprise, however, to find that the Independence Generation was moving away from democracy and politics at this time. Using European Social Survey data, we find in regression analyses (controlling for sex, region of resdience, and education) that the Independence Generation—those born in 1975–85 and who were between the ages of six and sixteen in 1991—were statistically 9 and 6 percentage points less likely (at a 95 percent statistical significance level) than their older or younger counterparts to report having voted in the last national election when they were surveyed in 2010 and 2012 respectively. It is this group who were twenty-five to thirty-five in 2010, who were trying to build their families and careers in the Ukraine of the 2000s, who became heavily disenchanted with the options available to them.

Zelensky and his team wanted to make it in the world, however, and thus they had little choice but to have at least some connection to oligarchs and the corrupt media sector, even if they were running the risk of being compromised in the process. And so ambitious Ukrainians looked to neighboring countries in the EU or to Russia. Just like them, Zelensky, who originally wanted to be a diplomat and studied international economics and law at his local university, abandoned that dream to follow a new one in showbusiness in Russia.[55]

Zelensky in showbusiness

The last time we left off from Zelensky and his hometown crew, they were competing in the Moscow-based KVN circuit. They had a great deal of success, winning one of the top two spots in the Moscow top tier, with the Kvartal core group at the center. They were the only team from Ukraine, and from Kryvyy Rih no less. Many were stunned that they had been able to beat the Muscovites. KVN invited Zelensky to break with the Kvartal group and remain as an editor, but he refused—not least because it would mean leaving his team behind—causing a conflict with the head of KVN, Aleksandr Maslyakov. Just before the Orange Revolution, by Zelensky's account, the team returned to Kyiv and made the first *Vechernyy Kvartal*, and this led KVN to consider Zelensky *persona non grata*.[56]

As already mentioned, for anyone ambitious in the cultural sector and the media in Ukraine, the Kvartal crew had no choice but to work for oligarchs and play by their rules, at least to some extent. As Zelensky later told an interviewer, because pretty much all the major channels were owned by oligarchs, he would inevitably work for one of them if he pursued a career in television.[57] Kvartal began producing for 1+1 in 2003. In informal conversations under Chatham House Rules with a producer from 1+1, it was clear that politics and the media at the channel completely blended, with producers often moving to work on political campaigns. And everyone who worked in the industry saw that payments were made in envelopes. What Zelensky and his team might or might not have seen personally is not in question, for if they did not see it, then they would certainly have heard of these practices. But politics at this time was not so clearly repressive and visibly corrupt as it had been during Kuchma's era—there was more freedom after 2004, but journalists nevertheless felt it necessary to engage in self-censorship to avoid upsetting powerful oligarchs or politicians.

Separately, I want to address the journalists of these channels!

Someone bought the channels, but not you.

You are not property! Not Medvedchuk's collection, not Rabinovych's servants.

You are the fourth branch of power, you are also servants of the people.

—Volodymyr Zelensky, 8 July 2019[58]

A great deal has been made of Zelensky's connections to Kolomoyskyy, who bought 1+1 in 2008 and was still the channel's owner when Zelensky returned to 1+1 in 2012. But it was Oleksandr Rodnyanskyy Sr. who owned the channel and was its general producer in 2003, and it is he who took Zelensky under his wing and mentored him. There was a sense that at 1+1 everyone was family of sorts, including Rodnyanskyy, who is said to have nurtured Zelensky and his team. Many people associated with the 1+1 family and even Rodnyanskyy's son would find themselves working in President Zelenksy's team further down the line. Not everything is clear-cut, of course; people in the know tell us that Rodnyanskyy's son was brought on board not by Zelensky himself, but by his first Prime Minister, Oleksiy Honcharuk. Nonetheless, the relationship was close enough and there were surely some hard feelings when Zelensky and Kvartal 95 moved to Inter TV in 2005, when Zelensky was only twenty-seven.

Inter's offer had been too good to refuse. In 2010, at thirty-two, Zelensky became general producer for the whole channel, and his business partner and long-time friend Serhiy Shefir, with Zelensky from their early KVN days, became his deputy.[59] This is where Zelensky's life changed dramatically. He was no longer a young actor, a troupe leader, but was building his own media empire. He was a major player in the Ukrainian media context and had a hugely popular show. Not only highly ambitious, by all accounts he was also a very hardworking producer. This is potentially why he was so able to adjust to the trying demands of the presidency and later the war. In researching Zelensky, we have been surprised at how few pay attention to the fact that he was managing the top television channel in Ukraine at such a young age and was doing so successfully while also leading the Kvartal group and acting in films and television series.

When Zelensky began working there, the TV channel Inter was associated with a pro-Russian editorial position and was owned by Valeriy Khoroshkovskyy, who was a caretaker owner for Dmytro Firtash while the latter was restructuring some of his businesses (Firtash bought back full shares in 2013). During the period when Zelensky worked at Inter, Khoroshkovskyy became head of Ukraine's Security Services (the SBU). Both Khoroshkovskyy and Firtash were among the wealthiest men in Ukraine, and Firtash is also believed to have ties to Russia. Zelensky said that most of his contact was with Khoroshkovskyy, seeing Firtash only once or twice on holidays.[60] For some who know the full story of Firtash's dealings in Ukraine, this is more than enough to cast a major cloud of doubt around Zelensky. Inter also came under scrutiny because it broadcast largely Russian-language content, including many Russian-made sitcoms. This would become a major point of attack during the election campaign in 2019.

At the same time, Inter was Ukraine's top channel, boasting a 25 percent share of the general audience (see Figure 3.13). For anyone interested in launching a media empire, it would be prudent to work at Inter. 1+1 came in second with a 20 percent share, with other channels trailing behind. Poroshenko's Channel 5 only received about 1.5 percent and 2 percent of the total audience share in 2005 and 2007, respectively, and for the whole of 2003–13 it did not even make the top ten. Thus, it would appear that the language used on television shows was not a priority for most Ukrainians, or not yet at least.

Although Zelensky says that he has performed for nearly all post-Soviet presidents, including those in Russia,[61] it was not until he became general producer at Inter in 2010 that he started to really feel the political pressure. Sometime after his election as president, Yanukovych tried to woo Zelensky, even inviting him to his opulent, privatized residence Mezhyhirya. To hear Zelensky tell it, there was heavy drinking, and Yanukovych effectively offered him the ability to grab $100 million from the budget of a different channel if he switched.[62] Zelensky continued to feel political pressure, and thus, to avoid getting embroiled politically, he claims that he delegated management of the news at Inter to someone else because he had constant conflicts with it. His point of view at the time, he said, was that the news would carry the channel's official version of events while Kvartal would present viewers with the real story.[63] Since the show had high ratings, he received other offers, including from Victor Pinchuk.[64] Channel 1+1, now owned by Kolomoyskyy, though, repeatedly made him offers to switch back, and in 2012 Zelensky and his team finally agreed to do so.

The Kvartal crew

The Kvartal 95 endeavor is perhaps as close to a family business as one can get without actually working with family. Indeed, the core were childhood and university friends. It is best to understand this group as a tight-knit crew—most of whom had been there from the very first days on KVN. This is the Kvartal *tusovka*, as Ukrainians would call it. But how did Zelensky get to know these people? The core group of actors and writers were mostly original members of the KVN troupe. They are also the main cast members for *Servant of the People*.

The Kvartal business, which was managed by Ivan Bakanov, a lawyer and Zelensky's childhood friend who would go on to head Ukraine's intelligence agency, was no exception from Ukraine's convoluted business structures. It involved two primary entities.[65] One is 95 Kvartal, founded by the Cyprus-registered company Green Family LTD, which originally was reported as listing a Cypriot (Lukas Kolokotronis) as its end beneficiary, but as of 2019 was reported as listing Zelensky, the Shefir brothers, and a Kolomoyskyy associate among the end beneficiaries. As Zelensky would discuss publicly, the portfolio of Green Family LTD also included shares in companies doing business in Russia prior to 2014. The other is Studio Kvartal 95, which is owned by Zelensky (99.99 percent) and his wife Olena Zelenska (0.01 percent). The Shefir brothers, Serhiy and Borys, whom Zelensky met during his time as part of the Zaporizhzhya-Kryvyy Rih Transit KVN troupe, were also major partners throughout the process. Serhiy Shefir, fourteen years older than Zelensky and later to become the latter's aide as president, was one of the main writers of the *Servant of the People* series and had also been Zelensky's deputy general producer at Inter, as noted earlier. In fact, Serhiy Sherfir continued to be a mentor of sorts to Zelensky throughout the years despite technically being his assistant and deputy.

As we have already made clear, it was during this period that Zelensky's showbusiness career started taking off, tapping into deep frustrations with the failure of the country's elites to eliminate corruption, political dysfunction, and poverty and Ukraine's increasing drift away from the European aspirations of the majority. As well as the issue of Ukraine joining the European Union, Zelensky's skits also featured Ukrainians working abroad in the EU and those who could afford it vacationing there. Europe was both a destination and standard of quality of life and democracy—and Ukrainians were depicted as wanting to be there.

The turn away from Europe

For almost as long as independent Ukraine has existed, Russia has opposed the idea of it ever joining NATO, but it was originally much less concerned about the European Union. Even into Putin's third term as president, the Kremlin saw Ukraine's EU membership as a distant prospect, the consequences of which were more technical and economic than geopolitical. This began to change, however, when the EU began offering certain post-

Soviet countries "association agreements" that would come with a "Deep and Comprehensive Free Trade Agreement." As these negotiations gathered steam in Ukraine and elsewhere in 2013, Moscow appears to have realized that these agreements were indeed deep and comprehensive and, if implemented, would take these countries a considerable way toward meeting the standards for EU membership. This clashed with Putin's efforts to push deep and comprehensive economic integration in the other direction, gathering post-Soviet countries and potentially others into an emergent Eurasian Economic Union.

Ukraine's president at the time, Yanukovych, had previously tried to have the best of both worlds, openly pursuing the EU Association Agreement while also humoring Putin in his efforts to integrate the post-Soviet space and specifically the Commonwealth of Independent States. When Putin's push came to shove in November 2013, Yanukovych did what most had expected: he suspended negotiations on the Association Agreement. While he claimed this was not the end, the signal was clear enough: Ukraine's Euro-Atlantic prospects were in jeopardy. Although not a surprise to those who supported the opposition, to many of his voters this was a sharp U-turn from his electoral promises only two years earlier.

Ukrainians, and especially members of the Independence Generation now entering or in their thirties like Zelensky, wanted to be successful and to live in a normal European country. They saw their chances of personal success as intertwined with the country's political and economic trajectory. To them, Yanukovych's U-turn signaled that their goals were unlikely to be met under his administration.

ORANGE IS THE NEW CORRUPTION

WE RECOMMEND OUR READERS LISTEN TO

"Ukrayino My Syla" by KOLA

Found on the "Ukraine Top 100" Playlist on Spotify, a playlist by Vova Zavadskyy

https://open.spotify.com/album/5jyoBJwlhcZOzG8W4a4pgb

The air here is mine
Here, every corner is home
It smells of love and honor
Here is my family, all my people
I am a Ukrainian,
I will forever be proud of this!

We stand side by side
One for all and all for one!
We are a force!
We are undefeatable—Ukraine!

—Authors' own translation

I will remind you of her words today: "[some] will fall into the ground of poetry..."

—Volodymyr Zelensky, reciting Lina Kostenko, 20 March 2022[1]

Great people of a great country!
A country of power. A country of freedom. The people of absolute moral leadership.
We have endured nine days of darkness.

...

We responded to the invasion as we can in times of greatest danger.
Responded with heroism. Solidarity. Mutual assistance.
We responded in Ukrainian.
So that the history of Europe will remember it forever.
It will tell children about it.
Show it to grandchildren.

...

Ukrainians are united from Uzhhorod to Kharkiv, from Kyiv to Kherson.

...

—Volodymyr Zelensky, 4 March 2022[2]

4

THE ART OF POLITICS

So that God will see us from above, we make maidans.

—Studio Kvartal 95 song[3]

Almost as soon as it became known that Yanukovych would be suspending talks on the EU Association Agreement on 21 November 2013, conversations between friends in Kyiv-based chat groups moved to public posts. Well-known activists and journalists—many of them members of the Independence Generation—started calling for people to come to *Maidan Nezalezhnosti* (Independence Square). Several posts immediately went viral. And so began the protests that were about to turn into a moment of mass mobilization. Some of the early risers, including journalists and opposition figures, gathered by a large baroque column erected in 2001 under Kuchma, just after he had weathered the "Ukraine without Kuchma" protest wave. For those aware of the scandals around its construction, it was not only tacky but a symbol of corruption and "Kuchmism" more generally. With each day, an encampment grew, beginning with an influx of university students on the first night and reaching an initial crescendo on the first Saturday, when an astounding

250,000 people turned up. There was a sense of déjà vu. A long-time activist and now a mother of two in her late thirties texted, 'yeah of course we are all going—but for ^#&* sake why do we have to do this again?' And so, the "Euromaidan" mass mobilization was born. Journalists quickly latched on to the catchy moniker combining the Ukrainian word for square (*maidan*, pronounced "my-DON") with a reference to the European Union. Ukraine's main opposition parties hopped on the bandwagon, setting up a concert stage a mere 450 meters from the main protest site in Kyiv, on European Square, even though most protesters regarded them as pathetic hangers-on.[4]

While it was the opposition parties and university students that grabbed much of the international attention, the Euromaidan actually reflected the political coming of age of the Independence Generation. In or around their thirties, not only did they now have experience in mass mobilization but the more successful among them also had more money, enabling them to exercise their sense of Ukrainian civic duty their own way, on their own initiative. And they were determined not to make the mistakes of 2004, when the momentum was co-opted by establishment figures like Tymoshenko and Yushchenko.

So just imagine their disappointment when events seemed to be repeating themselves yet again in the mobilization's aftermath. After a long chain of events including protesters rebuffing a bloody crackdown to topple the regime and Russia responding with an even bloodier invasion and land grab, the political spoils once again landed in the hands of an establishment figure. This time, it was consummate insider and oligarch Poroshenko—a member of every administration and regime coalition since Kuchma, including holding key posts in Yanukovych's government—who had rebranded himself as a revolutionary figure and co-opted the *maidan*'s radical ethos for his electoral victory. During Poroshenko's time in office, not least thanks to an active civil society born on the *maidan*, a great deal was accomplished, including the initial phase of decentralization and military reform. But, for ordinary Ukrainians, politics remained much the same. Corruption continued to fester, and Ukraine appeared to become even more deeply mired in poverty. It was this mass disappointment, more than anything else, that fueled Zelensky's rise to political prominence, setting him up for his presidential run.

In the pages that follow, we explore how it was possible for the hopes of the Euromaidan to have been crushed. What explains Poroshenko's plummeting approval ratings? And how did this context give rise to Zelensky's presidential campaign?

The Maidan was noisy …

We are wounded in our hearts, but still alive

We walk along the street, with a burning soul.

We are lied to, we laugh.

We are suffocated, we breathe.

We are torn, we sew,

We are blinded, we see.

—Studio Kvartal 95 song[5]

all the hopes of the Maidan again … It seemed like everyone was standing on the Maidan …

—Studio Kvartal 95 song[6]

The Euromaidan

Had Yanukovych simply waited the initial protests out, it is likely that he would have prevailed. Instead, he ramped up the violence, something even Kuchma before him had not dared to do. On the night of 29–30 November, his regime sent Berkut special forces to clear the protest encampment in Independence Square.

Scenes of brutality spread on social media and opposition television. There was security camera footage of Berkut forces chasing foreign and local journalists more than 900 meters uphill, and a film from one journalist's own camera of him being beaten while screaming "I'm a journalist [*presa*]!" For the protesters and much of the country at large, the Euromaidan was transformed. It was no longer just about Ukraine's path toward the EU; it was now also about the protection of basic human rights. A team led by Onuch collected on-site interviews, conducted focus groups, and carried out on-site protest participant surveys. In her field notes, she has information about a typical Donetsk-based mother who explained that she did not care about the EU and had even voted for Yanukovych but joined the protest because she wanted to live in a normal country where young people were not beaten, saying "it could have been [her] son [who was] beaten." There was a widespread sense that the regime had overstepped a line and reached a point of no return. Cities across the country began their own Euromaidans from the very first night, but now they grew larger, including even in the incumbent's hometown, Donetsk, where a small tent was erected and local activists demonstrated each day.

Overall, some 2 million people are estimated to have joined the Euromaidan protests at some point. Onuch managed to survey a large sample of the protesters over the course of the events and found that 26 percent were there because they wanted a democratic future for Ukraine, while 27 percent cited defense of their personal rights as citizens.[7] The Independence Generation across Ukraine tended to echo these sentiments. Data from the European Social Survey in 2013, immediately before the protests, show that members of this generation felt that Ukraine was much less democratic than it should be.[8] Onuch's survey also found that a similar proportion of protesters was motivated by wanting Ukraine to join the EU and the need to hold the police and government responsible for the violence perpetrated against ordinary citizens. Another finding was that motivations shifted as the repression ramped up, with the protests becoming more about the regime and European values and not simply Ukraine joining the EU.[9]

Onuch's data show that the typical protester was a member of the Independence Generation, with a median age of thirty-two and an average age of thirty-six.[10] The median protester was also employed full time, highly educated, and more likely than the general population to speak Ukrainian at work and in their private lives. While most said they had supported opposition candidates and parties in the preceding elections, around 2 percent admitted to voting for Yanukovych. Most of the protesters on the *maidan* were from Kyiv, 16 percent said they had traveled from western Ukraine, and 3 percent were from the south or east. Onuch's team noted that southeastern and formerly pro-Yanukovych protesters were reluctant to report this, answering "we are not from here," and thus it is likely that their participation has been underestimated. Research by Emma Mateo shows that Euromaidan protests were actually quite common in the southeastern cities and towns themselves.[11]

Where was Zelensky in all of this? His native oblast, Dnipropetrovsk, was home to some of the largest protest marches in the region. In the final weeks of the protest, *babushkas* (grandmothers) began storming local village councils. Local businesspeople even projected Tchaikovsky's *Swan Lake* onto city center buildings, the same ballet Soviet television infamously used to broadcast when a change in leadership was afoot. The message to Yanukovych was clear: your days are numbered. We know from informants that Zelensky and some of his Kvartal crew, based in Kyiv at the time, joined some of the protests and made donations to support activists and events on the ground. Later on in 2014 Zelensky also made a donation of

1 million hryvnyas to the Ukrainian Military and ATO needs.[12] But unlike so many of their generational peers, they did so without seeking a high profile or personal leadership roles. Support for this type of protest activity is also a theme in Zelensky's post-2014 performances.

> *If we didn't stand out on the streets of this city, then what country would I have been living in?*
>
> —Studio Kvartal 95 song[13]

Sadly, the regime learned the wrong lesson from its initial response and ramped up the repression as December rolled into January. Protesters responded in kind, turning to Molotov cocktails to defend themselves and push the regime back onto its heels. The violence culminated in a three-day stand-off in February, when the regime resorted to sniper attacks on unarmed people on the square. On 18–19 February, the bells of Kyiv's Mykhaylivskyy Monastery rang out in alarm. Onuch recalls an activist friend calling her: "Olyu, they are dying on the cold floor! Can we get some blankets from your house?"—Onuch's family's flat was within walking distance of the monastery. Few would or can forget that night, and not all would live to remember it, with 103 protesters and thirteen police losing their lives in those three days.[14] Yanukovych fled first to eastern Ukraine and then to Russia under the cover of night.

In the aftermath of these events, older political divisions among "democrats" re-emerged. These did not center on partisanship as usually understood in the West. Instead, they centered on a question of identity and strategy: Should democracy be sought by basing activism on the liberal and civic ideals of Ukrainianness, or could Ukraine only become truly democratic if it were culturally and linguistically Ukrainian as frequently understood in Halychyna, maximally walled off from Russian imperial and authoritarian influence and associated Soviet legacies?[15] This divide would come to be reflected in the discourses of post-Euromaidan politicians and would play out dramatically in the 2019 presidential election, as described in the next chapter. One aspect of this discourse involves the name that should be given to the events of 2013–14. Some dub them the "Revolution of Dignity" to assign it a certain weight, while others prefer different terms, in part to avoid belittling other mass mobilizations, which were also about a sense of dignity.[16] A more neutral term is the "Euromaidan" mass protest.

Russia launches its war

To the east, the Kremlin was watching closely. Having only just recovered from the largest opposition protests of the Putin era two years earlier, Russia's leadership was likely worried that the downfall of its man in Kyiv would set a bad example for its opponents at home.[17] It would be even worse if his downfall translated into a successful democratic Ukraine, making opposition to Putin seem even more attractive. "Hard" geopolitical realities were also at stake: Russia's most important naval base, home to its Black Sea Fleet, was in Sevastopol, a city on Ukraine's Crimean peninsula.[18] Many Russians had long seen Crimea as "Russian," having wound up in Ukraine only by historic accident.[19]

Putin acted quickly to try to snatch a victory from the jaws of defeat, first mobilizing unidentified "little green men" (read: Russian troops) to swiftly seize Crimea from a stunned Ukrainian military, some of the members of which defected to the Russian side. Recently released internal documents indicate that the transitional Ukrainian leadership decided not to fight for Crimea primarily to save lives, unsure whether its forces would be loyal to Yanukovych or the temporary government or even whether they had the capacity to resist, along with a sense that Crimea was not core Ukrainian territory.[20] The Obama administration's hesitant response is also likely to have discouraged Ukraine from militarily engaging with Russia, lest all-out war break out.[21] After mimicking a referendum, Russia annexed Crimea on 18 March 2014, the first forcible annexation of a neighbor's internationally recognized territory in Europe since World War II.

The loss of Crimea became a *cause célèbre*. Some Ukrainian nationalist and right-wing patriotic groups even took up the plight of an ethnic minority, the Crimean Tatars, descendants of the ethnic group that predated both Russians and Ukrainians on the peninsula. Zelensky and his Kvartal troupe reflect this sentiment in many of their skits, depicting colonial attitudes among Russian vacationers in Crimea and dedicating many songs to it. In fact, the troupe's discourse shifted in 2014. While they further dismayed many of their critics by continuing to sing primarily in Russian, they consistently sang about how the invaded territories will always be Ukrainian. The songs conveyed a sense that Ukraine's political elites were to blame, including for placing emphasis on language rather than civic unity.

Do not separate, loving Crimea
Do not separate, love
Don't vote at gunpoint
We will not tire of waiting for you.

—Studio Kvartal 95 song[22]

By April, however, Ukraine's government and military were regrouping, and when Russian forces began to foment an insurgency in eastern and southern Ukraine, the population and government mobilized. A combination of Ukraine's military and grassroots "volunteer battalions," some linked to far-right groups and others primarily Russian-speaking and financed by oligarchs, ultimately limited Russia's gains to the self-proclaimed "Donetsk People's Republic" (DNR) and "Luhansk People's Republic" (LNR) in parts of Ukraine's industrial and rural Donbas region.

Neither side gave in, leading war to become a grinding feature of life in this region, one that had taken the lives of over 13,000 people by the end of 2021—and causing misery for countless others who considered these areas home. By November 2014, the government estimated that nearly half a million people had had to be resettled after fleeing their homes in eastern Ukraine.[23] A 2014–15 ceasefire agreement through what became known as the Minsk negotiations did not stop the carnage, with both sides accusing the other of violating the resulting agreements. Many in Ukraine feared Russia would use the accord's provisions on special autonomy and representation for the occupied Donbas regions to sway Ukrainian politics long into the future.

> *But Luhansk, Donetsk … suddenly they hang the tricolor … I love my family for sure! All her beautiful cities. Kyiv–Lviv, on Donetsk–Dzhankoy. I will never share this land with a lowly person.*[24]
>
> —Studio Kvartal 95 song[25]

> *Whose Crimea, someone else's or ours? Let the colors be repainted for a while, but it will never become Russian!*
>
> —Studio Kvartal 95 song[26]

Kvartal's songs and skits, as well as Zelensky's solo speeches and interviews, make clear he opposed the violence, so perhaps he would have accepted some kind of compromise to end it. But his and Kvartal's commitment to Ukraine's territorial integrity came through even more clearly, including frequent references to Crimea as nothing other than Ukrainian. There was thus no uncertainty about what side they stood on: the side of Ukraine as their *rodina* (Russian for "motherland").

> *Let them lie, that we are getting stronger, here are new betrayals. From the separatists, and from the federalists. It's a shame to give in, it's worse to sell. But if we fall, we must get up and fight.*
>
> —Studio Kvartal 95 Song[27]

And who's there to vote for? It's always the lesser of two assholes and it's been this way for twenty-five years. You know what else? Nothing will change again. You know why? Because you, my dad, me, we'll once again vote for another shitstick! Yeah, because we all know he's an asswipe, but the other person is worse!

— Holoborodko, *Servant of the People*, Season 1, Episode 1

A consummate insider president

The Euromaidan made some politicians and broke others. Most dramatically, Yanukovych's Party of Regions found itself not only unceremoniously toppled but also discredited. Ironically, the parties that had been the most visible in the Euromaidan also emerged broken. As revolutionary victory had neared on 21 February 2014, world-famous boxer and UDAR Party chief Vitaliy Klychko (often spelled Vitali Klitschko), *Svoboda* (Freedom) Party leader Oleh Tyahnybok, and acting Fatherland Party leader Arseniy Yatsenyuk tried to seal the victory through a deal with Yanukovych that was widely seen as a betrayal.

But the Euromaidan made Poroshenko. Or, perhaps more accurately, remade him. Remade, because he was no newcomer to politics but had been a major player in the patronal politics of the two preceding decades. He was the consummate insider. Having made his money as a confectioner before expanding into the media and other industries, he was frequently counted among the country's oligarchs. So politically active was Poroshenko that he had been part of every president's governing team since the 1990s. He was even a founding member of the Party of Regions. Key to his survival was an impressive knack for jumping ship at the right time, leaving each sinking political vessel just prior to its demise. True to form, Poroshenko abandoned Yanukovych long before the spark that lit the Euromaidan mass mobilization. When the Euromaidan emerged, his Channel 5 covered the events in a positive light. When Poroshenko himself appeared on the *maidan*, he proved he could hold an audience as he inveighed for a European future and warned Yanukovych not to take Ukraine back to Russia's fold.[28]

Over the course of the Euromaidan, Poroshenko went from 2–4 percent in the presidential polls to over 20 percent, making him the frontrunner in the next presidential election.[29] In a pattern common in patronal polities, Ukraine's oligarchs quickly sought to get on the good side of the likely winner, striking deals that cleared some of Poroshenko's peskiest rivals out of the way—exactly the kinds of deals depicted on *Servant of the People*.[30] One of these was believed to involve Kolomoyskyy, the owner of the 1+1 television channel, who was considered to have been critical of Yanukovych prior to his ouster.[31] On 25 May 2014, Poroshenko became the first candidate ever to win a Ukrainian presidential election without a runoff, netting 55 percent of the vote to Tymoshenko's 13 percent (see Figure 4.1 for Poroshenko's vote share by oblast). Far-right candidates, such as Right Sector's Dmytro Yarosh, got less than 5 percent of the total vote combined, assuaging fears that fascism could gain traction in the crisis-ridden country.[32]

Zelensky himself reports voting for Poroshenko, as did his parents. The latter, he said, had always voted for parties, like the Party of Regions, that had their political bases in southeastern Ukraine, even after the Orange Revolution. "This is their region, what's to argue about?" After the Euromaidan, and with the start of war, things changed, even in the southeast. "Everyone had hope," he recalled, comparing the new president to a film that everyone says will be amazing.[33]

In the end, we supposedly changed power.

—Studio Kvartal 95 song[34]

Poroshenko may well have expected his historic win to translate into a similar victory in the upcoming parliamentary elections, giving him a majority in the Verkhovna Rada to carry out his agenda, notwithstanding Ukraine's divided-executive constitution. But it was not to be.[35] Some of his key supporters chose to run on separate tickets, and in the end his bloc won just 132 of the 421 seats in Ukraine's 26 October Rada elections.[36] While he was able to strike another deal with key power players to forge a majority coalition, the same kind of elite agreement that Zelensky's show was constantly skewering, this also meant he had to contend with the oligarchs' interests to get anything done.[37]

The winning parties, though, did usher in some eager changemakers. For one thing, the new Rada included forty-nine women, the largest number ever, along with several new faces. Among them were some prominent Euromaidan activists and journalists from the Independence Generation, including Mustafa Nayyem, Serhiy Leshchenko, Svitlana Zalishchuk, and Hanna Hopko. They would shake up several votes in the parliament, including going against their own parties when they felt it necessary. Despite being in Poroshenko's coalition, Nayyem and Leshchenko openly opposed and criticized him, including for corrupt practices.

The Poroshenko presidency

Poroshenko accomplished a great deal in his presidency.[38] While Ukraine could not push Russia out of Crimea and the areas claimed by the self-proclaimed DNR and LNR, it did prevent Russian forces from taking even more land. Reflecting strong popular support for a ceasefire over the summer of 2014,[39] and at the urging of US advisors,[40] Poroshenko pursued negotiations that after a failed effort now known as "Minsk I," produced the ceasefire known widely as "Minsk II." Among other things, the Minsk accords required Ukraine to amend its constitution, decentralizing authority and giving special autonomy to the occupied areas of the Donbas. It proved to be a ceasefire in name only. Ukraine insisted that free and fair elections uncontrolled by Russia should come first in the occupied territories, a position Russia refused to countenance. Accordingly, with each side blaming the other for violating the agreement, the fighting continued, and the death toll steadily rose, topping 4,000 by the end of 2014.[41]

It was under Poroshenko that Ukraine began major military reforms that proved vital to its survival as a state in 2022.[42] Most attention went to the integration of volunteer militias—sometimes associated with far-right symbolism and controversial political behavior—into its military structure, a move that inspired more doubt than hope among Ukraine's Western allies.[43] Yet Ukraine also decentralized its military command structure. While Russia had stuck with the Soviet military's longstanding practice of highly centralized control, Ukraine gave more operational authority to its commanders to make tactical decisions quickly as conditions change. According to security expert Mariya Omelicheva, this reform gave Ukraine's military an important advantage over Russia in the weeks after the Kremlin launched its all-out invasion in 2022, ultimately helping to save the country from being overrun.[44]

A wide range of other changes also took place on Poroshenko's watch. While the Minsk II agreement obliged Ukraine to decentralize political power, he avoided devolving authority to Ukraine's regions, the model advocated by Putin.[45] Ukraine instead ceded substantial new authority to local governments and allowed them to organize themselves voluntarily into larger local units called *hromadas*.[46]

Poroshenko also implemented a series of reforms framed as insulating Ukraine from pernicious Russian cultural influence as part of the Kremlin's "hybrid warfare." These included "decommunization," which banned Communist symbolism and ultimately the Communist Party of Ukraine itself, which still had a delegation in parliament as of the summer of 2014. As part of these reforms, the southeastern megopolis of Dnipropetrovsk, close to Zelensky's own Kryvyy Rih, became simply "Dnipro." Another such reform was "lustration," which barred people who had occupied key positions in the Yanukovych regime and certain others deemed supportive of that era's repression from running for or holding many state offices for a certain period of time.[47]

Affecting many people's personal lives more directly were bans on Russian TV channels and Russia's social media platforms, Vkontakte (VK) and Odnoklassniki, both of which had been highly popular in Ukraine (along with Facebook), as well as Russia's popular search engine, Yandex.[48] Ukrainian media also came under increasing restrictions. To support the Ukrainian language, a November 2016 law imposed quotas requiring a quarter of all radio songs to be in Ukrainian, with more required in successive years.[49] Television and radio stations with national audiences also had to make sure that at least three-quarters of their programming was in Ukrainian, with certain exceptions. Russian-language films had to have subtitles.[50] Beginning in 2014, Ukrainian authorities maintained lists of individual Russian actors supporting Crimea's annexation and denied them entry into or airtime in Ukraine.

It was at the Young Leninist summer camp in the Carpathians.

It's now called Stepan Bandera.

—Holoborodko's friends reminiscing about their youth,
Servant of the People, Season 1, Episode 7

Some of these "cultural" reforms had more public support than others. Hale and Kulyk found in early 2017 that two-thirds of all Ukrainian residents favored the state actively introducing the Ukrainian language into all spheres of life, a position even backed by many Russian-speakers. A majority of 53 percent opposed banning individual Russian films or performers, however.[51] Even as the Poroshenko era was coming to a close, in early 2019, 56 percent thought it was a mistake to ban individual Russian artists and films, and a plurality was against banning Russian TV and social media.[52] Zelensky was likely part of this 53 and 56 percent. Because they featured actors who had traveled without permission to Crimea, some of Zelensky's own films could not be shown in Ukraine for a period of time.[53] Zelensky openly criticized some of these policies, as well as those that punished actors and restricted access to certain cultural products.[54] To some, cultural reforms were simply a distraction from the many other problems facing the country.

More damaging for Poroshenko was that the economy failed to recover over the five years of his presidency, with yet more ordinary Ukrainians leaving the country to seek gainful employment. Figures 4.2–5 tell this story through data on unemployment, population, remittances, and poverty. Reform was not completely absent. In the financial sector, for example, National Bank chief Valeriya Hontareva spearheaded an effort to weed out insolvent banks that had enabled oligarchs to issue massive loans to themselves without ever paying them back.[55] Her reforms, including a partial floating of the hryvnya, helped stabilize the National Bank, were met with praise, and helped Ukraine get a $17.5 billion bailout package from the IMF.[56] This reform was marred by one insolvent bank that held nearly one-third of the country's individual deposits and was thus deemed "too big to fail." This was Pryvat Bank, co-owned by oligarch and then-governor of Dnipropetrovsk Kolomoyskyy, then in alliance with Poroshenko.[57] The National Bank bailed it out to the tune of $5.6 billion.[58] According to Standard & Poor's, Ukraine's losses approached 5 percent of its GDP.[59] An audit later found the bank to have engaged in "large-scale fraud" for a decade with over $5 billion unaccounted for. Although Kolomoyskyy denied any wrongdoing,[60] the government turned on him, nationalizing Pryvat in 2016. Hontareva left her post—citing political pressure.[61]

There is a crisis at the gate ... Oh!
I lie on the podium
I transfer hryvnya to bucks,
I am friends with Georgians.

—Kvartal 95 song, "We Are So Different"[62]

In highly patronalistic societies, corrupt practices can be tenacious, so it was perhaps to be expected that the high hopes for change ushered in by the Euromaidan would meet the same fate as the euphoria surrounding the Orange Revolution nearly a decade earlier. Within the first year of Poroshenko's presidency, Ukraine took several steps in the right direction, such as the creation of two new anti-corruption organs: the National Anticorruption Bureau of Ukraine, widely known by its acronym NABU, and the Specialized Anticorruption Prosecutor's Office (SAPO). Designed to be independent of political control and empowered to root out corruption among high officials, NABU was to hand cases over to SAPO for prosecution.[63] But before long, seemingly all state agencies involved in the fight against corruption began training their sights on each other, with the agency previously in charge of such initiatives, Ukraine's General Prosecutor's Office, at the center of it.[64] US Ambassador Marie Yovanovitch, who was closely monitoring Ukrainian anti-corruption efforts, came to believe that Poroshenko and his supporters were actively seeking to bring NABU and SAPO under their control, in part to thwart an investigation into illegal sales of Ukrainian biometric passports that investigators thought involved high-level government officials.[65] In another emblematic episode,

Poroshenko granted citizenship to former reformist Georgian president Mikheil Saakashvili and made him governor of Odesa, but when Saakashvili began accusing the government of undermining his efforts, he was stripped of his citizenship and all but booted out of the country. By the time Poroshenko left office, not a single top official had been convicted or jailed.[66]

Surikov: Channel 3 recently launched an independent investigation revealing what I have and more importantly what I do not have.

Journalist 1: But channel 3 is owned by you is it not?

Journalist 2: You recently donated computers to orphanages...

Surikov: That is right.

Journalist 2: But I know that money was not in the budget. I also know you paid for those computers out of your own expense.

Surikov: Let's not talk about me again ... I do help as I can. But how could I do otherwise? Every child deserves care.

Press Secretary: You did not introduce yourself.

Journalist 2: Oleh Bazylevych Channel 3.

—Exchange between journalists and President Surikov,
Servant of the People, Season 3, Episode 1

Perhaps most damaging of all for Poroshenko was the persistent stench of corruption that surrounded him, though the specifics were vehemently denied by the president himself. His son Oleksiy was given a spot near the top of the Poroshenko Bloc party list in the 2014 parliamentary elections. He refused to sell off his Channel 5 television station. And while he ceded management of his candy empire to the reputable international Rothschild firm, his wares were seemingly everywhere in Ukraine.[67] Other businesses of his were managed by his friends.[68] He did not sell important assets in Russia and Russian-occupied Crimea, though he argued this would have been impossible since Russia had frozen his assets and claimed that he did not receive any income from any sales in these places.[69] One joint American–Ukrainian investigation claimed to have exposed "secret meetings" that raised "questions of backdoor deals" between Poroshenko and Viktor Medvedchuk, a veteran behind-the-scenes operator and reputed oligarch whose relationship to Putin ran so deep that Putin became godfather to his daughter.[70] Thus while perceptions of corruption in Ukraine improved slightly under Poroshenko as Figure 4.6 shows, his conduct placed a cloud over any reforms that did take place. And the fiercest Independence Generation anti-corruption crusaders in his own parliamentary delegation were not afraid to call him out on it.

Poroshenko-era governments were also accused of at least tacitly supporting extralegal measures against media suspected of wittingly or unwittingly aiding Russia's cause. One of the most horrific of these was the July 2016 car bomb that killed Pavel Sheremet, a journalist at the opposition-minded Russian-language *Radio Vesti*, accused by many of being a Kremlin mouthpiece. Poroshenko himself denied any threat to journalists in Ukraine.[71] But reflecting worries that many in Ukraine had about such developments, especially in southeastern Ukraine, Zelensky himself would later make the failure to find Sheremet's killers one of his first questions to Poroshenko in their head-to-head debate.[72]

The old playbook returns: identity politics

In a last-ditch effort to turn the political tide as the 2019 election approached, Poroshenko sought to wrap himself in the anti-Russian cause more tightly than ever, ramping up an emphasis on cultural and largely symbolic issues. Political scientist Solomiya Kryvenko examined Poroshenko's last two speeches on Constitution Day (28 June) and found that they were strikingly "bimodal," tending to reflect us–them binaries with an emphasis on terms like "Russian aggressor" and "fifth column."[73] Accordingly, in August 2018, he ordered the Foreign Affairs Ministry to let the Ukraine–Russia friendship treaty lapse[74] and announced bills that would embed Ukraine's Euro-Atlantic orientation in the Constitution.[75] That same month, he launched legislation to make "Glory to Ukraine!" and the reply "Glory to heroes!" an official military salute.[76] It was also during this period that Poroshenko initiated a new law expanding on his prior promotion of the Ukrainian language.[77] He successfully championed a longstanding effort to have Constantinople grant the Ukrainian Orthodox Church *tomos* (official certification of autocephaly) and thus independence from the Moscow Patriarchate. In another triumph of this period, the EU granted what Ukrainians widely called *bezviz*, the right to travel to EU countries without a visa, which Poroshenko trumpeted as "a final exit of our country from the Russian Empire.[78] In late 2018, after Russia seized Ukrainian vessels, Poroshenko declared a period of martial law that would have upset the electoral calendar. Parliament forced him to scale it back so that it would end just before the campaign began and so that it did not cover all of Ukraine, though it still applied in regions where the president's support was weakest.[79] None of this saved him in the eyes of the public, as illustrated by Figure 4.7.

Poroshenko had some staunch supporters who were thrilled that they had finally found a politician who was willing to double down on issues related to language and religion, someone willing to support conservative national-patriotic views on these issues. To them, the unsavory whiff of his personal affairs and failures to tackle corruption and bread-and-butter issues could be forgiven, perhaps written off to the war. But many others viewed him differently, seeing more bad than good by the time he entered the fifth and final year of his presidential term. His presidency's shortcomings were not only experienced in the daily lives of ordinary Ukrainians but were also on vivid display on their television screens. Much of Season 3 of *Servant of the People* depicts problems with Poroshenko's policies, and many Kvartal songs and skits focused on Poroshenko's quirks and failings.

You are my oligarch!
Democracy's favorite
Three percent walker!
We are so poor … Seychelles are pale,
The banks are scattered,
Taxpayers!
We are so modest
… Country houses,
… I close my eyes and represent the people …
Crisis, hunger, delicious barbecue.

—Studio Kvartal 95, "We Are So Different"

Talking with a journalist just days before he announced his candidacy for president in December 2018, Zelensky remarked that if Poroshenko had been like a film that everyone in 2014 was saying would be amazing, he was now like that same film when it turned out to be mediocre. His main feeling about Poroshenko, Zelensky said, was now one of "disappointment."[80] Poroshenko himself summed up the national feeling well in a September 2018 address to parliament. "Most Ukrainians," the President lamented, "have not yet felt improvement in their welfare."[81] The stage was set—literally, as it happens—for Zelensky or someone like him to take up the baton and challenge the incumbent, somehow conveying that change was possible. But how?

Enter Zelensky

As Poroshenko's reputation waned, Zelensky's own standing among Ukraine's mass public waxed meteorically. His *Vechernyy*

Kvartal concerts increasingly gained must-see status, becoming not only sources of humor and sharp political satire but something like collective therapy for an increasingly disillusioned nation. A patronal democracy in full flower, full of vibrant competition, vile corruption, and colorful yet flawed political characters, Ukrainian politics provided an endless supply of material for Kvartal's alchemists to turn into television gold. Kolomoyskyy's 1+1 TV channel, which had broadcast *Vechernyy Kvartal* and employed Zelensky's team since 2012, could not have been more pleased with the crew's success. Moreover, the connection between Kvartal and society was far from one-sided. While Zelensky's troupe supplied a vitally needed release for the public, he was also learning a great deal about their needs and concerns as Kvartal toured the country, reaching nearly every major urban center between the Euromaidan Revolution and 2019. By the time he declared his candidacy, he had gained first-hand exposure to the struggles facing ordinary people, their frustration with continued corruption and the war, and the strengthening of civic national identity in Ukraine. "That is what touring the country will do to you," as one journalist put it in an interview, "you see the real Ukraine."[82]

Vechernyy Kvartal concerts were certainly sometimes off-color, not politically correct, and in some cases outright offensive, but they were always unpretentious. Some called them "full of gender and national (mostly Ukrainian-focused) stereotypes" with satire "on the verge of defamation and obscenity."[83] While not to everyone's taste, this mix resonated with millions of Ukrainian viewers. By one account, over 85 percent of the population claimed to have seen the show prior to Zelensky's election in 2019.[84] This obviously included voters. Many skits were highly political. Most of these sketches satirized the corrupt political elite. Claims that might be difficult to substantiate, such as connections between politicians and oligarchs, could easily be made into jokes, satire, or insinuation ("it's just a joke!"). Viewers would understand that there was typically some grain of truth behind the joke.

Kvartal's content became more political after the annexation of Crimea, as did the patriotic content of its songs, our analysis finds. One study of the show's skits and monologues estimates that "around a third of the show's airtime" between March 2017 and March 2018 was overtly political, and we find important political content implied even in many sketches seemingly addressing other themes (like petty corruption or civic responsibility).[85] Some skits depicted the realities of annexation and war. For example, in "*Krym nash*" (Russia's infamous cry of "Crimea is ours"), Zelensky and Kravets play a Russian family on vacation. The Russian tourist is brash, loud, gangster-ish, and extremely unappealing. When his wife asks: "Why did you not vacation here before?" he answers: "Because I did not like the Ukrainian Crimea, I like our Russian Crimea." A few minutes later, the troupe sings an emotional song about Crimea leaving Ukraine, quickly changing the mood.[86] The concerts would often end with lines about the army and Ukraine's heroes on the front lines. While high-brow electorates often dismissed the show entirely, considering it a vulgar *sovok* or *homo soveticus* brand of humor, its large audience would surely have noticed this emphasis on the political and patriotic.

Zelensky viewed such programming as having an important role to play in Ukraine's political life and thus already considered himself to be actively involved in politics. This is something of a running theme in his interviews. In one, he compares the role of political humor to that of a speed limit sign, a way of communicating to people behind the wheel (politicians) that they should adjust the way they are driving because there is dangerous road ahead.[87] Elsewhere, he further explained that "humor reflects society. Humor is a kind of easy way for any leader of the country (this is very important) to understand where he lives, in what kind of situation."[88] He took pains to emphasize that his relationship to humor was not simply that of an actor capable of landing punchlines written by others or singing and dancing. In one deeply autobiographical 2018 interview, the journalist playfully opened by asking whether 11 am, the time of their interview, was "early for an actor." Zelensky evinced a double-take at his interlocutor's assumption that being an "actor" defined his day, even being a "big actor" as the interviewer then corrected himself. "I am, after all, a producer," Zelensky emphasized, describing a bevy of leadership duties that regularly resulted in his sleeping only six hours per night and that made 11 am a "very late" time for him.[89]

Art imitates life, or is it the other way around?

In 2015, 1+1 and Zelensky's Studio Kvartal 95 aired the now-famous first episode of *Servant of the People*, a prime-time television series with Zelensky portraying a president named Vasyl Holoborodko. Holoborodko is a truly accidental president. In the first episode, he is shown as a committed high school history teacher whose students make little attempt to hide their complete indifference to learning anything about Mykhaylo Hrushevskyy, a historian and leader of Ukraine's first experience with modern statehood during World War I. With the students gone, he starts venting to a colleague, culminating in an expletive-filled rant in which he talks about everything an ordinary person like him would do to Ukraine's corrupt politicians if he were ever in charge. Outside the classroom, one of his students secretly films the tirade and posts it online. The video goes viral, and his students all come back telling him that their parents would vote for him. They crowdsource funds to get him on the ballot. His true chance comes, though, when on election eve Ukraine's shadowy oligarchs realize that their own candidates are all neck-and-neck, so they make a sporting bet to let the people decide and allow a free vote. Holoborodko thus surges to victory. The rest of the series is about how he manages this unexpected responsibility.

It is far less clear that Zelensky himself is so accidental. As the show raised his profile and people started to see him as a contender for the presidency, it was common for observers to wonder whether the show had made the real candidate or whether the real candidate had made the show for this reason. While its timing and success point in the latter direction, there is no conclusive evidence. Both Zelensky and Kolomoyskyy, owner of the show's television channel, deny it was created as a political vehicle for the lead actor's presidential bid. Instead, they claim they simply wanted to make a good show that might at most send a political message.[90] According to one report, the idea for the show emerged "several years" before its 2015 debut, which would date its origins to before the Euromaidan.[91] What we do know is that the show was developed by Zelensky and his longtime partners the Shefir brothers. We also know that both the initial idea and the concept was Zelensky's (as is noted in the credits) and that he often contributed to the writing and content, even claiming that "his [i.e. Holoborodko's] words are mine."[92] In fact, as well as being an actor, producer, and creator, he was also a de facto creative director of the project.[93] The show ran over three seasons and generated one feature film. The first season came out in 2015, the second (with associated feature film) in 2016–17, and the third was delayed and wound up coming out in 2019, timed to be broadcast on 1+1 during the actual presidential campaign.

Combining techniques ranging from silly physical humor to political innuendo in what might be called a cross between a bawdy family sitcom and *Veep* in the US or *The Thick of It* in the UK, the show is about Holoborodko's attempts to do good. He does not always succeed, making numerous mistakes along the way to humorous and dramatic effect. Some mistakes come from naïveté, others come from his initial failure to understand just how entrenched oligarchic control and corruption is in Ukraine. Four themes from the show would become particularly important in Zelensky's own presidential rise. The first is based around patriotism and civic duty. The show portrays two kinds of patriots. One set repeatedly describes themselves as such, despite many being corrupt and taking bribes. Others are patriots without ever saying so, simply trying to get things done out of a sense of civic duty and love for their country. Holoborodko and his team are in this latter category. But almost all the other politicians are, at least at times, motivated by securing personal benefits. A running joke is that elite politicians who call themselves patriots are often everything but. At their most sincere, they are caricatured as caring more about their ethnonational identities than about the country as a whole. A layer below the top, the show provides plenty of examples of good citizens devoted to state service. Strikingly, many are women. Presidential secretary Bella Rudolfivna, for example, has seen all the presidents come and go and, ultra-competent, can anticipate everything that Holoborodko might need. Serhiy Mukhin, a former actor turned minister of foreign affairs, also has a particularly capable assistant—Oksana Skovoroda—a name alluding to Hryhoriy Skovoroda, a Socratic philosopher whose mission was to teach. "She will turn you into a diplomat, into a professional person," he is told. A few are men, though: Holoborodko's laconic bodyguard Tolik also falls into this category, though his wife is portrayed as the brains behind his operation.

The second theme centers on corruption, or more broadly how patronalism is an everyday reality for both ordinary people and elites. Scheming oligarchs open the show's first episode, and their attempts at behind-the-scenes manipulation remain a key feature throughout the series. Their machinations are Holoborodko's chief obstacle until the establishment political elite cause the country's breakup in Season 3. The series also skewers the pervasive corruption in the government and among elected officials, right down to the luxury cars ordinary Ukrainians would see zooming recklessly through city streets or parking outside state buildings. In Season 1, Episode 12, Holoborodko is trying to crack down on corruption and calls a nationalist deputy in and asks him why he lives with his family in a modest 45-meter apartment instead of something much larger in the posh Koncha-Zaspa suburb. The deputy replies that his mother owns the latter house, not him. Viewers understand that he does in fact live in the flat registered in his mother's name to escape tax reporting requirements.

Even more important is the spotlight the show puts on how ordinary people contribute to the problem by playing along. This is the classic problem of patronalism: when corruption is so endemic in daily life, attempts to be completely honest can seem hopeless and materially suicidal, even stupid and pretentious. But by playing along, one only contributes to the sense that everyone does it.[94] The people playing along are often portrayed in a sympathetic light, such as the new minister of defense's wife in Episode 10, who, desperate to escape her poverty and start a family, frantically pleads with her upright husband to accept a bribe she calls a "lottery ticket." In Episode 12, the president learns his own father has been evading taxes and not licensing his taxi. The father replies, "Well, why should I pay tax if it's only going to be stolen?" and adds that the unpaid money is just enough for him to buy the cognac necessary to give as a gift to get an appointment for some surgery he needs. The show thus highlights the duty of ordinary citizens to fight malfeasance in their daily lives.

A third major theme emphasizes the importance of knowing one's history and learning from past mistakes. Holoborodko is a history teacher whom we first meet, as noted above, endeavoring to get his students to care about Hrushevskyy. The tirade that catapults Holoborodko to the presidency is his expletive-filled complaint that not enough people learn from history, instead studying only math—knowing how to add, subtract, and multiply their own assets. Throughout the series, various historical figures make cameos or receive mentions, ranging from Plutarch to Lincoln to Mazepa to Che Guevara to Yaroslav the Wise, the latter of whom says that "borrowing is a one-way ticket to slavery" when Holoborodko is meeting with the IMF. These appearances supply subtext to the surface-level discussions.

In one particularly interesting scene in Season 2, Episode 14, Holoborodko reunites with a more senior historian, the man who had handed him his high school teaching job upon reaching retirement age, at a new museum the latter is setting up. There are statues of some of the key Ukrainian leaders and figures central to the making of the Ukrainian state: King Ateas (who gathered the Scythian tribes), Bohdan Khmelnytskyy, Mykhaylo Hrushevskyy, Queen Olha (mother of Svyatoslav), and Nestor the Chronicler. Suddenly they come to life to give Holoborodko advice, but they turn out also to be his friends, his cabinet team. They say the "oligarchs are tearing Ukraine apart." King Ateas (Holoborodko) remarks that little is known about Scythian culture because its language was lost—a warning. Then just as suddenly as they came to life, they freeze up again. Holoborodko's predecessor as history teacher comes back in and gives him Hrushevskyy's book to read. The message could not be clearer: only those who know their history can avoid past mistakes, stand up to oligarchs, and succeed in building a modern Ukraine.

A fourth important theme in the show emphasizes that Ukraine's strength and successes have their roots in the country's diversity. The show frequently switches between Russian and Ukrainian. At times, this seems to have been done to convey an important message, yet at other times it is simply a reflection of how things are in the real world. There is an acceptance of this particularly Ukrainian linguistic complexity and all the tensions and funny moments that arise from it. What unites Ukrainians is more important than what divides them. And it is ordinary Ukrainians and not the political elite that are at the center of this unity. This theme is particularly stark in Season 3, which we discuss in the context of the election campaign during which it first aired in 2019.

The show's appeal is evident in the numbers. More than 20 million people watched its first season, which ended in December 2015. This was impressive for a country with a population of just over 40 million. It attracted the most viewers of any program in its time slot by a wide margin while also being the top show in the entertainment and artistic categories, according to a Ukrainian ratings agency.[95] The second season was also the highest-rated in its slot.[96]

Resonance with Ukrainian civic identity

The themes in Zelensky's work coincided and resonated with key features and trends in Ukrainian society, most notably an emphasis on civic identity, meaning above all an attachment to civic duty and Ukrainian statehood rather than an identification with an ethnonational collective identity, which has been an increasingly important feature of Ukrainian politics since at least 2014. We have found this repeatedly in our data from the UCEPS, IBIF, and MOBILISE projects,[97] as have a growing number of other political science studies. For instance, Grigore Pop-Eleches and Graeme Robertson document that most Ukrainians have a strong attachment to Ukraine as their homeland regardless of their nationality or language.[98] Kulyk reveals that residents of Ukraine have increasingly been "shedding" their Russianness and that the "Russian" minority is by now very small.[99] Aaron Erlich and Calvin Garner show that a large majority, even of "Russians" in Ukraine, subconsciously harbor primary attachment to Ukraine, not Russia.[100] In our own analysis, which we present in other parts of this book, this civic attachment is also correlated with growing support for EU and NATO membership from 2014 onwards. Our analyses also show that there has been a collapse of the support that had previously existed among some for Russian-oriented integration projects, such as the Eurasian Economic Union. Furthermore, when people think about what it means to be "Ukrainian," they increasingly think of civic rather than ethnocultural criteria. Even what it means to call Ukrainian one's "native language" is changing: for more and more people, your "native" language is Ukrainian simply by virtue of identifying with the Ukrainian state, regardless of whether it was actually the language one spoke as a child. Finally, many of those in Ukraine who support ethnocentric policies, such as restrictions on the use of Russian, are doing so only because they think this is temporarily necessary to protect Ukraine from Russian authoritarian interference, not because they want to exclude Russian-speakers on ethnic grounds. As Hale and Kulyk explain it, such people see themselves as aspiring to civic ideals, but make compromises in the short-term in order to realize them.[101]

Poroshenko's personalization of the battle against Russia and his emphasis on divisive themes sat somewhat uneasily with this development and mobilization of more civic forms of Ukrainian identity. This was particularly problematic for Poroshenko in the southeast.

Ripe for an outsider

These trends in identity came in tandem with massive disillusionment not only with Poroshenko but with the entire political status quo and pretty much all of the Ukrainian politicians that were part of it. In December 2017, a Democratic Initiatives survey found that the negatives outweighed positives for all prominent politicians when it came to measures of (dis)trust and (dis)approval. For Poroshenko, disapproval outweighed approval by 62 percentage points, with the presidential front-runner Tymoshenko not far behind at 53.[102] The demand for fresh faces became a common topic of political conversation. The same Democratic Initiatives poll also revealed that 67 percent of the public thought Ukraine needed new political leaders, while only 19 percent thought that Ukraine's problems could be solved by its current leaders.[103]

Entrenched power networks, which in Ukraine's case frequently featured reputed oligarchs as the most potent patrons, are typically well aware that their brand of politics breeds disillusionment. They therefore try their best to turn this political "lemon" into "lemonade."

Oligarchs are thus notorious for seeking out people whom the electorate might take to be a fresh face and organizing electoral campaigns around them, hoping to usher their own people into power by doing so. Examples sometimes given include the "Young Team" of big businessman and former Kyiv mayor Leonid Chernovetskyy, or the "New Faces" party of Irpin mayor Volodymyr Karplyuk.[104] Of special interest here is that Kolomoyskyy, owner of 1+1, was also believed to have a history of funding or otherwise aiding the formation of new parties. One of these, the uber-patriotic party UKROP, which was founded by a Kolomoyskyy associate after the Euromaidan Revolution, gained its first two seats in the Verkhovna Rada through by-elections in 2016.[105] It was thus rather common in Ukraine for new parties and new political figures to emerge, typically with oligarchs or other establishment figures lurking behind the scenes or ready to strike a deal when a price was set. The challenge for ordinary voters was to figure out which was which. Either way, such faces almost always became stale just as rapidly as they rose to prominence.[106] Indeed, in Ukraine, all four presidents prior to Zelensky had come from the high-level political elite of previous eras.

From TV to reality

In light of this desire for fresh faces, the idea that Zelensky could one day enter electoral politics was far from radical. In fact, his first invitation from a reputed oligarch to run for office came even before the *Servant of the People* series launched in 2015. By Zelensky's own account, Poroshenko invited him to join the Poroshenko Bloc's party list for the 2014 Rada elections.[107] Poroshenko ally Yuriy Lutsenko confirmed this account, saying the idea was for Zelensky to be on the list's highest profile "top five" set of candidates. But Zelensky declined.[108]

Another invitation reportedly arrived about a year and a half later from Andriy Bohdan, an advisor to Kolomoyskyy when the oligarch was governor of Zelensky's home oblast of Dnipropetrovsk. Bohdan reported getting to know Zelensky during this period through mutual acquaintances and wide-ranging political conversations when the performer was in town. After a district parliamentary seat became available in late 2015, while *Servant of the People* was still in its debut season, Bohdan suggested that Zelensky run for it in the upcoming by-election and that this could even serve as a platform for a future presidential bid. In Bohdan's rendering, Zelensky replied: "No ... I would become just the same as them. I would lose the faith of the people ... they will consider me just another deputy."[109] Despite this rejection, the idea of Zelensky launching a political career was clearly in the air. And we also know that the possibility had occurred to Zelensky himself.

According to accounts Zelensky personally has given, the idea of an actual presidential run in 2019 developed through a series of unanticipated events as the *Servant of the People* show took off. In the summer of 2017, he discovered that people with no connection to him or Kvartal 95 were trying to register a party with the same name as the show.[110] This forced him and his colleagues to start registering such a party themselves so as not to leave the possibility open for people to hijack his brand.[111] The Servant of the People Party was born, therefore, as what Zelensky called a mere "juridical nuance" with no initial intent that it would run for anything.[112] Ukraine's law on parties, however, requires a party to run for office in order to remain in good standing, something Kvartal's lawyers surely knew.[113]

But how to form a party? In Ukraine, a political party cannot simply be declared. Instead, it requires a long and potentially costly process of meeting state legal requirements for official registration. For example, aspiring parties must collect thousands of verifiable signatures of eligible voters in no fewer than two-thirds of the counties (*rayons*) of two-thirds of Ukraine's oblasts and hold an official founding party congress.[114] To circumvent such a process, which would have inevitably brought considerable fanfare as well as significant costs, Zelensky's team instead opted to take over and rename an existing party. This is a relatively common tactic in post-Soviet polities, which tend to have similar legislation, and some entrepreneurs make it their business to establish parties that exist primarily on paper before later supplying them to oligarchs or others who may one day want them, presumably for a price.

In Zelensky's case, the chosen vehicle was the Party of Decisive Change, which had only been registered in April 2016 and existed primarily on paper, led by the largely unknown former student activist Yevheniy Yurdyha.[115] To our knowledge, Yurdyha had no connection to the Kvartal team or Kolomoyskyy, and we have no information on whether or not there was some sort of price involved. The notion of "decisive change" surely fit what Zelensky was peddling on his TV show. In any case, the party's name was officially changed to Servant of the People in December 2017, and along with a new governing body consisting of people linked to Kvartal, a new party leader also appeared on the books: Ivan Bakanov, the lawyer and longtime manager of Kvartal's business and legal operations.[116] The process was managed by the legal firm Kachura Lawyers, which reportedly specializes in issues connected with party formation. This firm supplied (reportedly rent-free) the only premises listed for the party: 4 square meters of space in its offices.[117] The party later included the law firm's founder, Oleksandr Kachura, as the forty-ninth candidate on its inaugural 2019 Verkhovna Rada slate, a slot that proved high enough to win him a seat.[118]

The new Servant of the People Party thus simply appeared on the books as a technical change to an unknown pre-existing party, with no fanfare whatsoever. There was no announcement by Zelensky or the new party leaders—not even a social media mention of the event. But journalists noticed and started to inquire. When they did, they got essentially zero information beyond what was formally listed in the publicly available registration documents. When the free-spirited *Ukrayinska Pravda* called the phone number given in the registration right after it appeared, it was told no commentary was being given.[119] *Glavkom* visited its office space at Kachura Lawyers in the spring of 2018 but was informed that its leaders were not there and would not be there unless the party decided to become active.[120] The fact-checking non-profit organization *Chesno* (which means "honest") reached out to the press secretary of Kvartal 95 in the summer of 2018 but was told that party representatives could not respond to its questions about the party's plans and possible ties to Kolomoyskyy.[121] Even as late as October 2018, when *Ukrayinska Pravda* tried again, this time visiting the party office, its journalists were denied entry but told that they might be able to talk to someone in the future. They even claimed that it was almost impossible to find a picture of the party's purported leader, Bakanov, on the Internet.[122] It is hardly surprising, therefore, that some observers thought this all looked rather mysterious and even suspicious.

Journalists were not the only ones to take note when the party appeared, however. Democratic Initiatives included the party in its December 2017 polling on voter preferences and found, to many people's surprise, that 4 percent of the population were already prepared to vote for the party even before anyone knew much about it at all—only that it was linked to Kvartal and the TV show.[123] This was well in the range of actually winning a parliamentary delegation, given that the required 5 percent counts only actual voters, excluding people who do not vote at all from the denominator. Pollsters then began including Zelensky himself in their lists of potential presidential candidates, and he also registered in the five-percent range, which at that time in Ukraine actually put him among the leaders.[124] One survey from December 2017 shed some light on why this was the case: Zelensky was one of two national leaders for whom the ratio of political trust to mistrust was not widely unbalanced toward the latter, just behind Svyatoslav Vakarchuk, the lead singer for the popular rock group Okean Elzy who was also being touted around that time as a possible candidate. Although both their ratios were still slightly negative, they were much closer to being balanced than all other major politicians in Ukraine.[125] Similarly, a poll in April 2018 found that Zelensky was the most popular "second choice" among candidates, though another poll the next month found him in a statistical tie with Vakarchuk and long-time centrist politician Anatoliy Hrytsenko.[126]

After engaging in exactly zero registered public activity through the first half of 2018, the party finally came to life in the third quarter of 2018, less than a year before the March 2019 presidential elections. This activity came in the form of 4,600 hryvnya (around 160 USD), which the party said had come from membership dues, of which 10 percent were spent on bank services.[127] Shortly thereafter, billboards began to appear along Ukrainian streets, though payment did not appear on party ledgers. Their slogan read: "President—Servant of the People, Soon."[128] Zelensky explained the thinking behind the slogan in January of the following year: "This is our approach, mine in part. In principle, it saved us a lot of resources. The approach is very simple: it is an ad for ... *Servant of the People* 3 that could, if you correctly turn the key, also work for an election campaign."[129] In October, he was still publicly keeping his options open, telling interviewers that it was "too early" to talk about any political future for himself or his nascent party.[130]

Initially, the political establishment did not take the Servant of the People Party very seriously. Experts thought it unlikely that it would get very far, with some even claiming that it would not clear the 5 percent mark that was needed to win an official Verkhovna Rada delegation.[131] The mass public was also skeptical: despite their poor standing in the polls, Tymoshenko and Poroshenko remained the favorites to win the presidency, with one poll in September 2018 showing only 4 percent predicting a Zelensky win.[132] Speculation also ran rampant among political insiders that the Servant of the People Party was an oligarch project, most likely Kolomoyskyy's in the vein of UKROP.[133] One rumor reportedly circulating in parliament had it that Zelensky's run was actually orchestrated by Tymoshenko in order to stymie the outsider bid of Vakarchuk, the rock star.[134]

Zelensky at campaign's eve

As the fall of 2018 wound down, Zelensky was increasingly tracking among the leaders, and the political class increasingly took notice. In August 2018, the Razumkov Center and Democratic Initiatives asked potential voters for the motivations behind their voting intentions, and the top responses for Zelensky were that they were attracted to him as a person (48 percent), wanted fresh blood in the presidency (32 percent), thought that he genuinely cared about people like them (25 percent), or saw him as the lesser evil (23 percent). Perhaps the most significant finding here is that among all the politicians covered in the survey, Zelensky was the only one that a large share believed actually cared about them. Poroshenko's supporters, in contrast, cited the work he had done for Ukraine, his ideas and proposals, and that he was respected in the world. Tymoshenko's appeal lay mostly in her personality and the ideas and plans attributed to her.[135] And while Vakarchuk, a singer, sometimes figured among the leaders in the late 2018 opinion polls, his ratings did not take off like Zelensky's did, and he ultimately decided not to run. He did not endorse Zelensky, however, instead sniping that "the presidency, this is not a role in a TV series. The presidency is a serious job."[136]

Zelensky, however, was tapping into a rich seam of public sentiment. Our analysis of all KIIS tracking surveys during 2018, the year pollsters first began including him in their list of potential presidential candidates, finds that several categories of people were disproportionately ready to vote for him before he announced his candidacy. These included youth, the internet-savvy, people with mobile phones, residents of Ukraine's southeast, and people who preferred speaking Ukrainian rather than Russian or other languages. His would-be voters also tended not to have higher education and not to be from western parts of Ukraine.[137]

And just like that, enter Zelensky. In the next chapter, we turn to the innovative campaign that grew these early numbers into a record electoral victory.

We recommend our readers listen to "Chuty Himn"
("The Anthem Can Be Heard")

By Skofka

Found on the "United24: Music for Ukraine" Playlist on Spotify:

https://open.spotify.com/album/4CDvAEwF29rYx7Jg2bpl22

…in the clear sky, you can hear a thunder, the Sky is whistling, but you can hear the anthem! In the clear sky, there is cloudy smoke, the forest is burning, but the anthem can be heard!…

—Authors' own translation

And I will remind you of her words today:

"… an artist doesn't need awards …"

—Volodymyr Zelensky, reciting Lina Kostenko, 20 March 2022[1]

Great people of a great country!

…

Ukrainians are united from Uzhhorod to Kharkiv, from Kyiv to Kherson.

…

Ukrainians have shown themselves.

They did not allow themselves to be deceived in a cheap cynical show.

…

Russian propagandists thought of our people as of themselves. And they saw that Kherson residents are proud. And respect themselves. Respect Ukraine.

…

But I see how … our people remain Ukrainians.

How our people stay with our state, even temporarily finding themselves in the darkness.

If Russian politicians still have their eyes, they will be able to see what Ukraine is.

What our freedom is.

…

Even if you deprive us of oxygen, we will breathe deeply, to say: get out of our land!

Even in complete darkness we see the truth.

…

Because we are the warriors of light.

—Volodymyr Zelensky, 4 March 2022[2]

5

THE VIRTUAL INCUMBENT

It is New Year's Eve 2018, the night before one of the biggest holidays in Ukraine, a time when families come together to drink, eat, and sing carols. Some go to church, some decorate a tree, and some children—especially those in central and eastern Ukraine—await a gift-bearing *Did Moroz*, Father Frost, a Soviet-era holiday figure. The holiday means different things to different people. For some in Ukraine's west, Easter is a much bigger holiday, and children of many families receive gifts from St Nicholas on 19 December or on 6 January (Christmas Eve). But New Year's Eve is a big deal for everyone in some way, with every home having its own traditions. And in recent years, something of a new tradition had also begun—watching the *Vechernyy Kvartal* New Year concert—or keeping it on in the background while festivities rolled on at home.

This year, broadcast on 1+1, in the final hours before 2019, audiences were treated to an evening that began with Zelensky portraying a stressed Poroshenko struggling to prepare his New Year's address and then joining with actors playing other politicians to sing the blues—the declining ratings blues. At one point, Zelensky appears on stage in a bright blue *kombinezon* (a snowsuit typically worn by children during Ukraine's cold winters) for a funny, nostalgic take on what it was like for a child of his generation to experience the holiday. This year's holiday period was tense, coming shortly after Poroshenko had brought an end to a period of martial law covering part of the country, so the whimsical skits were a cathartic release for many viewers.

As midnight approached, 1+1 audiences were in for one more surprise. Zelensky comes out from behind the edge of a stage curtain, a decorated tree to his side, and greets his viewers. At first, he speaks in Russian, the language mostly used in the concert. He explains that everyone will greet the New Year very soon and then the *Vechernyy Kvartal* concert will continue. But now he tells viewers he has something to say personally, as himself, "Vladimir" Zelensky.[3] At this point, he switches to Ukrainian. Striking the same themes of civic Ukrainian identity and responsibility that had long been at the core of his connection with the public, he explains that the situation in the country is such that every Ukrainian has three paths they can take: to live as they do now (and that is OK); to move to another country, earn money there, and send it back to relatives (and that is also OK); or to live up to their civic duty and try to change their country. He announces that he has chosen the third option, the path of civic duty. Now, only minutes from the New Year, he ends the growing speculation: "I am running for president of Ukraine." He concludes his short address with the words: "Let's do this together. With the new year, with a new servant of the people." This line was a play on words in Ukrainian, since one way to wish someone a Happy New Year is simply to say "With the new year!" But in this context, what he said could also be understood as promising Ukrainians that they will have a new president (him) in the new year.

Observers noted that by letting Zelensky deliver his New Year's greeting when he did, the 1+1 television channel owned by reputed oligarch Kolomoyskyy was effectively handing Zelensky the slot typically reserved for actual sitting presidents to give their New Year's remarks.[4] Indeed, Zelensky's announcement bumped Poroshenko's own New Year's greeting on the channel to after midnight, although Zelensky himself said this was not intentional.[5] By law, 31 December 2018 also marked the official start of the presidential campaign season in Ukraine. President Poroshenko's address should therefore have been part of his inherent advantage as an incumbent, a status giving him the right to appear before voters in an official capacity that other candidates do not have. But by greeting the public first with his speech and forcing Poroshenko to go second and possibly be drowned out by the revelry at midnight, Zelensky was taking this advantage away from him. This turned out to be much like the rest of Zelensky's campaign. After all, many in the country were already used to seeing him as the president of Ukraine, albeit on a TV show rather than in reality. We now show how this played out and explain the factors behind his campaign's success.

> *In other words, a man ascended to the presidency who isn't under the control of any of us? That's rich.*
>
> —Oligarchs' discussion, *Servant of the People*, Season 1, Episode 1

A virtual incumbency advantage

So began Volodymyr Zelensky's campaign for the presidency. Its opening was very much characteristic of the whole endeavor. Recognizing that it represented something new and distinct, observers emphasized the role of the media in Zelensky's bid for the presidency, calling it a "virtual campaign" due to its reliance on social media platforms that have been important parts of American presidential campaigns since 2008.[6] While this was a striking element of the campaign, what is even more novel is how media were used, and perhaps even more remarkably how they were not used. There were no major ad buys, and no traditional campaign rallies designed to attract media coverage and hence exposure. Instead, the essence of Zelensky's campaign was simply to perform his job.

Political science tells us that this is the kind of campaign that only incumbents can run when seeking re-election.[7] Already in office, sitting presidents primarily want to be seen as presidential and as getting things done. And what better way to do so than meeting with foreign leaders, proposing legislation, and giving addresses to parliament—that is, simply doing their job, though in ways designed to bolster their presidential prospects. Sitting presidents' exclusive ability to do this is one key to their fabled "incumbency advantage."[8] Nor do sitting presidents need to strive for exposure in the same way that challengers do.

Thus, Zelensky was doing something akin to incumbent presidents. He was all over the media, although not always explicitly as a candidate. One is even tempted to say that more ordinary Ukrainians were regularly exposed to Zelensky in the role of fictional president than to Poroshenko as the real one. His *Vechernyy Kvartal* concerts, which dug into popular discontent with corruption and expressed desires for a united and European Ukraine, continued to run on 1+1, and he continued to star in them. He continued to perform with his comedy troupe throughout the country. Advertisements appeared on TV and billboards, but most of them were for his television programs. And the few that did advertise openly for his presidential bid did not mention his name, only "Ze President" and simple slogans like "The Epoch of Greediness Is Over."[9] And most widely noticed of all, he continued to play a president on TV.

The short third season of *Servant of the People* began and ended during Ukraine's official presidential campaign period, giving him an incumbent-like ability to appear presidential that only an actual incumbent could match. In fact, an incumbent might not have been able to match it, because by playing a fictional president in a world made up by the candidate and a production team of his supporters, who were also running his campaign, Zelensky was able to create scenarios designed to display precisely the kind of president he wanted people to think he would be. Incumbents are rarely so lucky, almost inevitably forced to respond to real-world events that can sometimes break good, but often also break bad. The themes Zelensky struck through all of his media performances continued to be those we have emphasized throughout this book, tapping into civic Ukrainian identity through concern for ordinary Ukrainians' material struggles, the challenges they face with corruption, civic duty, and calls to set aside ethnic, religious, and regional differences for the sake of a European-facing future.

At the same time as Zelensky was carefully cultivating his image and message as a "virtual incumbent," he did not alter his public persona. When American comedian Al Franken ran for the US Senate in 2008 after writing a humorous book about himself becoming an accidental president, he toned down the bawdier aspects of his comedy so that he could appear more like a serious politician and avoid offending voters.[10] Zelensky, on the other hand, remained the same old Zelensky. And pointedly so. He sung. He danced. He made off-color jokes. He appeared in a puffy blue *kombinezon* with clipped-on mittens dangling from his sleeves. He even ironically referred to himself as a "clown"—a true-to-self reaction to the way some media reported on his candidacy.[11] That is, somewhat paradoxically, he ran as the authentic Zelensky that Ukrainians felt they had known for years, someone who was not trying to conform to the appearance and behaviors of "normal" politicians in order to seek political office—all while he was also playing a serious but make-believe president on TV.

Zelensky was also a master at using social media, making direct appeals and sending his messaging through the right channels. By 2019, billboards were a campaign tactic of a bygone era. Now, a much wider audience can be reached with well-targeted social media posts. As many people we talked to freely admit, political analysts and Zelensky critics frequently failed to look for his message in the right places. They were slightly out of step, and he was getting so far ahead of them that it would be months until they caught up. Zelensky was younger, of the Independence Generation, and as one informant put it, he was a "mini-media mogul" who had made a career of knowing how to communicate to ordinary Ukrainians. In fact, detailed analysis of Zelensky's social media presence shows that the Zelensky we have seen in 2022 issuing direct video appeals to the public on a self-held mobile phone was in fact the same one running for office back in 2019.

Just after the first round of the 2019 voting, Zelensky had some 3.3 million followers on Instagram. By the second round, he had 3.8 million, and when he won the presidency, he had 4.7 million (at the time of this writing in mid-2022, it is 16.8 million). Poroshenko's Instagram, in contrast, had but 286,000 (now 375,000). Zelensky's Instagram posts alone were reaching more Ukrainians than some of Poroshenko's billboards. Poroshenko was not ready for a different approach. Mobilizing this virtual incumbency advantage to deliver his message to Ukrainian voters, Zelensky was thus able to defeat an actual incumbent in the biggest presidential landslide the country has yet known.

> *After my election victory, my six-year-old son said: "Dad, they say on TV that Zelensky is the president … So, it means that … I am … the president too?!" At the time, it sounded funny, but later I realized that it was true. Because each of us is the president.*
>
> —Volodymyr Zelensky, 20 May 2019, inaugural speech[12]

Making the leap

In his first major interview after announcing his run, Zelensky said that he had weighed the possibility for a year. His family urged him not to run, but most of his Kvartal friends were in favor of the idea. By the fall of 2018, he was leaning far enough toward doing it that he started putting together a campaign team.[13] The time seemed ripe. That fall, the National Bank raised its projected annual inflation rate from 8.9 to 10.1 percent,[14] Freedom House downgraded Ukraine's Internet Freedom rating,[15] the incumbent had issued a declaration of martial law that most saw as a power-grab, and the IMF was reporting that Ukraine had now sunk below Moldova to become the poorest country in Europe per capita.[16]

On 25 December, Zelensky reported that his party would run in the next parliamentary elections,[17] though he was still claiming not to have decided on the presidency.[18] When he finally announced that he planned to run for office, even his wife claimed to have found out from the TV.[19] One wonders exactly how Olena Zelenska—someone with an impressive satirical writing and producing career in her own right—might have felt at such a moment. She too was part of the Independence Generation and clearly at least partly responsible for helping develop what we have been calling the Zelensky Effect.

This is why I really do not want my pictures in your offices, for the president is not an icon, an idol or a portrait. Hang your kids' photos instead, and look at them each time you are making a decision.

—Volodymyr Zelensky, 20 May 2019, inauguration speech[20]

Reality show campaign

Zelensky described his strategy for winning the presidency as a kind of "reality show." This was first and foremost because it would be completely transparent: "I very much want an open presidential campaign ... I want people to see everything we do in real time: the creation of the team, the ... program, the congress, going to the Central Election Commission. We will broadcast all this ... we should have an ... open government."[21] This included crowdsourcing his campaign. On Facebook, Zelensky posted a video calling for people to send him what they saw as the top five problems facing Ukraine, promising to add them to his program.[22] Similarly, in a short Facebook video announcing he would debate Poroshenko one-on-one shortly before the runoff, he called on his followers to post the questions they would like to see him ask the president to his face.[23] Then, in the debate itself, he used his first opportunity to unleash a rapid-fire reading of highly pointed questions rooted in popular frustrations that he said people had sent him online.[24] He also pledged to openly select the best experts in different spheres to head state posts.[25]

The campaign, which adopted "Ze!" as a shortened version of Zelensky's last name and as an enthusiastic call to vote for him, employed a wide range of tactics to communicate with voters. Internet videos were one hallmark, a preferred way of reaching the public quickly, directly, often, and on a large scale. These videos tended to be short, often only about a minute long, designed to convey the point in an entertaining way before anyone, especially the younger generations, would have a chance to tune out. Typically posted on Instagram and Facebook and filmed selfie-style on what was apparently the candidate's mobile phone, the most successful went viral. With Zelensky's showbusiness acumen, and aided by his skilled Kvartal 95 production team, these videos proved a highly effective way of reaching large numbers of supporters with very little effort and at effectively zero monetary cost.[26]

In one such video, for example, Zelensky issued a one-minute Instagram response to a Poroshenko Bloc deputy who had just made the news for telling a journalist questioning him on possible corruption "go fuck yourself." In the post, Zelensky noted that as a media man, he took personal offense and issued a hashtag challenge for people to tell this deputy exactly what they thought and to call for him to "*idit' v sraku!*" (this translates loosely as "go to hell," but a more literal translation would be "go to the shitter.").[27] As another example, during the campaign itself, Zelensky posted a one-minute video on Facebook imploring Poroshenko to stop talking and take action on outstanding problems, such as getting Ukrainian sailors released from Russia.[28] This was not only effective but set Zelensky apart from all the other main candidates as someone from a new and modern generation.

Zelensky also continued to perform *Vechernyy Kvartal* concerts, which not only involved appearing on national TV but also touring the country. Zelensky did not have to go from hall to hall making stump speeches or organize typical campaign meetings with voters. He was already traveling the country and reaching voters there—but through the concerts, which required no organization other than what he had been doing. Zelensky emphasized that the concerts would not explicitly call for people to vote for him and that this would not technically constitute "campaigning" in the traditional, legal sense.[29]

The show even made fun of this flirtation with formal definitions of campaigning, showing that just like the other politicians he was not beyond being the butt of jokes. In doing so, he played a comedic caricature of himself. In one such skit, his campaign team gives him a "body double" who looks nothing like him except for a comically ill-fitting wig of tousled dark hair. Zelensky-playing-Zelensky decides to quiz the double to see whether the double knows enough about the real person to adequately do the job. A rapid-fire Q&A ensues, enabling the real Zelensky to convey personal details about himself and communicate key campaign messages in a humorous manner. Zelensky-playing-Zelensky: "Why do I not take money from Kolomoyskyy?" Double: "Because he is not offering you any."[30]

In at least one case, Zelensky wraps up the evening by turning to the audience just before the concluding song: "At the very beginning of the show we said there would be no campaigning. Was there any?" The video shows the audience smiling and shaking their heads. "What would be the sense of campaigning?" Zelensky goes on: "You people are smart! You know what to do on the 31st!"[31]

These campaign-period Kvartal concerts hammered home the aspects of Zelensky's appeal emphasized in earlier chapters as central to both his political and entertainment careers. Incumbent President Poroshenko, Zelensky's rival in the race, remained the butt of many jokes, a symbol of the country's pervasive corruption and inability to effect real reform. Musical elements inspired unity and hope, such as one concluding song sung by little girls about the need for adults to act and to think about the sort of country they will leave behind for them.[32]

Zelensky is portrayed as the Independence Generation's determined answer to the day's problems. In one skit that pokes fun at an "ordinary" Zelensky now with an over-eager security detail, his colleague and friend Yevhen Koshovyy sidles up to Zelensky-playing-Zelensky and asks whether he would be as determined to fight corruption as Singapore's strict Lee Kuan Yew, even jailing his friends. Zelensky-playing-Zelensky replies "well ... if I have to, then yes." Koshovyy responds, "I respect that. Strong decision. I'll definitely vote for you," then turns away and starts fiddling with his phone. Zelensky-playing-Zelensky asks him what he's doing, and Koshovyy replies, "deleting you from my friends."[33] Another skit—a particularly gendered one that aligns with Tamara Martsenyuk's critical work on masculinities in Ukraine[34]—compares his rivals' use of "political technologists" (consultants with reputations for manipulative practices) to consulting with a doctor on penile enhancement, with Zelensky ultimately walking in and announcing that their problem is an incurable disease to which the people need immunity.[35]

A critical part of the campaign, as already said, was the third season of the *Servant of the People* television show, which aired during the election period itself. Shortly before it began, Zelensky explained that the third season's airing so close to the voting "will help a lot. Because it is awesome promotion for the election campaign."[36] Indeed, the show amplified many of Zelensky's key themes, this time placing particular emphasis on the threat to national unity posed by ultranationalists in Ukraine's west and Russia-oriented, Soviet-nostalgic forces in its east. Some observers saw in this a "dangerously pro-Russian" villainization of Ukrainian "patriots," while Poroshenko called some of its themes "part of the hybrid war that Russia is conducting against our state."[37] But this was not what *Servant of the People*'s third season meant to the voters Zelensky was reaching.

Zelensky's message was that some politicians in Ukraine have been dividing the population along imaginary lines. Yes, there is no mention of Russia here, and this is undoubtedly an uncomfortable absence. But there is mention of Ukraine's enemies. And it is suggested that some of the elite have done a better job than Ukraine's enemies at dividing it. This notwithstanding, the show's main message is that, when taken to extremes, a focus on regional differences, on localism, on cultural or linguistic divisions, can be used to split the country into pieces. Rather than replicating the myth of a Ukraine divided into two neat halves, the last episode makes clear that there are many different histories and versions of Ukraine and Ukrainianness. The take-away is that what unites ordinary people is much stronger than these localized histories, cultures, and ways of being. In order to bring the country together, the fictional President Holoborodko decides to make Ukraine the most successful country there is. The pieces will all be happy parts of the whole when they see that it is better to stay together. The theme of a united Ukraine under one civic national identity traces both backwards and forwards in time for Zelensky, harking back to the dissident discourse he inherited from the 1970s and '80s and hailing forward to his powerful rhetoric of resistance after Russia's full-scale invasion of 2022.

The *Servant of the People* series was working for the campaign even before its third season aired. Trailers for it were already being broadcast in late 2018. One, for example, showed Zelensky's make-believe accidental President Holoborodko driving on a bad road and cursing at real-life politicians. In another trailer, Holoborodko is asked to set out his dream for the future of Ukraine, to which he replies that it is a normal life for ordinary Ukrainian families, whereupon the video depicts scenes of peace in the Donbas and Ukraine hosting the Olympics in Crimea.[38] When Zelensky was asked whether the ads could also be a form of electioneering, he slyly replied to one journalist, "No one has ever done this," allowing ample room for interpretation.[39] New billboards advertising *Servant of the People 3* also appeared during the campaign, this time with the slogan "Servant of the People: President, No Matter What."[40]

Just before Zelensky declared his candidacy, journalist Dmytro Hordon asked him whether he thought people were being misled if they decided to vote for Zelensky with the Holoborodko character in mind. Zelensky replied that of course there are differences between him and the fictive president, since the real person is neither a teacher nor poor ("I am a top-manager," he emphasized). "But in principle, his words are mine. This is not simply a film that was written for me. We all wrote it together, thought through everything together."[41]

Behind the scenes

In the context of Ukraine's patronal politics, where deceptive "virtual politics" are the norm, journalists and opponents quite understandably wanted to know whether what Zelensky was telling them was really the whole story.[42] The way in which his presidential bid was rolled out left room for suspicion, with the party suddenly appearing with no fanfare at all in 2017, no activity on its books until less than a year before the election, and very little information about it being made public by the people purporting to be its leaders. Could it be that Ukraine's backroom dealers had gained enough sophistication to seek power by parodying and lambasting their own cynical methods for obtaining power? This would be taking virtual politics to a new, postmodern level.

Another way to look at the question is to think about the challenges facing anyone who wants to effect change in a highly patronalistic polity, especially someone who wants to do so through media. As Zelensky himself explained in his interview with Hordon, all major television outlets in Ukraine are essentially owned or controlled by people he would call oligarchs.[43] Anyone wanting to be on TV has little choice but to work for at least one of them. Making such a deal does not mean that they then become the oligarch's puppet. Relations between patrons and clients in countries like Ukraine can be complex. Oligarchs might take someone on since they think what they are doing serves their interests, but this also works the other way around. People at lower levels of the informal patronal hierarchy are constantly trying to use those in higher positions to improve their own lot. As mentioned, after he becomes president in the *Servant of the People* show, Holoborodko's family is besieged by phone calls from relatives, friends, and people they barely know hoping they can get the new president to help them obtain better jobs or housing. In electoral and media politics, then, it is indeed quite plausible that Zelensky has been using others more than others have been using him. But the history of patronal politics in Ukraine and many other countries indicates that the chances of the chief patron having zero influence are low. But not zero.

And it can be very difficult for observers to tell the true reformers from the puppets until we see what they do later on.

Journalists in Ukraine, who initially seemed to be suspicious of the campaign, tried their best to uncover any dirt that might exist on Zelensky as his presidential ambitions came into greater focus. *Ukrayinska Pravda* rightly observed that Zelensky had made hardly anything known about the nuts and bolts of his campaign. The paper found that while he had initially met with some political technologists in the summer of 2018, they did not come to an agreement, and the Kvartal 95 team decided to run the presidential effort itself, only occasionally engaging the services of some trusted figures for particular tasks.[44] The effort was led by Bakanov, Zelensky's childhood friend who was a key manager of Kvartal's business and political activities.[45] Others reported that a few characters of dubious reputation were working on Zelensky's presidential bid behind the scenes, though Zelensky denied they played key roles. He did, though, admit that his extended team included people he did not know personally, as might be expected for such a campaign.[46]

> *Oligarch 1*: *I had nothing to do with this.*
> *Oligarch 2*: *Oh please...*
> *Oligarch 1*: *If he's not yours, then he's got to be Rustem Ashotovich's man.*
> *Oligarch 3*: *Gentlemen, I swear, I've had nothing whatsoever to do with Holoborodko.*
>
> — Oligarchs' exchange, *Servant of the People*, Season 1, Episode 1

One of the most important questions about Zelensky's campaign is his relationship with Kolomoyskyy, which Poroshenko portrayed as one of puppet-master and marionette—in posters in Kyiv and other cities, for example—but which Zelensky portrayed as almost incidental. When Zelensky ran for president, the reputed oligarch had fallen out of favor with Poroshenko, with his Pryvat Bank nationalized, his right-hand man arrested for alleged kidnapping and murder, and his assets frozen.[47] Kolomoyskyy fled to Geneva in 2016 and then on to Israel (where he holds citizenship) in the summer of 2018.[48] Poroshenko's team framed this as going after a corrupt oligarch, though others saw it as Poroshenko turning on a former ally. Kolomoyskyy was believed to be the fourth richest man in Ukraine as of 2021 (with an estimated fortune of $1.8 billion), though this is not too far off from Poroshenko himself (with an estimated $1.6 billion).[49] What is not disputed is that Kolomoyskyy and Zelensky had a good professional relationship. Channel 1+1, after all, made considerable money from the Kvartal team's successful programming, and the Kvartal team had access to one of the country's biggest television audiences. Zelensky and Kolomoyskyy also shared a love of humor. When asked which oligarch had the best sense of humor, Zelensky named Kolomoyskyy, while others have also reported on the businessman's wit.[50]

Journalists had a hard time determining just how far and deep this relationship went. Most obviously, Kolomoyskyy's 1+1 was incredibly supportive of Zelensky politically. This went well beyond giving prime-time slots to his shows, which, as well as *Vechernyy Kvartal* and *Servant of the People*, also included other programs like the satirical current affairs show *Chistonews*. The most-trusted and most-watched channel for news in Ukraine as of February 2019,[51] 1+1 was found by the National Council on Television and Radio Broadcasting not to have broadcast a single negative story on candidate Zelensky during the period of its monitoring.[52] The same organization found that the satirical *Chistonews* also cast all but Zelensky in a negative light.[53] The channel's bias was also widely perceived among the public.[54] Some noted that the "day of silence" right before the election, when campaigning is prohibited by law, featured a whole array of programming linked to Zelensky, including two airings of

Kvartal concerts and one episode of *Chistonews*.[55] During the campaign, 1+1 also broadcast a documentary on Ronald Reagan, an American actor turned president, voiced by none other than Zelensky.[56] Such programming led monitors to question whether this was in fact an illegal form of unregistered campaigning, but 1+1 replied that campaign restrictions did not apply as the programs featured Zelensky as an actor, not a candidate.[57] This was Zelensky's business, just as Poroshenko had kept performing his duties as president during the campaign.

But this tells us nothing about where the initiative came from. Zelensky was a top producer for 1+1, so it is hardly surprising that his network colleagues would seek to work to his advantage politically, whether consciously or subconsciously. At a minimum, it can be concluded that Kolomoyskyy chose not to prevent the use of his channel in this way. It was quite clear that he preferred Zelensky over Poroshenko, whom he now considered a political and economic enemy. Indeed, asked which he wanted more, Poroshenko's resounding defeat or Zelensky's victory, Kolomoyskyy replied the former.[58] Zelensky also said that the positive coverage on 1+1 could be explained by the fact that this channel's staff simply knew him well enough to know he had nothing to hide.[59] Either way, the two men had clearly aligned interests in both business and politics. And reading between the lines, Zelensky was claiming to be using Kolomoyskyy's 1+1 rather than the other way around.

The other major political link between Kolomoyskyy and Zelensky was Andriy Bohdan, a lawyer who had worked closely with Kolomoyskyy since the latter's days as the governor of Dnipropetrovsk but who also began working for Zelensky's campaign and ultimately became the first head of Zelensky's presidential administration. Investigative journalists revealed that Zelensky and Bohdan made repeated trips to Kolomoyskyy in exile, though neither said these involved Zelensky's presidential bid.[60] Kolomoyskyy said that both he and Zelensky understood that no such meetings were necessary and could only compromise the latter's reputation.[61] Kolomoyskyy admitted that Bohdan regularly informed him about the campaign. But he claimed Bohdan worked for Zelensky as a separate initiative—after all, lawyers commonly have multiple clients—and that he exercised no influence on the businessman's behalf.[62] Probing journalists found evidence that Zelensky was making at least some use of services beyond media that Kolomoyskyy's network was equipped to provide, such as security, but even this reportedly came more specifically from 1+1.[63] Kolomoyskyy claims he gave Zelensky advice only once or twice over the half-year before the election,[64] and Zelensky emphasized whenever he could that no one could influence him.[65] Moreover, the candidate vowed, he would not be returning nationalized banks to anyone.[66] "We are not friends," Zelensky emphasized. "We are from different generations."[67]

Some reports found circumstantial evidence that other powerful figures might be backing Zelensky's bid. These included such people as Interior Minister Arseniy Avakov and the Surkis brothers, known widely as Kuchma-era oligarchs.[68] But none of these reports were able to claim that these figures had organized Zelensky's campaign, and it was to be expected that powerful figures would begin to place bets on likely winners as the election neared.

Sometimes, investigative journalists were surprised to find that some of the seemingly dubious aspects of Zelensky's campaign actually checked out. For example, a team of journalists from *Schemes*, a venture known for its tenacious reporting, looked through records on the Zelensky campaign's funding and noticed suspiciously large donations from members of the general public.[69] To investigate, journalists turned up on the doorsteps of some of these donors and probed them about the money. It turned out that the contributions were genuine. For example,

Serhiy and Svitlana Ivashkovskyy from Odesa oblast donated almost 3 million hryvnya by selling a building they owned. Approached by journalists, Serhiy said "I respect him [Zelensky] not only as a comedian but also as a person who speaks the truth to one's face." Serhiy explained that he had decided to sell a second house he owned for $280,000 to make the donation. Zelensky thus appears to have struck a chord that resonated unusually deeply with at least some of the Ukrainian public.

> *Holoborodko: A common person can't become president.*
>
> Student: *Why not?*
>
> *Holoborodko: First, to register…one must deposit at least 2 million hryvnyas.*
>
> …
>
> *Student: Sure, but you know about crowdfunding, right?*
>
> *Holoborodko: What?*
>
> *Student: We started raising funds online… You've almost got two million in the account.*
>
> —Holoborodko's exchange with his history class students,
> *Servant of the People*, Season 1, Episode 1

> *… each of us is the president.*
>
> *From now on, each of us is responsible for the country that we leave to our children …*
>
> *Our European country begins with each one of us.*
>
> *We have chosen a path to Europe, but Europe is not somewhere out there.*
>
> *Europe is here [points to head]. And after it appears here, it will be everywhere, all over Ukraine.*
>
> —Volodymyr Zelensky, 20 May 2019, inauguration speech[70]

Zelensky's campaign themes

Some commentators disparaged Zelensky for failing to offer a real policy alternative or even a clear vision of where he would take the country—in effect, for being a populist.[71] Zelensky did not put forward detailed legislative proposals that could be introduced on day one—with the exception of his repeated mentions of canceling immunity from prosecution for members of parliament, which he did right away—but his "virtual incumbent" campaign was far from vacuous. Instead, we argue, four major themes came through that powerfully connected with a significant share of voters, forging a core of support that ultimately attracted others who saw him at least as a lesser of evils.

> *... to our defenders ... I will do everything I can to make you feel respect. This means decent ... secure salaries, living conditions, vacation leaves after the combat missions and your and your families' holidays. We must not just talk about NATO standards—we must create those standards.*
>
> *... many other problems ... trouble Ukrainians ... shocking utility tariffs, humiliating wages and pensions, painful prices and non-existent jobs ... the ... roads that are being built and repaired only in someone's prolific imagination.*
>
> —Volodymyr Zelensky, 20 May 2019, inauguration speech[72]

One such theme was a promise to care for the material interests of ordinary people, both by taking the fight against corruption seriously and shifting state priorities to privilege ordinary people rather than the elite. In the first question he posed to Poroshenko in the 19 April runoff debate, Zelensky went straight for the jugular with a question he said Ukrainian voters had given him: "How is it that Ukraine is practically the poorest country but has the richest president in all of its history?"[73] The idea he communicated is that corruption, poverty, and inequality are not matters of technocratic policy but of political will.

The *Servant of the People* series also conveyed this idea: Ukrainians knew what needed to be done; they just need someone with a strong will to stand up to insidious pressures. For example, many politicians had promised to revoke the immunity of deputies from prosecution, but time and again they had failed to deliver. The question was not about policy details but about commitment. For an anti-corruption drive to have any success, the leader would have to be clean and zealous. One of Zelensky's greatest triumphs was to convince a large number of skeptical Ukrainians that he really cared enough to make a difference.

> *Both Crimea and Donbas have been our Ukrainian land, but the land where we have lost the most important thing—the people.*
>
> *Today we have to return their minds—that's what we have lost.*
>
> *... authorities have not done anything to make them feel Ukrainians [sic] ... they are our people, they are Ukrainians ... being Ukrainian is not a line in the passport—being Ukrainian is here [points to heart] ... for sure ... the soldiers who are now defending Ukraine, our heroes, some of whom are Ukrainian-speakers, while others—Russian-speakers. There, in the frontline, there is no strife and discord, there is only courage and honor.*
>
> —Volodymyr Zelensky, 20 May 2019, inauguration speech[74]

A second theme emerging from Zelensky's campaign appearances was to bring peace. Unlike Poroshenko, Zelensky said that he would even be willing to sit down with Putin to bring a halt to the killing, potentially making compromises with the enemy.[75] "The first thing that I want is to stop the shooting," he averred in his first major interview in 2019: "These agreements, I think, are not very complicated. It seems to me that it is possible to come to agreement. First—stop killing. This is important—to save our people." Asked with whom he would negotiate, Zelensky said that first he would like to get the Minsk process working again, but that he would perhaps bring in other Western countries. He made it clear that Ukraine should do all it can to regain its territories but argued that this did not exclude a potential ceasefire agreement.[76] While the theme of ending war with Russia was noticeably absent from *Servant of the People 3*, it did appear in Zelensky's public statements during the campaign. For example, he called it his number one priority during his debate with Poroshenko.

The third season of *Servant of the People* and his Kvartal performances of 2019 emphasized the need for Ukrainians themselves to come together to resolve their country's problems: east and west, Ukrainian-speaking and Russian-speaking. This was also the third theme of his campaign. Zelensky stressed what Ukrainians had in common rather than issues that might divide them. The contrast was sharp with Poroshenko's approach, which gave primary emphasis to issues that appealed to specific parts of the population—such as autocephaly, the law on language, and martial law—but that could spark controversy among others.

When asked about Poroshenko's language law, Zelensky attempted to show how this might be accomplished:

> We should not squeeze out those who speak in other languages. And in Article 10 [of the Constitution] it is stated: The state language is Ukrainian. Everyone knows Ukrainian. If people in the east don't know it, they will learn it. There they speak *surzhyk* [an informal hybrid of Russian and Ukrainian], but we will not give *surzhyk* legal status—this would not be good. So, this is it, there is the Ukrainian language—the state language. But talk however you'd like, I say.[77]

This statement carried particular weight given that it came from someone of his background, someone from Ukraine's industrial southeast who is not only of Jewish rather than ethnically Ukrainian heritage but who primarily spoke Russian in both his personal and professional lives.

Similarly, touching on divisions in how different groups of Ukrainians remember important parts of their history, Zelensky argued that Ukrainians should remember their past, acknowledging its problems (like communism), but not try to erase their memory.[78] Zelensky proposed adopting the same approach to the policy of decommunization:

On the whole, I am OK with decommunization. Society has made its choice, and that is fine. There are undeniable heroes. Stepan Bandera is a hero for a certain percentage of Ukrainians, and this is normal and cool. This is one of those people who defended the freedom of Ukraine.

But this did not mean, he said, that every street needed to be renamed for Bandera. Wrapping up his thoughts, he said that more care needs to be taken to unite Ukraine, with tensions being so high in society.[79] The "national idea" of Ukraine is something entirely different, according to the message he conveyed. Something deeply civic. Asked by the journalist Hordon what this idea is, Zelensky replied that Ukraine is "an awesome, very liberal, free country."[80]

The fourth theme was of Ukraine's path to Europe. Despite widespread accusations from Poroshenko and other skeptics that Zelensky was a "Russian project," the vision that emerges from his public statements and performances is one of a Ukraine firmly embedded in Europe. Zelensky said that the question is not whether it would be good for Ukraine to join the EU and NATO but instead whether they will accept Ukraine as a member. If they do, he promised to support it.[81]

A final campaign promise, which he may yet decide not to keep, was that he would do all this in a single term:

If I am elected, I will be the kind of person who people first sling mud at (this is what is happening, I am already feeling it), then who people learn to respect, then whose departure they cry about. Because I think a president should stay only for a maximum of five years.[82]

Rivals' campaigns

The real-world incumbent, Poroshenko, doubled down on appropriating for himself the struggle against Russia in ways that many found divisive. His slogan was "Army, Language,

Faith" (*Armiya, mova, vira*), which some referred to simply as *ArMoVir* and resembled a sort of religious belief. This was something that distinguished him from his virtual incumbent rival, whose emphasis was explicitly on what united Ukrainians at a level that transcended particular languages, faiths, and security strategies. As one of Poroshenko's campaign insiders described his strategy in the second half of 2018, the idea was to portray the president as the only leader who has actually revived the Ukrainian army and who is now capable of standing up to the aggressor.[83] He similarly positioned himself as the only statesman able to unite the West against Putin, reminding voters that it was under his watch that the EU gave Ukrainians visa-free status for entering the EU. Since Poroshenko's ratings were abysmal, this strategy was aimed at restoring faith in his leadership specifically in western and central Ukraine, people who had voted for him in 2014 but were now planning to vote for other candidates.[84]

In addition to branding Zelensky incompetent and a Kolomoyskyy puppet, Poroshenko's appearances highlighted the need for a strong and proven leader to defend Ukraine against the Russian threat, replete with warnings of "fifth columns" operating in the country. This category most explicitly included forces related to Putin-connected Medvedchuk but could also be read as applying to almost anyone who criticized his leadership in a time of war.[85] Indeed, in January 2019, Poroshenko explicitly said that a vote for anyone else was a vote for Putin.[86]

This strategy appealed to Ukraine's cultural establishment and a subset of western Ukrainians, a group too small in number to win a runoff but sufficient to get Poroshenko past the first round. Many in this minority saw themselves as seeing through the virtual incumbent's façade, fearing his incompetence in a job he had no business seeking. They backed Poroshenko's cultural and social policies, which they believed to be the only way to wall off Russian influence and the threat posed by Moscow.

What often, though not always, went unstated was a suspicion that Zelensky and his supporters were not truly "conscious Ukrainians." As one of Ukraine's leading thinkers, and our respected colleague, put it just after the election, Zelensky's was in fact a "Little Russian" (*malorosiyskyy*) project rather than a truly Ukrainian one, using a term for Ukraine from the pre-Soviet Russian Empire that implied a vision for contemporary Ukraine in which it was subordinate to its neighbor, "Great Russia."[87] Billboards appeared shortly before the 21 April runoff showing Poroshenko and Putin in a Photoshopped stare-down—with no Zelensky in sight and the slogan "April 21: The Final and Crucial Choice."[88]

Poroshenko and his supporters also accused Zelensky of having links to the Russian government, calling his patriotism into question.[89] In the end, these accusations were at least as flimsy as charges that Poroshenko himself was double-dealing with Russia. Zelensky and Poroshenko both had business interests in Russia prior to 2014, and both had repeatedly made clear that they had done all they could to separate themselves from these business ties without simply surrendering their assets to Russians.[90]

Using his own position as president during the runoff period, Poroshenko traveled as president to France and Germany, where he met Emmanuel Macron and Angela Merkel, respectively.[91] Zelensky responded by also traveling to France and meeting with Macron.[92] Poroshenko also used the eve of the election, when formal campaigning was banned, to sign a decree confirming a plan for Ukraine to join the EU and NATO, which he said would secure the irreversibility of the country's European and Euro-Atlantic course.[93] With the president self-financing his campaign, his Channel 5 television station was found to have been presenting the news in a way that was favorable to him,[94] a bias also recognized by the public.[95]

The campaign of the political veteran Tymoshenko, the front-runner prior to Zelensky's rise, never gained traction. She and

Poroshenko spent much of the time prior to the first round of voting accusing each other of having links to Russia, representing corrupt interests, and failing to do what they were now promising when they held power—and denying each other's charges. The most Russia-oriented forces, including those tied to Medvedchuk, also failed to gain ground, with many of their former supporters finding a better expression of their discontent in the young showman. Zelensky also proved able to appeal to members of this constituency (and others) through his symbolizing the political arrival of a new generation, the Independence Generation.

The election results

In a race in which some eighty-three candidates had originally registered an intention to run,[96] the first round of voting ended with election first-timer Zelensky in the lead, though without enough votes to avoid a runoff, garnering 30 percent of the total. Poroshenko edged out Tymoshenko for the second runoff slot by 16 to 13 percent, followed by the relatively pro-Russian Opposition Platform's candidate with 12 percent.[97] A poll taken right after the results were known found that a three-fifths majority expected Zelensky to win.[98] And win he did, with a historic 73.22 percent of ballots cast, far ahead of Poroshenko's 24.45 percent to claim the largest margin of victory in Ukrainian presidential election history.[99] As it turned out, Zelensky won every single region of Ukraine save one, Lviv oblast, and even there Poroshenko's win was decisive only in the city itself (see Figure 5.1).

This landslide does not mean that the nation rallied fully around Zelensky's vision. Polls showed that as many as two-fifths of his supporters were voting as much against Poroshenko as for Zelensky.[100] But it is not true that people saw Zelensky simply as an empty vessel into which they could pour their own hopes and dreams, as some have argued.[101] While his coalition was diverse, this was precisely the point: to try to find common Ukrainian ground.

Leveraging a nationally representative sample of 2,000 adult residents of Ukraine from shortly before the voting it is possible to identify more precisely who Zelensky's voters were. Figures 5.2 and 5.3 summarize the findings from an Ordinary Least Squares (OLS) econometric analysis, which is useful for confidently identifying correlations in data that are highly unlikely to be random. For each factor, the dot represents our best estimate of the magnitude of its effect, and the lines radiating out from the dots capture 95-percent confidence intervals—that is, we have 95 percent statistical confidence that the effect lies within that range. We consider a variable to be having an effect if we can confidently rule out zero effect. The patterns we find are interesting. First, people in Ukraine's southeast were more likely than others to vote for Zelensky in the presidential election and his Servant of the People Party in the July 2019 parliamentary election, which we describe further in the next chapter. Zelensky voters also stand out as people who are more likely than others to have been considering leaving the country and migrating abroad. With at least 90 percent statistical confidence, we find such people were 3 percentage points more likely to vote for the Servant of the People Party and 4 percentage points more likely to vote for Zelensky. And younger voters clearly broke in Zelensky's favor. Other interesting findings include that people who spoke Ukrainian at work were 7 percentage points more likely to vote for Zelensky, economic transition winners were 6 percentage points less likely to cast a ballot for him, and those dissatisfied with the government were 3 percentage points more likely to vote for the Servant of the People Party.

Hope, ridicule, and anxiety

Zelensky's victory centered on his embodiment, real or imagined, of the civic and not ethnolinguistic and conservative image of a "good Ukrainian." Simply put, Zelensky's articulation of the Ukrainian nation connected with the median voter better than Poroshenko's. Internationally, though, his victory was often framed differently. The Kremlin reacted smugly, by all accounts thinking this would be its chance to push the inexperienced "comedian" around. Putin sent simple congratulations and said he respected Ukrainians' choice.[102]

Commentators in the United States, the UK, and other Western countries were generally surprised by the result. We analyzed the top ten pages of English-language articles that mention Zelensky during the election period in 2019 using the Google News search function. To most journalists in this sample, he was simply a comedian (125 mentions, comedy 41, and comic 30), an actor (41 mentions), a clown (19 mentions), or a joker (16 mentions). In fact, the term candidate (117) was mentioned fewer times than comedian. There was not one mention of producer or major media player. Kvartal was mentioned 25 times, "Servant of the People" 74, while Kolomoyskyy was mentioned 93 times. Zelensky himself was obviously mentioned most (784), Ukraine was second (641), president was third (348), and Poroshenko came in fourth at 314 mentions. The Western story was clear: an inexperienced Netflix star has just won the presidency in a country riddled with corruption (129 mentions) and an oligarch is connected to the whole thing, though few mentioned that Poroshenko was also widely regarded as an oligarch. This is how many in the West saw Zelensky and his electoral victory. They were not looking deeply into his long and successful career, and many were worried that this was the wrong person to have in the presidency with a war going on.

Perhaps most important in all of this, though, is that Ukraine was actually proving to the world that it is an increasingly stable and consolidated democracy. Despite war with Russia and the Kremlin's efforts to destabilize the country, an incumbent had been ousted at the ballot box and there was a peaceful transition of power. Indeed, perhaps this is one of Poroshenko's most important contributions to Ukrainian history: having lost a largely free and fair election, he stepped down and made way for a new leader. Of course, Zelensky was inexperienced in many ways, as were some of the new faces he brought to power. Mistakes were inevitable, as he had foreseen in the *Servant of the People* series. We now turn to his very real presidency.

We recommend our readers listen to “Kohaytesya Chornobryvi” (“Make Love to Each Other Blackbrowed”)

By Jerry Heil

Found on the “Top Songs—Ukraine” Playlist on Spotify:

https://open.spotify.com/album/5VEnWSE4uemvxXN7ezdH0W

Make love to each other, blackbrowed,

But not with Muscovites!

—Authors’ own translation. The lyrics are also part of the Poem “Katryna” by Taras Shevchenko (the Bard of Ukraine) and include citations of Zelensky’s wartime speeches.

And I will remind you of her words today:

… "destiny rewards him …"

—Volodymyr Zelensky, reciting Lina Kostenko, 20 March 2022[1]

Today is a hard day, but a happy day.
We are fighting for our state absolutely on all fronts: south, east, north, near the rich places of our beautiful country…
… Everyone who has already joined the defense of the country or can help the defense—stop the enemy wherever you can.
Cover the special signs that saboteurs leave on roads, that saboteurs leave on buildings.
Burn enemy vehicles with everything, everything you can.
If even kindergartens are a valid target for the invaders, you should leave them no chance.
All thoughts and prayers of Ukrainians are with our military.
We believe in them, we care about them.
We protect our state.
The night will be hard, very hard.
But it will be morning.
Glory to Ukraine!

—Volodymyr Zelensky, 24 February 2022[2]

6

PRESIDENT "ZE!"

A car alarm goes off outside a typical run-down five-story apartment building in Kyiv. A high school history teacher, having fallen asleep reading Plutarch, stirs and then panics. He has overslept! His rush to get ready for work is a comic scramble. Living with his parents and his sister's teenage daughter following his recent divorce, he doesn't know how to iron his shirt or even where the iron is kept. His turn for the single bathroom finally comes up, but just as he settles in to read a current affairs magazine featuring the prime minister, there is a knock at the door. Men in suits enter. One is the prime minister himself, who then gravely states the teacher's full name. Emerging from the bathroom still in his underwear, the worried teacher gulps and confesses his identity. Then the prime minister replies: "Good morning, Mr President!" The teacher is stunned, his family dumbfounded. He had let his students crowdfund a campaign after his secretly videotaped rant against politics as usual had gone viral, but he had never expected to win in Ukraine's oligarch-dominated political system. And so the premise for the TV show *Servant of the People* is set: a completely accidental president, Vasyl Holoborodko, must now cope with the job.

The (fictive) prime minister is Stanislav Chuyko, who accompanies a still-stunned Holoborodko in a luxury car to the presidential administration. Anxiously watching news reports about his surprise election on a TV screen in the back seat, Holoborodko instinctively grabs the handle just above the car door. Chuyko reminds him that he is not commuting in a tram. Embarrassed, Holoborodko lets go. But seeing his distress, the prime minister extends some sympathy. If it would make him more comfortable, he can hold on. The president-elect accepts this small social mercy, clinging on to the handle as if for dear life. In the hours and days that follow, Holoborodko meets his security detail (which he thinks he does not need), the outgoing president (who refuses to leave and locks himself in the presidential office), and the presidential administration staff (who make clear they have seen many presidents come and go). When presented with a speech he is expected to give at his own inauguration that turns out to be a word-for-word copy of US President Abraham Lincoln's Gettysburg Address, it dawns on him that no one expects him to be his own man, let alone his own kind of president.

The character Zelensky plays ultimately decides to follow his gut and stay true to himself. Walking into the Verkhovna Rada on his inauguration day, he intentionally takes the wrong route to the podium (one with fewer cameras) and then delivers his own speech, one placing primary emphasis on civic duty and the role citizens have to play in their democracy. Next, he fires his security detail and the bloated administration staff (including its masseurs) and replaces problematic officials with trusted members of his own team (all friends from the same high school). Holoborodko and his team then embark on radical reforms, though they face attempts to thwart or corrupt them at every turn. Persevering, and sometimes resorting to non-transparent methods that make them feel less-than-comfortable, they get some of these reforms done but face an increasing backlash from oligarchs, establishment politicians, mass media, and even ordinary citizens. But none of it stops them. They are on a mission to make Ukraine better for ordinary citizens.

This is clearly how Zelensky wanted Ukrainians to see his presidency. Through this TV show, he had prepared them for the likelihood that he would face a steep learning curve and make some mistakes along the way. But he had also set some high expectations. In a vibrant and unruly patronal democracy like Ukraine's, such expectations would be hard for anyone to meet in normal circumstances, even a highly competent and dedicated reformer. But Zelensky's presidential tenure would turn out to be far from normal. In fact, the "normal" period he likely expected lasted only about nine months. At that point, the COVID-19 pandemic set in, only to be followed by Russia's full-on invasion two years later. Moreover, the first months after his 20 May 2019 inauguration were of necessity consumed by team-building and the 21 July parliamentary elections that would decide whether he had a hope of passing his agenda into law and getting a cooperative prime minister.

This chapter examines how the now-real "President Ze" fared prior to 24 February 2022. His presidency marked the ascendancy of the Independence Generation, which now occupied key positions of influence throughout the country. So the story is no longer about this generation's rise, but about their growing leadership of the country as a whole. For a newcomer to elected office facing a debilitating global health crisis, he and his team were able to accomplish a remarkable amount. In addition, Zelensky as president did not reverse the most important substantive policies of his predecessor, even accelerating many of them, making for a great deal of continuity in policymaking. But we also find many bumps in the road, things left undone, and continuities with the corrupt system and patronal political practices he had inherited, though we find important signs that progress was being made on corruption. More fundamental, though, was how he did it, continuing to strike his signature themes of civic national identity, the duty of all citizens to their country, Ukraine's European orientation, and a desire for peace, finding the latter challenge the most stubborn of all.

Style as substance

The style Zelensky brought to the presidency turned out to have strong roots in his past lives as an actor-producer and as a presidential candidate, and this same style continues to be his today as he leads Ukraine after Russia's 2022 attack. Most noticeably for the public, he did not change the way he communicated with citizens upon assuming office. This includes his preference for personalized, direct, and curated appeals. His speeches are designed to be highly accessible to ordinary Ukrainians (the country's "median voter") and frequently delivered through short videos on social media. As those close to the administration told us, he often writes his own speeches, though in the busiest of times he will give staffers an outline to flesh out before giving it a final edit himself. His KVN-honed talent for extemporaneous speaking also serves him well; even today, some of his speeches actually are impromptu, off-the-cuff recordings. This approach is authentic to him, as much as it is purposely managed and delivered. Critics sometimes complained that he seemed to avoid extended questioning from potentially critical media, and indeed his direct appeals allowed him to reach constituents unfiltered by potentially critical eyes. His now-famous green T-shirt would also make appearances during his presidency, usually in meetings involving military themes, symbolizing an informality that he also sought to convey at times, though he would frequently appear in a suit.

This style, symbolizing a direct connection with the people of Ukraine, resonated with his longstanding substantive emphasis on civic Ukrainian identity and the duty of ordinary people to improve their country. This message takes center stage from his very first appearance as president. In his inaugural speech, Zelensky focused on the need for ordinary citizens to exercise their democratic civic duties not only through elections but also by doing what they can personally to fight systemic corruption. His presidential messaging also consistently emphasized the need to bring unity to the country and to find a path to peace. To some, this particular message appeared naïve, while to others it seemed to be typically "Zelenskyesque" pathos, grounded in humanist values. It does appear that he truly believed that negotiations could bear fruit even in the face of Russia's ongoing occupation of Crimea and parts of the Donbas. As he himself put it: "The path to peace is not easy ... I know that we can do it."[3] This patriotic and civic-duty-oriented rhetoric struck a chord with many ordinary people, including millions who recognized these themes from his famous political satire over the previous two decades. Zelensky's focus on civic Ukrainian identity was perhaps most prominent when the COVID-19 pandemic put him in the position of leading the nation through the country's most deadly public health crisis since World War II. He often concluded his addresses to the nation during this period with "protect yourselves, protect others, protect Ukraine."

To some of the new president's opponents, this message seemed hollow or gimmicky, if not outright dangerous. As Chapter 5 has shown, while the 2019 presidential election was a major moment of rallying for Ukraine's population, it also arguably consolidated two political poles that came to sandwich Zelensky's large and broad center. Political scientists have a term for something like what happened, when intense political competition leads people to become so emotionally involved in their side that they become predisposed to overemphasize negativity in the actions of the other side and positivity in those of one's own side. This term is "affective polarization."[4] In using this term, we are not arguing that Ukraine itself is a polarized country, but that it does have two small political poles that behave that way, bookending the majority middle ground.

On one side of the political spectrum, Zelensky faced fierce opposition from a rather openly pro-Russian opposition. But they were split on what "pro-Russian" would and should mean. One group was quite outwardly pro-Russian Federation and advocated accommodating Kremlin interests in order to build a future partnership with Moscow. This group was personified most powerfully by Medvedchuk, the oligarch whose daughter had Putin for a godfather and who was now a leader in the Opposition Platform—For Life party. Others were pro-Russophone and authoritarian in orientation but still remained Ukrainian-state-centered, ultimately siding clearly with Ukraine after Russia launched its all-out war. Before that point, though, it could be difficult at times to tell exactly who was in which camp. Both parts of this group generally saw Zelensky for what he was, a European-oriented politician committed to democracy and reform, which put them strongly at odds.

On the other side of the political spectrum, the 2019 election led to a congealing of the self-described "25-percenters," those who had voted for Poroshenko but were much more suspicious of Zelensky than loyal to Poroshenko personally. While not all adopted the label "25-percenter," and while many sought new standard-bearers after Poroshenko's defeat, their most fundamental fear was that Zelensky would not prove to be a real "conscious Ukrainian." That is, they argued, he was not someone who had a true understanding of what it means to be Ukrainian as opposed to Russian or Soviet, and therefore he was not someone who knew how Ukraine needed to be transformed to protect itself against the Russian aggressor and more broadly to realize its national potential.[5] Seeds of such doubt seem to have emerged from Zelensky's Russophone and southeastern upbringing, the perception that he was a product of low "Soviet" or *sovok* culture, and that he did not articulate their vision of what a "good" or "patriotic" Ukrainian looks like. These seeds of doubt deeply ingrained, they were quick to find signs that he was unfit for the job or—for the more conspiracy-minded—something much worse: part of a revanchist Russian plot.

If Zelensky's brand of Ukrainian identity politics was a gimmick, it was a remarkably intellectually consistent and solidly grounded one that connected powerfully with millions of Ukrainians. In fact, Zelensky's presidential rhetoric was strongly—even fiercely—patriotic, just pulling at different Ukrainian national heartstrings than the 25-percenters were used to plucking. Instead of language, religion, and the Russian threat, Zelensky emphasized the state, civic duty, shared history, the importance of Ukraine's diversity, and the common quotidian experiences that bound Ukrainians together. Rather than fear, Zelensky struck the emotional chords of sympathy and hope, even in the face of misery and difficulty. This comes through clearly in the following passage from his January 2020 greeting to Ukrainians on Unity Day:

> Exactly 101 years ago, one of the most significant events in the history of Ukrainian statehood and national liberation struggle took place ... The reunification into a single, independent state and was solemnly proclaimed on 22 January 1919 ... Sophia Square in Kyiv.
>
> In all corners of Ukraine, this was met with enthusiasm and inspiration: at last there was a chance to build a united and independent country. Unfortunately, it was lost. ...
>
> ... It's been over 100 years. Did we draw any conclusions from this story?
>
> It teaches us a simple yet vital principle for Ukraine: only together are we strong ... But in search of this unity, we again quarrel: "And how can we, so different and dissimilar, unite?" ...

> ... the sense of nation as a whole emerges not only due to common traditions, culture and religion. There are also values. Which are acceptable for every corner of Ukraine. And by which in the future Ukrainians could be identified in every corner of the planet. Values of integrity and honesty. Good manners and tolerance. Values of freedom and democracy. The desire for economic welfare and prosperity. The desire to be wealthy. Values of respect for the law, private property and respect for one another.
>
> I am Ukrainian. Because I live according to the law.
>
> Always ready to protect my homeland when needed.
>
> I am a role model for the post-Soviet space: in defense of my rights, protection of the freedom of speech, the rule of law, civil society, zero tolerance for corruption.
>
> I am Ukrainian. Because I am a responsible citizen. I pay taxes.
>
> I don't drive against the lights, I park properly, I never drive drunk. I care about the environment. I'm learning to think critically.
>
> I am Ukrainian—because we are the best in sports, science, IT.
>
> I live a healthy lifestyle. I study foreign languages.
>
> I support equal opportunities for men and women.
>
> I respect the rights of representatives of all national minorities and all religions ...
>
> ... This list can be supplemented for a long time ...
>
> ... To be strong, one must become united.
>
> To become united, one must be strong ...
>
> —Volodymyr Zelensky, 22 January 2021[6]

The "Ze Team"

In patronal politics, the chief political actors are typically not "parties" per se but instead extended power networks of people joined by actual face-to-face connections that can involve both personal loyalties and the material interests of the individuals involved.[7] The biggest reputed oligarchs like Kolomoyskyy, for example, might have people connected to him in multiple political parties, not just one. And when a political juggernaut arises like Zelensky's Servant of the People Party, oligarchs' networks (and other major power networks) can be expected to try to get some of their own people included so as to gain access to power. When such people act, therefore, they may not act in their party's publicly stated interest but instead try to work within it to advance the interest of the network they represent, sometimes at cross-purposes with the party leadership and membership.

Zelensky faced just such a situation after his own election, and since he simply did not have enough personally trusted friends with the right qualifications to fill every post, it was inevitable that he would wind up taking on personnel from a variety of sources and striking alliances with a diverse array of actors, resulting in internal competition among factions and personalities on top of the institutional rivalries that will be more familiar to readers in, say, the United States or the UK. Nevertheless, for the sake of simplicity, in these pages we follow a common informal practice in Ukraine by referring to a single "Ze Team" consisting of all people widely considered as such.

Some key members of the Ze Team had been with him for years. Most noteworthy here is childhood friend Ivan Bakanov, a lawyer who had handled Kvartal 95's legal and financial affairs from the beginning and whom Zelensky had entrusted to set up the Servant of the People Party. Zelensky named him to a post where a leader would naturally want only the most trusted individuals: head of the Security Service of Ukraine (SBU). He occupied this post until the summer of 2022. Another Kvartal 95 figure, Serhiy Shefir, still served as Zelensky's main advisor as of the second half of 2022.

Other Ze Team members joined through processes both transparent and opaque during the campaign and Zelensky's presidency itself. In a few instances, Zelensky held an open online competition, much as envisioned in the *Servant of the People* TV series. One such contest was for the job of administration spokesperson, with 4,000 people tossing their hats in the ring. The winner was a young journalist with experience working at the online EspresoTV and the major ICTV and Inter television channels, and who had also been a communication consultant for the World Bank and had contributed articles to the *New York Times*. Despite this impressive CV, which also included training at Warsaw and Yale Universities, some in the media, including some with similar pedigrees, were quick to question her qualifications.[8] It was clear from the start that Ukraine's mass media were not going to go easy on the new president.

Zelensky's appointments signaled different things to different observers and were generally received with skepticism. The most eye-catching for many observers was Zelensky's decision to name one of Kolomoyskyy's lawyers, Andriy Bohdan, as his chief of staff (head of the presidential administration). This seemed to confirm the speculation that the reputed oligarch had played a large role in Zelensky's election and would have outsize influence over his presidency. Countering this signal, though, was the new president's decision to appoint Oleksandr Danylyuk as the head of the National Security and Defense Council. Danylyuk had been minister of finance in the Poroshenko-era government that had nationalized Pryvat Bank, and during the campaign he had affirmed the nationalization was done correctly and indicated no compensation should be paid to former owners like Kolomoyskyy.[9] Announcing Danylyuk's appointment to his team, Zelensky said that "his only minus is that Oleksandr is a former minister. I think that in order to destroy the old system such specialists are needed."[10] Within a year, both Bohdan and Danylyuk would be replaced. The latter was succeeded by the former mayor of Luhansk, Oleksiy Danilov, while Bohdan's duties were assumed by Andriy Yermak, a lawyer who had worked with Inter TV when Zelensky was general producer. As he had worked for a Party of Regions deputy in the Verkhovna Rada, Yermak's appointment was not uncontroversial, though he had also served as a campaign representative for future post-Euromaidan Prime Minister Arseniy Yatsenyuk.[11] Also controversial was Zelensky's attempt to install Georgia's former president, Mikheil Saakashvili—whose citizenship he restored right after assuming office—as deputy prime minister for reforms. When the Rada rejected this appointment, Zelensky instead named him executive committee chief for the advisory National Reform Council.[12] Other appointments, like Dmytro Kuleba being named deputy prime minister for European affairs, were near universally praised, as such figures were widely seen in expert and diplomatic circles as competent and uncompromised.

Once Zelensky's party had won control of the Verkhovna Rada and could select its own prime minister, the Ze Team brought aboard a young prime minister, Oleksiy Honcharuk, and with him came a team of internationally recognized academics. These included Tymofiy Mylovanov (a University of Wisconsin–Madison PhD) as minister of economic development and trade, and Oleksandr Rodnyanskyy Jr (a Princeton PhD and assistant professor at Cambridge) as economic advisor. The Rada victory also enabled Zelensky's party to choose the new parliamentary speaker, Dmytro Razumkov, though he was linked by some to the Party of Regions and was replaced as speaker by Ruslan Stefanchuk in late 2021 after a scandal we discuss later in the chapter.[13]

Filling important posts was difficult not only because it was hard to find people who were qualified and honest but also because some of the best potential candidates among the 25-percenters refused to work with the new president, even on reforms they themselves had long advocated. One of this book's authors personally observed someone boasting to civil society leaders that they had refused to accept an important role Zelensky was offering them in July 2019. Partly as a result, key posts in both government and presidential administration were left unfilled for extended periods.

Because the new president did not have an established political brand and extensive patronal network of his own from which to fill key posts, the Ze Team was frequently reshuffled. Sometimes the movement was upwards, once it had been proven that someone was exceptionally good at their job. This was the case, for example, in Kuleba's 2020 promotion to foreign minister. In another example, current Prime Minister Denys Shmyhal was originally director of a company in Lviv belonging to Rinat Akhmetov (though he denies ever meeting the reputed oligarch). He entered a Zelensky Facebook competition for governor of that province and lost, but captured Zelensky's attention and was soon made governor of neighboring Ivano-Frankivsk.[14] He was promoted in February 2020 to the position of minister of regional development and the following month was named to replace Honcharuk as PM.[15]

Yet more often, the personnel movement was in the other direction, often in the wake of regular scandals. In one, the thirty-five-year-old Prime Minister Honcharuk was recorded badmouthing the president, saying Zelensky had a "primitive understanding of the economy."[16] He kept his post on that occasion but was replaced in 2020 after a series of new conflicts. Sadly, with him left several excellent ministers like Mylovanov. Others left following accusations of corruption. The Servant of the People Party, for example, booted from its delegation Oleksandr Yurchenko (accused by NABU of corruption), Yevheniy Shevchenko (for meeting with and praising Belarus dictator Aleksandr Lukashenko), and Lyudmyla Buymister (for voting against Zelensky's centerpiece Law on Oligarchs).[17] Zelensky held all this up as evidence that he was serious about battling corruption even among his own team.[18] The media and his opponents, though, regularly called him out for having harbored reputedly corrupt people on his team in the first place. And protesters would let the president hear their anger when he did not remove such officials, as students and other activists have repeatedly done over a minister of education and science accused of plagiarism.[19]

The 2019 parliamentary campaign and the Independence Generation

Zelensky's presidential victory by no means gave him full power over the executive branch. This is because Ukraine has a divided-executive constitution by which executive power is split between the president and a prime minister who is beholden primarily to parliament. This means that without control of parliament, a president would be unable not only to pass legislation freely but also to implement policy in many important spheres that ministers oversee. This put a premium on his party's gaining control of the Verkhovna Rada, something Poroshenko had not been able to achieve. Zelensky and his team moved quickly, seeking to capitalize on the momentum from his landslide presidential win. While the president did not have the power to simply order the Rada's dissolution, the overwhelming nature of his April victory convinced enough of the deputies that he had a mandate to do so and that early elections should be held. They were ultimately held on 21 July 2019.

Ukraine's parties scrambled to put together their party lists, and none found this more challenging than the Servant of the People Party, which had never before contested a parliamentary election and did not have a stable of experienced party hands. The party's strategy was to nominate fresh faces that would represent a broad spectrum of Ukrainian society, cutting across all major social cleavages.

During the campaign, Servant of the People built on Zelensky's strategy of pledging to tackle the bread-and-butter issues about which voters cared deeply. In particular, the party focused on ending corruption, embarking on reforms framed as facilitating EU accession, and working toward peace, all of which resonated strongly with the electorate. Surprisingly, its main opponents outside the pro-Russian camp (Poroshenko's European Solidarity, rock star Svyatoslav Vakarchuk's *Holos*, and Poroshenko-era prime minister Volodymyr Hroysman's Ukrainian Strategy) did not focus on such concerns. Instead, led by European Solidarity, these parties emphasized the cultural issues and warnings about fifth columns that had previously proven to generate strong but regionally concentrated support. After the presidential election, and with the upcoming parliamentary election in view, therefore, they doubled down on framing Zelensky as a threat to Ukrainian ethnonational ideals like the future of the Ukrainian language and hence as a threat to Ukrainian statehood. But Ukraine had changed since 2014, and Zelensky's approach was more in line with Ukraine's growing sense of civic identity and unity. Zelensky's opponents on this side of the spectrum were also largely competing for the same electorate and wound up dividing it up among themselves. Holos (meaning "Voice") seemed to follow the Zelensky playbook to the letter, insisting on new faces, a social media presence, and free concerts, but it lacked a policy profile that would separate it from European Solidarity. The pro-Russian parties followed their usual strategy, emphasizing social issues important in the southeast and the need to work with Russia rather than resist it.

International observers generally found the elections to be free and fair, though the competitors skirted the campaign spending and media coverage rules in much the same way they had in the presidential contest three months earlier. TV channels linked to Poroshenko ran an hours-long "marathon" on the theme

"Russian revanche or a European future?" Channels 1+1 and Inter gave Servant of the People and Zelensky favorable coverage, with the former continuing to air *Vechernyy Kvartal* and the *Servant of the People* TV series. Vakarchuk's famous band, Okean Elzy, also performed at free concerts around the country.

The results left no room for doubt. It was another landslide victory for Zelensky. In fact, this was the first time since independence that a single party had gained an outright majority in parliament, with 254 out of 450 seats.[20] The biggest losers were Poroshenko's European Solidarity, which lost 107 seats, and *Samopomich* (which retained but one of the 33 seats it previously held). Holos won twenty seats, including an outright win in Lviv, the only locality that had overwhelmingly voted for Poroshenko in the presidential runoff back in April. Overall, the votes received by the Servant of the People Party demonstrated that it had nationwide support across the country, as Figure 6.1 shows.

One important result was to bring into parliament many new people, large numbers of whom were representatives of the Independence Generation. All of the Servant of the People Party's deputies were political newcomers, and 63 percent of parliament now consisted of political novices. According to Gwendolyn Sasse's assessment, 97 percent held a higher education degree (31 percent law, 31 percent economics, and 27 percent management) and 10 percent had been educated abroad for at least part of their studies.[21] There were more women, more younger deputies, and generally fewer "old faces" from the 2000s and 2010s.

Reforms: continuity and change

As president, Zelensky continued to pursue some of the reforms started by his predecessors as well as introducing new ones. All of his reforms shared an emphasis on a common, inclusive Ukrainianness and were framed as helping Ukraine meet its Euro-Atlantic aspirations. The need for banking and land reforms, and ending immunity from prosecution for Ukraine's deputies, were all presented as necessary for Ukraine to be able to sit at the European Union's table as an equal and not just as "a neighbor." Zelensky also framed his continuation of some of his predecessor's policies and reforms as part of a president's civic duty to support the country's laws. His role as reformer, therefore, was couched in civic and democratic duty, which in turn rallied more people to support these policies—if not him directly.

Often to the surprise of many, Zelensky decided not to reverse some of Poroshenko's more controversial reforms, including the language law that had been rushed through parliament and signed by outgoing President Poroshenko shortly before Zelensky's inauguration.[22] Part of the law had come into effect in 2019, but other parts still needed to be rolled out in the years that followed. That this reform did not designate Russian as a minority language in the same way it did other regional languages was problematic for some liberal groups and human rights watchdogs.[23] While many had expected the southeastern and native Russian-speaking Zelensky to undo the law with his solid parliamentary majority, he instead enforced the legislation, citing his duty as president to uphold laws that had been passed democratically. A more cynical interpretation is that he did not dare seek its repeal, as many supporters of this law were openly threatening a "new maidan" if he tried. But as someone whose speeches often stressed that it does not matter what language one speaks in order to be a good citizen of Ukraine, he understood nothing would be gained by inflaming the ethnolinguistic divides that repealing the law would have unleashed. Fighting these kinds of battles was his predecessor's modus operandi, not Zelensky's.

Perhaps even more surprising was Zelensky's enforcement of Poroshenko-era bans of certain Russian cultural products. In fact, in February 2020, the Ukrainian Cinema Agency banned Zelensky's own 2012 film *Eight First Dates*. It was blacklisted because its cast included Yekaterina Varnava, a Russian actress who in 2017 had been declared *persona non grata* in Ukraine after visiting Crimea without the permission of Ukrainian authorities.[24] Just as strikingly, his government also extended bans on Russian television and media. All of this was indeed surprising because, prior to becoming president, Zelensky had spoken out against both laws. These moves not only showed a level of democratic consolidation, continuity, and stability that Ukraine had not previously seen between presidential tenures; they also quickly dispelled, at least for some, the idea that Zelensky's election was part of a revanchist Russian plot.

As well as upholding many of the laws passed under Poroshenko, Zelensky also accelerated or extended some of them. This was the case, for example, with reforms involving finance and the National Bank.[25] Also hugely important was his acceleration of the military reforms launched under his predecessor. These reforms not only strengthened the military but improved its readiness for the all-out Russian invasion just months later.[26] Zelensky also took ongoing decentralization to a new level. In July 2020, with overwhelming support from Servant of the People and several other parties, the Rada approved a bill reorganizing *rayons* (roughly the equivalent of American counties), fully scrapping Soviet-era divisions and creating 136 units out of the previous 490.[27] In March 2021, Zelensky and his team launched the "New Village" program that forged state–business partnerships to improve living conditions in rural areas (building modern spaces, administrative service centers, post offices, medical centers, stores, concert halls, movie theaters, and sports complexes).[28] As Tymofiy Brik and Jennifer Murtazashvili have documented, the decentralization reform was important in reinforcing senses of local civic duty that plugged in well to Zelensky's larger development of national civic identity and strengthened Ukrainian resistance to Russia's invasion.[29]

But it is the third set of reforms and policy successes, those initiated by Zelensky's party and government and making up a big chunk of his electoral promises, that gave his presidency its strongest claim to success. Four major reforms stand out in this category. One was to roll out the *Diya* app and other important e-democracy platforms and programs in Ukraine. Diya allows Ukrainians to use digital identification documentation, providing for greater transparency in the provision of state services that has proven life-saving in the context of the war. A second was a new Electoral Code, which finally stripped parliamentarians of immunity from prosecution, something many politicians had called for over the years but none had pushed through. The third was a law banning Rada nepotism, prohibiting close relatives from being appointed aides or consultants to elected deputies at all levels in Ukraine.[30] Fourth and finally, Zelensky achieved something else that many of his predecessors had tried but failed to do, namely pass a ground-breaking land reform that brings Ukraine in line with EU accession requirements.

A last grasp at peace

Upon assuming the presidency, Zelensky ushered in a sense of optimism that a new, pragmatic approach to Russia could end the carnage in Donetsk and Luhansk oblasts that had begun in 2014. As he and those around him described it, the approach was based above all else on the need to protect the lives of Ukrainians. Negotiations were the key, including sitting down and talking with Putin himself to reach an agreement. The 25-percenters were quick to brand this naïve, and Russia's leader would soon leave no doubt that he considered Russia and Ukraine a single nation and that his price for ending the conflict was no less than the surrender of Ukraine's sovereignty, as we will discuss in

Chapter 7. This was antithetical to what Zelensky himself had long stood for, but the new president clearly hoped that he could persuade the Kremlin to accept something less by displaying more pragmatism than had Poroshenko in recent years.

The Kremlin would certainly not be bowled over by the new Ukrainian president's political gravitas. In the first public appearance where he mentioned Zelensky by name, at the St Petersburg International Economic Forum on 7 June 2019, Putin snarked:

> Judging by everything I've seen, he is a good specialist in the area he has worked in until now. He is a good actor. [Laughter.] I am serious, and you are laughing. But it is one thing to play someone and another to be someone. Obviously, acting requires talent. Many talents. You can change your role every ten minutes. The prince and the pauper—every ten minutes, and you have to be convincing in every role. This is really a talent. In order to deal with the affairs of the state, one needs different kinds of qualities.[31]

Despite being ridiculed by the Kremlin, Zelensky's approach to Russia did produce some limited results. One was the 2019 prisoner exchange he successfully negotiated in his first meeting with Putin. In his campaign and his earlier Kvartal 95 performances, Zelensky had called for the release of the famous Ukrainian filmmaker Oleg Sentsov, who had been languishing in a Russian prison since 2014. These negotiations won the release of Sentsov, then near death following a hunger strike, along with lesser-known but no less important political and war prisoners. This was seen as a major achievement domestically, something Ukraine's previous president had been unable to make happen.

But Zelensky's attempts to find a more lasting settlement foundered. In an initial move to deescalate, over opposition charges he was "capitulating to Russia," Zelensky unilaterally withdrew Ukrainian troops from battle lines in eastern Ukraine. But Russia and its self-proclaimed Donetsk and Luhansk "People's Republics" did not reciprocate, so Ukraine reengaged.[32] He also stared down opposition charges of national betrayal in late 2019 by endorsing the "Steinmeier Formula," a plan informally named after Germany's foreign minister, which set out a path to realizing the Minsk II accords that Poroshenko had committed Ukraine to in negotiations in 2014–15 (described in Chapter 4). It called for the reintegration of the occupied parts of the Donbas by recognizing them as distinct units and changing Ukraine's constitution to grant them special autonomous status after they held elections, a move critics feared would give Russia a permanent foothold in the Ukrainian state.[33] Zelensky argued the formula did not concede any territory and that to qualify for the agreement, the new local elections would have to be held under Ukraine's constitution and without Russian troops present and have to be validated by OSCE observers. This, he averred, was Ukraine's best hope of ending the bloodshed and ultimately returning the lost territories.[34] Zelensky's Verkhovna Rada majority, though, was not the supermajority required to amend the constitution, and other parties refused to give him the needed votes.[35] And in any case, Russia had shown no sign of holding up its end of the bargain, including when it came to allowing truly free and fair elections in the territories in question.

Importantly, although willing to negotiate a peace, Zelensky continued to be unwaveringly committed to upholding Ukrainian territorial integrity, a theme that can also be traced back to 2014 and his Kvartal 95 and *Servant of the People* performances. In August 2020, for example, he vowed Ukraine would get Crimea back.[36] He turned the tables on some post-Euromaidan leaders now accusing him of capitulating to Russia: "Those who gave away part of our territory without a fight should give testimony, not sermons on patriotism."[37]

Overall, Zelensky probably represented Ukraine's best available effort to come to some kind of working relationship with

Putin's Russia without sacrificing its sovereignty and territorial integrity. But in the end, the Kremlin insisted that Ukraine make offerings of exactly those things that Zelensky, his followers, the 25-percenters, and the overwhelming majority of Ukrainians would never bring to the altar. This mutual realization by both the Kremlin and Zelensky set the stage for Russia to attempt its own final solution to what it called "the Ukraine problem" in February 2022. US intelligence on Putin indicates that "the Russian leader ... saw a window of opportunity closing" to restore Ukraine to Moscow's orbit.[38] This is because the Kremlin had thought it was getting what it wanted with Zelensky's election in 2019 but by 2022 had realized something like the opposite was the case. While Ukrainians had decisively rejected Poroshenko's brand of nationalism in favor of someone who advocated a negotiated settlement and seemed to be a manipulable neophyte, Zelensky's Ukraine had not only failed to submit but was now making even more headway than ever on a Euro-Atlantic course.

As it became bitterly apparent that no acceptable compromise would be found, Zelensky began paying more attention to the different ways in which Russia was trying to get its way in Ukraine. And this meant dealing with Ukraine's more Russia-oriented opposition and media. This presented Zelensky with a classic dilemma of democracies at war: How is it possible to balance democracy and freedom of speech against the risk that the enemy will exploit them, especially when many mass media and politicians are believed to be highly corruptible?

We have already noted that Zelensky accelerated the closures of Russian-owned media outlets. But as Russian rhetoric and propaganda escalated, he found himself pressing even harder in a direction he had surely not anticipated before his election. Zelensky's own rise to high politics had coincided temporally with the political return of reputed oligarch Medvedchuk, Putin's close family friend, who in late 2018 assumed a leadership position in what became the Opposition Platform—For Life party. Reputed to have been Kuchma's manipulative gray cardinal leading up to the Orange Revolution as presidential chief of staff, Medvedchuk had been sanctioned by the United States in 2014 for his involvement in Russia's annexation of Crimea, among other things.[39] With the 2019 Verkhovna Rada elections, the Opposition Platform—For Life outpaced Poroshenko's European Solidarity to become the largest opposition party in the Rada.[40] Zelensky thus had what many regarded as a Russian fifth column in parliament. But to go after it directly would raise concerns about Ukraine's democratic trajectory. As we discuss below, he ultimately framed this battle as one against a class of oligarchs rather than a class of ideologies.

The good, the bad, and the ugly

Just as democratic leaders must wrestle with tradeoffs between freedom of speech and possible enemy exploitation of this freedom when focusing on national security, so too do they face a dilemma when it comes to combating pervasive corruption. Do you prosecute and jail opposition figures believed to be corrupt, potentially even including the previous administration? To some the answer might seem an obvious yes. The problem is that going at corrupt opposition also brings political advantage to oneself, which can look very much like the same old selective prosecution of patronal regimes past, undermining one's credibility as a reformer. Yet, to give one's predecessors a pass is also fraught with peril for reformers. One of the reasons people lost faith in Presidents Yushchenko (after the Orange Revolution) and Poroshenko (after the Euromaidan) was that hardly any senior figures from the previous Kuchma and Yanukovych regimes (respectively) were actually jailed through due process.

Dilemmas even extend to prosecuting corruption in one's own ranks: do it, and questions arise about why you had any corrupt people in your team in the first place; avoid it, and you can be accused of selective prosecution, itself a form of corruption.

Whether or not leaders go after other corrupt politicians, therefore, it can be very hard to tell the sincere reformers from the imitators. In Zelensky's case, we find evidence of a slow start followed by a genuine anti-corruption drive that opted to accept the risks of prosecuting political friends and foes alike but that also involved some questionable decisions that his opponents have been quick to latch onto. Here we focus on his struggles, first, with Ukraine's notorious judiciary and, second, with the oligarchs.

Judiciary

The Ze Team sent early signals they would seriously fight corruption, and one of the most important was the promise to strengthen Ukraine's independent anti-corruption agencies, especially NABU.[41] One early move was to replace Prosecutor General Yuriy Lutsenko,[42] widely believed to be in a turf battle with NABU that was hindering its effectiveness.[43] As a result, reports political scientist Ivan Gomza, through January 2020 "NABU managed to improve cooperation with the police, the Public Prosecutor's Office, and even SAPO, building up to 500 cases, making this the most successful phase in its entire history."[44]

A backlash from many of NABU's critics and rival institutions soon followed, resulting in what seemed like the same old in-fighting within Ukraine's judiciary. Just a year into Zelensky's presidency, one of his own party's deputies, someone also formerly working for Kolomoyskyy at 1+1, initiated a Constitutional Court case that resulted in an August 2020 ruling that the head of NABU had been appointed illegally.[45] This set off a public relations war, with different parts of Ukraine's judiciary accusing each other of corruption.[46] Zelensky soon jumped in, initiating bills to reboot the Constitutional Court and strengthen NABU's independence in 2020 and 2021.[47] The deputy initiating the Constitutional Court case was later expelled from the Servant of the People Party.[48] Some observers believed Zelensky would still covertly try to gain control over NABU and other agencies,[49] but it has remained in place and by and large preserved its independence. That being said, signs of judicial in-fighting continued even after Russia launched its February 2022 attack.

De-oligarchization

The oligarchs were front and center of Zelensky's anti-corruption rhetoric, the *Servant of the People* series, and much of his political satire. After a series of less systematic moves, Zelensky eventually declared a policy of "de-oligarchization" in April 2021, the centerpiece of which would become a new Law on Oligarchs adopted at the end of that same year.[50] This law created a legal definition of "oligarch," forced those who met it to formally register as such, imposed restrictions on the political activities of those on this list, and barred them from participating in the privatization of state assets, among other things.[51] Falling into this category was anyone who met three of the following four criteria: taking part in political life, having significant influence on mass media, being an end beneficiary owner of a monopoly, and having a net worth of more than a million times the country's official minimum wage.[52] Observers widely agreed that both Poroshenko and Kolomoyskyy would meet these criteria,[53] with other high-profile figures cited including Akhmetov, Firtash, Medvedchuk, and Pinchuk.[54] The oligarchs had their apparent defenders in the Verkhovna Rada. In fact, this is what reportedly catalyzed the removal of Servant of the People Party deputy Dmytro Razumkov as parliamentary speaker: he had called for a delay in this legislation.[55]

Upon the bill's passage, Zelensky warned the oligarchs: "When the state's angelic patience ends, someone is going to start experiencing hell. You can test us, or you can simply help your state."[56] And indeed, by the time of Russia's 2022 invasion, most of Ukraine's major reputed oligarchs appeared quite unhappy in one way or another, with each one and their supporters accusing Zelensky of attempting to usurp power at their personal expense. We now focus on three reputed oligarchs with distinct relationships to Zelensky, though moves against and discontent among others were evident too—including Dmytro Firtash,[57] Pavlo Fuchs,[58] the Surkis brothers,[59] and Rinat Akhmetov.[60]

In a politically savvy move, Zelensky made Medvedchuk the first poster boy for the de-oligarchization campaign. His main TV channels were shut down, his assets frozen, and he was placed under house arrest. In a special article marking the start of the campaign, Zelensky announced:

> For the first time in many years, the number of oligarchs in Ukraine has not grown but has shrunk. Minus Medvedchuk. He has been deprived of the capability of using media assets and state property to the detriment of the country. There will be future minuses so long as all oligarchs do not become simply big businessmen.[61]

These moves drew considerable ire not only from Medvedchuk's partisan supporters in Ukraine but from the Kremlin as well.

Poroshenko was also in the crosshairs. And here the reformer's dilemma was made stark by the international community. The US Embassy in Kyiv even warned that "the justice system should not be used for the purpose of settling political scores," a message understood as referring to Poroshenko's possible arrest.[62] Prime Minister Shmyhal replied that it was necessary to go after him as all should be equal before the law.[63] And go after him they did, with investigators and prosecutors seemingly raining criminal cases upon the ex-president for various forms of alleged corruption over the course of 2019 and 2020. In 2021, Zelensky even linked Poroshenko to Medvedchuk, accusing him of profiting from the war based on investigative journalist reports citing leaked Medvedchuk telephone conversations.[64] Poroshenko denied these accusations, calling them false, libelous, a form of political persecution, and part of a Kremlin narrative.[65] The prosecutorial moves were popular, though. One poll in June 2020 found that 51 percent of the population believed the prosecutions to have been justified, while only 30 percent considered them primarily political.[66] While Poroshenko has not yet met Medvedchuk's fate, he did take pre-emptive action to avoid falling into the new legal category of "oligarch," selling off the two media outlets he owned (Channel 5 and *Pryamyy*) to former and current employees[67] and transferring the ownership of his chocolate business to his son.[68]

The "litmus test" for Zelensky's sincerity, as one senior US State Department official put it, would be his treatment of the person widely suspected of being his own chief political patron, Ihor Kolomoyskyy,[69] who had returned from his self-imposed exile in Israel just days after Zelensky's election, signaling that he now felt "safe."[70] He was to be disappointed. For one thing, Zelensky kept his promise not to return Pryvat Bank to its former owners, with the Verkhovna Rada even adopting a new law preventing the return of nationalized or liquidated banks, or even providing the former owners with monetary compensation.[71] Zelensky was not only failing to do Kolomoyskyy's bidding but actively tightening the screws on him as well. Not only did Zelensky replace Bohdan with Yermak as head of the presidential administration just two months before declaring de-oligarchization,[72] but his authorities also arrested a former deputy chairman of Pryvat Bank (Volodymyr Yatsenko) for alleged embezzlement as he was attempting to flee the country in Kolomoyskyy's private jet.[73] In

March 2021, the Anti-Monopoly Committee found the Pryvat holding group guilty of anti-competitive practices, slapping it with a big fine.[74] At the dawn of 2022, Zelensky could still be criticized for failing to lodge actual criminal charges against Kolomoyskyy, unlike Poroshenko.[75] But in July 2022, Zelensky appeared to deliver a different *coup de gras*: Ukraine reportedly stripped Kolomoyskyy of his citizenship, citing a law against dual citizenship and the fact that he held passports for Israel and Cyprus.[76] While a major blow against a reputed oligarch, this move was controversial, smacking of old-style politics and Poroshenko's own stripping of Ukrainian citizenship from his political opponent Saakashvili.

Zelensky's critics tended to focus on what they saw as the persecution of "their own" reputed oligarch, and sometimes said at the same time that Zelensky was only weakening oligarch power to take their place in Ukraine's political economy for himself.[77] The Law on Oligarchs, some charged, could pave the way for selective targeting since the National Security and Defense Council (led by Zelensky himself) would decide who meets the definition and goes on the registry.[78] Whatever the president's ultimate motives, though, the drive against the oligarchs appears to have been sincere, though it was sidetracked by Russia's 24 February 2022 attack.

The Trump impeachment scandal

Shortly after assuming office, Zelensky found himself embroiled in a different scandal, one involving consummate insider politicians, oligarchs, backroom dealing, extrajudicial activities, and threats of impeachment. While this sounds wild, this time it was not a scene from the *Servant of the People* television series, nor a Kvartal 95 skit; nor were the actors driving it even Ukrainians. We are talking about the events involved in the December 2019 impeachment of US President Donald Trump.

During Poroshenko's time in office, Trump associates had been trying to pressure Ukrainian officials into supporting the American president's reelection chances. For one thing, they were attempting to dig up dirt on Hunter Biden, who had joined the board of a large Ukrainian company (Burisma Holdings) while his father Joe Biden was vice-president under Barack Obama. In particular, former New York Mayor Rudy Giuliani, at the time working as a Trump aide and lawyer, was trying to build credibility for a claim that the American then-vice-president had tried to protect his son by pressuring Ukraine to remove Prosecutor General Viktor Shokhin in 2016. The rub is that Shokhin was not actively investigating the company at the time, as confirmed by his aide.[79] The Trump team was also interested in bolstering its assertion that the consequential 2016 hacks into the Democratic National Committee servers, widely linked to Russia, may in fact have come from Ukraine, a notion the Mueller Commission had already debunked.[80]

What Trump and Giuliani wanted most of all, according to reports and various investigations, was for Ukraine to announce an official investigation of the Bidens and the 2016 DNC hack. This would lend credibility to their narratives while also tarnishing the reputation of the elder Biden, widely—and ultimately correctly—believed to be Trump's most likely Democratic Party challenger in the 2020 presidential elections. US Ambassador Yovanovitch believed that the man Poroshenko had tapped to succeed Shokhin as prosecutor general, Lutsenko (2016–19), was engaging these attempts, thinking Trump and company could in return help him politically at home. Poroshenko, it has been reported, was ready to make the announcement sought by Giuliani.[81]

Zelensky's win derailed these machinations, and so he himself became a Trump team target while he was still just president-elect. According to reports, Giuliani first sought to approach Zelensky through Kolomoyskyy, thinking like many observers that he was Zelensky's patron. The Ukrainian businessman recalls having replied to Giuliani's representatives (Lev Parnas and Igor Fruman) when they arrived: "Did you see a sign on the door that says, 'Meetings with Zelensky arranged here?' They said, 'No.' I said, 'Well then, you've ended up in the wrong place.'"[82] Ultimately, Trump diplomats Kurt Volker and Gordon Sondland reached Zelensky both directly and through Andriy Yermak, the future presidential chief of staff who was then a close advisor.[83] These efforts culminated in the infamous 25 July 2019 phone call between Trump and Zelensky. In all these communications, the message was understood to be that if Zelensky wanted to guarantee good relations with the US under Trump, including getting a White House meeting and even badly needed military aid, he would need personally to announce the desired investigations.[84]

When the contents of the phone call began to become more broadly known late in the summer, Zelensky claimed he had not felt pressured, apparently doing his best to forge good relations with President Trump.[85] But, of course, this was tremendous pressure, putting Zelensky in the awkward position of having to choose between his anti-corruption stance and vitally needed military support (and good relations with Ukraine's most important international partner more generally). Kvartal 95 could not have drawn up a more dramatic dilemma to face a fictional president than Zelensky now found himself confronting. Had the Trump team's bullying and advice on how to navigate the American president not become public, it is not clear whether Zelensky would have eventually made the requested announcement. He had indicated in the infamous phone call that he would look into everything and take it very seriously, but as of 25 July he had only just won the parliamentary election and was still putting together his team. Ultimately, he never gave Trump what he wanted. Nonetheless, his involvement in the scandal was not a good look for a president who was still having to battle the widespread international media trope of his being a "comedian" or actor in over his head.

Not all international coverage was unflattering during this period, though. The Senate impeachment trial took place just after the tragic shooting down of Ukraine International Airlines flight PS752 by the Iranian military.[86] Ukrainian, Canadian, and Iranian citizens died. In a study of the tandem Canadian–Ukrainian response, Onuch and Orysiya Lutsevych demonstrate that Ukraine's diplomats (like the ambassador to Canada, Andriy Shevchenko) and politicians were able to lead from the front, and on an even playing field with their Canadian counterparts. Zelensky, in his typical humanist style, issued a trademark direct appeal and sent condolences to his citizens invoking the civic nation:

> Dear Ukrainians!
>
> In these difficult days for each of us, I want to say the following.
>
> I will return all the dead to their relatives and friends, they will be able to say goodbye to them in a human way.
>
> We will honor their memory with dignity.
>
> All the guilty will be punished.
>
> We will return to Ukrainians not only a sense of security and justice, but also the confidence that Ukraine will always protect you, no matter where you are on the planet!
>
> —Volodymyr Zelensky, 11 January 2020[87]

He had also acquitted himself relatively well in his first meeting with Putin in late 2019. Overall, Zelensky's first tests on the international stage showed he was capable of being presidential, raising his currency in Ukraine and abroad, though his image still had a long way to go.

Pandemic

Unfortunately, Ukraine would soon face more hardship. In February–March 2020, like everywhere else around the globe, the COVID-19 pandemic hit. In a country where so many were already so poor, the pandemic further devastated the economy before any of the early Zelensky reforms could have an effect. Indeed, Zelensky took the health threat very seriously, initially ordering a lockdown and advocating social-distancing measures, eventually settling on restrictions that would vary in severity depending on how hard-hit a given locality was by the virus. Comparative studies have given Ukraine mixed reviews on its coronavirus response from a health perspective, with some suggesting Zelensky relaxed the country's policies too soon.[88]

But with the economy in tatters, the lockdowns were received negatively by many small business owners and informal workers, the backbone of the Ukrainian economy. Some local politicians channeled this sentiment, framing the country's coronavirus strictures as overreach on the part of the central government, the Kyiv elite, or Zelensky personally. It certainly did not help that some in Ukraine did not believe COVID-19 was real or thought garlic would be enough to prevent infection. In fact, according to MOBILISE project data in December–February 2022, a shocking 48 percent of the population believed the conspiracy theory that the virus was a weapon created in a lab. The health crisis also foregrounded the early instability in the Zelensky Team. In the first two months of the pandemic, between March and April, Zelensky went through two health ministers, with one lasting only twenty-six days.[89]

Perhaps the greatest strength of Zelensky's coronavirus response was his communication. His traditional presidential style proved very effective in conveying clear and effective messages around what to do and what not to do. In our research together with Kulyk and Sasse, we found that Zelensky regularly connected pandemic rule-following with being a good Ukrainian citizen. He also linked the personal "take care of yourselves and your loved ones" with the collective "take care of all of Ukraine" in his regular briefings and speeches. Furthermore, an analysis of his shorter Instagram videos shows that he began every clip with *budte zdorovi* (be healthy). These messages were even more convincing when he repeated them after it became known his wife Olena had contracted COVID-19 in June 2020, meaning he himself had to go into partial self-isolation.[90]

As of January 2021, according to MOBILISE project data, a plurality of 47 percent believed that Ukraine's local politicians were handling the crisis well or very well, but only 29 percent thought Zelensky was doing the same. Interestingly, approval of his virus response went up to 43 percent by December–February 2022, with 54 percent now approving of the local politicians.[91] Our statistical analyses of IBIF project survey data (together with Sasse and Kulyk) reveal that those who were more afraid of COVID-19 and those personally affected by it were more likely to be among those who approved of Zelensky's handling of the pandemic. Over time, Zelensky relaxed his approach, and Ukraine's lockdowns became far less severe than those of other countries, such as Canada or Poland.

Geopolitics was not absent from pandemic politics in Ukraine. In February 2021, Zelensky barred the Russian Sputnik V vaccine even after it got reasonably positive assessments in some international studies.[92] There was simply no faith in anything coming from Russia. Instead, Zelensky sought vaccines from India and the global COVAX system, as well as Pfizer and AstraZeneca directly. To increase uptake, Zelensky personally got vaccinated with AstraZeneca as commander in chief together with soldiers on the frontline.[93] Rather than simply roll up his sleeves, though, Zelensky took off his whole shirt, instantly drawing comparisons with well-known bare-chested photos of a certain autocratic Russian leader. We heard claims from some folks in the know that this part of the PR outreach was not planned, and that his shirt was simply too tight to be rolled up to his biceps.

Zelensky and the people

Zelensky's approval ratings ebbed and flowed throughout the first two and a half years of his presidency. The country was experiencing multiple simultaneous crises, and even if none were a product of Zelensky's actions, he was still the one that people were going to hold accountable. The pandemic, though, brought an overall decline, with his disapproval ratings topping his approval ratings in the KIIS polling agency's measures for first time in June 2020, with 38 percent approving and 45 percent disapproving of his actions as president.[94] Nevertheless, Zelensky's Servant of the People Party surprised observers in October of that same year by winning the most mayoral competitions and the most local deputy seats nationwide among political parties. And where it did lose, the party generally came second. The political neophyte was gaining stature. Though he was still far from the historic figure Zelensky appeared to be envisioning for himself in the *Servant of the People* series.

At the same time, Zelensky's connections with the electorate had shifted a little bit during his actual presidency relative to what they were during his nascent candidacy in 2018 (described in Chapter 4) and during the election campaign (discussed in Chapter 5). Analyzing all KIIS omnibus surveys that asked Ukrainian citizens how they would vote from the start of 2020 through the February 2022 eve of Russia's all-out invasion, and controlling for the time periods involved, we find stability in his disproportionate appeal to youth, people without higher education, and residents of Zelensky's own home southeast. But unlike

2018, he was now drawing especially strongly from people who identified as Ukrainian by nationality (which we have argued earlier reflects primarily a strong civic connection to the Ukrainian state) at the same time he was appealing rather evenly across Ukrainian and Russian language preferences. Moreover, Ukraine's western regions no longer stood out for opposing him.[95]

In the next chapter, we will present evidence that Zelensky's presidency—including both his Euro-Atlantic messaging and the reforms he pursued—helped bring many new people to positions of support for a Euro-Atlantic orientation for Ukraine despite his declining poll numbers. We will show that in this pandemic- and crisis-ridden period, Ukraine experienced a strengthening of a sense of civic duty, growing readiness to engage in political action, and increasing support for democracy. If the Kremlin had interpreted continued dissatisfaction in Ukraine with potential support for Russian invaders, which it strongly appears to have done, it was to be badly mistaken. This is the story we tell in the next chapter. A story of how and why millions of "Zelenskys" rose up to defend their country. A story of the Zelensky Effect.

We recommend our readers listen to "Vova, yibash yikh blyat"

By Myusli UA

Found on the "Ukraine Top 100" Playlist on Spotify, a playlist by Vova Savadskyy:

https://open.spotify.com/album/6dG164KSddFfZI6VirzCjB

I want to address the president

. . .

I want to address Volodymyr Zelensky

. . .

there has never been such a president before
And there will not be another such president

. . .

You are the only one who could unite people
You're the only one who did

. . .

I did not vote for you in the first round
But I'm ready to give up my life right now

—Authors' own translation

And I will remind you of her words today:

"When one has a nation, she is already a person …"

—Volodymyr Zelensky, reciting Lina Kostenko, 20 March 2022[1]

Now I will say one thing:
I stay here.
I stay in Kyiv.
On Bankova Street.
I am not hiding.
And I am not afraid of anyone.
As much as it takes to win this patriotic war of ours.

—Volodymyr Zelensky, 7 March 2022[2]

7

THE ZELENSKY EFFECT AT WAR

I love my country as she is
Sometimes her head is a mess
European, Asian
Or free-spirited Cossack.

I love my country like crazy
"Still hasn't died yet," I sing, raising the flag.
And more than once they divorced/divided us
But after all, I don't have another land.

—Kvartal 95 Song, "It Seems to Be"[3]

The former president of Ukraine is in prison. Independent exit polls indicated he had won the recent election, yet the official results held that he had lost. EU election observers refuse to hear any complaints from his team. In prison, he learns of a massive state crisis emerging in his absence, a political scenario that surely reminds the Independence Generation of the tumultuous 1990s. Politicians were reverting to the old ways of Ukrainian politics, cutting behind-the-scenes deals and taking their slices of the profiteering pie. A populist leader plunges the country into a downward economic spiral. There is no money. Debt and inflation are skyrocketing. The masses take to the streets and turn violent. The ultimate winners are radical nationalists under the slogan "Freedom! Surname! Country!" When citizens turn against them, the nationalists declare: "If the country is not with me, then *u sraku* [to the shitter] with that country." Ukraine cycles through six presidents in eighteen months, and foreign leaders meet to decide if they should step in. They do not. To salvage their own power, political leaders resort to divide-and-rule tactics, manipulating local populations by emphasizing regional, ethnic, and linguistic divisions. The country breaks apart into twenty-eight units, each a self-proclaimed independent state ruled by a patronal leader who plays up some myopic localized identity to create enemies that justify their rule. Ukraine is now divided between a "Legitimate Ukraine," a "Great Ukraine," a "Kingdom of Halychyna," the "Crimean Emirate," a "North" and a "South Kherson," and even an "SSSR," the Russian-language acronym for USSR that in this case refers instead to *Soyuz Svobodnykh Samodostatochnykh Respublik*, or the Union of Free Self-Sufficient Republics. Ukraine as we knew it no longer exists. Someone says: "We need a Ukrainian de Gaulle ... that's the only option."

Fortunately for Ukrainians, this was not a real moment in their history but a scene from the *Servant of the People* TV series, Season 3, Episode 2. And it of course turns out that Holoborodko is the only person with any hope of bringing the fighting fragments back together as one united country. Spoiler alert: He succeeds. Alerts are even less necessary when we say that he does so by focusing on a civic identity that unites Ukrainians.

In this fictional account, the real enemy is faceless and nameless. Russia is only alluded to. In real life, the threat to Ukraine's survival comes primarily from the Russian Federation and its imperial ambitions. Putin resolved all doubts about his intentions with Russia's military actions on 24 February 2022. Comparing himself to empire-builder Peter the Great, he initiated an all-out military effort to "return" what he calls misguided, breakaway parts of a greater Russia to the motherland. What this *Servant of the People* episode does is to emphasize the importance of what unifies Ukrainians. It also makes the point that ordinary Ukrainians do not need a Russian enemy to understand the importance of Ukrainian unity. And it was precisely this kind of unity that became vital to Ukraine's survival against its aggressive neighbor less than three years later.

Sitting down today to watch this episode, which was intended for viewing during the 2019 election campaign, one cannot help but imagine what Zelensky was thinking as he sat in his underground bunker as Russian tanks first rolled into the country and enemy artillery pounded the entire country on 24 February 2022. He is the real and legitimate president, but of a Ukraine that was already broken into five parts—this had happened in 2014 at the hands of Russian forces, which had orchestrated pseudo-referendums and declarations of independence in Crimea, the special-status city of Sevastopol, and the self-proclaimed Donetsk and Luhansk "People's Republics." He must have been watching in anger and horror as cities across the country were being bombed in Moscow's attempt to tear the country further apart. One wonders whether he thought at all about the fictional character he had created and played only three years earlier, or whether he experienced any regrets about leaving his previous life to take on the grave national responsibility he now bore.

Regardless, his wartime leadership proceeded first and foremost from an emphasis on the same Ukrainian civic unity that he had both reflected and developed in the entertainment sphere and now as president for well over a decade. His attention thus turned immediately to ensuring that Ukraine's 44 million citizens did not split apart in the face of Russia's assault, ensuring they maintained the unity needed to defeat it. As it turns out, despite the fears of his critics, he proved to be extraordinarily well positioned to accomplish just this. For one thing, Zelensky was precisely the sort of "ordinary Ukrainian" that Putin had expected would greet his invading army with flowers, a seeming *sovok* from southeastern Ukraine whose native language was Russian. And as one journalist put it, he was also a "super average" citizen whom people widely believed shared their general outlook on life.[4] In a country with millions of Zelenskys, his own acts of resistance and his appeals to their sense of patriotic duty would carry exemplary weight.

But he was also an ordinary Ukrainian in a way no one else could be. First and foremost, he is an extraordinary communicator, someone whose native skills had been refined over decades in the entertainment industry. His career has demonstrated a profound capacity to connect with what political scientists call the median voter, with those who find themselves in the middle of the political spectrum.[5] At no time can such skills be needed more than at war, when inspiration and morale can decide the outcome. He proved up to the job. In fact, we will show that much of his success as wartime leader reflected not only the same sense of civic patriotism that he had long represented and championed before the war but also many of the same techniques he had long used to do this championing, including his savvy use of mobile phones and social media. He also knew where his expertise ended. For example, he did not attempt to micro-manage military decisions.

The Zelensky Effect at war's eve

Prior to 24 February, Zelensky's public standing seemed to be on the same track that had bedeviled all four Ukrainian presidents before him: high hopes followed by growing disappointment and frustration. Such a pattern is not unusual in economically struggling countries where patronalism is the norm. Almost inevitably, the problems prove too entrenched to be fixed immediately, if the leader even tries.[6] While the last chapter presented evidence that Zelensky seemed to be trying, the result was similar. MOBILISE project data show that an astonishing 37 percent of the population in 2021 and 2022 either did not have enough money for food or only enough for "the most basic items." And over three-quarters of the population reported that corruption was a major problem. In February 2022, right before Russia's new assault, 37 percent of Ukrainians were considering migrating abroad. Readiness to take to the streets in protest was at a seven-year high, reaching 60 percent. After winning a record-breaking landslide in 2019, Zelensky's approval ratings were now decidedly under water, dropping to just 33 percent in the days before 24 February.

While the larger pattern seemed familiar, Zelensky was in fact faring better with the public than had his predecessors. While Poroshenko had also faced war, his successor was additionally confronted with the COVID-19 pandemic and its economic consequences, forcing the difficult policy choices discussed in the previous chapter. MOBILISE data show that nearly half the population, 45 percent, personally knew someone who had died from the virus as of February 2022. In this light, it is noteworthy that Zelensky's approval ratings remained higher than those of his predecessors at comparable points in their presidential tenures, including Yushchenko's roughly 5 percent and Poroshenko's ballpark 15 percent.[7] Moreover, Zelensky's ratings did not decline steadily over time, as they had risen to 55 percent in January–February 2021 before reaching their low a year later.

But the situation in Ukraine was far from rosy nonetheless. So if someone, say a leader of a large neighboring state with territorial ambitions, were making a calculation about whether the context might allow for a quick invasion and occupation, they might take such data as signaling that the country was filled with potential collaborators. In fact, reports have emerged that Russia's FSB did just this, commissioning surveys across Ukraine asking similar questions that appear to have led them to just this conclusion.[8]

What Russia overlooked is that people can be extremely dissatisfied with their government and even disagree vociferously on how to correct their country's problems without ever wavering in their commitment to the country itself. And as we have described in previous chapters, attachment to all things Ukrainian had been steadily on the rise, an effect only heightened by 24 February and the ensuing events. Researchers have shown that the standard census question on nationality tends to capture identification with the Ukrainian state as a civic, as opposed to ethnic, entity.[9] And as Figure 7.1 shows, almost 90 percent of the country identified as "Ukrainian" throughout the Zelensky era; only a handful selected "Russian" or anything else. Growing by large margins during this period were support for democracy, acceding to the EU, and joining NATO (Figures 7.1, 7.3). Figure 7.2 also shows pronounced increases in Ukrainians' personal sense of civic duty, including the duty to vote, engage in civil society, and protest about the most important problems facing the country. Indeed, research by Oleksandra Keudel has shown that there can be plenty of room for civic participation even in highly patronalistic polities.[10] Since Russia's invasion threatened these things, it should not have been surprising that Ukrainians fought back, and fiercely.

It was no coincidence that these values spread under Zelensky. In a detailed analysis published elsewhere, Onuch employed OLS econometric analysis to identify strong patterns among responses from people whom the MOBILISE project interviewed multiple times over the course of 2019–22. This exercise strongly indicates that Zelensky himself (or at least least his party and policies) was actually leading people to support democracy, the EU, and NATO when they had not done so before. People who had voted for the Servant of the People Party, for example, were 9 percentage points more likely than others to be among those who shifted to supporting democracy (Figure 7.4). There is less than a 5 percent chance that this pattern is random. Onuch finds an even larger effect (24 percentage points) for people who had not originally voted for the party but later came to support it.[11] Extensions of the same analysis show that the party's supporters were also more likely to come to support NATO membership during the Zelensky presidency, as were those in the country's southeast.[12]

In short, Zelensky and his party have brought more undecided Ukrainians to both Euro-Atlantic and pro-democratic positions, strengthening pre-existing trends. This is a key part of the Zelensky Effect. Had Russia understood it, perhaps it would not have done what it did on 24 February.

Russia's misguided march to war

In early 2021, with the Delta variant of COVID-19 giving new life to the pandemic, Russia undertook something of a dress rehearsal for its eventual attack, mobilizing its massive army to positions near Ukraine. International tensions ratcheted up, but soon the troops packed up and mostly returned to their normal stations. While the Russians were not invading now, Zelensky's National Security and Defense Council chief later said it was at this point that his administration began preparing for all-out war with Russia, coming to believe that the Kremlin was preparing to reinstall the ousted Yanukovych in Kyiv.[13] Additional signs were soon to materialize.

As Ukrainians were preparing for their thirtieth Independence Day on 24 August, and with the Independence Generation now roughly between thirty-seven and forty-six years of age, Putin personally published an article that ominously denied almost everything they stood for. The 12 July screed, called "On the Historical Unity of Russians and Ukrainians," mixed fact with liberal doses of fiction and wishful thinking to make a case that Ukrainians were nothing other than wayward Russians whom the West had wickedly deceived for centuries.[14] It was not news that he harbored such views. At one point in 2008, he infamously told US President George W. Bush that Ukraine was not really a country and had regularly endorsed characterizing Ukraine as *malorossiya*, a "Little Russia" that had become separated from "Great Russia."[15] The Russian public echoed such views of Ukraine: while they generally did not advocate it becoming part of Russia and tolerated its existence as an independent state, they frequently viewed it as an illegitimate hodgepodge of regions that did not really belong together.[16]

The letter was disturbing to Ukrainians in part because it laid out some potential justifications for military aggression and occupation of all of Ukraine. The word cloud in Figure 7.5 summarizes our content analysis of this text, with words in the largest fonts being used most frequently. While many have attributed Putin's obsession with Ukraine to tensions with the West over NATO expansion, "NATO" does not appear in the top ten, 100, or even 300 mentioned words. In fact, it is mentioned only twice. His article instead grounds Russian interest in Ukraine as primarily cultural and ethnonational, focusing a great deal on language, notions of historical lands, and Orthodoxy. "Russians and Ukrainians were one people—a single whole" wrote Putin. He uses the term "Ukraine" much more frequently than "Russia" (75 mentions to 53), perhaps ironically reinforcing the idea of Ukraine as a separate entity in struggle with Russia.

Putin clearly thought this would also resonate with a considerable number of Ukrainians. "I am confident that true sovereignty for Ukraine is possible only in partnership with Russia," he opined.[17] But he was clearly unfamiliar with the trends in Ukrainian national identity that we have discussed in previous chapters, trends that show an increasing identification with things Ukrainian, a growing dissociation with things Russian, and a larger commitment to the Ukrainian state. So, to those studying the subject, it was small wonder that his words provoked a massive backlash across the whole country, regardless of language and region. Many a mocking meme appeared on the Internet in Ukraine, one of the most prominent presenting different versions—some cartoon, some real-life photos—of the painting *Zaporizhian Kozaks* [Cossacks] *Writing a Letter to the Turkish Sultan*, depicting a group of Kozaks huddled around a table, writing a profane and humorous reply to Sultan Mehmed's demand that they submit to Ottoman rule.

As 2021 rolled on, the signs mounted. In October, Putin's supposedly pro-Western sidekick Dmitriy Medvedev published his own article echoing Putin's claims and adding new justifications for a potential invasion. Zelensky, Medvedev wrote, "has certain ethnic roots" that he abandoned after becoming president, now serving Ukrainian nationalism much like some German Jews collaborated with the Nazis.[18] Later that fall, the world's intelligence services noticed that Russia was once again strengthening its army along Ukraine's northern and eastern borders. The UK and the United States warned of having received actionable intelligence that Russia and its collaborators in Ukraine were planning to stage a coup in Kyiv in February 2022.[19]

Zelensky and the Ukrainian government played down any talk of a possible invasion.[20] Our understanding, based on our conversations with policy insiders and government interlocutors, is that while some Ukrainian intelligence did contradict US and UK warnings, the country's authorities intentionally minimized the possibility in order to prevent a run on Ukraine's already fragile economy and avoid mass panic and flight for as long as possible. Journalists have now also confirmed this in subsequent interviews with Zelensky himself and key members of his team.[21] But as noted already, Ukrainian security officials claim to have been preparing for the unthinkable since Russia's early 2021 mobilization. These preparations reportedly included some of the crackdowns described in the previous chapters on reputedly corrupt courts they believed were prepared to work with Russian plans, as well as shutting down media linked to Russian interests through reputed oligarch Viktor Medvedchuk.[22] Military preparations were also underway, including secretly placing some units in strategic positions around the country. The public downplaying of the threat's immediacy, though, led some in Ukraine and abroad to doubt that the government was ready to respond to the threat or that it was even taking it seriously.[23]

Warnings from Western intelligence of an imminent invasion grew by the day.[24] In response to reports that the invasion might happen on 16 February 2022,[25] Zelensky announced a day of national unity on 14 February and told all Ukrainians to raise flags, hang them outside their windows, and wear their *vyshyvankas* (shirts with traditional embroidery) to show that the country was united. Once again, he did so by highlighting the strong sense of state attachment in the country and among its people.

> *Great people of a great country!*
>
> ...
>
> *We are told that February 16 will be the day of the attack.*
> *We will make it the Day of Unity ...*
> *We will hoist national flags, put on blue and yellow ribbons and show the world our unity.*
> *We have one great European aspiration.*
> *We want freedom and are ready to fight for it*
>
> ...
>
> *Today is not just Valentine's Day.*
> *It is the day of those in love with Ukraine.*

We believe in our own strength and continue to build our future together.
Because we are united by love for Ukraine, united and unique.
And love will win.
...
Love Ukraine!
We are calm! We are strong! We are together!
Great people of a great country.

—Volodymyr Zelensky, 14 February 2022[26]

That evening, Zelensky posted a Valentine's Day message to his wife Olena Zelenska on his official Instagram page.[27] He was doing all he could to show that he was staying calm in the face of what he called "a very stressful time." At a press conference a few days later, his sarcasm about Russia not having invaded on the 16th was misunderstood as him doubting the accuracy of US and UK intelligence. Our sources indicate that few in Ukraine's leadership seriously doubted the intelligence was solid. Instead, the question was whether there was anything that could be done to shift Kremlin plans short of sacrificing territorial integrity and sovereignty. As history has shown, no such possibility was found.

Putin's Orwellian announcement

On 21 February, the day after the closing ceremony of the Beijing 2022 Winter Olympics, the Kremlin staged a Security Council meeting at which one member followed the other in giving justification for formal intervention to "protect" what Russia brands the Donetsk and Luhansk People's Republics (the "DNR" and "LNR," respectively).[28] The meeting was tense, with Putin publicly scolding several of the council's members. This was Kremlin political theater in full force. It was all meant to look as if we were watching the events live, but it was clear that it had been taped and edited. That evening, television stations around the world would interrupt their news streams as a speech by Putin was released. Sitting at a much smaller desk than usual, the Russian president launched into a summary of his July 2021 article.

Performing a content analysis of this speech (Figure 7.6), we see similar patterns to those observed in the July letter, but with a few changes. One change is that NATO and Western aggression now took center stage. In fact, "NATO" is the third most mentioned in the speech (40 times), just behind "Ukraine" and "Russia" (62 and 61, respectively). In addition, Putin suggests an answer to the "why now" question: he mentions the year 1922 three times. This is the year of the formal founding of the USSR, and 2022 would mark its 100th anniversary. He blames Ukrainian "nationalists" and "Lenin" for historical mistakes in "creating" Ukraine, each getting equal mention (10 times). "Empire" and "Nazi/Nazism" (applied to Ukraine) are mentioned 6 times each. The term "Donbas" is only mentioned 8 times, and the so-called DNR and LNR only get two mentions in the whole speech. This makes clear that the speech was about the entirety of Ukraine, not just specific parts of it. That night Russian tanks "officially" entered Donetsk and Luhansk oblasts, seeking to provoke the Ukrainian army.

The Russian president would once again appear on screens worldwide the morning of 24 February, Kyiv time. On this occasion, he announced the start of a "special military operation" aimed at guaranteeing the security of what he called the DNR and LNR and, ominously, "demilitarizing" and "de-nazifying" Ukraine. This added a new twist to the old Kremlin narrative that Ukrainians were misguided Russians currently ruled by an illegitimate neo-nazi regime propped up by the West as a way of weakening Russia. Calling it what it was, an "invasion" or even simply a "war," would become a crime in Russia. Putin's speech was also released after Zelensky's office had put out the Ukrainian president's own late-night video that we described earlier, the one appealing to ordinary Russians in Russian not to go along with their misguided leader.

Analysts immediately noticed that Putin was at the same unusually small desk, even wearing the same suit and tie, as in his 21 February video. This was the second half of the pre-recorded speech from three days ago. By pre-recording, the Kremlin could release it at any time, declaring the assault's start without tell-tale signs of elite movements that could tip foreign intelligence off about the attack's precise timing. Our content analysis shows that the 24 February episode stood out from the previous one for its clear focus on "Russia." This term was mentioned 35 times, with "Russians" coming second (25 times) and the "military" and "Ukraine" sharing third (12). "War" was mentioned 11 times, but not as a description of what Putin himself was launching. "NATO" once again fell out of the top mentions, though it came up 9 times. "Donbas" was not even among the top thirty terms (5 mentions).

Putin's announcement of a "special military operation" came at the conclusion of the speech. With the skies cleared of civil aviation, Russia immediately began raining destruction on cities and military targets across the entirety of Ukraine, with the shells coming first. Then, evoking scenes from a previous era, long lines of tanks and other destructive equipment rolled across Ukraine's border from Russia and its ally Belarus in the north and east. Other Russian forces advanced from within parts of Ukraine that Moscow had already occupied, including Crimea in the south. The movements indicated what Western intelligence had long been warning: Russia's goal was first and foremost to seize Kyiv to install a new Russia-friendly government, a move Moscow would frame as "restoring" the "legitimate" Yanukovych regime that had been overthrown in 2014 by what Kremlin media have branded a "nazi junta."

This plan also counted on local-level regime change in Ukraine's cities and towns, figuring that often-corrupt Ukrainian politicians would be quick to defect to the Russians once it made a dramatic show of force and offered the right price. That the invading forces were unprepared for much resistance or a longer war is strong circumstantial evidence that Russia expected all this to happen very quickly, with few Russian military casualties. And Putin had even said as much, letting slip in a conversation with the EU president back in 2014 that he thought his forces could take Kyiv in two weeks.[29]

Things could hardly have gone more badly for the Russians in the days that followed. We have already described these events in Chapter 1 and will not revisit them here. We simply repeat that Ukraine's military turned out to be much more effective than expected and that, rather than defecting, ordinary Ukrainians turned out en masse using everything at their disposal to thwart Russia's advances, even if all they had was their bare hands. The most important result was to win the battle for Kyiv, ensuring Ukraine's survival as a state, even though some territories in Ukraine's southeast remained contested at the time of this writing.

This accomplishment clearly belongs to the Ukrainian people as a whole rather than to any individual. But Zelensky played an important role in leading the people at this pivotal moment. What was his role? In Season 3 of the *Servant of the People* series, a history professor asks his students what makes a good state leader and how they would describe such a person. The students answer: "Decisive, intelligent, sincere, well educated, hard-working, democratically minded, good at policy and economy, a true professional, and good-looking." The professor laughs and says: "It is important that the president is the face of the nation ... But what shouldn't they be?" The students answer: "Greedy, stupid, indecisive, angry, selfish, not true to his words, two-faced, and ugly." Zelensky's show had set a high bar.

Zelensky's initial response

The bombs begin to fall, the sirens begin to roar, foreign journalists standing on borders with Russia and Belarus can see tanks crossing into Ukrainian territory, a CNN team unexpectedly films a Russian paratrooper group descending from a helicopter in Kyiv near the Hostomel military airport. Russia's all-out effort to conquer Ukraine is here. Zelensky, like millions of ordinary Ukrainians waking up to the sound of explosions, stays as calm as he can in a secure location separated from his family, not knowing if he will ever see them again. Some Ukrainians seek shelter in their basements and metro stations, some with small children flee to safer zones in the west of Ukraine. But the broad majority of the adult population organize their friends and neighborhoods, start volunteering, or line up at their local military and territorial defense offices to enlist. To put it mildly, this was clearly not what Putin had been expecting.

Ukrainians were united, they were fighting back, and they had a leader who was quickly proving to be a powerful role model for ordinary citizens, demonstrating by example how to act and how to speak about this foreign threat on their state's soil.

> *Citizens of Ukraine.*
>
> *What are we hearing today? These are not just explosions of rockets, battles, the roar of aircraft. This is the sound of a new iron curtain falling and closing Russia off from the civilized world. Our national task is to ensure that this curtain does not pass through our Ukrainian territory, but in the homes of the Russians.*
>
> *The Ukrainian army, our border guards, police forces, and special services stopped the enemy's attacks. In the language of the conflict, this can be called an operational pause.*
>
> *In Donbas, our Armed Forces are working perfectly, the Kharkiv direction is very difficult, the forces to protect the city are working, they are reliable, they are our guys.*

> *The most problematic situation today is in the south. Our troops are fighting fiercely in the suburbs of Kherson. The enemy is pressing from the occupied Crimea, trying to advance towards Melitopol.*
>
> *In the north of the country, the enemy is slowly advancing in the Chernihiv region, but there is someone there to hold him. The defense is reliably built in the Zhytomyr region.*
>
> —Volodymyr Zelensky, 24 February 2022[30]

Perhaps most importantly of all, Zelensky physically stood his ground in Ukraine. Evacuation offers were made, but he did not flee. By doing so, he set an important example not simply for ordinary Ukrainians who might have been contemplating whether to fight for their nation's freedom but also for the governors and mayors in Russia's sights: they must stand firm. And for the most part, they did.[31] He was also demonstrating a contagious confidence in the ability of his country's military and people to fend off the Russian attack.

This is why the famous line "The fight is here; I need ammunition, not a ride!" resonated so broadly in Ukraine and around the world. This quotation, reportedly made to a US official offering to evacuate him from Kyiv in the first hours of the war, was initially attributed to Zelensky in an Associated Press report that relies on a single source, but subsequent efforts to confirm its authenticity have been unsuccessful. Yet it so perfectly captured Ukraine's spirit of resistance that the Ukrainian Embassy in the UK tweeted it out a day later (see Figure D). The embassy did not say whether its tweet was based on the original AP story or separate sources, though the ambassador, Vadym Prystayko, was a key member of Zelensky's team, having previously been deputy head of the presidential administration, foreign minister, and minister for EU integration, so he would have been in a good position to obtain an accurate quotation. Regardless, the quota-

Figure D. Ukrainian Embassy to UK tweet

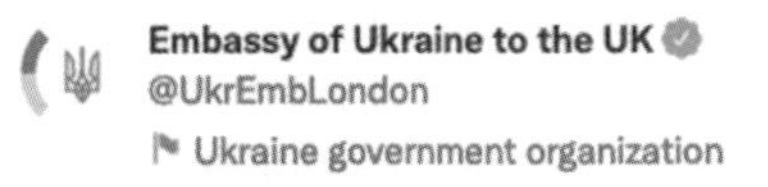

"The fight is here; I need ammunition, not a ride." - @ZelenskyyUa on the US evacuation offer.

tion is now widely attributed to Zelensky and firmly established as wartime lore.[32]

More immediately important than the "ammunition" line for Ukrainians, though, was one of his first recorded videos. This now-famous appeal received nearly 15 million views on Instagram alone. It conveyed the simple but crucial message: "The president is here ... we are all here ... citizens are all here ... we are all here defending our independence and our state, and this is how it will be going forward ... glory to Ukraine. Glory to our heroes."[33] The message was that he was safe, secure, and in charge. Ukraine would not capitulate.

Commander in chief

Sometimes, what leaders don't do is as important as what they do. In Zelensky's case, his effectiveness as a military commander in the early war period stems from the trust he had in his generals and other military experts. In those first few hours and days of the Russian invasion, he did not intervene where it was not necessary to do so. The army was prepared, and the security services were able to act (though with some notable defections, as in the Kherson region). Thus, while Zelensky was informed about the military situation and coordinated Ukraine's response, our informants suggest he let the generals and military professionals make the key decisions on the ground. This was also in keeping with the military reform that began in 2014, a reform that included decentralizing tactical decisions to commanders on the ground, where it was often clearer what needed to be done. There was no micro-managing of strategy and battles. His job was to get them the support, arms, and funds they needed—and to show leadership and resolve in order to raise the morale of those at the front.

Russia's own military strategy, based on false assumptions about the readiness of Ukrainian society to capitulate when presented with a show of Russian force, was grossly flawed from the beginning. That is, the Kremlin mistakenly believed Ukrainians' attachment to their state and their civic national identity was not very strong. The Russians had thus not anticipated that building-by-building, face-to-face combat would be necessary to take Ukraine's major cities, instead expecting them to quickly defect. This led the Russians to refrain from sending in enough troops to have any hope of success. Russia also chose initially to focus on the deployment of paratroopers, an elite force in Russia with little capacity to engage in hand-to-hand combat and population management. This tactic can only work if the local population does not fight back. The Russians were thus expecting the paratroopers (like their "little green men" had done in 2014) to come in and swiftly take over localities and major structures with the help of defectors. Instead, Moscow's forces were met with determined local resistance, well-organized security services monitoring their movements, and a military that had been dramatically improved since 2014. And because the Ukrainian army and local farmers were stopping large, easy-to-target Russian caravans, the paratroopers were left with little support.

Thus, while Ukraine's army was better trained and better organized in 2022 than it had been in 2014, it is the civic national identity factor that explains why hundreds of thousands joined the territorial defense force, millions volunteered in other ways, and hundreds of farmers stole Russian tanks. This, we argue, was at the heart of Ukraine's early battlefield victories. This Ukrainian civic identity was what had produced not only Zelensky, but 44 million Zelenskys, with Zelensky himself playing a significant but still small and symbolic role in advancing this process. The Zelensky Effect at war, then, is how all this came together starting 24 February 2022.

Communicator in chief

What Zelensky did in the early days of the war, first and foremost, was to reinforce, mobilize, and amplify the civic Ukrainian nation in its resistance to Russia's armies through appeals he would issue morning and evening. These appeals were effective both for their format and for what their words conveyed to Ukrainians.

How he says it

Zelensky's wartime addresses followed a familiar format. As he did before the war, and as he had done even before becoming president, he communicated with the population directly and frequently through short, often selfie-style videos that could be circulated quickly and widely on social media. He even used the same tone of voice, for the most part.[34] This low-production-value style conveyed a sense of authenticity, and it is indeed what most in Ukraine have come to expect from him, notwithstanding some more highly produced material.[35] And he is obviously very experienced in delivering messages this way. To Ukrainians who had been watching him closely over the years, this was very much the same Zelensky that had been around before, though his bloodshot eyes, paler skin, and distressed facial expressions would sometimes betray the gravity of the situation in which he now found himself.

As the war dragged on, the format of his appearances evolved in certain ways. When the war first starts, we see him in front of a podium, visibly tired but still in his suit.[36] This quickly changed to a series of T-shirts and jumpers that are now emblematic of Zelensky's wartime image (although there was an army-green *vyshyvanka* too).[37] In the past, his go-to casual look had been a turtleneck, but now it became a plain green T-shirt,[38] sometimes adorned with a symbol like that of the Ukrainian Army or the Ukrainian national trident,[39] or even with the text "I am Ukrainian."[40] Not all of this was new, though. Zelensky's now-famous green T-shirt, for example, had been a staple of his public wardrobe for years, pulled out for meetings with soldiers and visits to military posts both during his presidency (multiple examples can be found on his Instagram) and, even before that, when he and his Kvartal 95 troupe started going to the front and performing for servicepeople in 2014.[41] The podium, a staple of presidential crisis appeals, also gave way throughout March to his desk, wherever it might be. All this marked a symbolic shift to a less formal format while making clear that he was still at work, as all Ukrainians should be. As the war continued, and as Ukraine achieved several battlefield victories, the podium has returned but typically only for occasions when foreign state leaders visit Ukraine.

Not all of Zelensky's appeals came from behind a podium or desk. At times, he would venture outside, at very high risk to his own security and life. The idea, of course, is not to demonstrate personal bravery but to reflect and inspire the resolve, strength, and bravery of his army and his fellow citizens. In one such speech from 23 March, one can see his security detail in the background.[42] On 9 April, Zelensky took a walk through Kyiv's city center with UK Prime Minister Boris Johnson, meant to display how safe Kyiv had become. In later speeches, like one filmed on Ukraine's central Khreshchatyk Street right before the 9 May Victory Day, no security is in sight.

What he says

Some have told us that Zelensky seemed to have changed his messaging after 24 February, with his former critics in particular saying that Russia's full-on assault had apparently given birth to a "new" Zelensky, one for whom even they could muster support.[43] To investigate, we used NVivo software to examine transcripts of his speeches from the presidential website, combining this with close readings of posts on Zelensky's official Instagram account and appeals on his Twitter and Telegram accounts. We find that his wartime appeals reflect the same general message we have found in his communications for years.

We identify five major themes in these communications that have become especially important for his role in rebuffing Russia's invasion in 2022. First, Zelensky always addresses all citizens of Ukraine, citizens of a great country. Second, he makes frequent statements about Ukrainian unity. Third, he consistently criticizes elite actors who are not doing enough, including telling them to come back on their private planes in a speech in February, while simultaneously emphasizing the civic responsibility of ordinary citizens (to protect democracy in 2019, to protect health during the COVID-19 pandemic, and to protect the country from invasion in 2022). Fourth, he unfailingly stresses Ukrainian values, which in his view are European, democratic, civic, liberal, and inclusive, and juxtaposes them with the Kremlin's or the oligarchs' value systems. Fifth, he consistently connects personal and collective national responsibility. As previous chapters have shown, such themes also featured systematically in Kvartal 95 skits and the fictional president Holoborodko's monologues in the *Servant of the People* television series.

One of Zelensky's first wartime video appeals is an excellent example, with the words speaking for themselves:

> My dear Ukrainians ... I promised I would regularly turn to you with information ... It is important to get information from official sources. Putin has begun a war with Ukraine, a war with all of the democratic world ... He wants to destroy my country, he wants to destroy OUR country, all that WE were building, thanks to which we are all living ... I turn to the army ... You can, you will, you are unbreakable because you are Ukraine ... To all Ukrainians who are on our territory, we are not giving in to panic. We are doing everything that is necessary to support the Ukrainian army ... Together we MUST save Ukraine, save the democratic world, and WE WILL do this ... Glory to Ukraine![44]

Particularly important here is how he frames his own experience and that of Ukrainians as being the same, frequently through terms like "my dear Ukrainians [*moyi dorohi*]" and "all Ukrainians." Also crucial is the emphasis he places on citizenship, "great citizens of a great country," stressing both the capacity and strength of purpose that citizenship gives while also highlighting the responsibility that "citizens" have to stay calm and do all they can to work for the defeat of the Russians.

Interestingly, he does not ask Ukrainian citizens to help him personally, as leaders sometimes do in times of crisis. Boris Johnson, Justin Trudeau, and Joe Biden all made such personal appeals for people to help them fight the COVID-19 pandemic.[45] Zelensky's message is that it is not him Ukrainians are working for or helping but Ukraine, the state, and the army that defends them. As we noted in the previous chapter, this was also Zelensky's approach in his pandemic-era speeches, in which he would frame calls to social-distance and wear a mask as something "we as Ukrainians are doing together" to protect and save all Ukrainians as a matter of civic duty. Similarly, it is rare for Zelensky to present a list of "his" accomplishments or what "he" has done unless it is to inform Ukrainians about people with whom he has spoken or met. When he lists accomplishments, he typically assigns credit with words like "we" (all Ukrainians), "our" (Ukrainian) army or men and women at the front, or "you" ("my fellow Ukrainians"). This self-effacing, credit-sharing use of "we" and "us" is also documented in Tayisiya Chernyshova's study of Zelensky's political communications during his first year in office.[46] When he does use "I," he is most often mentioning how he is staying in Ukraine, how he is speaking to leaders, how he is awarding medals to heroes of Ukraine, and how he believes in Ukraine. Thus, his words indicate an effort to sustain and deepen a collective feeling of identity and belonging, a common sense of responsibility, and affirmation of other Ukrainians' actions and bravery in the defense of Ukraine.

One revealing way to see what changed and what stayed the same in his public appeals is to examine the frequency with which he uses key words in his speeches. We do this using NVivo software on the Zelensky appeals available to us from 2019 through mid-2022. The word clouds in Figures 7.7–8 summarize the results, with larger fonts reflecting more frequent use of the word. In 2019, the focus was on the state of Ukraine, the country, and its institutions, including the presidency, which was mentioned frequently in the sense of his responsibility to all Ukrainians. In 2020, there remained a focus on citizens and the state, albeit with new elements coming to the fore related to the coronavirus, health, and the heroes of that year: doctors and medical professionals. In 2021, his speeches again focus on citizens, the state, the country, and Ukraine's independence. But as the year went on, references to security, war, and Russian aggression also increased.

Comparing the word clouds from Zelensky's wartime and pre-wartime speeches in 2022 alone, one is struck by his emphasis on the people of Ukraine as commander in chief from 24 February through 31 July 2022, when we were finalizing our analysis. During this period, we found Zelensky mentioned "Ukraine" some 1,726 times and "people" 1,238. As the war continued, his speeches shifted in tone, placing more emphasis on "Russia" (mentioned 905 times), "Russians" (1,150), "occupiers" (309), "military" (295), and "freedom" (286 mentions). One thing this pattern reflects is the president's juxtaposition of the value Ukraine places on freedom with Russia's lack thereof. Indeed, in one 24 February speech, Zelensky switched to Russian and spoke directly to the Russian people, reminding them that "the Ukrainian nation is free."[47] Such contrasts with Russia help Zelensky also affirm Ukraine's pro-European vector, a theme that Yuliya Lyubchenko and her coauthors confirm strongly characterized the major speeches he made during his first year as president.[48] He also highlights this freedom when stressing that Ukraine needs help. On 25 February, he declared "We defend our freedom and land. But we need effective international assistance"[49] while also connecting it to the bravery and determination of Ukrainians by saying "it was a difficult but courageous day!"[50]

Although "country," the "state," and "Europe" (649 mentions when counted together with "European" and "Europeans") all make the top twenty, "peace" is not discussed nearly as often, with just 330 mentions. Thus while Zelensky may have started out as a candidate of peace challenging Poroshenko's presidency of war, now he too has become a war president. It is in this battlefield context that he frequently mentions Mariupol (280 mentions), where some of the most horrific war crimes have been perpetrated. This is even more than he mentions Ukraine's capital city "Kyiv" (187 mentions), which also withstood a ferocious battle. "Kharkiv," "Kherson," and "Donetsk" received many mentions too: 137, 64, and 34, respectively. No other Ukrainian place name makes it into the top 500 mentions, although many are mentioned at least once. While "artillery," "attacks," "combat," and "missiles" are all mentioned frequently, "democracy" (34 mentions, with 49 more for "democratic") and "responsibility" (36) also feature in the top 500, providing evidence that these along with citizenship and Europeanness make up the core of Zelensky's rallying cry. His messaging during the six wartime months we have been able to analyze in detail is thus all about the whole civic Ukrainian nation, unifying everyone within it and expressing its will to resist.

Rallying around the flag

The term "rallying around the flag" refers to an upsurge in patriotic sentiment during conflicts that also has the effect of boosting people's support for their incumbent leaders.[51] Political science has long told us that there are two reasons for this.[52] First, innate psychological instincts guide people to feel tighter bonds with their communities when under threat, a feeling that translates into a greater willingness to trust and feel positively about community leaders.[53] Second, independent media and opposition politicians tend to stop criticizing the country's leadership, instead deferring to the need for national unity, and this cues their followers to become more supportive of the state's authorities.[54]

From this perspective, it is unsurprising that Zelenksy's standing in public opinion would soar to unprecedented heights after 24 February. This is clear from data collected for us by KIIS in 2022. When we asked a nationally representative sample of Ukrainians how they would vote as late as January and February 2022, almost immediately before Russia's new invasion, only 18 percent said they would support the incumbent's re-election. But when KIIS was able to resume its polling for us in May and July 2022, as Figure 7.9 illustrates, his electoral support had increased fourfold to well over 70 percent. Notably, this is 70 percent of the entire population, so his dominance among people who plan to vote and have decided upon their choice is even greater.

Also in line with what political science tells us about rallying around the flag, our data show that this surging pro-Zelensky sentiment has come with an increase in positive feeling for Ukraine as a whole, including for Zelensky's vision of a Ukraine defined primarily by civic rather than ethnic criteria. The sets of three lighter-color bars in Figure 7.10, depicting surveys taken between 2019 and Russia's 2022 invasion, show what we have discussed earlier: Zelensky's presidency did not much change identity itself. When he was in office prior to the all-out war, there were no significant increases in the share of the population saying they spoke Ukrainian in private life, the percentage saying they considered Ukrainian their native language, or the portion identifying Ukrainian as their nationality, an indicator we have said earlier tends to reflect attachment to the Ukrainian state more than ethnicity.[55] These quantities all rise well outside the margin of error after the start of the war, as the sets of two darker bars in the same figure show.[56] Moreover, our July 2022 survey (Figure 7.11) finds that 90 percent of Ukrainians generally agree that "All who consider Ukraine their fatherland belong to the Ukrainian nation, regardless of nationality, language, or religion." While 84 percent already adhered to this highly inclusive civic notion of Ukrainianness in 2017, when the country's citizens were asked the same question, what is striking is that the share saying they "fully" agreed shot up from 44 percent in that survey to 69 percent in the July 2022 poll.[57] Similarly, the share of people expressing the maximum value when asked their level of pride in Ukrainian citizenship leapt from 59 percent in April 2020 to 82 percent in July 2022. While wartime public opinion data must be treated with care, we are confident these figures do not boil down to underreporting of people with other views due to reasons such as population movements, instead reflecting a genuine increase in attachment to a civic notion of Ukraine.[58]

The surge in attachment to the state has manifested most dramatically in survey data on whether Ukrainians intend to leave the country (see Figure 7.12). As noted throughout this book, large numbers of Ukrainians have long harbored ideas of emigrating. Actual emigration rates have also been high, including during Zelensky's time in office. This has, in fact, been something of a preoccupation of Zelensky's, trying to counter many Ukrainians' feeling that they needed to go abroad for a better life. In the wartime context of 2022, however, readiness to leave the country plummeted to less than 5 percent of the adult population currently in Ukraine. Anecdotally, we find the same in our conversations with many of our family, friends, and colleagues who remain in Ukraine. This includes women, who unlike men can legally leave the country: they are overwhelmingly choosing to stay to help defend and support Ukraine.

Rallying around the flag is, though, a complicated phenomenon. Social scientists are beginning to recognize this, going beyond overly simplistic interpretations that posit a simple connection linking conflict, a rise in patriotism, and a rise in leadership support. In a recent study, Hale points out that conflicts typically produce intense social pressures to conform, including pressures to appear patriotic. This, he finds, can lead people who privately harbor critical views of the country's leader not to divulge this to pollsters, a phenomenon that can inflate survey estimates of leaders' support.[59] Samuel Greene, Graeme Robertson, and Gulnaz Sharafutdinova also find that similar social pressures can lead people to jump on the bandwagon, either taking their cues on what to believe from others or simply not wanting to be left out of a powerful and emotional social movement.[60]

It is thus little surprise that we find such phenomena in Ukraine, where Zelensky had faced intense opposition along with considerable mass ambivalence prior to the war, and where the "conflict" at hand is literally a matter of personal and national life or death. Indeed, our findings indicate that support for Zelensky is, for many, part and parcel of patriotism in wartime Ukraine. Our July 2022 survey thus finds 31 percent affirming that criticizing Zelensky is unpatriotic, with only 30 percent completely denying this is the case. People also widely believe Zelensky is hugely popular and would win another landslide if a new election were held, as can be seen in Figures 7.13 and 7.14. Clearly, Zelensky's public support is currently bolstered by considerable social pressure generated by the war.

How large is the share of people who are dissembling in the face of such pressures when telling pollsters they support Zelensky, and how much of his support is wholehearted? Social scientists have developed a clever technique to tell, called a "list experiment," which we adopted in our July 2022 survey. First, we presented the whole nationally representative sample of respondents a list of three famous and non-controversial people and asked them how many they thought were doing their jobs well. Crucially, the only answer we record is their count, a number from 0 to 3. Second, we divide the sample completely randomly into two parts and, for only one of these parts, add a fourth individual to their list: Zelensky. Because the only reason the average count will be significantly higher in one of the two randomly selected groups than the other is the addition of the fourth item, the difference in the average counts of each group yields an estimate of the share of people who genuinely approve of Zelensky's job in office. And so long as the experiment is well designed, which checks confirm ours to be, respondents never have to reveal whether they approve of Zelensky specifically or not.[61] All they have given us is a number of people they support, and we have no idea whether that number includes Zelensky for any given individual.

Figure 7.15 reports the findings. Two take-aways are evident here. First, we do find evidence of substantial dissembling: 28 percent of our respondents said they approved of the job Zelensky was doing when asked directly but withheld that support when their lack of support could not be attributed to them personally. This is to be expected. Like democracies typically do, Ukraine has fierce internal political divisions, but they are divisions that stop at the national border. Our analysis thus shows that the war has not washed away older political sentiments. But perhaps even more important is that our study strongly confirms that Zelensky holds the genuine support of three-fifths (or 60 percent) of Ukrainians as of July 2022. This is a 26-percentage point increase from the December 2021–February 2022 survey data MOBILISE collected right before the start of the war (33 percent). This is an impressive majority that reflects a remarkable turnaround, giving Zelensky a substantial degree of moral authority when he speaks in the name of—and to—Ukraine's civic nation, calling on it to mobilize.

The masses respond with mobilization

The importance of all this lies in what so many ordinary Ukrainians were moved to do in the wake of Russia's 24 February attack. The wartime surveys we have been discussing thus also confirm what we already knew anecdotally from our friends and analysis of numerous other available data points: Ukrainians were doing what they could to aid the nation's survival.

We asked Ukrainians "Since the Russian invasion of Ukraine on 24 February 2022, have you participated in any of the following actions and, if so, which one(s) [choose all that apply]?" There were five options to choose from (Figure 7.16). About 60 percent said they were making donations, around 32 percent were volunteering in their communities, 3–4 percent were engaged in civil resistance, 6 percent had joined the territorial self-defense, and 2 percent had joined the military. There was also an "other" open text option—and we were inundated with hundreds of other responses. People wanted to make sure that their contribution to the war was being recorded. Maybe they were not getting 1.4 million retweets a day—but these are their acts of resistance to Russia's invasion and occupation, the acts that are what gave Zelensky and other leaders of Ukraine the "*natkhennya*" (akin to spiritual inspiration) to keep going. People mentioned that they hosted refugees, assisted the army and territorial defense, created aid organizations, organized bomb shelters, carried sand to make barriers, supported people as psychologists, delivered medicines, distributed informational materials, helped find housing for IDPs, prepared Molotov cocktails, organized support chats, made welded anti-tank hedgehogs, helped dogs left behind, engaged in partisan resistance, wove nets, and sewed body armor. These answers highlight the main thesis of our book—Ukrainians have a profound sense of civic attachment and civic duty to defend their democracy, and each ordinary citizen (Zelensky included) is doing what it is in their basic capacity to do.

We thus return to the theme that Ukraine is a country of 44 million Zelenskys. Some make powerful speeches and videos while interacting with foreign leaders to get support for the country and for the army—and some milk their goatlings to ensure those at the front get enough protein to fight and endure. Or as one of our survey's respondents said when asked how they had supported the war effort, "We united with neighbors and shared what we could, helped each other."

Rallying international opinion

Zelensky has also proven remarkably successful at translating all of this into an effective effort to rally international opinion to

Ukraine's side, particularly in the West. A recent study by Marta Dyczok and Yerin Chung finds that one key to this success was a regular series of speeches given to foreign audiences.[62] Our own independent analysis concurs. Virtually "traveling" to major Western power centers, he would deliver online addresses to the likes of the German Bundestag, the US Congress, the UK Parliament, or Ukrainian student societies. In these speeches, he focused primarily on building up sympathy for the Ukrainian cause, often by drawing parallels with critical moments of his "host" country's own history, and conveying the immediacy and urgency of Ukraine's need for foreign support. Here he was, a former media celebrity and hugely successful businessman turned president refusing rescue, wearing a simple T-shirt, speaking before world leaders who were sitting comfortably in their expensive suits inside posh chambers in free countries while he was in a bunker working to defend his country, quite literally fighting for his and his family's lives. He was earnest and did not mince words, a common refrain being that "Ukraine is strong, but it cannot do it alone." Avoiding the temptation to resort to shaming the West, Zelensky instead inspired them with Ukrainians' resolve and fighting spirit. In contrast to his speeches oriented to Ukrainians, in which he would evoke their senses of civic national duty, his addresses to foreign audiences appealed to their humanity. He spoke of families torn apart, war crimes being perpetrated, and Ukraine's desperate need for help against a much larger and stronger foe.

While these speeches would make the biggest headlines, his short Internet-savvy videos and social media posts also proved tremendously effective in reaching foreign audiences, being highly accessible, easily translatable, and readily shared. To help us document this effect, we turned to our friends at New York University's Social Media and Political Participation (SMaPP) Lab, including Megan Allison Brown, Joshua Tucker, Sarah

Graham, and Jason Greenfield. At our request, they kindly examined all 2,299 tweets ever posted from Zelensky's presidential Twitter account, @ZelenskyyUa, covering the period from 25 April 2019 through 11 July 2022.[63] Figure 7.17, which they created for us, shows the rolling seven-day average of the number of these tweets per day over the course of this period.[64]

This analysis reveals some important patterns. For one thing, Zelensky's Twitter activity has generally been increasing over time since 2019, clearly reflecting his administration's view that this form of communication is effective. The trend is not smooth, though: there is a huge spike in March 2022, when it was becoming clear to all that the war was not going to end anytime soon, and the Ukrainian government was doing as much as it could to communicate to the world what was happening and what Ukraine needed to defend itself. While Zelensky did not use his speeches to communicate what he did, this is what the Twitter account was used for, often reporting whom he had met with and for what purpose.

The SMaPP analysis also shows that the world responded to these tweets. Figures 7.18 and 7.19, which the NYU team also created at our request, present the mean number of likes and retweets per Zelensky tweet during the same period (also presented as each day's rolling seven-day average). These figures show a high level of positive response by other Twitter users relative to the pre-war period, with a spike again in March.[65]

Zelensky's combination of formal appeals and social media posts helped fuel a massive international response, one that has helped encourage leaders across the West to aid Ukraine and sanction Russia. Google Trends allows users to track the frequency of searches that include certain keywords, and Figures 7.19–20 report the frequency of searches for "Zelensky" and "Ukraine" over time. Accordingly, the numbers in these figures represent search interest relative to the highest point, with 100 representing "the peak popularity" for a term and 50 meaning that the term was "half as popular" while "0 means there was not enough data for this term."[66]

As can be seen, there was precious little interest in either of these terms until February 2022, a pattern that may have factored into Putin's apparent belief that he could get away with invading the country. After the invasion, searches for these terms spike into the millions, again with a peak in March before trailing off to much lower levels, albeit figures that are still high when compared with those before 2022. The interest was truly global, not even limited to the West. Twitter data, analyzed by SMaPP for us (Figure 7.21), provide a somewhat more nuanced picture, revealing an initial spike in tweets containing some version of the name "Zelensky" around the time of the Trump impeachment scandal. This, though, is completely overwhelmed by March 2022, during which time over 1.4 million tweets about Ukraine's president were being posted daily.

The importance of Zelensky's direct appeals can be found by looking at the content of hundreds of articles written about Zelensky in English since 24 February. Identifying a sample of 100 such pieces using the Google News search function, we find much material on his bravery, but a large share of the stories are framed around some form of surprise that a comedian appeared to be a highly effective leader. More critical takes suggest Zelensky is using the only skill he has, his talent for communication. By speaking directly to people around the world in his formal speeches and social media, Zelensky can to some extent circumvent this rather simplistic media pigeonholing in order to get his broader message across.

Ukraine's civic nation

What has made Zelensky a good leader in his country's time of national peril is not simply that he understands his fellow citizens. Most important is that the masses see in him one of themselves. Speaking to his fellow citizens and to foreign audiences, his specific words and deeds have arguably mattered less than what he represents: a Ukrainian civic attachment to the state and a fiery resolve to defend their values, including their hard-fought political and social openness and their European orientation. By personally resisting Russia, he has sent an important signal of resistance on behalf of the whole civic Ukrainian nation, a nation full of Zelenskys defined by citizenship rather than any ethnic litmus test. And he does so as a representative of the Independence Generation, a cohort now in positions of national influence, many with older children who are themselves increasingly coming to defend Ukraine and its values.

This combination could not have been more deadly to Putinism. Zelensky personifies the vacuity of Putin's narrative on Ukraine, which, as we have seen, mistakenly questions Ukrainians' loyalty to Ukraine outside the country's western region of Halychyna and among those who grew up speaking Russian. Inversely, Putin's meandering speeches about how Ukraine is not real and how Ukrainians do not exist fall flat among a population that has developed an even stronger attachment to citizen-centered democracy and a sense of civic duty—not least because their history of civic struggle is pointedly and frequently referenced by Zelensky, who switches between Ukrainian and Russian with ease.

As we write, the war's ultimate outcome is yet to be decided. But Ukraine's achievements in fending off total conquest are already of great historic import. In the chapter that follows, we reflect on where Ukraine has come from and where it may yet go.

We recommend our readers listen to:

"Dobroho vechora (Where Are You From)"
By Probass and Hardi

Found on the "Ukraine24" Playlist on Spotify.

https://open.spotify.com/track/0O3TZYgwaRadNprRONZ7iX

Good evening
We are from Ukraine

—Authors' own translation

And I will remind you of her words today:
… "There's no need to think meagerly …"

—Volodymyr Zelensky, reciting Lina Kostenko, 20 March 2022

We were all bombed in Kyiv last night. And we all died again in Babyn Yar—from a missile strike. Although the whole world promises constantly—never again.

For any normal person who knows history, Babyn Yar is a special part of Kyiv. A special part of Europe. A place of prayer. A place of remembrance for the hundred thousand people killed by the Nazis. The place of old Kyiv cemeteries. Who should you be to make it a target for missiles? You are killing Holocaust victims for the second time …

… But why was it bombed?
This is beyond humanity.
Such a missile strike shows that for many people in Russia, our Kyiv is completely foreign.
They know nothing about our capital.
About our history.
But they have an order to erase our history.
Erase our country.
Erase us all.

—Volodymyr Zelensky, 2 March 2022[1]

We have survived in our history and on our land two world wars, three Holodomors, the Holocaust, Babyn Yar, the Great Terror, the Chornobyl explosion, the occupation of Crimea and the war in the east.

We do not have a huge territory—from ocean to ocean, we do not have nuclear weapons, we do not fill the world market with oil and gas. But we have our people and our land. And for us—it's gold. That is what we are fighting for.

We have nothing to lose but our own freedom and dignity. For us, this is the greatest treasure. They wanted to destroy us so many times. They failed.

They wanted to wipe us off the face of the earth. They failed.

They backstabbed us. And we are on our feet.

They wanted us to be silent. But the whole world heard us.

We've been through so much!

And if someone thinks that, having overcome all this, Ukrainians—all of us—are scared, broken or will surrender, he knows nothing about Ukraine ...

... Glory to Ukraine!

—Volodymyr Zelensky, 3 March 2022[2]

We have survived the night that could have stopped history. History of Ukraine. History of Europe. Russian troops attacked the Zaporizhzhya nuclear power plant. The largest in Europe. It alone could be like six Chornobyls. Russian tanks knew what they were firing at. Direct aiming at the station. This is terror of an unprecedented level. There are fifteen nuclear units in Ukraine. And the Russian servicemen have completely forgotten about Chornobyl. About this world tragedy.

Russian people, I want to address you. How is that even possible? Together in 1986 we struggled with the consequences of the Chornobyl disaster. You must remember the burning graphite scattered by the explosion. Victims. You must remember the glow above the destroyed power unit. You must remember the evacuation from Pripyat and the 30 km zone. How could you forget it? And if you have not forgotten, then you cannot be silent.

—Volodymyr Zelensky, 4 March 2022[3]

8

UKRAINE'S FUTURE HISTORY

Fast-forward to 2049. A professor of history—yes, yet another history teacher—is beginning his class. The lecture room is pristine white. Stylish graphics hang on the wall, and careful observers might notice they depict the same famous historical figures that had adorned Vasyl Holoborodko's classroom before he became president. But this is a university, and these are medical students. The lesson begins. It will be about the great Ukrainian state crisis of 2019–22, "the so-called second destruction," recalls the professor in an effort to spark the students' interest. One student who had arrived late is confused about what class this is, asking whether it is economics or business. No, he is told, it is history. The med students all have one question: Why on earth do future doctors need to learn history?

This is a great question, affirms the professor. Does anyone in the class know the answer, he asks? One student pipes up: "Maybe as a break from normal lectures?" The professor takes the question with good humor but asks if anyone has any other ideas. None follow. Another student follows up on the original question: Why do doctors need to learn about ancient people when they will be treating people who are alive today? The teacher credits the student with making a good point, but presses on: Who else is against history lessons? Every student raises their hand. Still cheery, the professor replies that if history is only good for a break from the routine, they might as well put down their tablets, sit back, and enjoy the discussion.

Life is very good in modern-day Ukraine, the professor begins to explain. In 2049, Ukraine is in the G20, among the leading countries in economic development. But it was not always this way, he goes on. Three decades ago, it was normal for a teacher's salary not to be enough to pay the bills. Patients had to bring their own syringes to the hospital. Old age and poverty were practically synonymous. And no one seemed to mind their country being used as Europe's dumping ground for old cars and expired medicines. Each generation is different, he reminds them, and history allows us to compare today, tomorrow, and yesterday. He asks: Who was the president back in 2019? Only on the third try do the students get this right. The professor then tells the story of how the fictive Vasyl Holoborodko was released from prison and made it his mission to put Ukraine back together again after it had split up into "molecules." In disbelief, they listen attentively. Ukraine came back together again, they learn, not because of the president but because of its people. Because ordinary Ukrainians from one part of the country came to the aid of those from the other. When Ukrainians are united, no enemy can tear them apart. And it is vital to know one's history to avoid repeating it.

* * *

Just as the first episode of *Servant of the People* had begun with a history teacher's outrage over society's historical ignorance, the final season's final episode struck the same theme, bookending a series replete with historical references and calls to learn from history. To understand the actions of Zelensky and millions of

Ukrainians as history unfolds before our eyes today, it pays to consider how history has influenced and produced both leader and country. As this book has shown, Zelensky himself frequently talks about Ukraine's rich history and its agents ranging from Soviet-era dissidents to figures shaping Ukrainian statehood centuries earlier. His presidential speeches, too, are steeped in history, a collective history of all Ukrainians. In the remaining pages of this book, we examine what his use of this history tells us, and what history may lie in store for him, his Independence Generation, and Ukraine as a country.

History and Ukrainian nation-building

By regularly referencing history, Zelensky the president and Zelensky the performer before him are not only evoking, but actually building up and strengthening, Ukrainians' contemporary sense of national civic identity. Social scientists have long studied the idea of "nation" and widely agree that a sense of shared history lies at its heart, a feeling of linked fate that leads people to perceive that their own personal interests are inextricably tied to those of the larger community, their country, their land.[4] Creating a sense of common experience, therefore, is part and parcel of nation-building. This is one key reason why mass education, which typically involves the teaching of national history, is so strongly associated with national consciousness and loyalty.[5] Media with national scope, even entertainment, can also serve this purpose through the telling of history both as it has already happened and as it is happening in current events.[6]

Zelensky's performances, poking fun at the petty triumphs and travails of everyday life for millions of ordinary people living in post-Soviet Ukraine, helped viewers put their finger on exactly how they all shared a rich common fate that transcended the country's linguistic, national, and religious diversity. This common fate included a shared struggle with the realities of patronalism in everyday life and politics, including widespread corruption and poverty, as well as moments of enormous national hope and inspiration. This nation-building message of shared struggle reconciles what to Vladimir Putin seem antithetical: dissatisfaction with one's standard of living and love for one's country. "I love my country simply as it is," goes a Kvartal 95 song from April 2014, even though it can be "a mess" (*bardak*) in its head.[7]

The role of history in Zelensky's nation-building efforts is perhaps nowhere clearer than in the Kvartal 95 song "Country of Strong People."[8] This piece, performed as the concluding number in a 2017 concert, tells the history of Ukraine as experienced by the Independence Generation, with iconic video images from each period appearing on a giant screen in the background while the performers, including Zelensky, sing almost wistfully. Beginning as Ukraine's declaration of independence appears behind them, the song opens: "Maybe we should have gone along with everyone else, but we have always been expecting something better." And while "our first step" turned out to be "on a rake," "this is logical—we had just learned to walk." In some ways pure schmaltz, the troupe pulls it off powerfully, taking audiences on a guided tour through the hardships and dreams of each major period in post-Soviet Ukraine's history—Kravchuk, Kuchma, the Orange Revolution. Each time "we" keep hope alive and try, but each time disappointment follows. "A Maidan of honest people. You remember how those hands did not steal at all? But they did not go on to build, build a country of honest people." The number evokes recent memories of Donetsk hosting European soccer championship games, of vacationing in Crimea, and of Ukrainian director Oleg Sentsov, jailed at the time in Russia, making films. The concluding message, central to Zelensky's appeals over the course of two decades, is a call to civic duty:

> It is not worth seeking out the guilty other than ourselves
> It is not important who is in power old and new

What is important is uprightness in your head
Nobody will make the country except you.[9]

In our own rendering of Ukrainian history in this book, we have emphasized how different groups in Ukrainian society came to attach their sense of Ukrainianness firmly to a democratic and European development path in different periods. From the perspective of the Independence Generation, the early risers were the dissidents of the late Soviet era and the activists of the 1990s and 2000s. Their commitment and attachment to the Ukrainian state has not waned. The Independence Generation experienced a differential conversion, some joining the national cause as soon as they were in their twenties, with the Orange Revolution being something of a coming-out party, while others waited until their thirties rolled around. Zelensky was in this latter group, whose turn to political activism came full flower through Kvartal 95 programming with the Euromaidan and the events immediately following. Then came those Ukrainians who took this position after Zelensky's landslide election and the first two-and-a-half years of his presidency. Finally, we find a group of late risers, people ultimately provoked by Russia's all-out invasion, occupation, and war. They too, though, now have all the hallmarks of stalwarts whose attachment to the state and its democracy look unwavering. A very large critical mass of Ukrainians, we argue, has now converged around a vision of the Ukrainian nation grounded in civic national identity, democratic ideals, and a European orientation. Ukraine's receipt of EU candidate status is a major symbol of this convergence and will surely help anchor it into the future.

History and the Russian other

Zelensky's emphasis on history in his entertainment and his presidency has also served another important purpose: distinguishing Ukraine from Russia. For the Independence Generation,

Ukraine's long association with Russia is itself history, a relatively unhappy time that took up only a small share of their lives. The story of post-Soviet Ukrainian politics, then, is a story of experiences that Ukrainians share as Ukrainians, and that Russians do not share despite the many cultural commonalities that continue to exist. Ukrainians' emphasis on democracy, or at least restive pluralism, as a central element of Ukraine's history adds another level of distinctiveness to the Ukrainian experience. Research by Mikhail Alexseev and Serhiy Dembitskyy finds that war with Russia since 2014 has strengthened Ukrainians' sense that their democracy distinguishes them from Russia, giving them added motivation to resist the advances of their increasingly authoritarian neighbor. This effect has surged since 24 February 2022.[10] Indeed, Zelensky's production sometimes traces Ukraine's roots to a rebellious Kozak tradition that predates Moscow's rule and implies a "free-spirited" national idea.[11] This is a country, after all, whose people have a history of regularly mobilizing en masse to drive out unwanted rulers, including those seeking to take them away from Europe and toward Russia. The dangers of failing to understand Ukrainian history are thus evident in the actions of Putin, whose ignorance of it encouraged him to order a murderous invasion in the belief that Ukraine would quickly capitulate and return to Russia's political orbit.

There are lessons here for those in the West seeking to understand Russia too. It is understandable that people might conclude, having witnessed Russia perpetrate perhaps the grossest military atrocity in postwar Europe by invading Ukraine, that we need to focus more of our attention on understanding Russia. To be sure, it is vital to understand why Russia does what it does, as well as what might lead it to behave differently. But one of the biggest lessons of 2022 is surely that we cannot understand Russia without also understanding Ukraine (as well as Russia's other neighbors, especially those on which many Russians may have imperial designs). And this means understanding not only Ukraine's relationship with Russia but Ukraine in its own right, including everything from its domestic politics to its economy to its society. How can we know what Russians are misunderstanding about Ukraine if we do not ourselves have a correct understanding of it? And without understanding Russia's misunderstandings, instead implicitly interpreting Ukraine largely through a Moscow-centric lens, we risk making some of the same analytical mistakes that Russian leaders themselves have made. This, we fear, was partly why Western intelligence agencies—while correctly predicting Russia would invade as 24 February approached—were so wrong in their warnings that Kyiv would likely fall within days.

We would go even further. Ukraine is one of Europe's largest countries, and one whose global importance in the supply of grain and sunflower oil (for example) has only become fully appreciated since it has been under attack. It, as with other countries previously in Russia's shadow, therefore needs to be given much more attention in its own right. Understanding Ukraine, its history, culture, and society, is vital to our understanding of contemporary Europe and beyond.

History in the making

Zelensky no longer plays a history teacher on TV. Instead, he has become a writer and producer of history in the realest possible sense. Or more precisely, a co-writer and co-producer. This is because he is doing all this together with Ukraine as a nation, which in fact deserves primary credit for defending the country's independence through its powerful sense of civic duty.

As we can see from Figures 8.1–3, Ukrainians' resolve and democratic expectations have only further hardened, views with which Zelensky's public speeches have been firmly aligned. As of

July 2022, more Ukrainians oppose compromises to end the war than they did even two months prior. And 75 percent think the country should never consider giving up any territory. Only 7 percent agree that Ukraine should be willing to put everything on the negotiating table in order to seek peace. Furthermore, more Ukrainians are convinced now than in May that any peace deal should be put to a referendum.

Looking at these data, one might well wonder: Will it be possible to meet these expectations? If not, and if Zelensky attempts to recognize this reality and stop the killing with a peace deal, the current state of public opinion indicates that sharp divisions among Ukrainians are likely to follow. While one hopes for a complete and unambiguous Ukrainian victory, this could be the next big challenge for Zelensky's presidency: Could he "sell" a peace deal of his own to Ukrainians as well as his Western allies? And can he prevent the allies from imposing one on Ukrainians?

One possibility is that, not wanting to disappoint anyone, he might simply avoid making any kind of deal. Before embarking on his path to the presidency, he was working to unite Ukrainians. That has now largely been accomplished, with unintended assistance from Putin. So, the question is whether Zelensky will be ready, when and if circumstances dictate, to try to direct this unity in the direction of a settlement. Zelensky owes his political rise, in part, to a reputation as someone who cares about ordinary people, who values human life. And he continues to say this has not changed with the start of this war. If peace may be divisive when war brings politically useful unity, will he choose one over the other?

What history is in store for Zelensky?

The British famously voted Winston Churchill out of the prime minister's seat right after he had led them in the Grand Alliance's historic victory over Nazi Germany in World War II. Grateful for his victory, the population wanted someone else to lead their post-war rebuilding. In the case of France's Charles de Gaulle, however, wartime wins anchored lasting political loyalties.

Zelensky's own political future beyond the war is thus uncertain even if Ukraine wins the war. Many of Poroshenko's 2019 voters, in particular, have mixed emotions. On the one hand, having doubted Zelensky's, and perhaps some of his voters', commitment to the country, they are greatly relieved to see him standing up strongly against the Russians. On the other hand, from the point of view of some, it is vexing that a man they view as a fundamentally incompetent president with questionable patriotic credentials is the one reaping the political credit for the heroic deeds of the nation that they themselves have championed from the beginning. Kyiv-Mohyla Academy National University political scientist Olexiy Haran, himself a prominent pre-war critic of Ukraine's president, argues that Zelensky is simply doing what any ordinary Ukrainian would and should do in his position, and in this sense he deserves support. But Ukraine's resistance is not about the president leading the people, he goes on, instead being about how Ukraine's self-organizing society "shows our leaders how to behave." Haran's central point is the following: Zelensky's patriotic critics have "decided to postpone all the criticism, and all of our internal problems and discussions, until the end of the war. Then, we are a democracy. We will have a democratic discussion, and we will decide." Alluding to what he feels were presidential missteps in the lead-up to and conduct of the war, he predicts that: "There will be a lot of things we will discuss after the victory."[12] Even in summer 2022, some of these tensions occasionally bubbled up to the surface. For example, some critics blasted Zelensky after he admitted to the *Washington Post* that he had publicly downplayed Western warnings of an imminent invasion in order to avoid panic and economic collapse, leading his critics to cry reckless deception.[13]

Our data indicate that a substantial minority in Ukraine feels this way about the president. While survey data show Ukraine is strongly united around Zelensky now, the analysis we presented in the previous chapter still finds that 12 percent openly withhold approval of the job he is doing, while another 28 percent quietly harbor reservations while outwardly voicing support. This still leaves a solid majority who both privately and publicly approve of his leadership. That said, post-war discussions and the re-emergence of political debate will likely shift the opinions of at least some Ukrainians, at which point some old patterns in political behavior are likely to re-emerge.

Probing regularities in Zelensky's support to identify lines along which future political debates may break, we find that his wartime appeal is remarkably even across the country's regions as of July 2022. The small minority who are openly critical today, we find, tend to be older, male, and (perhaps reflecting the elite's initial skepticism of Zelensky) highly educated. Also more likely to be open critics are those who dissociate themselves from Ukrainian nationality (and the civic attachment to the state it implies) as well as from Ukrainian ethnocultural identity, not to mention former Poroshenko voters and people who do not consider Zelensky a truly "conscious Ukrainian."[14]

We also commissioned the KIIS polling agency to ask the population several questions about how they perceive various qualities of Zelensky's leadership in July 2022. Figure 8.4 shows the results when we asked people which of Ukraine's possible future candidates for president would be most competent for leading the country to victory in the war with Russia. Zelensky comes first with 65 percent of the responses, far ahead of second-choice Poroshenko's 5 percent (19 percent said there is no difference among the politicians or did not venture an answer). This figure, though, also shows that fewer people (55 percent) are confident Zelensky would be most competent for leading the postwar reconstruction, and the share saying there is no difference or who refuse to answer rises to 28 percent. That said, there is no one else who comes even remotely close (Poroshenko is second with 4 percent). And perceptions of his leadership qualities appear quite solid. As Figure 8.5 reports, as of July 2022, at least four-fifths of the population perceived him as intelligent, strong, and honest. On the metrics we included, it is interesting that his weakest showing is on the statement that he "really thinks about the interests of people like you," but even here he rates 79 percent agreement. Noteworthy for those of his critics who have doubted whether the southeastern and originally Russian-speaking president with Jewish roots is a true "conscious Ukrainian," we find such doubts are decisively rejected by 88 percent of the population. This reflects the broader integration of what some have called *sovoks* into the Ukrainian national project.

Overall, Ukrainians clearly feel he represents them and leads them well. Figure 8.6 indicates that his support is emotionally deep: most feel positive emotions when reflecting on his leadership. If the war were to end today, therefore, our analysis suggests he would indeed be the kind of president he once said he wanted to be, someone "at whom people first sling mud ..., then whom people learn to respect, then whose departure they cry about."[15]

What history is in store for the Independence Generation?

The members of the Independence Generation are now in power, and they are powerful. While every generation is doing its part in the war, assuming roles of both soldier and leader, this is the moment at which this particular cohort has come into its own. With their very specific experiences of being born under communism, watching the wild 1990s unfold, and seeing the Ukraine of 2021–2, they know exactly what they have and are fighting for.

Most have shed the sense of "post-Sovietness" that even the generation right before them struggled to escape, yet they still have enough experience with unfortunate pasts to be determined not to allow the same histories to repeat themselves. Unlike in Russia, where the ruling elite is still dominated by older generations of politicians with formative years in the Soviet era, in Ukraine the Independence Generation is not going back on the shelf. If viable alternatives to Zelensky as president are to emerge with large-scale political support in the near future, they are likely to emerge from his generation, or at least will have to draw heavily on its members. They will thus likely become the most influential voices shaping Ukraine's history after the war.

What history is in store for Ukraine?

As for what Ukraine's real-world history will be as of 2049, this generation's hopes are high, and the expectations of its leaders are even higher. Our role as political scientists is not to dissuade them from pursuing lofty ends, though accumulated research tells us that few politicians will be able to deliver on all that is now expected, even with a decisive victory over Russia. With the war largely sealing the effort, Ukraine has now made one major important step along the road of the progress so many of its citizens desire: the creation of a vibrant, inclusive civic nation with an associated sense of civic duty and democratic orientation. But patronalism can exert a powerful pull: so long as a feeling continues that "everybody does it" when it comes to corrupt practices or the skirting of formal procedures in favor of personal connections, these practices are likely to continue. Similarly, politicians can find it tempting to try to compensate for poor economic performance, or to distract from their own corruption or their failure to root it out, by resorting to divide-and-rule tactics along ethnocultural lines. EU candidate status will help push against such inertia. But what Ukraine needs most of all is to use the sense of unity generated in response to the war to effect thoroughgoing change.

The dangers of returning to "patronal politics as usual" in Ukraine are real, and there is an even greater danger: that Ukraine may shift from the patronal democracy it has typically been, with its characteristic pluralism by default, into a much more authoritarian patronal polity.[16] When opposition re-emerges in Ukraine once the war ends, as we have argued it is likely to do, Zelensky and his successors might be tempted to return to previous practices and amass power for themselves—even if the initial aim is only to push through reforms or rebuild the country. These are justifications that would-be reformers across Eastern Europe, Latin America, and elsewhere have time and again used, often sincerely, when seeking constitutional changes that concentrate power in the presidency, only for this ramped up "presidentialism" to set in motion processes that sooner or later undermine the needed reforms and often lead to some form of dictatorship.[17]

While widely seen as necessary to defeat an enemy bent on conquest, we see in some of Ukraine's pre-war and wartime moves the potential to threaten postwar democracy. These include the consolidation of all private television channels into a single state wartime broadcaster and the suspension of certain Russia-oriented political parties without clear due process. Zelensky's erstwhile critics frequently harbor concerns about this, worried that he may not give up this control when he has to shift attention from war to construction. No leader, after all, relishes being criticized or—in their view—lied about, as typically happens in any true democracy. It will thus be vital for Zelensky to strike a strongly liberal balance that addresses national security yet without threatening democracy. This does mean tolerating some risk, showing confidence that the Ukrainian civic nation that has rallied so strongly against Russia's army will not simply succumb to the Kremlin's messages when they are heard.

Zelensky's popularity could also pose a threat to democracy should he come to equate his own political fate with that of the country. The polling we have presented shows that there is simply no one in Ukraine today who has anything close to Zelensky's stature and popular support as a political leader. Will that lead him to conclude that he needs to hang on to power, effectively denying others the chance to gain the needed stature? Perhaps the greatest thing that US President George Washington ever did, even after leading the country to independence, was to step away from the presidency at a time when this seemed all but unthinkable, setting a precedent for the transfer of power. As we saw earlier, shortly before being elected, Zelensky declared that a president should only serve a single five-year term. This is why he once said he hoped people would "cry" when he left office.[18] If he revises this view now that he is actually in power, and is re-elected, Ukrainian democracy may come to depend on whether he will at least abide by the country's two-term limit.

Throughout this book, we have also noted that the rise of civic national identity in Ukraine, an identity that places civic duty and attachment to the state above all other lines along which the nation might be defined, has been consistently challenged by a different vision of Ukrainian identity. This alternative connects national identity to ethnocultural identity and external threats linked to many of those who do not share certain ethnocultural traits. It connects the concept of being a good and reliable citizen with speaking the right language, holding the right view of the country's history, and revering the right cultural figures. There is thus a strong likelihood that Ukraine will again become divided over this question, creating a further risk that politicians will take this too far, seeking political gain by capitalizing on these emotional issues when they need the support of localities where one view or the other is more prevalent. History is indeed rife with instances of countries facing enemies, especially countries traumatized by extremely brutal war crimes like those perpetrated by Russia, resorting to more exclusive definitions of the nation in an effort to wall off foreign influence.[19] Such moves can sometimes lead to division, oppression, and internal conflict, ironically at times weakening the country and opening up opportunities for exploitation. In Ukraine's wartime context, the risk is that some might doubt the endurance and strength of a civic Ukrainian path, leading to a hardening of more extreme nationalist positions according to which true national security and prosperity can only be achieved through some kind of ethnic purification. Fortunately, we do not see signs that this is currently happening in Ukraine. Research by Alexseev and Dembitskyy reinforces our findings that, if anything, the war seems to have strengthened Ukrainians' commitment to liberalism and inclusive ideas of the nation.[20]

War may even create an opportunity in the wake of tragedy. Russia's 2022 invasion has produced an extraordinary sense of Ukrainian national unity—at least for the time being. And much can happen in a moment well seized. While Georgia's Mikheil Saakashvili can be criticized for many things he did in office, even some of his fiercest critics acknowledge that he successfully capitalized on the 2003 Rose Revolution to immediately and dramatically eliminate petty corruption in everything from the previously notorious traffic police to basic state services.[21] In his case, the revolution served up a moment of mass euphoria in which people saw that change was possible, having directly witnessed far more people than expected standing up for change in this highly patronalistic polity. His brilliance was thus not so much to propose a technically impressive anti-corruption plan as to convince millions among the elite and the masses that things actually *would* change.[22] Because only when people are fully convinced change is coming will they wholesale alter their own behavior, adapting to the new expected reality, thereby making it happen in a virtuous self-fulfilling prophesy. Formulating attractive proposals is relatively easy; convincing people that things will change is much more difficult.

The outcome of the war may offer Zelensky, the Independence Generation, and the rest of the country just such a moment. The president will need to find a way to translate the population's will to fight into an equally strong conviction that the old ways are no longer possible, and then to follow through personally on the promises his fictional history teacher Holoborodko first made in his expletive-filled rant in *Servant of the People*'s opening episode. The people have done most of the work for him. The people who make up the nation, the nation that made Volodymyr Zelensky. Let us hope this moment ultimately arrives, and that he lives up to it.

UKRAINE'S FUTURE HISTORY

The first episode of the fictional Servant of the People series ends with a Dzidzio song. We find it fitting to end our book on the very real Zelensky Effect with Dzidzio's rendition of that which unites all Ukrainians: their civic national call to arms. The very same one those little Independence Generation children were singing in 1991. The one reverberating in their hearts as they defend their country in whatever way they can.

Hence, we recommend our readers listen to "The National Anthem of Ukraine", sung by Dzidzio:

https://open.spotify.com/album/1UhycE07R3g01d3vZG3WTB

APPENDIX OF FIGURES

Figure 1.1. Approval of President Zelensky 2019–22

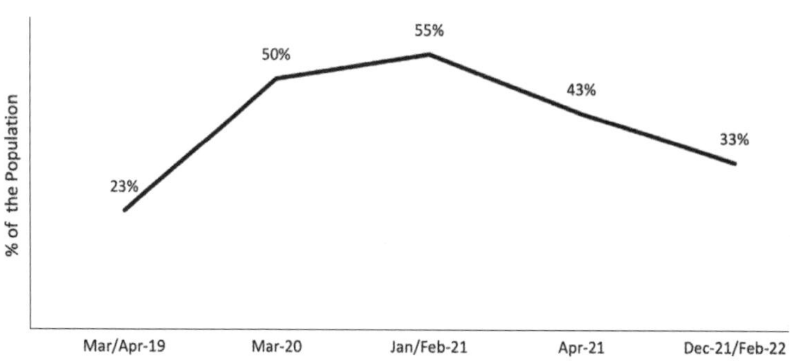

Authors' calculations. Data source: MOBILISE Project.[1]

Figure 1.2. Transparency International, Corruption Perception Index Score For Ukraine 1998–2019

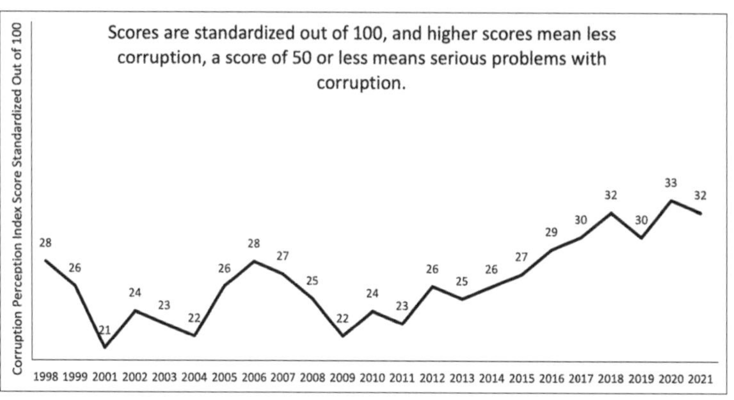

Authors' calculation. Data source: Transparency International.[2]

Figure 1.3. Civic Duty to...
2021–2 (pre-24 February 2022)

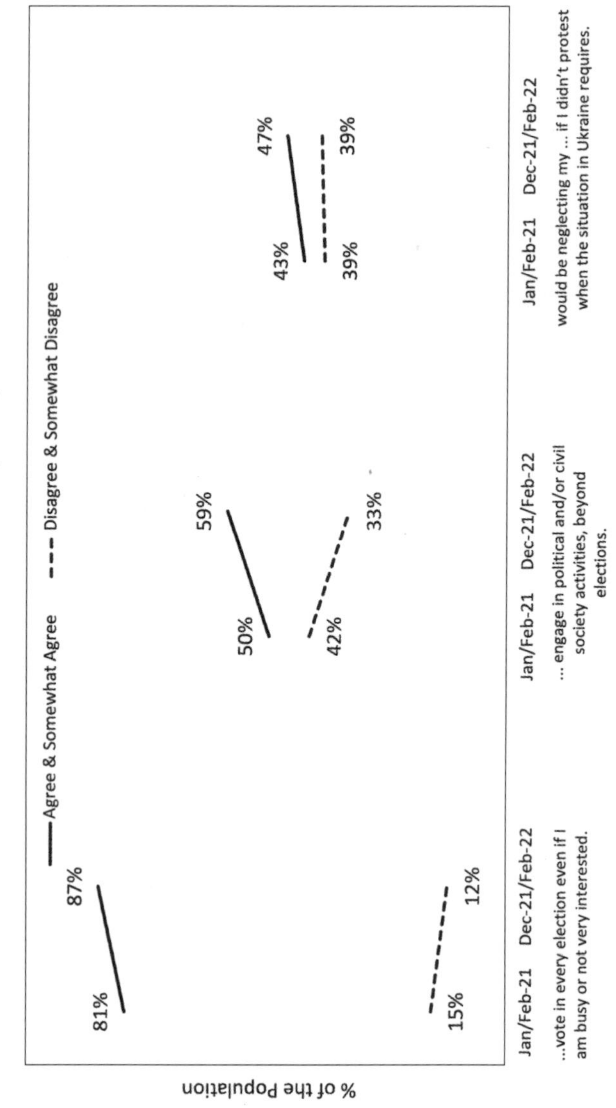

Authors' calculations. Data source: MOBILISE Project.[3]

APPENDIX OF FIGURES

Figure 1.4. Support for Democracy Among Ukrainians
With Which of the Following Statements Do You Agree Most?

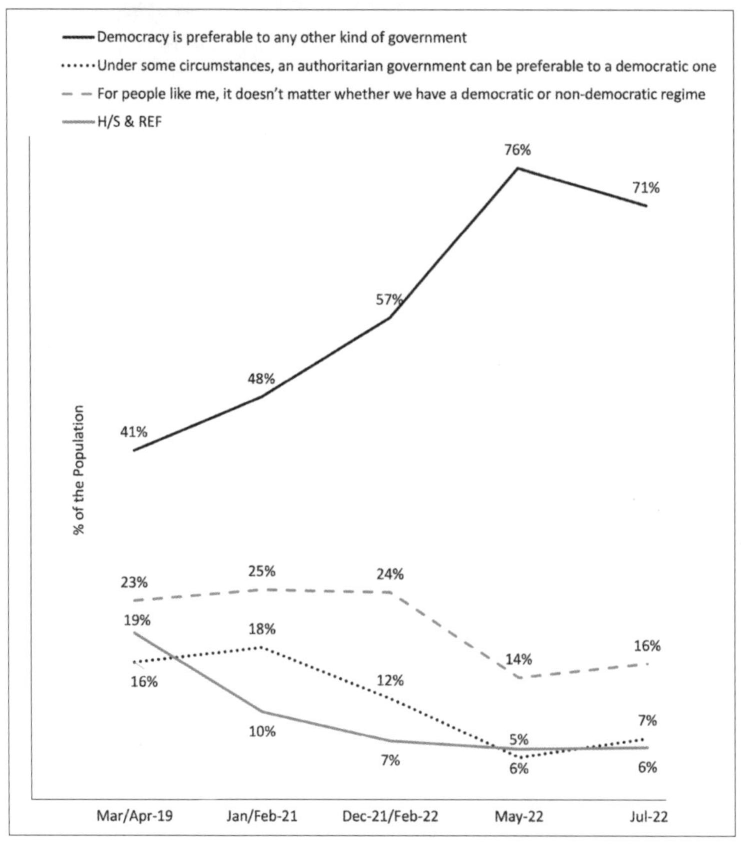

Authors' calculations. Data source: MOBILISE Project.[4]

Figure 2.1. Map depicting regions where dissident leaders were born

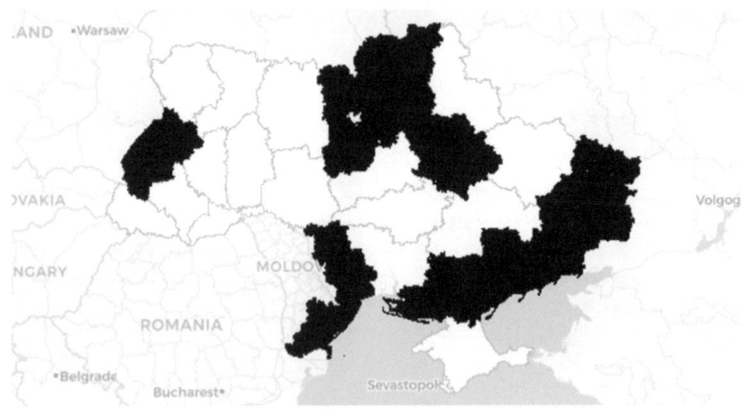

Authors' calculations.

Figure 2.2. Word frequency analysis of Leonid Kravchuk's inaugural address, 5 December 1991

Authors' calculations.[5]

APPENDIX OF FIGURES

Figure 2.3. Inflation Rates in Ukraine 1989–97

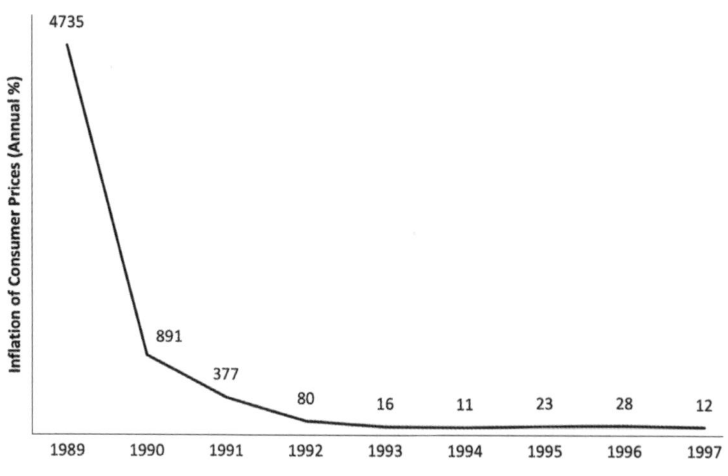

Authors' calculations. Data source: World Bank.[6]

Figure 2.4. Adults (ages 15–49) Newly Infected with HIV in Ukraine 1990–2020

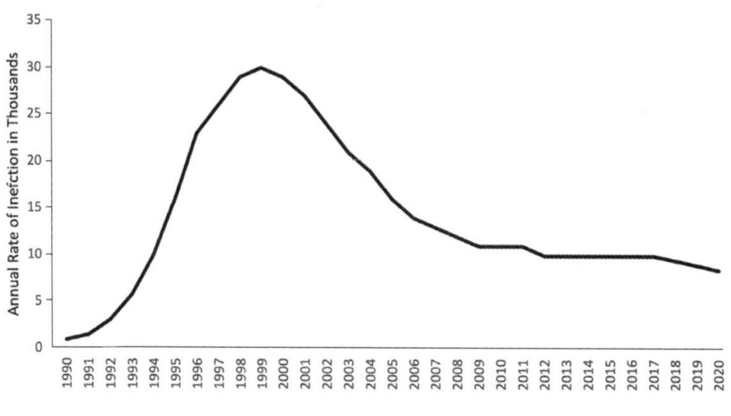

Authors' calculations. Data source: World Bank.[7]

Figure 2.5. Unemployment Levels in Ukraine 1991–2021

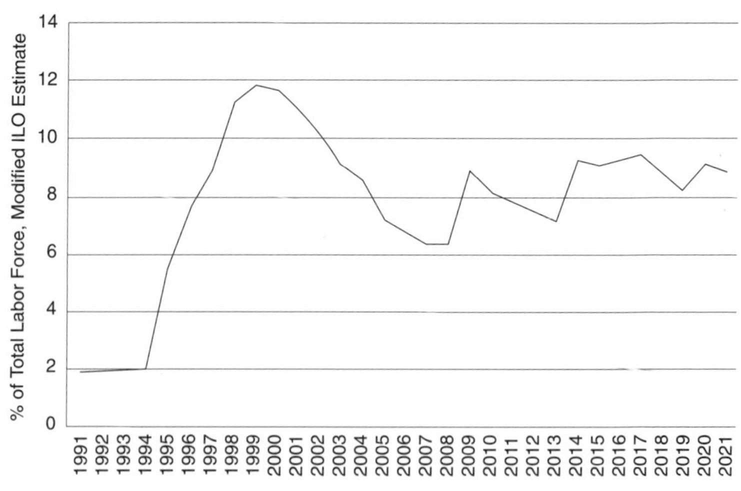

Authors' calculations. Data source: World Bank.[8]

Figure 2.6. Population Growth 1978–2004 (annual %)

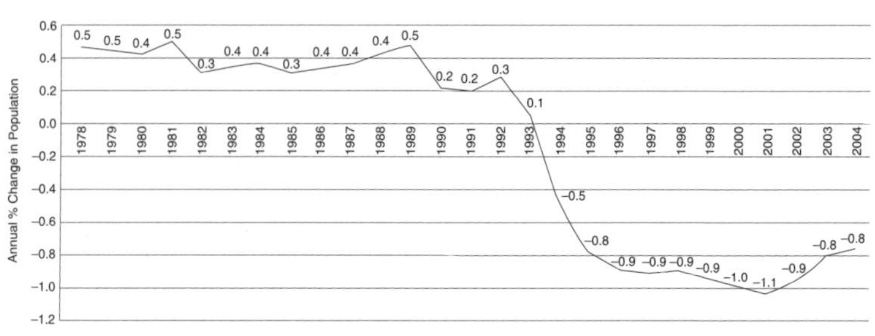

Authors' calculations. Data source: World Bank.[9]

APPENDIX OF FIGURES

Figure 2.7. Ukraine's GDP Per Capita 1987–2001

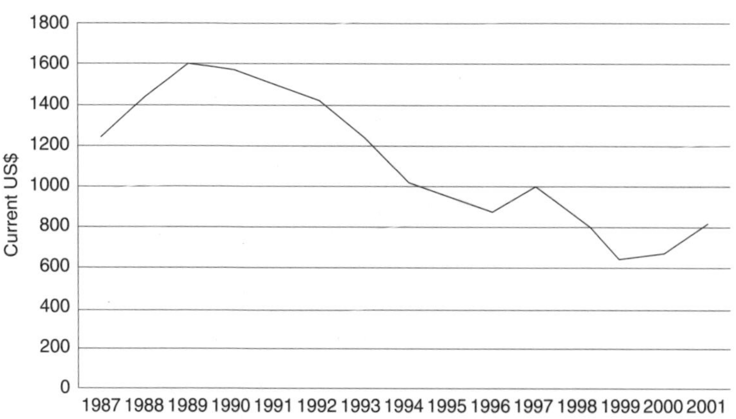

Authors' calculations. Data source: World Bank.[10]

Figure 2.8. Population of Kryvyy Rih 1978–2004

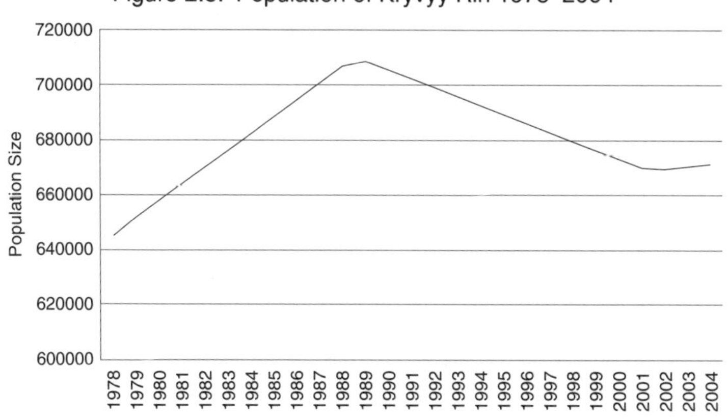

Authors' calculations. Data source: World Population Review.[11]

Figure 2.9. Percentage of votes for Kuchma in 1994 runoff per oblast

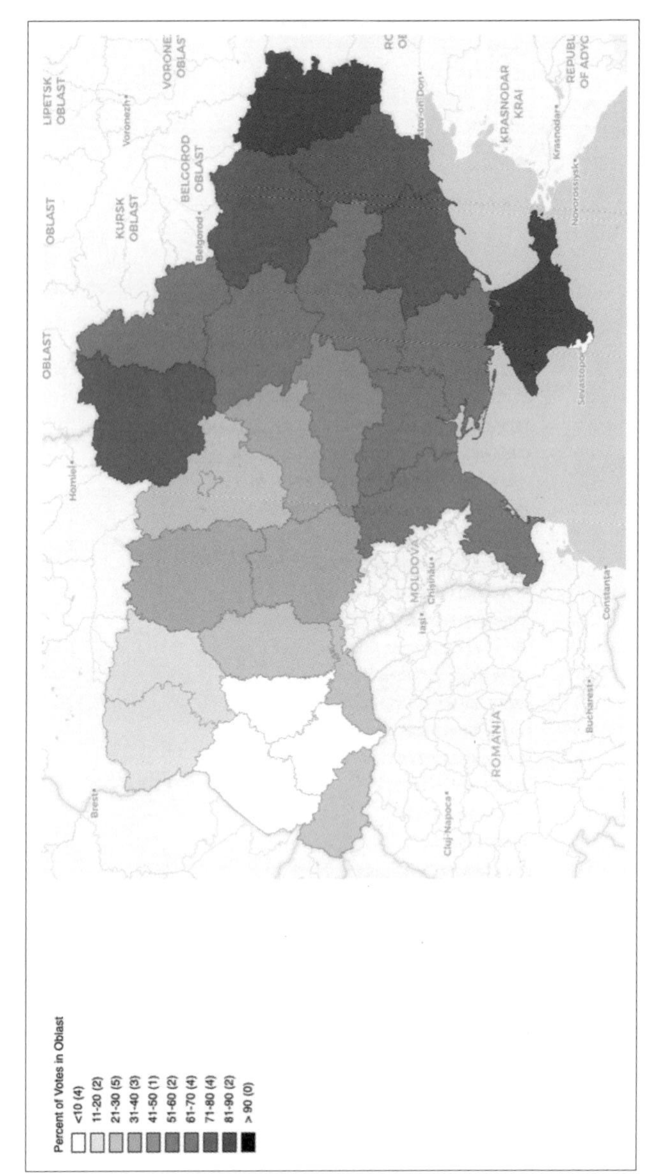

Authors' calculations. Data source: Central Electoral Commission.[12]

Figure 2.10. Perentage Point Change in Self-Declared Nationality by Oblast, 1989–2001 Censuses

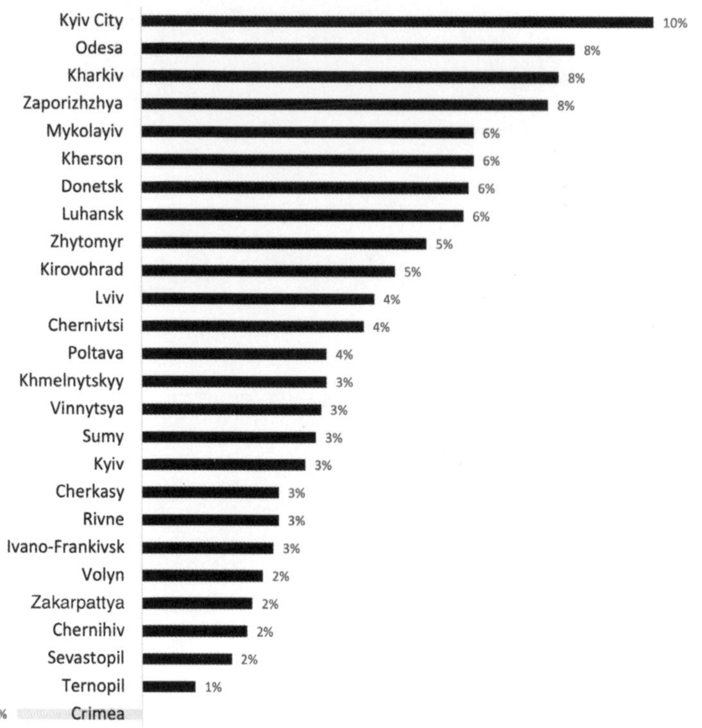

Authors' calculations. Data source: Ukrainian State Statistics.[13]

Figure 2.11. Percentage of votes for Kuchma in 1999 runoff per oblast

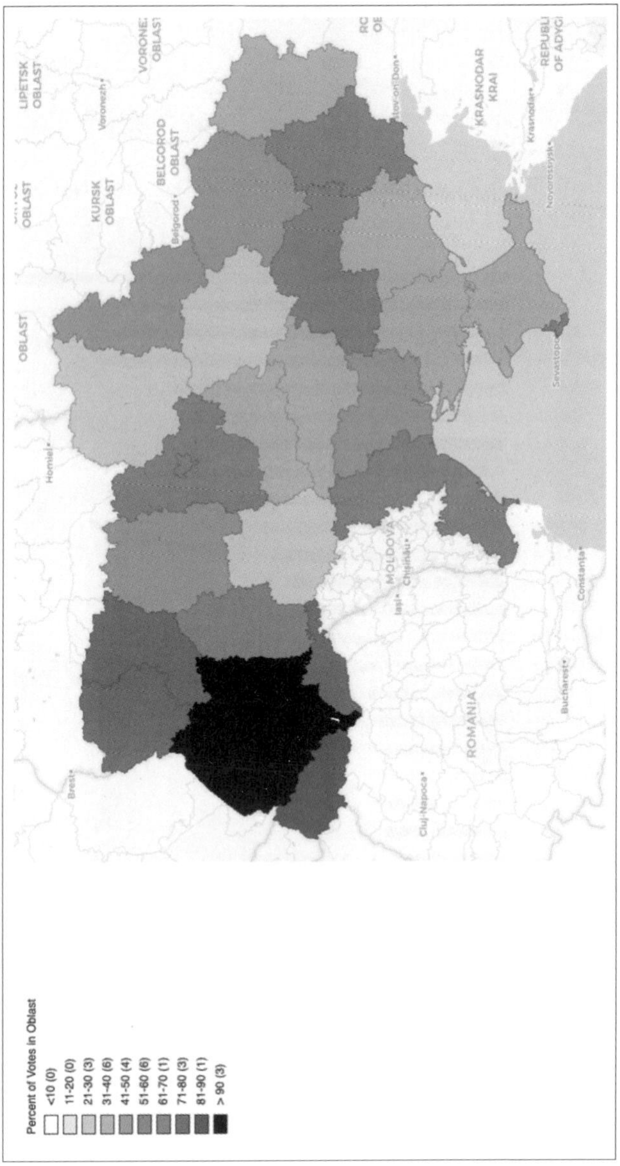

Authors' calculations. Data source: Central Electoral Commission.[14]

Figure 2.12. Candidate vote in oblast by percentage of residents who declared Russian and Ukrainian nationality (2001 Census)

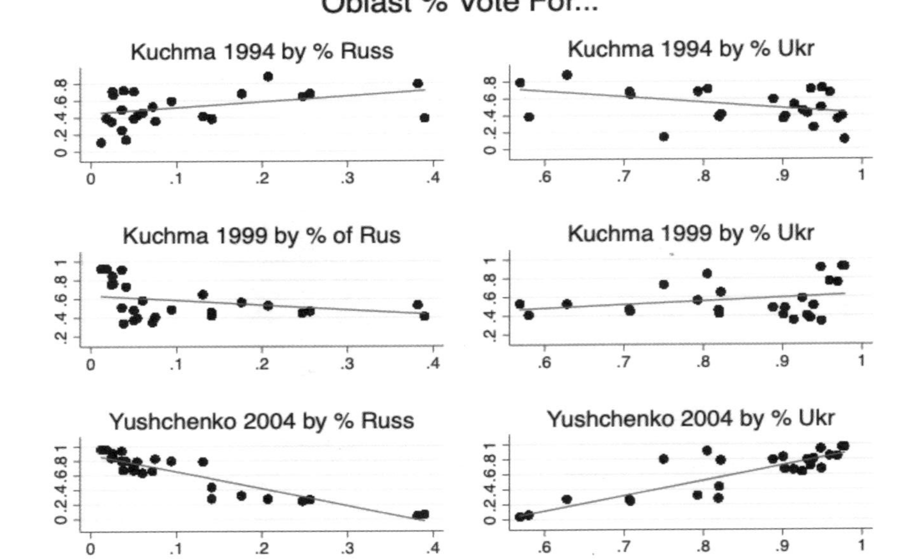

Authors' calculations. Data source: Ukrainian State Statistics and Central Electoral Commission.[15]

Figure 2.13. Percentage of votes for Yushchenko in 2004 December runoff in oblast

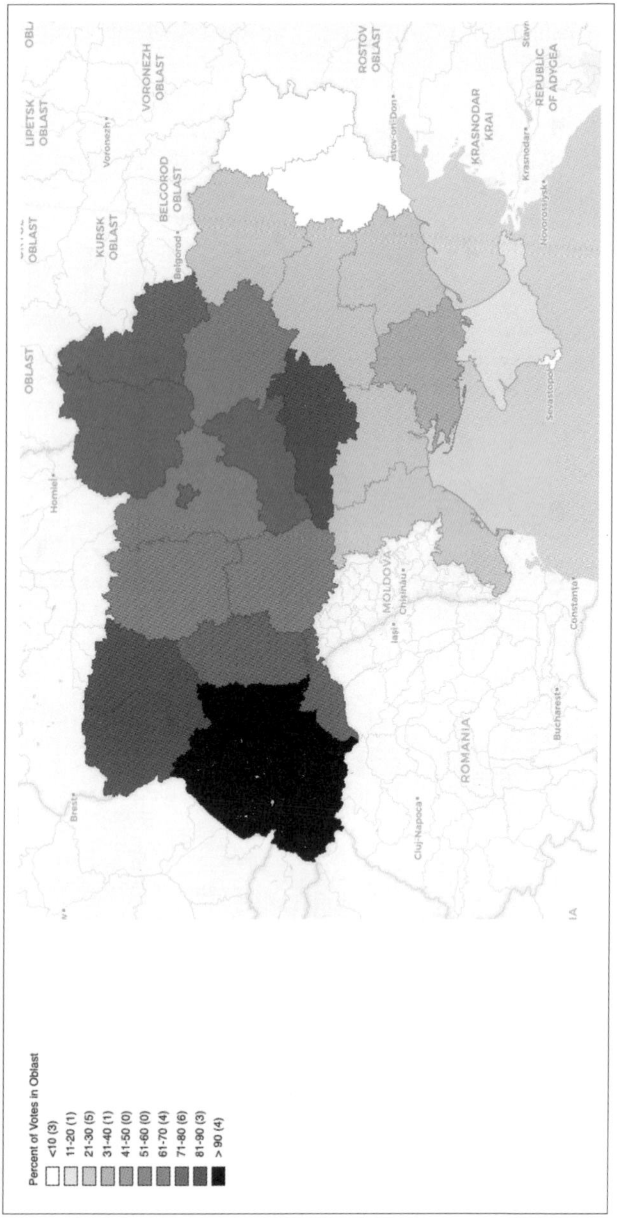

Authors' calculations. Data source: Central Electoral Commission.[16]

APPENDIX OF FIGURES

Figure 3.1. Freedom House Nations in Transit Indicators

(ratings are on a scale of 1 of 7:1 = highest level of democratic progress, 7 = lowest)

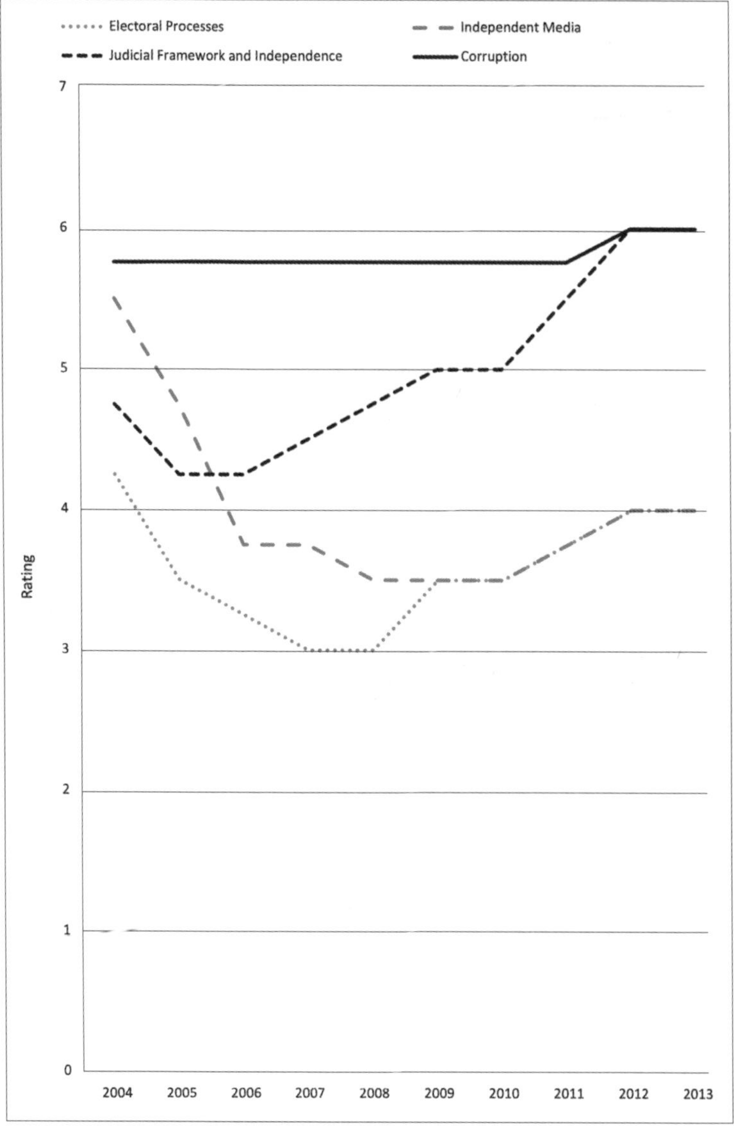

Authors' calculations. Data source: Freedom House.[17]

Figure 3.2. Levels of Democracy in Ukraine 2003–13 by Polity Index

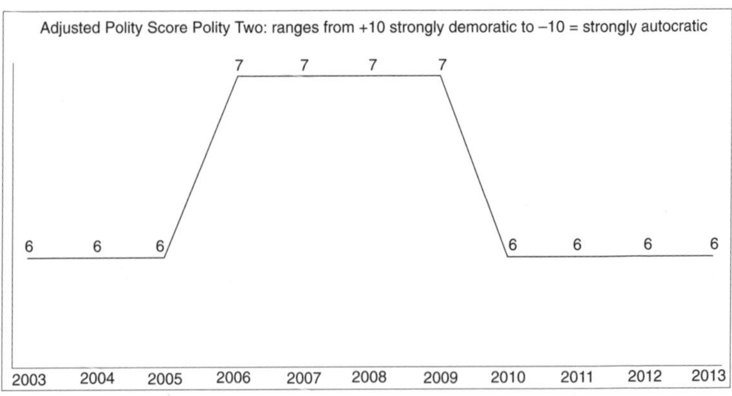

Figure 3.3. V-Dem Scores for Ukraine 2003–13

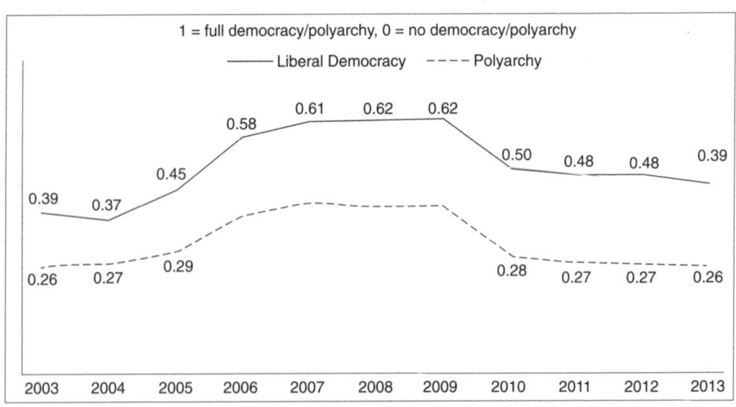

Authors' calculations. Data source: Polity[18] and V-Dem.[19]

APPENDIX OF FIGURES

Figure 3.4. How Satisfied With The Way Democracy Works in Country... Data From ESS (2004–2012)

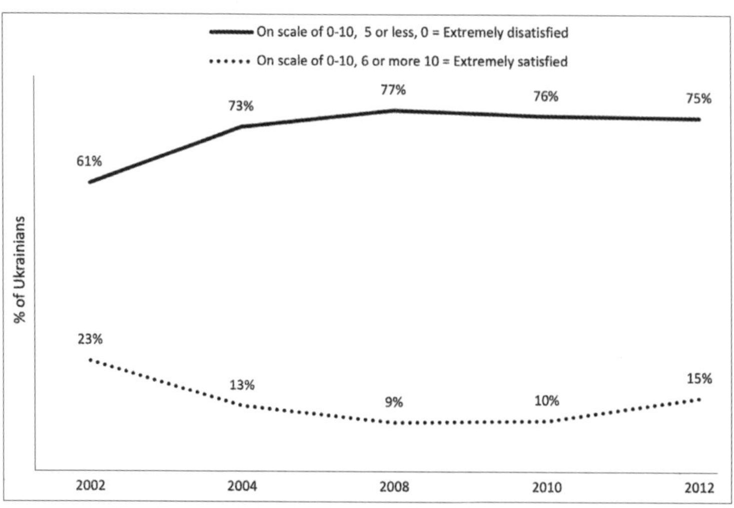

Authors' calculations. Data source: European Social Survey Rounds 2002, 2004, 2008, 2010, 2012.

Figure 3.5. Transparency International, Corruption Perception Index Score for Ukraine 2003–13

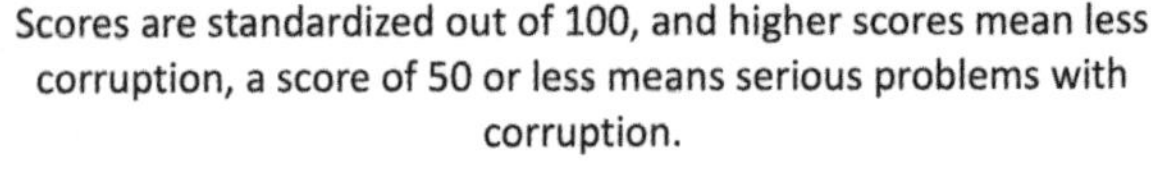

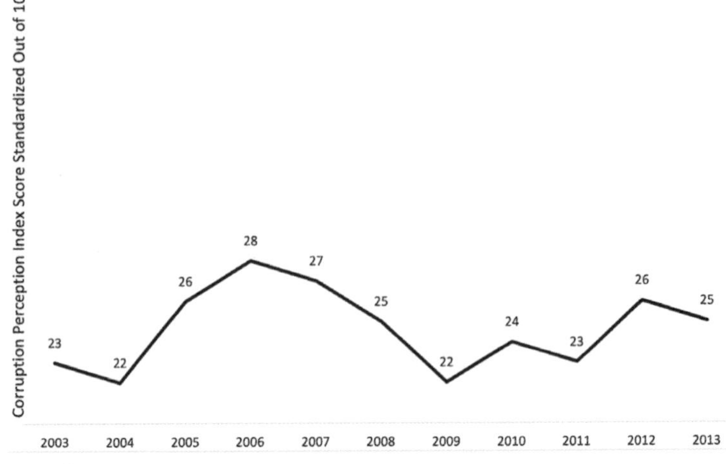

Authors' calculations. Data source: Transparency International.[20]

Figure 3.6. Ukraine's GDP Per Capita 2003–13

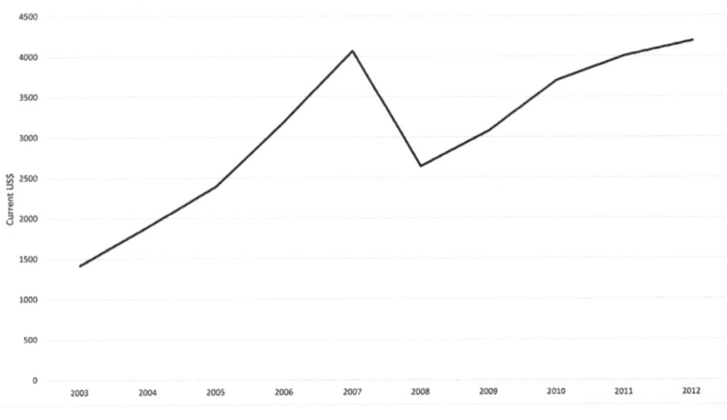

Authors' calculations. Data source: World Bank.[21]

Figure 3.7. Poverty in Ukraine 2003–13

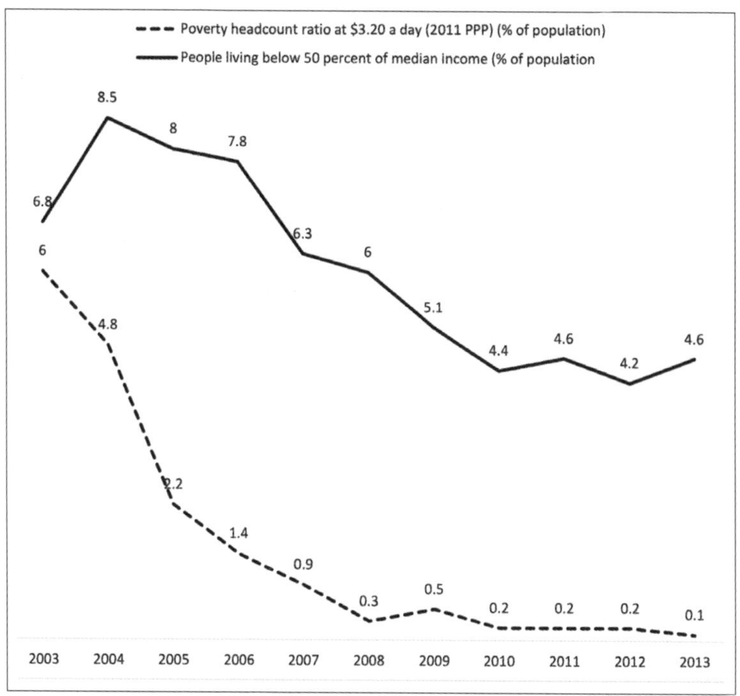

Authors' calculations. Data source: World Bank.[22]

Figure 3.8. Unemployment Levels in Ukraine 2003–13

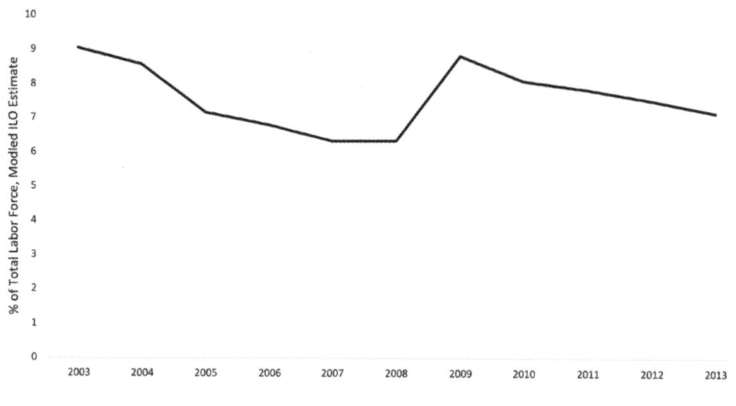

Authors' calculations. Data source: World Bank.[23]

Figure 3.9. Inflation Rates in Ukraine 2003–13

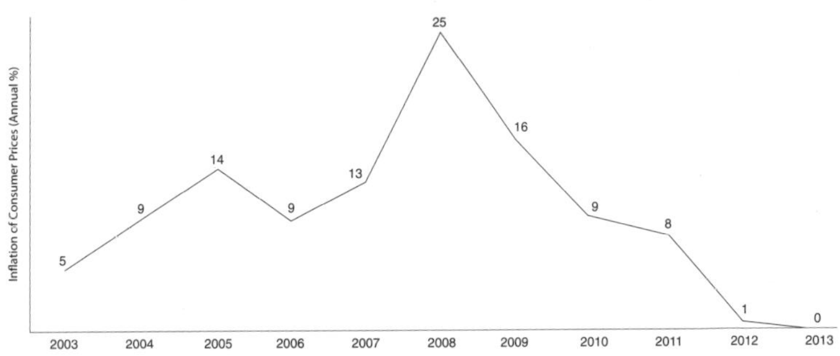

Authors' calculations. Data source: World Bank.[24]

Figure 3.10. Population of Ukraine 2003–13

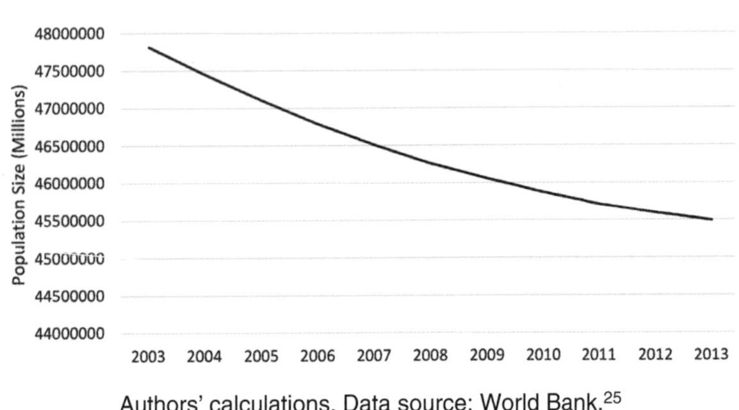

Authors' calculations. Data source: World Bank.[25]

Figure 3.11. Remittances as Share of GDP in Ukraine 2003–13

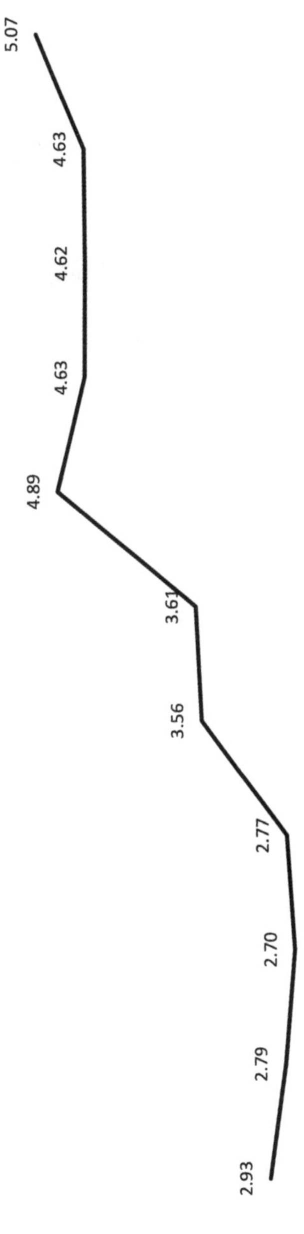

Authors' calculations. Data source: World Bank.[26]

Figure 3.12. Percentage of votes for Yanukovych in 2010 runoff in oblast

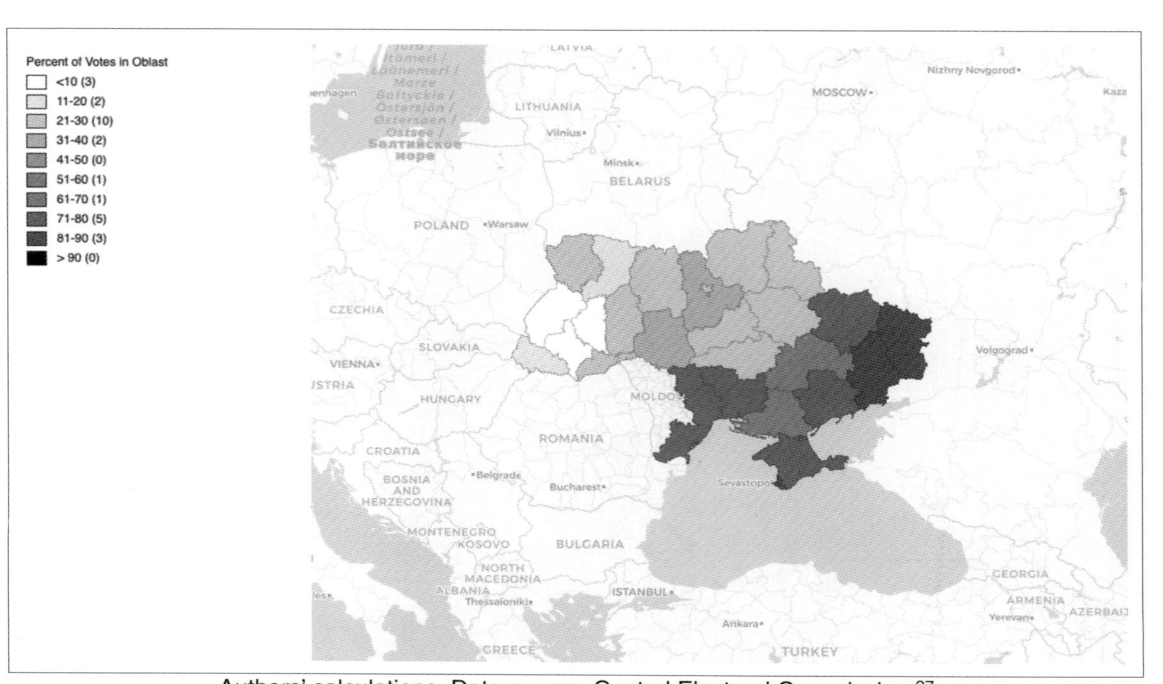

Authors' calculations. Data source: Central Electoral Commission.[27]

Figure 3.13. Top TV Channels by Audience Share 2003–13

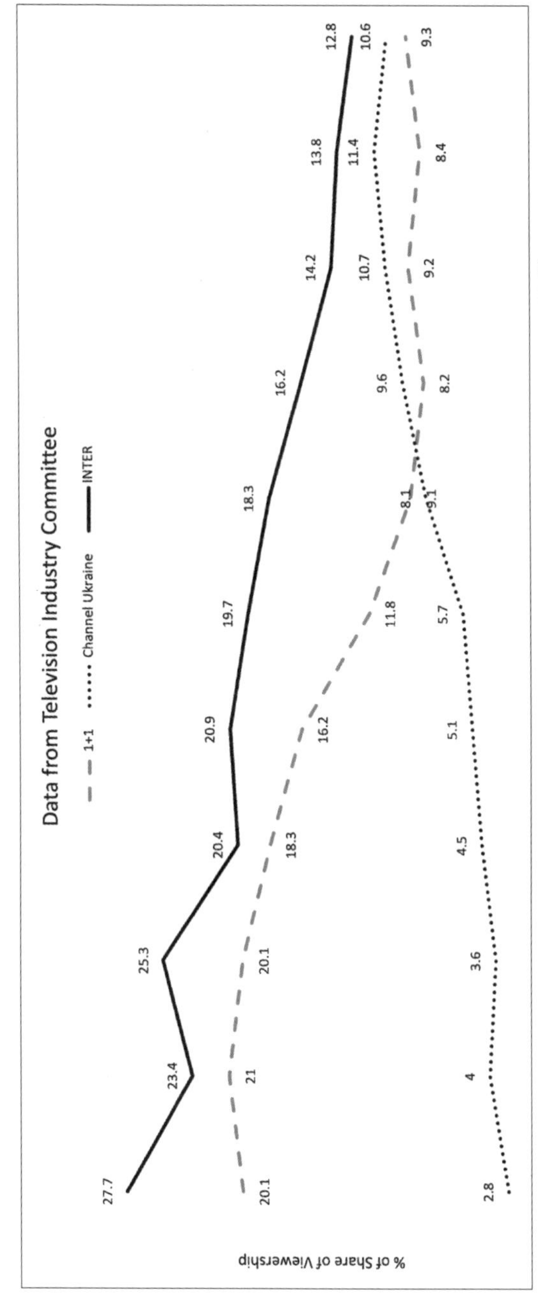

Authors' calculations. Data source: Television Industry Committee (TIC).[28]

Figure 4.1. Percentage of Vote for Poroshenko in 2014 in oblast

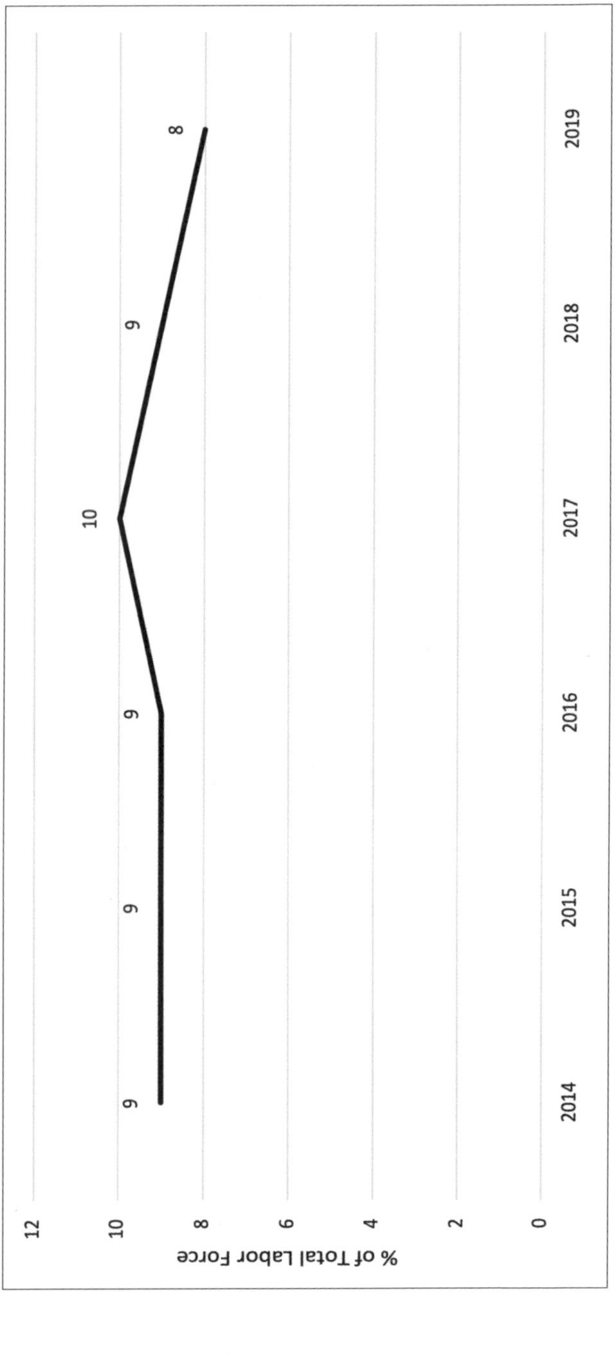

% of Total Labor Force

12
10
8
6
4
2
0

9 9 9 10 9 8

2014 2015 2016 2017 2018 2019

Authors' calculations. Data source: Central Electoral Commission.[29]

APPENDIX OF FIGURES

Figure 4.2. Unemployment Levels in Ukraine 2014–19

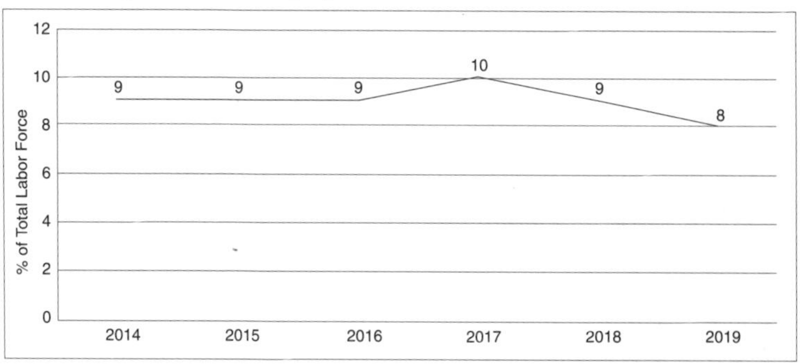

Authors' calculations. Data source: World Bank.[30]

Figure 4.3. Population of Ukraine 2014–19

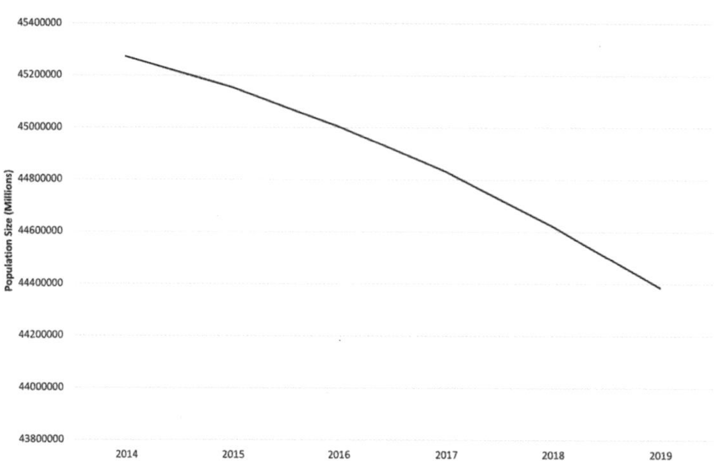

Authors' calculations. Data source: World Bank.[31]

Figure 4.4. Remittances as Share of GDP in Ukraine 2013–18

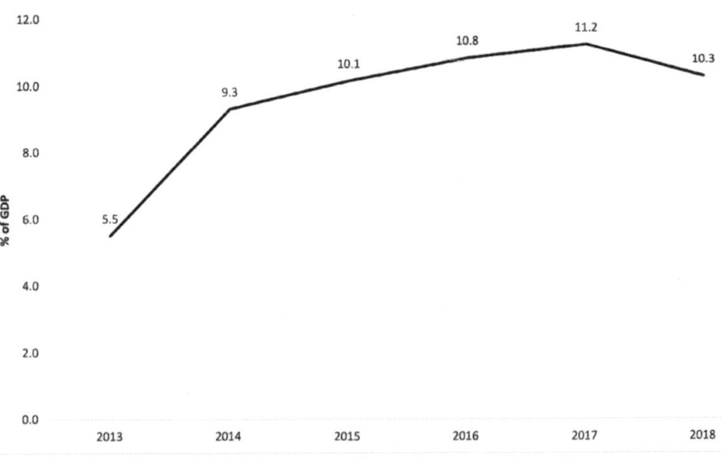

Authors' calculations. Data source: World Bank.[32]

Figure 4.5. Poverty in Ukraine 2014–19

- - - Poverty headcount ratio at $3.20 a day (2011 PPP) (% of population)

—— People living below 50 percent of median income (% of population)

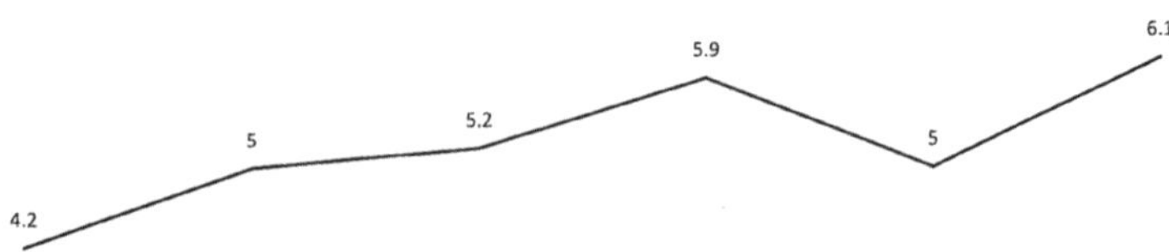

Authors' calculations. Data source: World Bank.[33]

Figure 4.6. Transparency International, Corruption Perception Index Score for Ukraine 2014–2019

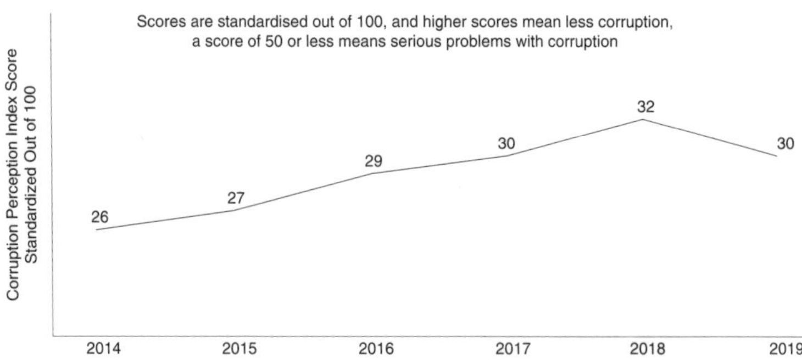

Authors' calculations. Data source: Transparency International.[34]

Figure 4.7. Poroshenko's Job Approval as President 2014–18

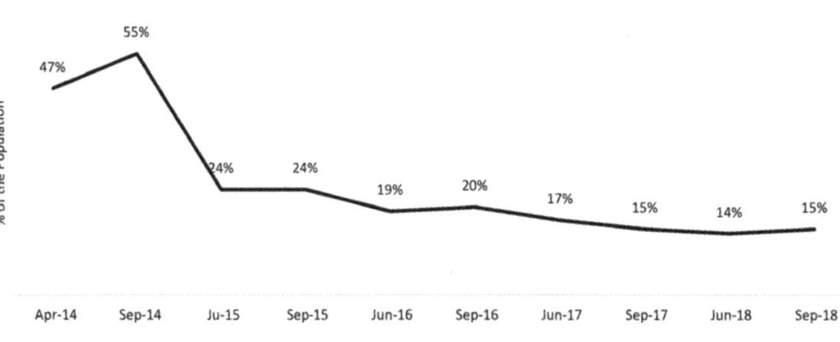

Authors' calculations. Data source: Rating Group.[35]

Figure 5.1. Percentage of votes for Zelensky in 2019 runoff in oblast

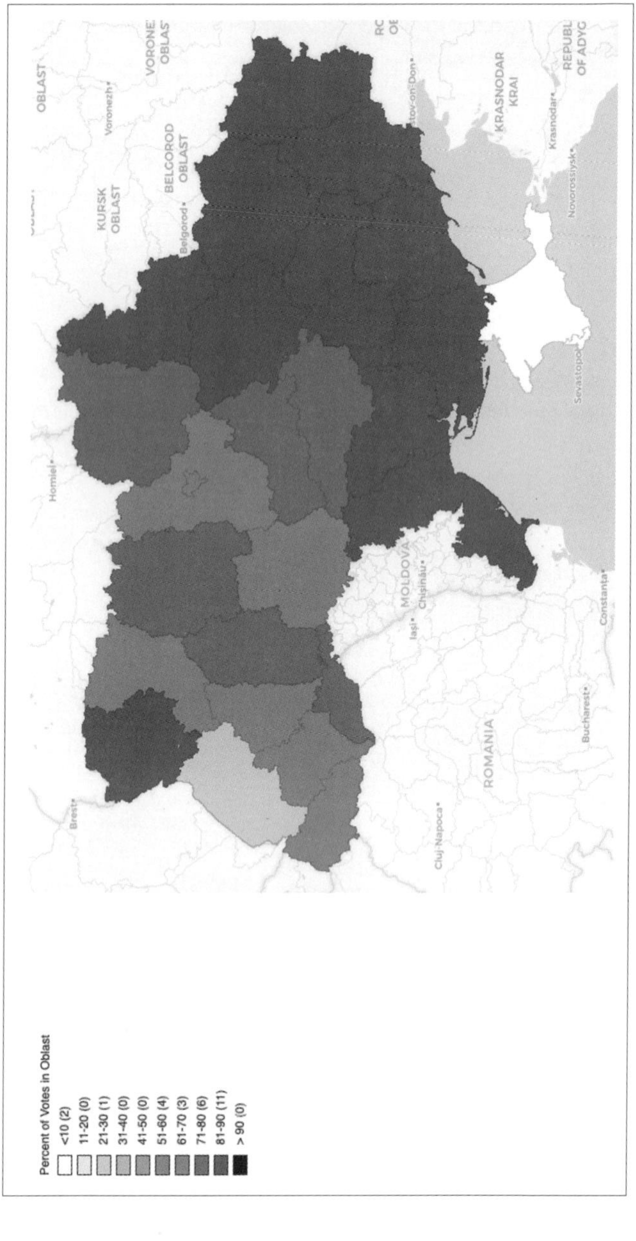

Authors' calculations. Data source: Central Electoral Commission.[36]

APPENDIX OF FIGURES

Figure 5.2. Correlates of Zelensky vote intention

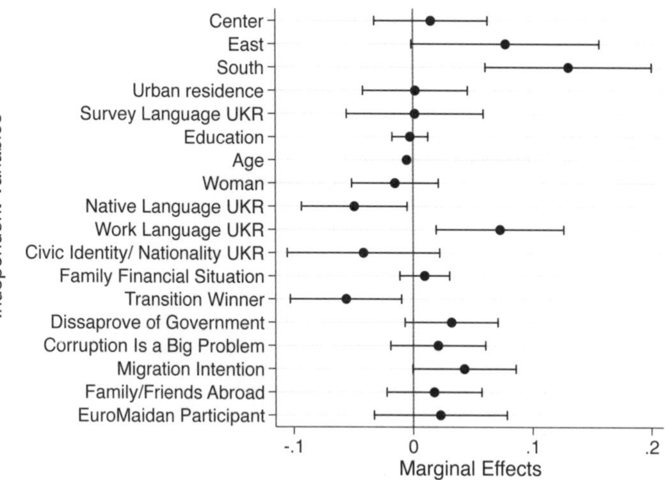

Figure 5.3. Correlates of Servant of the People Party vote intention

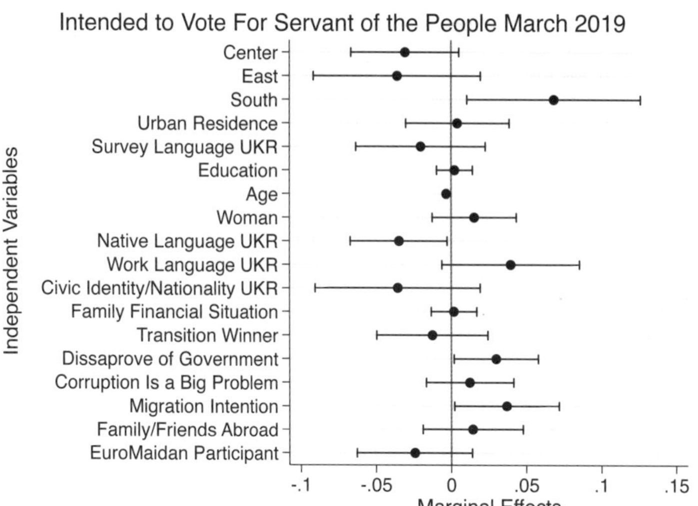

Figure 6.1. Percentage of vote for Servant of the People Party in 2019 parliamentary elections in oblast

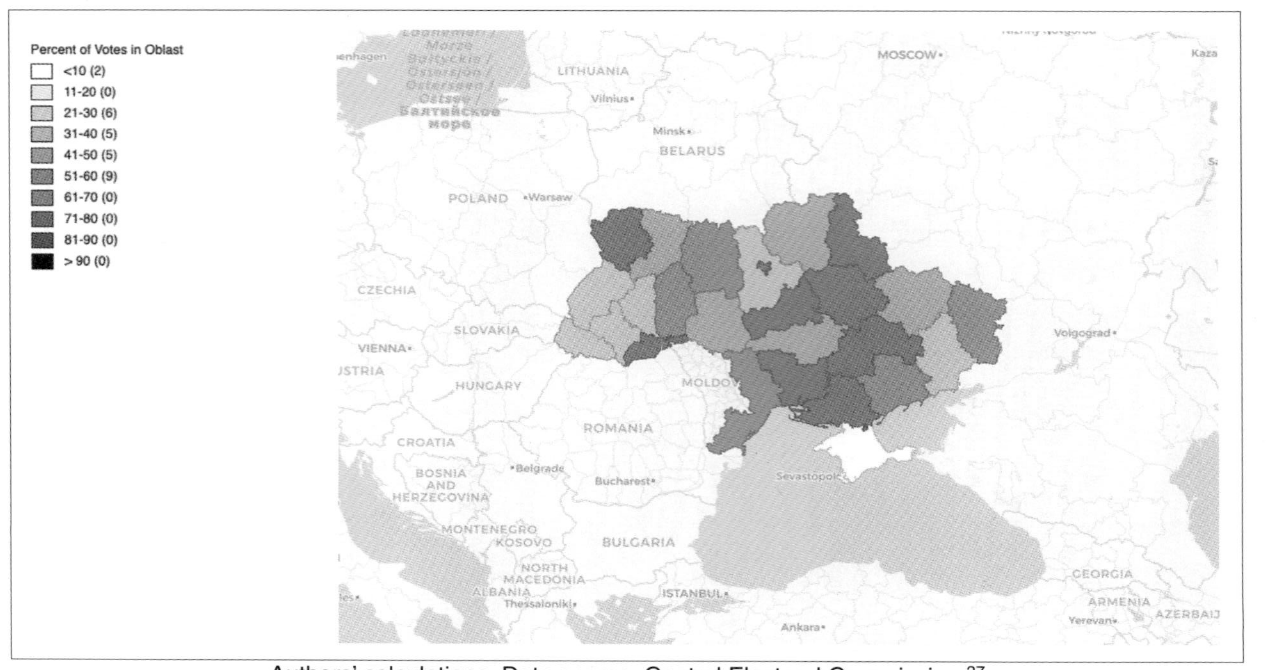

Authors' calculations. Data source: Central Electoral Commission.[37]

APPENDIX OF FIGURES

Figure 7.1. The Zelensky and War Effects on Identity and Political Dispositions 2014–22

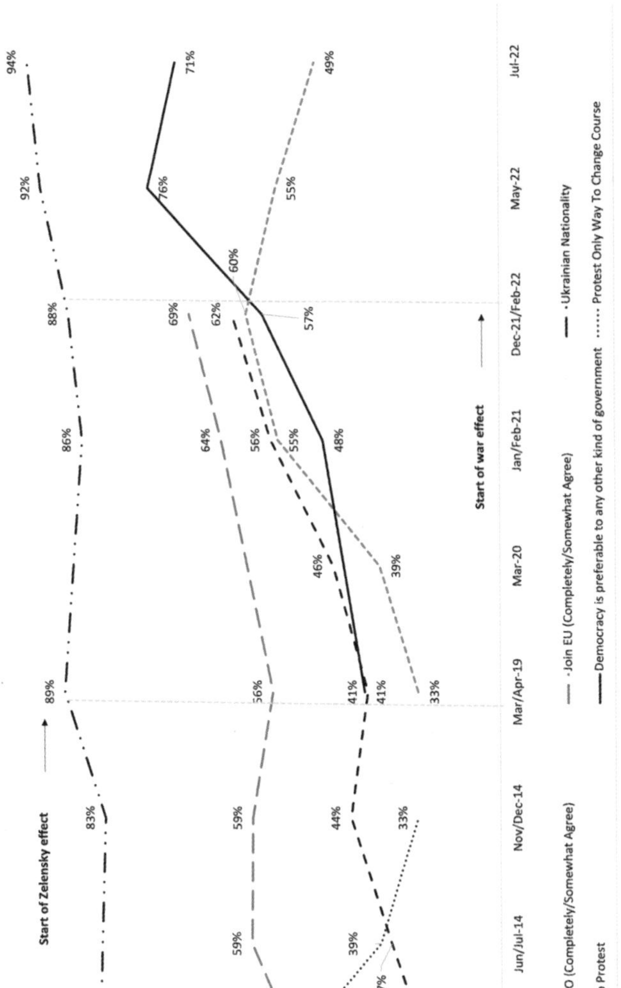

Authors' calculations. Data source: MOBILISE project.[38]

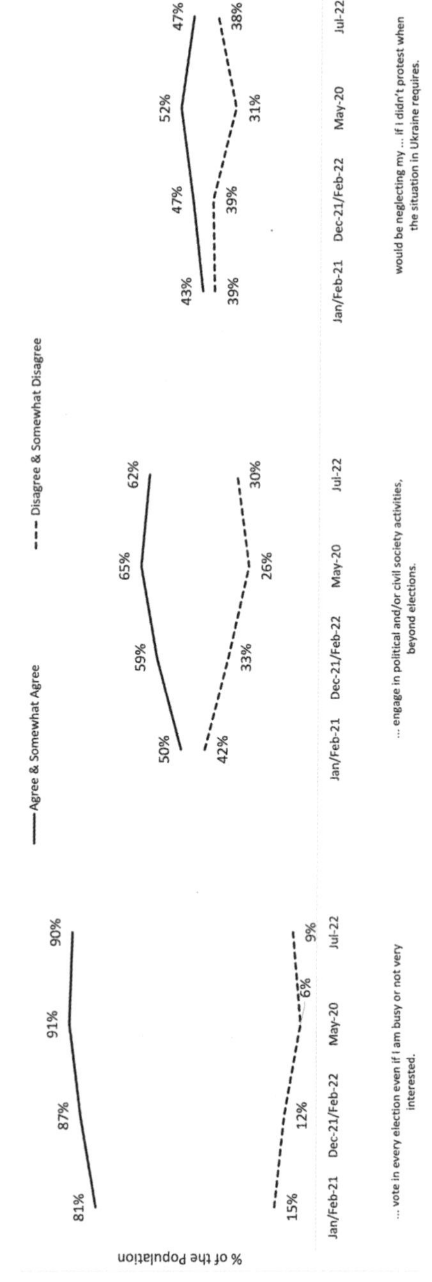

Figure 7.2. Civic Duty to ...
2021–22 (including post-24 February 2022)

Authors' calculations. Data source: MOBILISE project.[39]

Figure 7.3. Support for Democracy Among Ukranians With Which of the Following Statements Do You Agree Most?

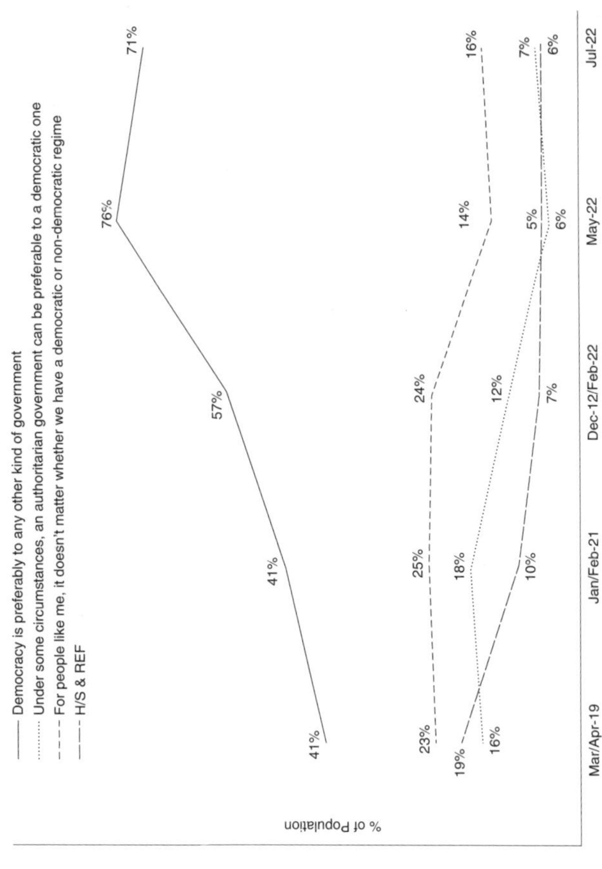

Authors' calculations. Data source: MOBILISE project.[40]

Figure 7.4. Who moved to support democracy?

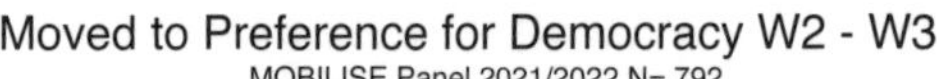

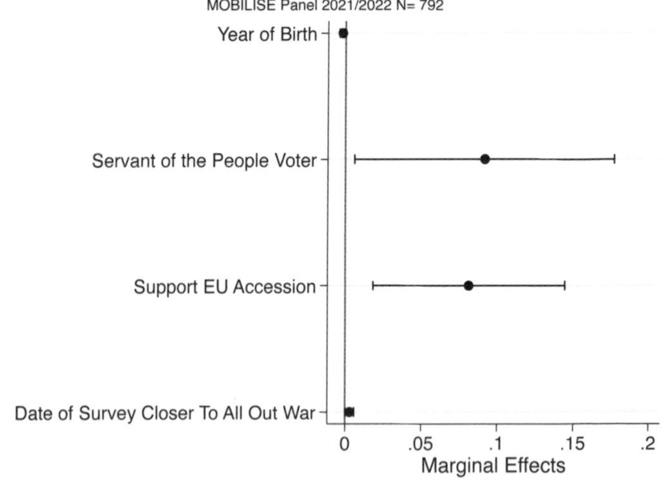

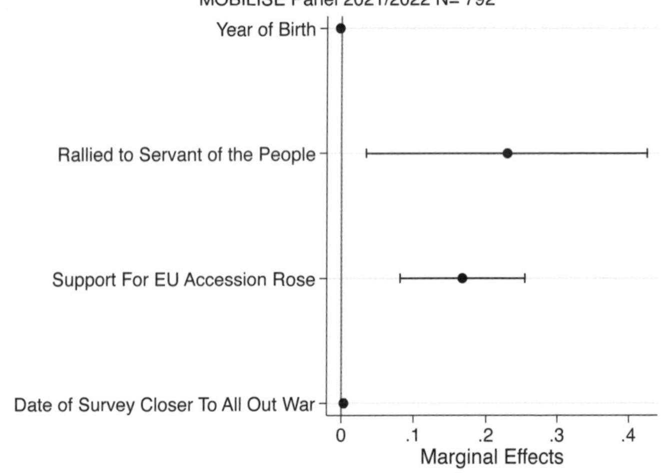

Authors' calculations. Data source: MOBILISE project.[41]

Figure 7.5. Word frequency analysis of Putin's article, 12 July 2021

Authors' calculations.[42]

Figure 7.6. Word frequency analysis of Putin's speech 21 February

Putin's speech 24 February

Authors' calculations.[43]

APPENDIX OF FIGURES

Figure 7.7. Word frequency analysis of Zelensky's speeches 2019

Zelensky's speeches 2020

Zelensky's speeches 2021

Authors' calculations of Zelensky's speeches in 2019, 2020, and 2021.

APPENDIX OF FIGURES

Figure 7.8. Word frequency analysis of
Zelensky's speeches 2022 pre-24 February

Zelensky's speeches 2022 post-24 February

Authors' calculations of Zelensky's speeches in 2022.

Figure 7.9. Percentage of Ukraine's Saying They Would Vote for Zelensky When Asked: If elections for president of Ukraine were to take place soon, for whom would you vote?

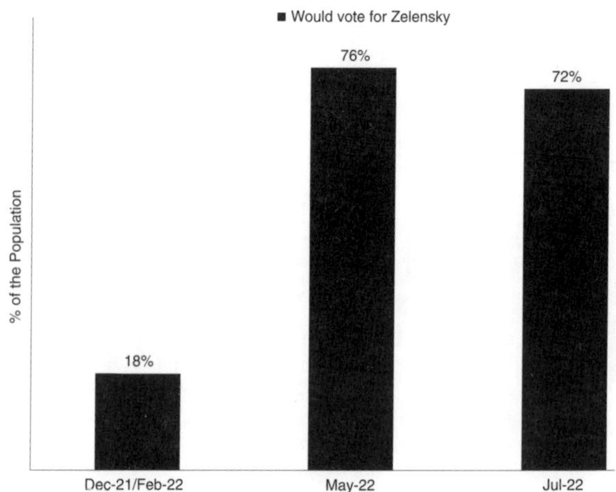

Authors' calculations. Data source: MOBILISE project.[44]

Figure 7.10. Ethnolinguistic and Civic Identity Among the Ukraine Population 2019–22

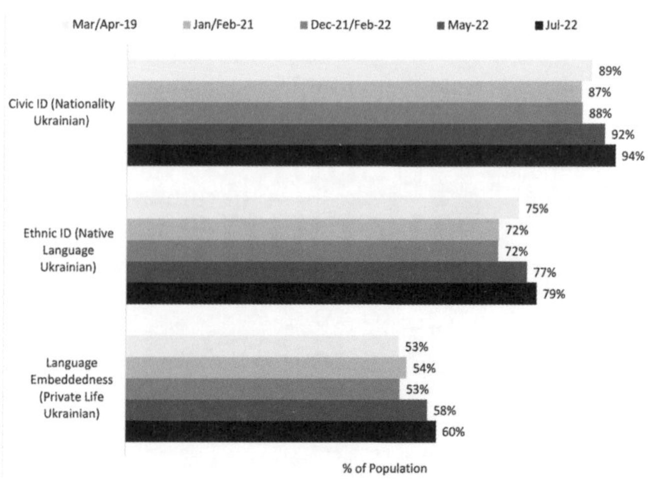

Authors' calculations. Data source: MOBILISE project.[45]
Typology and operationalization.[46]

Figure 7.11. The Ukrainian Nation Includes All Those Who Consider Ukraine Their Home

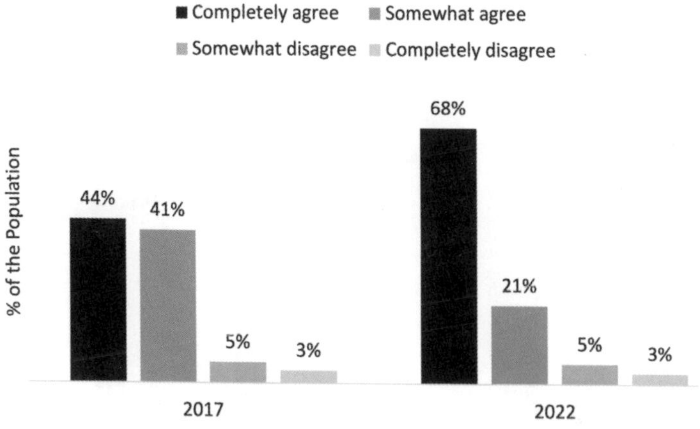

Authors' calculations. Data source: MOBILISE project.[47]

Figure 7.12. Intention to Migrate...

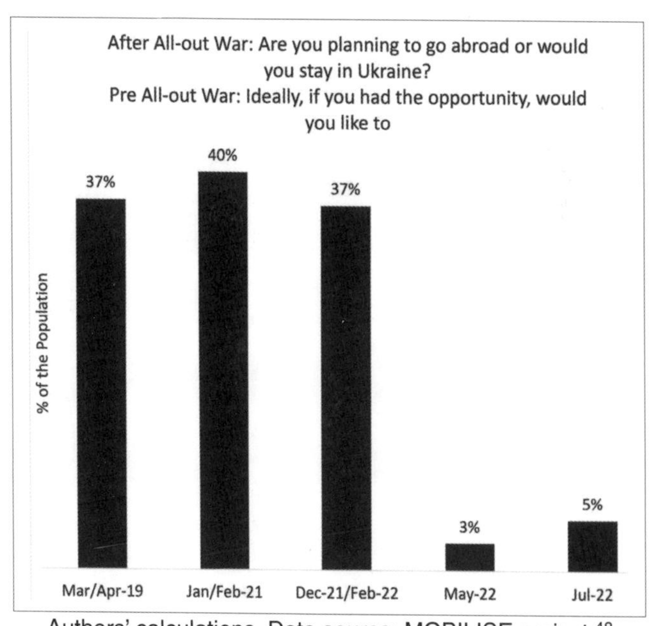

Authors' calculations. Data source: MOBILISE project.[48]

Figure 7.13. Percent Agreeing and Disagreeing that Zelensky Would Win a Large Majority if Presidential Elections Were Held Now and All Ukrainians Could Vote

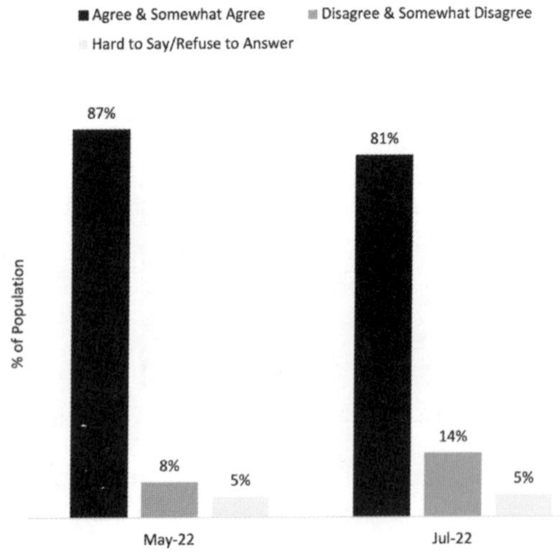

Authors' calculations. Data source: MOBILISE project.[49]

Figure 7.14. Percent Agreeing and Disagreeing That Zelensky Would Win a Large Majority if Presidential Elections Were Held Now and All Ukrainians Could Vote, by Macroregion

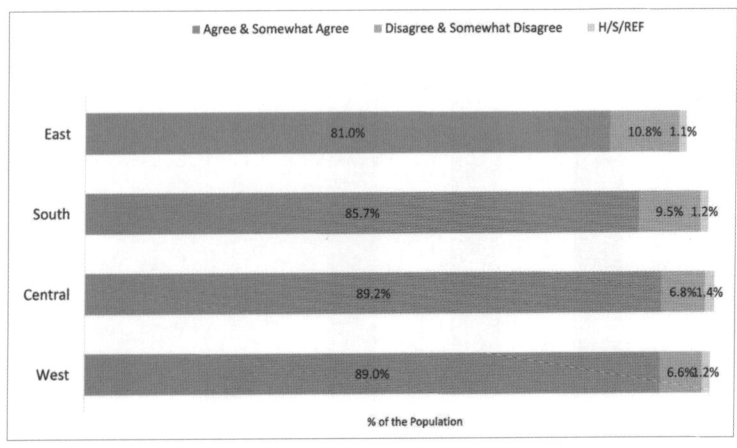

Authors' calculations. Data source: MOBILISE project.[50]

Figure 7.15. Share Approving Zelensky's Actions as Ukraine's President July 2022

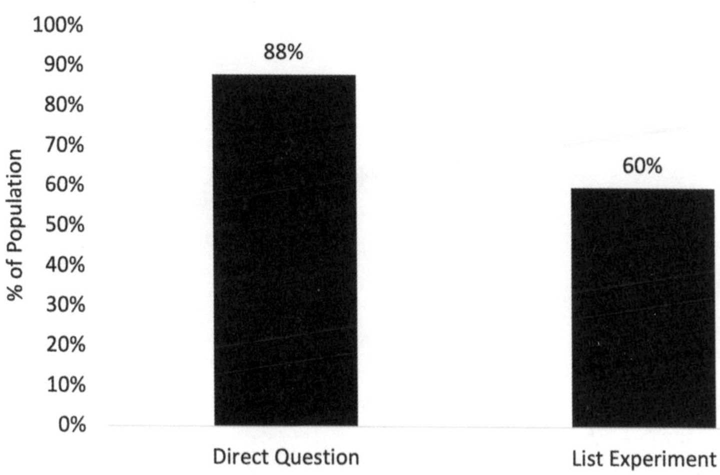

Authors' calculations. Data source: MOBILISE project.[51]

Figure 7.16. Since the Russian invasion of Ukraine on February 24, 2022 have you participated in any of the following actions and if so, which one/s [choose all that apply]?

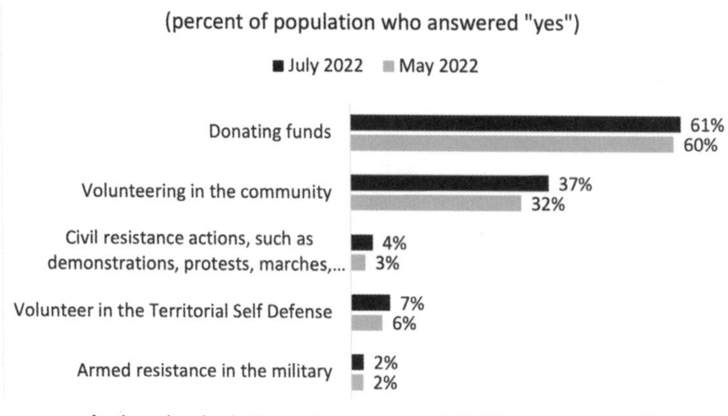

Authors' calculations. Data source MOBILISE project.[52]

Figure 7.17. Count of Zelensky Tweets Over Time

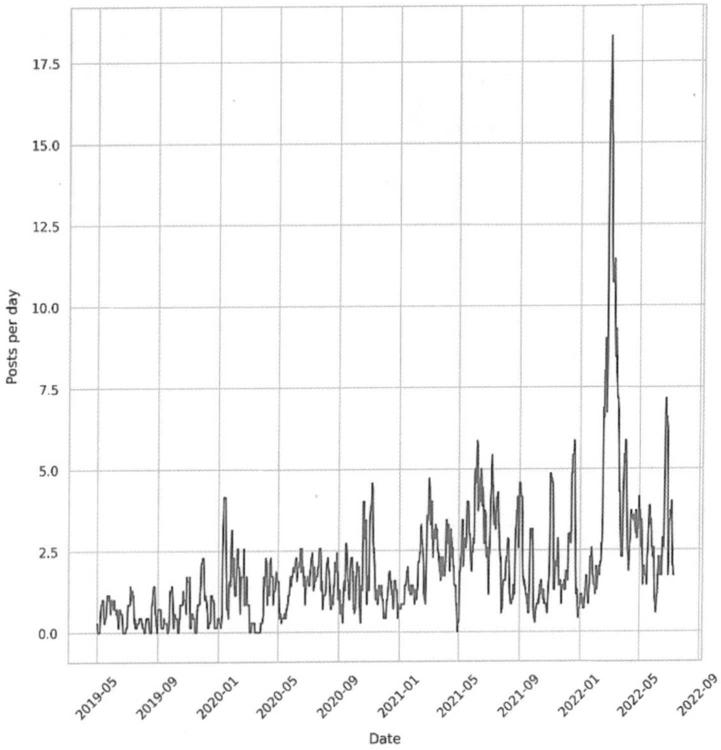

SMaPP Lab Team calculations of SmaPP Lab data.

APPENDIX OF FIGURES

Figure 7.18. Mean Likes Per Zelensky Tweet Over Time

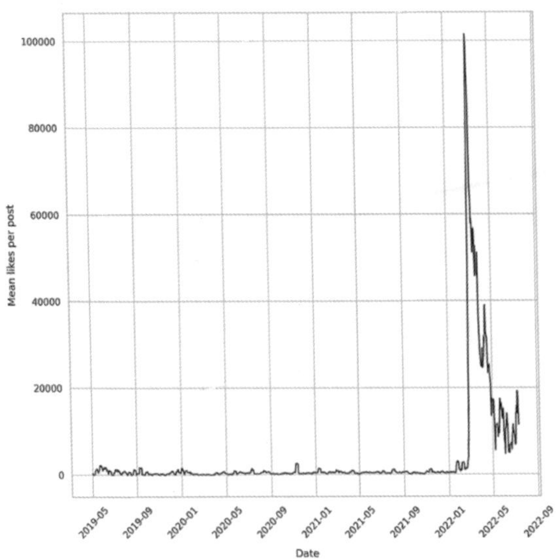

Mean Retweets Per Zelensky Tweet Over Time

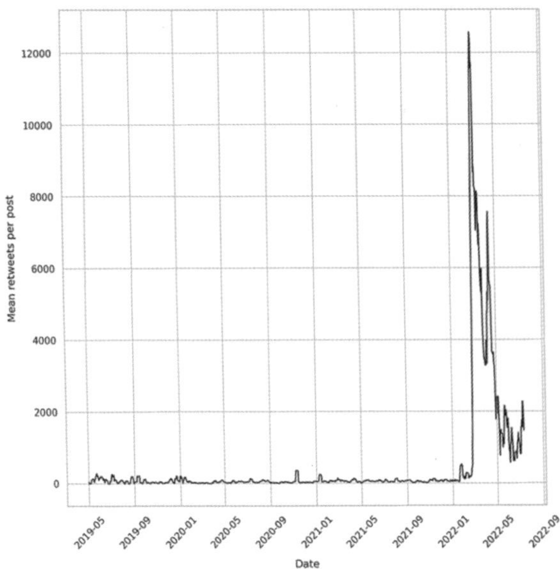

SMaPP Lab Team calculations of SmaPP Lab data.

Figure 7.19. Global Interest in Zelensky as Measured by Google Trends

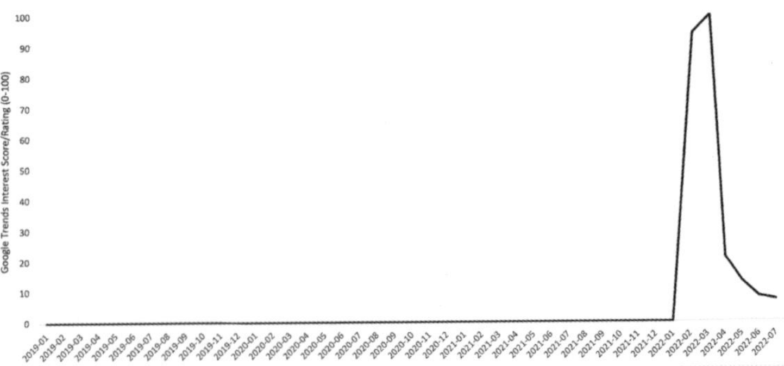

Authors' calculations. Data source: Google trends key term "Zelensky."

Figure 7.20. Global Interest in Ukraine as Measured by Google Trends

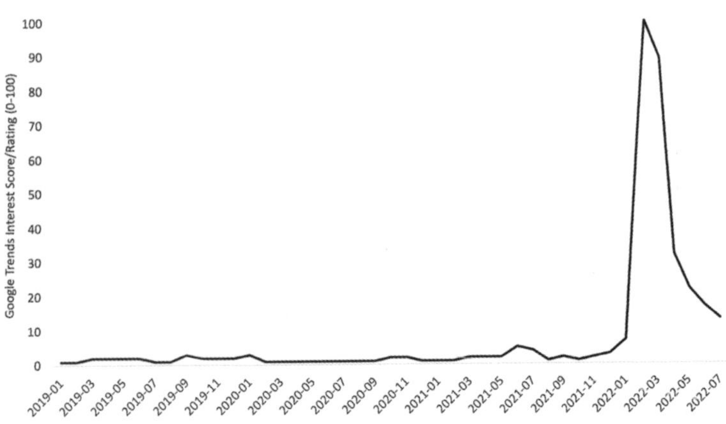

Authors' calculations. Data source: Google trends key term "Ukraine."

Figure 7.21.Count of Tweets Mentioning Zelensky Over Time

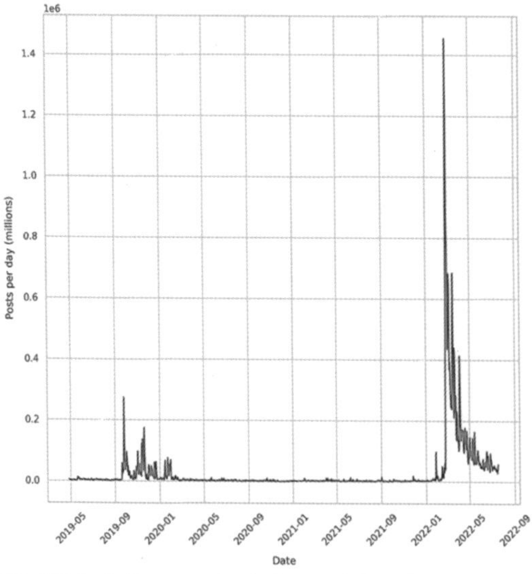

SMaPP Lab Team calculations of SmaPP Lab data.

Figure 8.1. Some Say That Ukraine Should Never Consider Giving Up Any of its Territory, Whereas Others Say Some Territory Could Be Sacrificed if Absolutely Necessary for a Deal That Could End the War and Bring Ukraine Lasting Peace. Which of the Following

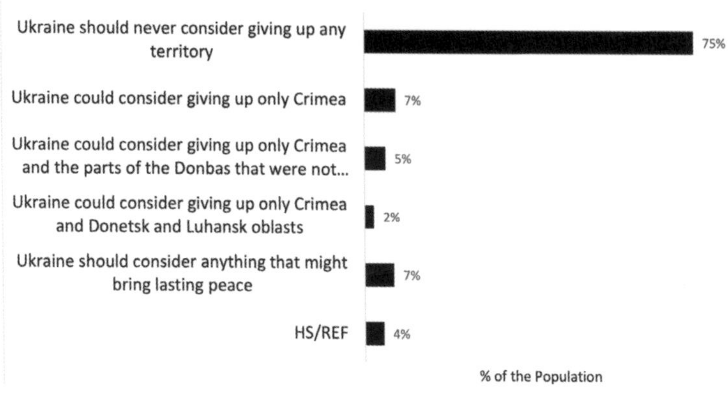

Authors' calculations. Data source: MOBILISE KIIS Omnibus July 2022.[53]

Figure 8.2. The Ukraine Government Should Not Make Any Compromises in Negotiations

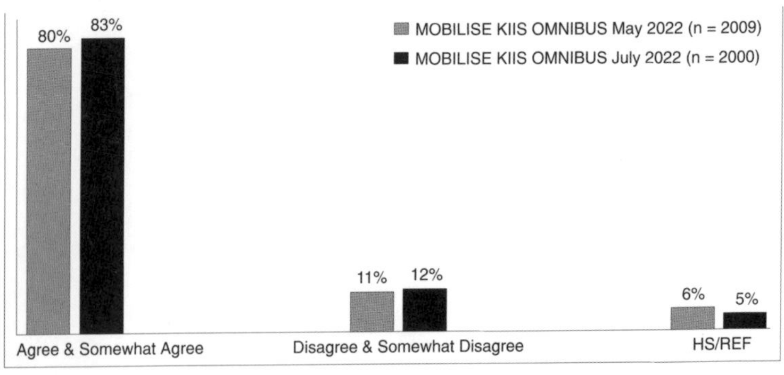

Figure 8.3. Any Negotiations Results Between Ukraine and Russia Should Be Put to a Referendum

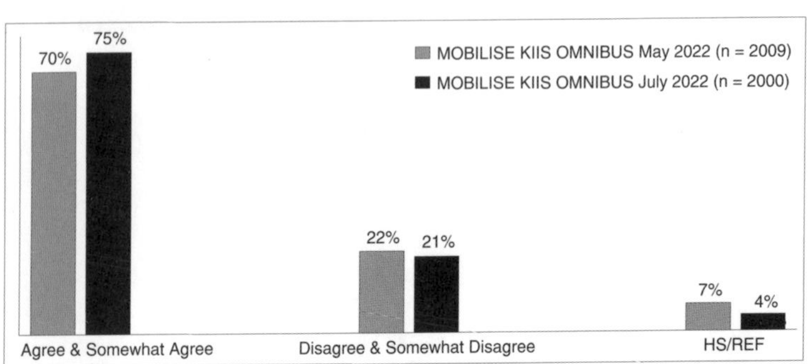

Authors' calculations. Data source: MOBILISE KIIS Omnibus May and July 2022.[54]

APPENDIX OF FIGURES

Figure 8.4. Which Politician Is Most Competent to...

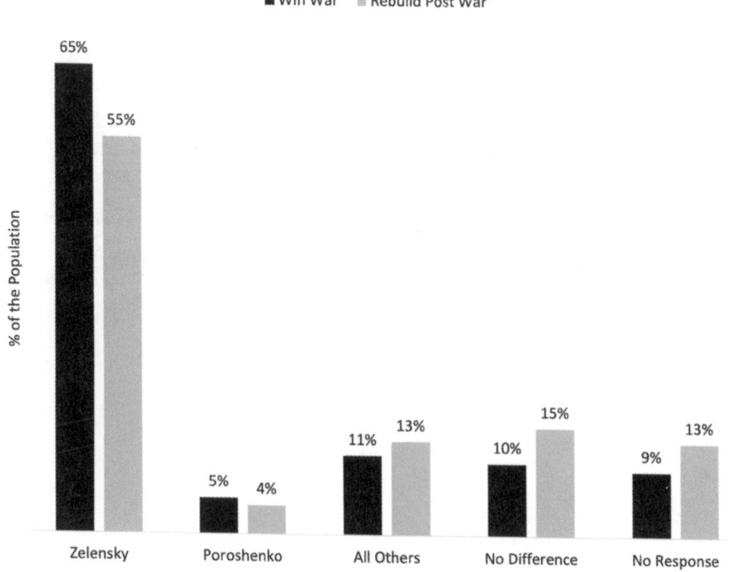

Authors' calculations. Data source: MOBILISE KIIS Omnibus July 2022.[55]

Figure 8.5. Does Zelensky Have the Following Traits?

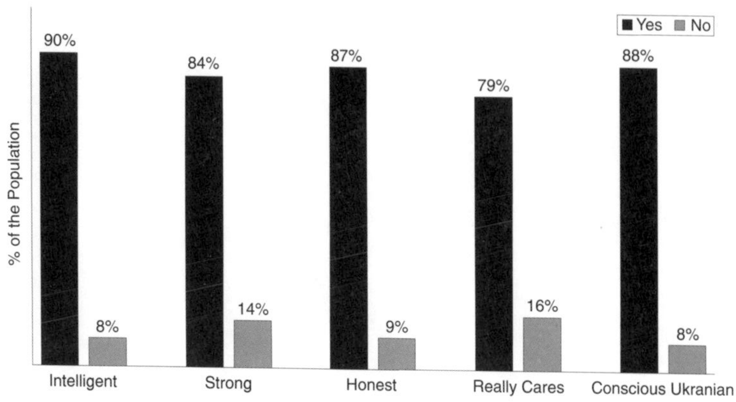

Authors' calculations. Data source: MOBILISE KIIS Omnibus July 2022.[56]

Figure 8.6. Which Words Best Describe Your Attitude to Zelensky?

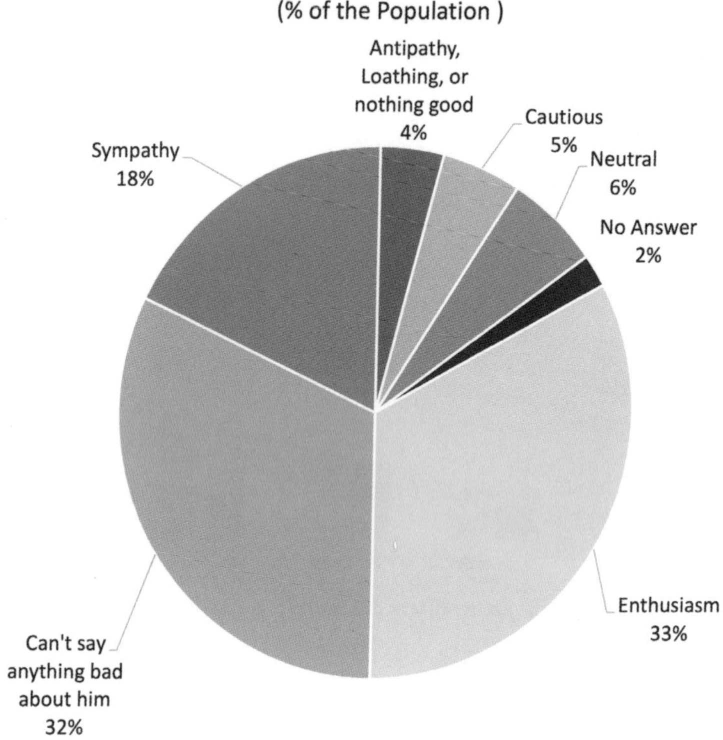

NOTES

1. GLOBAL HERO

1. Office of President of Ukraine,"The more Russia uses terror against Ukraine, the worse the consequences will be for it—address by President Volodymyr Zelenskyy," Official Website of the President of Ukraine, 20 March 2022, https://www.president.gov.ua/news/sho-bilshe-rosiya-zastosovuye-teroru-proti-ukrayini-girshi-n-73685
2. Office of the President of Ukraine, "Address by the President of Ukraine," Official Website of the President of Ukraine, 24 February 2022, https://www.president.gov.ua/en/news/zvernennya-prezidenta-ukrayini-73137
3. Dmytro Hordon, "Zelens'kyy," gordonua.com, 26 December 2018, 10:31, https://gordonua.com/ukr/publications/zelenskyi-yakshcho-mene-oberut-prezydentom-spochatku-budut-polyvaty-brudom-potim-povazhaty-a-potim-plakaty-koly-pidu-609294.html
4. Office of President of Ukraine, "Zelensky Speech: Ukrainian President's Last Appeal to Russian Public before Invasion Began," *Foreign Policy*, 23 February 2022, https://foreignpolicy.com/2022/02/23/zelenskys-desperate-plea-for-peace
5. While we wrote this book quickly in the immediate aftermath of Russia's 2022 invasion, it is based on decades of research each author has conducted on and in Ukraine, as well as Olga Onuch's personal experiences as a Ukrainian. We were also able to conduct considerable additional research in the time between the idea for this book emerged and publication. For a detailed description of our data and many of the analyses we rely upon, see our online appendices available at www.zelenskyeffect.com
6. Glenn Kessler, "Zelensky's Famous Quote of 'Need Ammo, Not a Ride' Not Easily Confirmed," *Washington Post*, 6 March 2022, https://www.washingtonpost.com/politics/2022/03/06/zelenskys-famous-quote-need-ammo-not-ride-not-easily-confirmed

7. Manveen Rana, "Volodymyr Zelensky Survives Three Assassination Attempts in Days," *The Times*, 3 March 2022, https://www.thetimes.co.uk/article/zelensky-survives-three-assassination-attempts-in-days-xnstdfdfc; Namita Singh, "Zelensky Has Survived More than a Dozen Assassination Attempts, Adviser Claims," *The Independent*, 10 March 2022, https://www.independent.co.uk/news/world/europe/ukraine-zelensky-assassination-attempts-russia-b2032759.html
8. "National Poll: Ukraine during the War (February 26–27, 2022)," Rating Group, 27 February 2022, http://ratinggroup.ua/en/research/ukraine/obschenacionalnyy_opros_ukraina_v_usloviyah_voyny_26-27_fevralya_2022_goda.html; "National Poll: Ukraine at War (March 1, 2022)," Rating Group, 1 March 2022, http://ratinggroup.ua/en/research/ukraine/obschenacionalnyy_opros_ukraina_v_usloviyah_voyny_1_marta_2022.html
9. We employed Way Back Time Machine to trace this development: https://web.archive.org/web/20190507152644/https://twitter.com/ZelenskyyUa/
10. See www.dataforukraine.com
11. Olga Onuch, David Doyle, Evelyn Ersanilli, Gwendolyn Sasse, Sorana Toma, and Jacquelien Van Stekelenburg, "MOBILISE 2022: Ukrainian Nationally Representative Survey, KIIS OMNIBUS May; (N=2009)," 24 May 2022.
12. Robert Putnam, *Making Democracy Work* (Princeton: Princeton University Press, 1993).
13. Olga Onuch, David Doyle, Evelyn Ersanilli, Gwendolyn Sasse, Sorana Toma, and Jacquelien Van Stekelenburg, "MOBILISE 2022: Ukrainian Nationally Representative Survey Wave Three; Version 2 (with Oversample, N=1218)," 16 February 2022.
14. Alexander J. Motyl, "Ukraine's Novice President Is in Serious Trouble Already," Atlantic Council (blog), 5 March 2020, https://www.atlanticcouncil.org/blogs/ukrainealert/ukraines-novice-president-is-in-serious-trouble-already; Motyl, "Ukraine's Pretend President Now Faces a Real Test," *Foreign Policy* (blog), 22 April 2019, https://foreignpolicy.com/2019/04/22/ukraines-pretend-president-now-faces-a-real-test; Alexander Motyl and Adrian Karatnycky, "Volodymyr Zelensky's Moment of Reckoning," *The American Interest* (blog), 19 May 2020, https://www.the-american-interest.com/2020/05/19/volodymyr-zelenskys-moment-of-reckoning; Nina L. Khrushcheva, "Ukraine Sends in the Clown," *Project Syndicate*, 30 April 2019, https://www.project-syndicate.org/commentary/ukraine-election-zelensky-trump-by-nina-l-khrushcheva-2019–04
15. Alisa Sopova, "Opinion: Maybe We'll Be Better Off with a Clown as President," *New York Times*, 18 April 2019, https://www.nytimes.com/2019/04/18/opinion/ukraine-election-clown-president.html; Dmytro Gorshkov and Olga Shylenko, "Zelensky: Ukrainian Clown or Political Wonder Boy?," *Times of*

Israel, 20 April 2019, https://www.timesofisrael.com/zelensky-ukrainian-clown-or-political-wonder-boy; "Ukrainian 'Clown' Zelensky Leading Polls Ahead of Presidential Vote," *Bangkok Post*, 8 February 2019, https://www.bangkokpost.com/world/1626022/ukrainian-clown-zelensky-leading-polls-ahead-of-presidential-vote; Tamila Varshalomidze, "Comedian Wins Ukraine's Presidential Vote," *Al Jazeera*, 22 April 2019, https://www.aljazeera.com/news/2019/4/22/volodymyr-zelenskyy-wins-ukraines-presidential-vote; Volodymyr Zelensky, interview, "Volodymyr Zelenskyy: 1 kvitnya—ofihennyy den' dlya peremohy klouna," *Ukrayins'ka Pravda*, 21 January 2019, 06:00, https://www.pravda.com.ua/articles/2019/01/21/7204341

16. William Jay Risch, "Who's Laughing Now? What Volodymyr Zelensky's Presidential Win May Mean for Ukraine Studies," *NewsNet: News of the Association for Slavic*, East European and Eurasian Studies 59, no. 3 (June 2019): 2–7.
17. Michael Bociurkiw, "Opinion: The Dangers of Electing a Comedian as President," CNN.com [italicize, 11 February 2022, https://www.cnn.com/2022/02/11/opinions/ukraine-president-zelensky-comedian-russia-bociurkiw/index.html; Anthony Lloyd, "Ukraine 'Must Act like Churchill to Face Russia' Says Former President," *The Times*, 27 January 2022, https://www.thetimes.co.uk/article/ukraine-must-act-like-churchill-to-face-russia-says-poroshenko-after-being-charged-with-high-treason-5fd0z7k5l; "Ukraine's Former President Accuses Kyiv of Risking National Unity," *Financial Times*, 21 December 2021; Olga Rudenko, "The Comedian-Turned-President Is Seriously in Over His Head," *New York Times*, 21 February 2022, https://www.nytimes.com/2022/02/21/opinion/ukraine-russia-zelensky-putin.html
18. Peter Baker, "Trump Acknowledges Discussing Biden in Call with Ukrainian Leader," *New York Times*, 22 September 2019, https://www.nytimes.com/2019/09/22/us/politics/trump-ukraine-biden.html; Renato Mariotti, "Trump Didn't Bribe Ukraine: It's Actually Worse Than That," *Politico Magazine*, 21 September 2019, https://politi.co/2VhS1Rn; Desmond Butler, "AP Sources: Ukraine's Zelensky Was Feeling Pressure from Trump Administration," *PBS NewsHour*, 18 November 2019, https://www.pbs.org/newshour/politics/ap-sources-ukraines-zelensky-was-feeling-pressure-from-trump-administration; Greg Sargent, "Opinion: Five Vile Things Trump Did to Zelensky and Ukraine That You Forgot About," *Washington Post*, 1 March 2022, https://www.washingtonpost.com/opinions/2022/03/01/vindman-zelensky-ukraine-putin; "Trump Impeachment: The Short, Medium and Long Story," *BBC News*, 5 February 2020, https://www.bbc.com/news/world-us-canada-49800181
19. Dimitry Medvedev, "Why Contacts with the Current Ukrainian Leadership Are Pointless," *Kommersant*, 11 October 2021, https://www.kommersant.ru/doc/5028300

20. "Lavrov Calls Ukraine's Zelensky 'Unstable,' Capable of 'Anything,'" *TASS*, 22 February 2022, https://tass.com/world/1408421
21. Joe Middleton, "Putin Tells Ukrainian Military to 'Take Power into Own Hands' and Overthrow Zelensky," *The Independent*, 25 February 2022, https://www.independent.co.uk/news/world/europe/putin-ukraine-zelensky-army-russia-speech-b2023350.html
22. Henry E. Hale, *Patronal Politics: Eurasian Regime Dynamics in Comparative Perspective* (New York: Cambridge University Press, 2015).
23. Ibid.
24. Erik S. Herron, *Normalizing Corruption: Failures of Accountability in Ukraine* (Ann Arbor: University of Michigan Press, 2020).
25. Henry E. Hale, "Ukraine: The Uses of Divided Power," *Journal of Democracy* 21, no. 3 (July 2010): 84–98.
26. Olga Onuch, *Mapping Mass Mobilization: Understanding Revolutionary Moments in Ukraine and Argentina* (London: Palgrave MacMillan, 2014).
27. Onuch, *Mapping Mass Mobilization*; Olga Onuch, "'Maidans and Movements: Legacies, Innovations, and Contention in Independent Ukraine," in *The Power of Populism and People: Resistance and Protest in the Modern World*, ed. Nathan Stoltzfus and Christopher Osmar (London: Bloomsbury Academic, 2021).
28. Ruth Berins Collier and David Collier, *Shaping the Political Arena: Critical Junctures, the Labor Movement, and Regime Dynamics in Latin America* (Princeton: Princeton University Press, 1991).
29. Emily Channell-Justice, Emily. 2022. *Without the State: Self-Organization and Political Activism in Ukraine* (Toronto: University of Toronto Press, 2022); Tetyana Lokot, *Beyond the Protest Square: Digital Media and Augmented Dissent* (Lanham, Maryland: Rowman & Littlefield, 2021).
30. Mykola Riabchuk, "Ukraine: One State, Two Countries," *Transit* 23 (2002), https://www.eurozine.com/ukraine-one-state-two-countries; Riabchuk, "Two Ukraines?" *East European Reporter* 5, no. 4 (1992); Andrej N. Lushnycky and Mykola Riabchuk, eds, *Ukraine on Its Meandering Path Between East and West* (New York: Peter Lang, 2009).
31. Pollsters and scholars typically identify four regions, east, west, south, and center. In the simplified and less formal discourse we discuss here, the "East" consists of what scholars and pollsters call east and south while the "West" comprises the west and center. When testing and controlling for posited macro-regional patterns, we follow KIIS's delineation: Western macro-region: Volynska, Zakarpatska, Ivano-Frankivska, Lvivska, Rivnenska, Ternopilska, Khmelnytska, Chernivetska oblasts; Central macro-region: Kyiv city and Kyivska, Vynnytska, Zhytomyrska, Kirovohradska, Poltavska, Sumska, Cherkaska, Chernihivska oblasts; Southern macro-region: Dnipropetrovska,

Zaporizhzhska, Mykolayivska, Odeska, Khersonska oblasts; Eastern macro-region: Kharkivska, Donetska, Luhanska oblasts.

32. Rebecca Kaplan, "Ukraine Crisis: A Look at the Country's Internal Divisions," *CBS News*, 4 March 2014, https://www.cbsnews.com/news/a-look-at-ukraines-internal-divisions; Jana Kobzova and Svitlana Kobzar, "The Partition of Ukraine," *RAND*, 17 April 2014, https://www.rand.org/blog/2014/04/the-partition-of-ukraine.html; Yegor Grygorenko, "Is Ukraine Divided?," *VoxUkraine*, 14 March 2014, https://voxukraine.org/en/83; "Ukraine's Sharp Divisions," *BBC News*, 23 April 2014, https://www.bbc.com/news/world-europe-26387353; Glenn Kates, "Ukraine's East–West Divide: It's Not That Simple," *RFE/RL*, 27 February 2014, https://www.rferl.org/a/ukraine-east-west-divide/25279292.html; Brian Whitmore, "Is It Time for Ukraine to Split Up?," *The Atlantic*, 20 February 2014, https://www.theatlantic.com/international/archive/2014/02/is-it-time-for-ukraine-to-split-up/283967; Shaun Walker, "Ukraine: Tale of Two Nations for Country Locked in Struggle over Whether to Face East or West," *The Observer*, 15 December 2013, https://www.theguardian.com/world/2013/dec/15/ukraine-protests-analysis-two-nations
33. Roger B. Myerson and Robert J. Weber, "A Theory of Voting Equilibria," *American Political Science Review* 87, no. 1 (1993): 102–14; Thomas Romer and Howard Rosenthal, "The Elusive Median Voter," *Journal of Public Economics* 12, no. 2 (1979): 143–70; Randall G. Holcombe, "The Median Voter Model in Public Choice Theory," *Public Choice* 61, no. 2 (1989): 115–25.
34. Richard Sakwa, *Frontline Ukraine: Crisis in the Borderlands* (London: Bloomsbury, 2014).
35. See: Dominique Arel and Valeri Khmelko, "The Russian Factor and Territorial Polarization in Ukraine," *Harriman Review*, no. 9 (1996): 81–91; Elizabeth A. Clark and Dmytro Vovk, "'The Orthodox Identification of Militants Is an Element of Their Understanding of the Russkiy Mir': Interview with Dr. Ihor Kozlovsky 1," in *Religion during the Russian–Ukrainian Conflict*, eds. Elizabeth A. Clark and Dmytro Vovk (New York: Routledge, 2019), 213–18; Keith Darden and Anna Grzymala-Busse, "The Great Divide: Literacy, Nationalism, and the Communist Collapse," *World Politics* 59, no. 1 (October 2006): 83–115; Serhiy Kudelia and Johanna van Zyl, "In My Name: The Impact of Regional Identity on Civilian Attitudes in the Armed Conflict in Donbas," *Nationalities Papers* 47, no. 5 (2019): 801–21; John O'Loughlin, Gerard Toal, and Vladimir Kolosov, "Who Identifies with the 'Russian World'? Geopolitical Attitudes in Southeastern Ukraine, Crimea, Abkhazia, South Ossetia, and Transnistria," *Eurasian Geography and Economics* 57, no. 6 (November 2016): 745–78; "'Nobody Wants Us': The Alienated Civilians of Eastern Ukraine," *Crisis Group*, 1 October 2018, https://www.crisisgroup.org/europe-central-asia/eastern-

europe/ukraine/252-nobody-wants-us-alienated-civilians-eastern-ukraine; Daniel J. Mitchell, "Ukraine, Ethnic Division, Decentralization, and Secession," *Forbes*, 3 March 2014, https://www.forbes.com/sites/danielmitchell/2014/03/03/ukraine-ethnic-division-decentralization-and-secession

36. A similar point is made by Taras Kuzio, "Russia-Ukraine Crisis: The Blame Game, Geopolitics and National Identity," *Europe-Asia Studies* 70, no. 3 (2018): 462–473.
37. David L. Stern, "Ukraine's Zelensky Alleges Russia Plotting Coup against Him for Next Week," *Washington Post*, 26 November 2021, https://www.washingtonpost.com/world/europe/ukraine-zelensky-russia-coup/2021/11/26/16e51c80–4e0d-11ec-a7b8–9ed28bf23929_story.html; "Ukraine–Russia Conflict: Zelensky Alleges Coup Plan Involving Russians—BBC News," *BBC News*, 26 November 2021, https://www.bbc.co.uk/news/world-europe-59428712; "SBU Says Probe Launched into Alleged Coup Plot," *UkrInform*, 10 November 2021, https://www.ukrinform.net/rubric-polytics/3359831-sbu-says-probe-launched-into-alleged-coup-plot.html
38. James Youniss, Jeffrey A. McLellan, and Miranda Yates, "What We Know about Engendering Civic Identity," *American Behavioral Scientist* 40, no. 5 (1997): 620–31; Miranda Yates and James Youniss, eds, *Roots of Civic Identity: International Perspectives on Community Service and Activism in Youth* (Cambridge: Cambridge University Press, 1999); Charles Tilly, "Citizenship, Identity and Social History," *International Review of Social History* 40, no. S3 (1995): 1–17; Chantal Mouffe, "Citizenship and Political Identity," *October* 61 (1992): 28–32; Lynn Jamieson, "Theorising Identity, Nationality and Citizenship: Implications for European Citizenship Identity," *Sociológia: Slovak Sociological Review* 34, no. 6 (2002): 506–32.
39. Henry E. Hale, "Explaining Ethnicity," *Comparative Political Studies* 37, no. 4 (2004): 458–85, https://doi.org/10.1177/0010414003262906
40. Henry E. Hale, *The Foundations of Ethnic Politics: Separatism of States and Nations in Eurasia and the World* (New York: Cambridge University Press, 2008).
41. Robert Hariman and John Louis Lucaites, "Performing Civic Identity: The Iconic Photograph of the Flag Raising on Iwo Jima," *Quarterly Journal of Speech* 88, no. 4 (2002): 363–92.
42. Maxwell McCombs and Paula Poindexter, "The Duty to Keep Informed: News Exposure and Civic Obligation," *Journal of Communication* 33, no. 2 (1983): 88–96; Aaron C. Weinschenk, "Personality Traits and the Sense of Civic Duty," *American Politics Research* 42, no. 1 (2014): 90–113; William H. Riker and Peter C. Ordeshook, "A Theory of the Calculus of Voting," *American Political Science Review* 62, no. 1 (1968): 25–42; Joel Westheimer and Joseph Kahne, "Educating the 'Good' Citizen: Political Choices and Pedagogical Goals," *PS: Political Science & Politics* 37, no. 2 (2004): 241–7; Russell J. Dalton, *The Good Citizen: How*

a Younger Generation Is Reshaping American Politics (Washington, DC: CQ Press, 2015); Vera Vogelsang-Coombs and Larry Bakken, "Dynamic Interpretations of Civic Duty: Implications for Governance," *International Journal of Organization Theory & Behavior* 6, no. 3 (2003): 442–60; Loren E. Lomasky and Geoffrey Brennan, "Is There a Duty to Vote?" *Social Philosophy and Policy* 17, no. 1 (2000): 62–86; André Blais and Carol Galais, "Measuring the Civic Duty to Vote: A Proposal," *Electoral Studies* 41 (2016): 60–9; Fernando Feitosa and Carol Galais, "How Stable Is the Sense of Civic Duty to Vote? A Panel Study on the Individual-Level Stability of the Attitude," *International Journal of Public Opinion Research* 32, no. 2 (2020): 344–53.

43. Lowell Barrington, "Citizenship as a Cornerstone of Civic National Identity in Ukraine," *Post-Soviet Affairs* 37, no. 2 (2021): 155–73; Barrington, "A New Look at Region, Language, Ethnicity and Civic National Identity in Ukraine," *Europe-Asia Studies* 74, no. 3 (2022): 360–81; Barrington, "Is the Regional Divide in Ukraine an Identity Divide?," *Eurasian Geography and Economics* 63, no. 4 (2021): 465–90; Lowell Barrington and Erik S. Herron, "One Ukraine or Many? Regionalism in Ukraine and Its Political Consequences," *Nationalities Papers* 32, no. 1 (2004): 53–86; Gwendolyn Sasse and Alice Lackner, "War and Identity: The Case of the Donbas in Ukraine," *Post-Soviet Affairs* 34, nos. 2–3 (May 2018): 139–157.; Gwendolyn Sasse, "The Role of Regionalism," *Journal of Democracy* 21, no. 3 (2010): 99–106; Olga Onuch and Henry E. Hale, "Capturing Ethnicity: The Case of Ukraine," *Post-Soviet Affairs* 34, nos. 2–3 (2018): 84–106; Olga Onuch, Henry E. Hale, and Gwendolyn Sasse, "Studying Identity in Ukraine," *Post-Soviet Affairs* 34, nos. 2–3 (2018): 79–83; Grigore Pop-Eleches and Graeme B. Robertson, "Identity and Political Preferences in Ukraine: Before and After the Euromaidan," *Post-Soviet Affairs* 34, nos. 2–3 (2018): 107–18.

44. Volodymyr Kulyk, "Language Identity, Linguistic Diversity and Political Cleavages: Evidence from Ukraine," *Nations and Nationalism* 17, no. 3 (2011): 627–48; Kulyk, "National Identity in Ukraine: Impact of Euromaidan and the War," *Europe-Asia Studies* 68, no. 4 (2016): 588–608; Kulyk, "Identity in Transformation: Russian-Speakers in Post-Soviet Ukraine," *Europe-Asia Studies* 71, no. 1 (2017): 1–23; Kulyk, "Language Identity, Linguistic Diversity and Political Cleavages: Evidence from Ukraine," *Nations and Nationalism* 17, no. 3 (2011): 627–48.

45. Volodymyr Kulyk, "Shedding Russianness, Recasting Ukrainianness: The Post-Euromaidan Dynamics of Ethnonational Identifications in Ukraine," *Post-Soviet Affairs* 34, no. 2–3 (2018): 119–38.

46. Olga Onuch, *Mapping Mass Mobilization*; Olga Onuch and Gilles Serra, "The Protest Calculus: Why Ordinary People Join in Post-Electoral Protests," Working paper presented at a Nuffield College Workshop, Nuffield College,

Oxford, UK (November 2010); Onuch, "Why Did They Join En Masse? Understanding 'Ordinary' Ukrainians' Participation in Mass-Mobilisation in 2004," *New Ukraine/Nowa Ukraina* 11 (2011): 89–113; Onuch, "The Maidan Past and Present: Euromaidan and the Orange Revolution," in *Ukraine's Euromaidan*, eds. David R. Marples and Frederick V. Mills (New York: Columbia University Press, 2015).

47. John E. Mueller, *War, Presidents and Public Opinion* (New York: John Wiley & Sons, 1973).
48. William D. Baker and John R. Oneal, "Patriotism or Opinion Leadership? The Nature and Origins of the 'Rally Round the Flag' Effect," *Journal of Conflict Resolution* 45, no. 5 (2001): 661–87; Adam J. Berinsky, *In Time of War: Understanding American Public Opinion from World War II to Iraq* (Chicago: University of Chicago Press, 2009); Marc J. Hetherington and Michael Nelson, "Anatomy of a Rally Effect: George W. Bush and the War on Terrorism," *PS: Political Science and Politics* 36, no. 1 (2003): 37–42.
49. Henry E. Hale, "Authoritarian Rallying as Reputational Cascade? Evidence from Putin's Popularity Surge after Crimea," *American Political Science Review* 116, no. 2 (2021): 1–15.
50. Samuel A. Greene and Graeme B. Robertson, *Putin v. the People: The Perilous Politics of a Divided Russia* (New Haven: Yale University Press, 2019).
51. Gulnaz Sharafutdinova, *The Red Mirror: Putin's Leadership and Russia's Insecure Identity* (Oxford: Oxford University Press, 2020).
52. Paul B. Baltes, "Longitudinal and Cross-Sectional Sequences in the Study of Age and Generation Effects," *Human Development* 11, no. 3 (1968): 145–71; Gosta Carlsson and Katarina Karlsson, "Age, Cohorts and the Generation of Generations," *American Sociological Review* 35, no. 4 (1970): 710–18; Neal E. Cutler and Vern L. Bengtson, "Age and Political Alienation: Maturation, Generation and Period Effects," *Annals of the American Academy of Political and Social Science* 415, no. 1 (1974): 160–75.
53. Anja Neundorf and Kaat Smets, "Political Socialization and the Making of Citizens," *Oxford Handbook Topics in Politics*, online edn, 6 August 2015, https://doi.org/10.1093/oxfordhb/9780199935307.013.98; Marc Hooghe and Dietlind Stolle, "Age Matters: Life-Cycle and Cohort Differences in the Socialisation Effect of Voluntary Participation," *European Political Science* 3, no. 2 (2003): 49–56; Grigore Pop-Eleches and Joshua A. Tucker, *Communism's Shadow: Historical Legacies and Contemporary Political Attitudes* (Princeton: Princeton University Press, 2017).

2. THE INDEPENDENCE GENERATION

1. "The more Russia uses terror against Ukraine, the worse the consequences will be for it—address by President Volodymyr Zelenskyy."

2. Office of President of Ukraine, "Address by the President to Ukrainians at the End of the First Day of Russia's Attacks," Official Website of the President of Ukraine, 25 February 2022, https://www.president.gov.ua/en/news/zvernennya-prezidenta-do-ukrayinciv-naprikinci-pershogo-dnya-73149
3. We employ the translations of dialogue from the Servant of the People series as it appears in the English language subtitles found in the version of the show streamed on Netflix.
4. Olga Onuch, "'Maidans and Movements."
5. Mark Beissinger, *Nationalist Mobilization and the Collapse of the Soviet State: A Tidal Approach to the Study of Nationalism* (Cambridge: Cambridge University Press, 2002); Vladimir Paniotto, "The Ukrainian Movement for Perestroika—'Rukh': A Sociological Survey," *Soviet Studies* 43, no. 1 (1991): 177–81.
6. Office of President of Ukraine, "Speech by President Volodymyr Zelensky on the Occasion of the 30th Anniversary of Ukraine's Independence," Official Website of the President of Ukraine, 24 August 2021, https://www.president.gov.ua/en/news/promova-prezidenta-volodimira-zelenskogo-z-nagodi-30-yi-rich-70333
7. It is in part for you all that we write this book!
8. Office of the President of Ukraine, "Speech by the President of Ukraine during the Independence Day Festivities," Official Website of the President of Ukraine, 4 August 2019, https://www.president.gov.ua/en/news/vistup-prezidenta-ukrayini-pid-chas-urochistostej-z-nagodi-d-56937
9. Valerie Bunce, "The Political Economy of the Brezhnev Era: The Rise and Fall of Corporatism," *British Journal of Political Science* 13, no. 2 (1983): 129–58; Stephen Kotkin, *Armageddon Averted: The Soviet Collapse, 1970–2000* (New York: Oxford University Press, 2008).
10. "Sixtiers," Kharkiv Human Rights Protection Group, Virtual Museum, Virtual Museum of the Dissident Movement in Ukraine (2004), http://archive.khpg.org/index.php?id=1162803362
11. "Ukrainskyy Visnyk," Kharkiv Human Rights Protection Group, 2004, http://archive.khpg.org/en/index.php?id=1127288239
12. Although not a binding treaty, the Helsinki Final Act (or Helsinki Accords or Helsinki Declaration) is the result of several years of negotiations (called the Helsinki Process) and includes a series of documents finalized and signed in August 1975 at the Conference on Security and Co-operation in Europe, which was held in Helsinki. A. M. Rusnachenko, *The National Liberation Movement in Ukraine* (Kyiv: O. Teliha Publishing, 1998).
13. Kharkiv Human Rights Protection Group, interviews by the Kharkiv Human Rights Protection Group of individuals involved in the Ukrainian Helsinki Group and/or the dissident movement, 2004, http://archive.khpg.org/en/index.php?r=17

14. Bohdan Krawchenko et al., *Ukraine after Shelest* (Edmonton: Canadian Institute of Ukrainian Studies, University of Alberta, 1983).
15. Osyp Zinkevych, "Ukrainian Helsinki Group," in *Encyclopedia of Ukraine*, vol. 5, 1993, http://www.encyclopediaofukraine.com/display.asp?linkpath=pages%5CU%5CK%5CUkrainianHelsinkiGroup.htm
16. Hordon, "Zelens'kyy."
17. Olga Onuch, *Mapping Mass Mobilization: Understanding Revolutionary Moments in Ukraine and Argentina* (London: Palgrave MacMillan, 2014).
18. Anatoliy Dol′chuk, "Chervnevi podiyi 1963 roku v Kryvomu Rozi," *Maidan-INFORM*, 23 January 2007, https://maidan.org.ua/static/mai/1169503541.html
19. Office of the President, "The More Russia Uses Terror against Ukraine, the Worse the Consequences for It."
20. Marko Robert Stech, "Holoborodko, Vasyl," in *Encyclopedia of Ukraine*, 2007, http://encyclopediaofukraine.com/display.asp?AddButton=pagesHOHoloborodkoVasyl.htm
21. Onuch, *Mapping Mass Mobilization*; Onuch, "'Maidans and Movements"; Onuch, "Maidans Past and Present: Comparing the Orange Revolution and the EuroMaidan," in *Euromaidan*, ed. David Marples (London: Columbia University Press, 2015); Onuch, "The Revolution on the Granite (1990): The Legacy Contention in Independent Ukraine," *New Eastern Europe*, 2017.
22. Anton Drannik, "'Sozdatelyam 'Slugi naroda' ya dolzhen butylku'—Vasyl' Goloborod'ko," *Vesti UA*, 19 April 2019, 06:00, https://vesti.ua/strana/333315-sozdateljam-sluhi-naroda-ja-dolzhen-butylku-vasyl-holoborodko; Roman Grivinskii, "Istorik protiv 'matematikov,'" *Den'*, 16 November 2015, 13:58, https://day.kyiv.ua/ru/article/media/istorik-protiv-matematikov; *Kinopoisk*, https://www.kinopoisk.ru/series/942397/, accessed 25 August 2022; Vladimir Runets, "'Menia zovut Tot, U Kogo Ukrali Imia," *Nastoyashchee Vremya*, 14 April 2019, 08:36, https://www.currenttime.tv/a/goloborodko-poet-zelensky-tv-ukraine-surname/29877307.html
23. Stanislav Markus and Volha Charnysh, "The Flexible Few: Oligarchs and Wealth Defense in Developing Democracies," *Comparative Political Studies* 50, no. 12 (2017): 1632–65; Stanislav Markus, *Property, Predation, and Protection* (Cambridge University Press, 2015).
24. Sergei I. Zhuk, *Rock and Roll in the Rocket City: The West, Identity, and Ideology in Soviet Dniepropetrovsk, 1960–1985* (Baltimore, MD: Johns Hopkins University Press, 2017).
25. "Poverty Headcount Ratio at $1.90 a Day (2011 PPP) (% of Population)," World Bank, 2022, https://data.worldbank.org/indicator/SI.POV.DDAY?locations=UA

26. "Intentional Homicides (per 100,000 People)," World Bank, 2022, https://data.worldbank.org/indicator/VC.IHR.PSRC.P5?locations=UA
27. Elizabeth Brainerd, "Winners and Losers in Russia's Economic Transition," *American Economic Review* 88, no. 5 (1998): 1094–116; Joshua A. Tucker, Alexander C. Pacek, and Adam J. Berinsky, "Transitional Winners and Losers: Attitudes toward EU Membership in Post-Communist Countries," *American Journal of Political Science* 46, no. 3 (2002): 557–71.
28. Vlad Mykhnenko, "State, Society and Protest under Post-Communism: Ukrainian Miners and Their Defeat," in *Uncivil Society? Contentious Politics in Post-Communist Europe*, ed. Cas Mudde and Petr Kopecký (London: Routledge, 2005), 89, 105–25. For more on workers' contention in the 1980s see: David R. Marples, *Ukraine under Perestroika: Ecology, Economics and the Workers' Revolt* (Alberta: University of Alberta Press, 1991).
29. Alyona Vyshnytska, Anastasia Vlasova, and Vladyslav Kudryk, "Strike: Donbas Miners Recall Protests of the '90s," *Hromadske International*, 23 September 2019, https://en.hromadske.ua/posts/strike-donbas-miners-recall-protests-of-the-90s
30. Maksym Kazakov, "How Workers in Ukraine's Metal Industry Are Fighting for Wages, Rights and Democracy," *Open Democracy*, 4 June 2018, https://www.opendemocracy.net/en/odr/how-workers-in-ukraine-metal-industry-are-fighting-for-wages-rights-democracy
31. "Population, Total: Ukraine," World Bank, 2022, https://data.worldbank.org/indicator/SP.POP.TOTL?locations=UA
32. "Kryvyi Rih Population 2022 (Demographics, Maps, Graphs)," *World Population Review*, 2022, https://worldpopulationreview.com/world-cities/kryvyi-rih-population
33. "Wayback Time Machine Archive of 'Oleksandr Semenovych Zelensky, Kryvyy Rih Economic Institute,'" Kryvyy Rih Economic Institute, https://web.archive.org/web/20190107072148/http://www.kneu.dp.ua/zelenskij-oleksandr-semenovich
34. Office of the President of Ukraine, "Speech of the President of Ukraine Volodymyr Zelensky at the 16th Annual Meeting of the Yalta European Strategy" [authors' translation], Official Website of the President of Ukraine, 13 September 2019, https://www.president.gov.ua/news/vistup-prezidenta-ukrayini-volodimira-zelenskogo-na-16-j-sho-57257
35. Central Election Commission, "Presidential Election Reports, 1991–2014," 2014, http://www.cvk.gov.ua
36. Hordon, "Zelens'kyy."
37. Ibid.
38. Office of the President of Ukraine, "Address by the President Following the Meeting of the National Security and Defense Council," Official Website of

the President of Ukraine, 4 June 2021, https://www.president.gov.ua/en/news/zvernennya-glavi-derzhavi-za-rezultatami-zasidannya-radi-nac-68849

39. By "oligarch" in this book, we refer to big businesspeople who appear in a given country's political discourse.
40. Hale, *Patronal Politics*.
41. Zhuk, *Rock and Roll in the Rocket City*.
42. Ibid.
43. Agata Wierzbowska-Miazga and Tadeusz A. Olszański, "Poroshenko, President of Ukraine," OSW Centre for Eastern Studies, 28 May 2014, https://www.osw.waw.pl/en/publikacje/analyses/2014–05–28/poroshenko-president-ukraine
44. Ibid.
45. Paul D'Anieri, *Understanding Ukrainian Politics: Power, Politics, and Institutional Design* (Armonk, NY: M. E. Sharpe, 2006); Hale, *Patronal Politics*.
46. Faceless, nameless oligarchs, *Servant of the People*, Season 1, Episode 1
47. "Inaugural Speech of the President of Ukraine Volodymyr Zelensky," Office of the President of Ukraine, 20 May 2019, https://www.president.gov.ua/news/inavguracijna-promova-prezidenta-ukrayini-volodimira-zelensk-55489
48. Juliane Besters-Dilger, "The Ukrainian Language in Education and Mass Media," *Harvard Ukrainian Studies* 29, no. 1/4 (2007): 257–93.
49. Office of the President of Ukraine, "Speech by President Volodymyr Zelenskyy on the Occasion of the 30th Anniversary of Ukraine's Independence."
50. Oxana Shevel, "Nationality in Ukraine: Some Rules of Engagement," *East European Politics and Societies* 6, no. 2 (2002): 386–413; Kulyk, "Shedding Russianness"; Barrington, "Citizenship as a Cornerstone of Civic National Identity in Ukraine."
51. Onuch, *Mapping Mass Mobilization*; Benedetta Berti and Olga Onuch, "From the Colour Revolutions to the Arab Awakening: EU Approaches to Democracy Promotion and the Rising Influence of CEE States," in *Democratization in EU Foreign Policy: New Member States as Drivers of Democracy Promotion*, ed. Berti, Kristina Mikulova, and Nicu Popescu (London: Routledge, 2015); Olga Onuch, "Survey on Orange Revolution Protest Participation" (Nuffield College, Oxford: Ukrainian Protest Project, Funded by British Academy Newton Fellowship and John Fell Fund, 2010).
52. Kataryna Wolczuk, "Integration without Europeanisation: Ukraine and Its Policy towards the European Union" (European University Institute (EUI), Robert Schuman Centre of Advanced Studies (RSCAS), 2004), http://ideas.repec.org/p/erp/euirsc/p0133.html; Wolczuk, "Ukraine and the EU: Turning the Association Agreement into a Success Story," *European Policy Centre Policy Brief*, 23 April 2014," http://www.epc.eu/pub_details.php?cat_id=3&pub_id=4360&year=2014. For more on EU-Ukraine relations we recommend: Rilka Dragneva-Lewers and Kataryna Wolczuk, *Ukraine between the EU and Russia:*

The Integration Challenge (London: Springer, 2015). For how Ukrainians view the EU we recommend: Natalia Chaban and Anatoliy Chaban, "Communicating Europe beyond Its Borders: Imagining the EU in Ukraine Post-Maidan," *European Foreign Affairs Review* 23 (2018). For more on youth views of Ukraine's EU accession see: Olga Onuch and Cressida Arkwright, "Ukrainian Youth and Ukraine in Europe: A Cohort Analysis of the Drivers of Attitudes toward the EU," *Demokratizatsiya: The Journal of Post-Soviet Democratization* 29, no. 4 (2021): 409–448.

53. Serhii Plokhy, *The Gates of Europe: A History of Ukraine* (New York: Basic Books, 2015).
54. Hordon, "Zelens'kyy."
55. Ibid.
56. Ibid.
57. Ibid.
58. Ibid.
59. "Volodymyr Zelensky President of Ukraine," *Liga*, 24 January 2022, https://file.liga.net/persons/vladimir-zelenskii
60. Hordon, "Zelens'kyy."
61. Ibid.
62. Ibid.
63. "Old KVN 1961–1971," *Amik.Ru*, 27 July 2014, https://web.archive.org/web/20140727085404/http://www.amik.ru/page/8.html
64. "AMIK.RU—Kak eto vse opyat' nachinalos'. 1986 g.," *Amik.Ru*, 27 July 2014, https://web.archive.org/web/20140727074442/http://www.amik.ru/page/9.html
65. "Three Generations of Owners of the Ukrainian Media," Kharkiv Human Rights Protection Group, 2006, https://khpg.org//en/1154132546; Marta Dyczok and O. V. Gaman-Golutvina, *Media, Democracy and Freedom: The Post-Communist Experience* (New York: Peter Lang, 2009); Marta Dyczok, "Information Wars: Hegemony, Counter-Hegemony, Propaganda, the Use of Force, and Resistance," *Russian Journal of Communication* 6, no. 2 (2014): 1–4; Oleksiy Sorokin, "Oligarchs' TV Channels Give Away Owners' Presidential Choices: Mar. 29, 2019," *Kyiv Post*, 29 March 2019, https://www.kyivpost.com/ukraine-politics/oligarchs-tv-channels-give-away-owners-presidential-choices.html
66. Andrew Wilson, *Virtual Politics: Faking Democracy in the Post-Soviet World* (New Haven: Yale University Press, 2005).
67. Lucan Way, *Pluralism by Default: Weak Autocrats and the Rise of Competitive Politics* (Baltimore, MD: Johns Hopkins University Press, 2016).
68. Keith Darden, "Blackmail as a Tool of State Domination: Ukraine under Kuchma," *East European Constitutional Review* 10 (2001): 67–71.

69. Office of the President of Ukraine, "Address of the President of Ukraine Regarding the Unity of Ukrainian Society," Official Website of the President of Ukraine, 14 February 2022, https://www.president.gov.ua/en/news/zvernennya-prezidenta-ukrayini-shodo-yednosti-ukrayinskogo-s-72893
70. Onuch, *Mapping Mass Mobilization.*
71. Ibid.
72. Ibid.
73. Hordon, "Zelens'kyy."
74. Valerie Bunce and Sharon Wolchik, *Defeating Authoritarian Leaders in Postcommunist Countries* (Cambridge: Cambridge University Press, 2011); Paul D'Anieri, "Explaining the Success and Failure of Post-Communist Revolutions," *Communist and Post-Communist Studies* 39, no. 3 (2006): 331–350.
75. Onuch, *Mapping Mass Mobilization.*
76. Ibid.
77. "Ukraine Presidential Election: 31 October, 21 November and 26 December 2004, OSCE/ODIHR Election Observation Mission Final Report," Warsaw: Office for Democratic Institutions and Human Rights, OSCE, 11 May 2005.
78. Onuch, "Survey on Orange Revolution Protest Participation"; Olga Onuch, "Why Did They Join En Masse? Understanding 'Ordinary' Ukrainians' Participation in Mass-Mobilisation in 2004," *New Ukraine/Nowa Ukraina* 11 (2011): 89–113; Onuch, *Mapping Mass Mobilization*; journalist focus group Ukraine, 18 August 2008, NaUKMA, Kyiv. Ordinary citizens focus group Ukraine no. 2, 27 July 2009, NaUKMA, Kyiv.
79. Henry E. Hale, "Formal Constitutions in Informal Politics: Institutions and Democratization in Eurasia," *World Politics* 63, no. 4 (2011): 581–617.
80. "The Tenth Day of Resistance," *Ukrayins'ka Pravda*, 1 December 2004, https://www.pravda.com.ua/articles/2004/12/1/3004876
81. To Vadym, Tanya, Olesya, and Taras who sang this song in Bucha whilst discussing Borshch—we will do this again when Ukraine is free of its occupants!

3. ORANGE IS THE NEW CORRUPTION

1. Office of the President of Ukraine, "The More Russia Uses Terror against Ukraine, the Worse the Consequences for It."
2. Office of the President of Ukraine, "Address by the President of Ukraine," Official Website of the President of Ukraine, 25 February 2022, https://www.president.gov.ua/en/news/zvernennya-prezidenta-ukrayini-73165
3. Hordon, "Zelens'kyy."
4. Onuch, *Mapping Mass Mobilization.*

5. Onuch et al., "MOBILISE 2019: Ukrainian Nationally Representative Survey Wave One; Version 2 (with Oversample, N=2000)."
6. Hale et al., "Ukrainian Crisis Election Panel Survey (UCEPS)."
7. Olga Onuch, "Who Were the Protesters?," *Journal of Democracy* 25, no. 3 (2014): 44–51; Onuch, "Why Did They Join En Masse?"; Onuch and Serra, "The Protest Calculus."
8. Unnamed black Pora activist, 15 July 2009, author's interview.
9. Author's interview, unnamed yellow Pora activist, 13 July 2007; Author's interview, unnamed, yellow Pora activist, 13 August 2008; Author's interview, unnamed yellow Pora activist, and *Nasha Ukrayina* campaign coordinator in Kharkiv, 14 July 2007.
10. Taras Kuzio, "Rise and Fall of the Party of Regions Political Machine," *Problems of Post-Communism* 62, no. 3 (2015): 174–186.
11. Onuch, *Mapping Mass Mobilization.*
12. Author's interview, unnamed yellow Pora activist and journalist, 18 July 2007.
13. Hale, "Formal Constitutions in Informal Politics"; Onuch, *Mapping Mass Mobilization*, Chapters 7–8; unnamed Kuchma presidential administration insider, 7 July 2008, interview.
14. Author's interview, unnamed Polish embassy in Ukraine insider, 13 July 2008; Author's interview, unnamed Canadian Embassy in Ukraine insider, 13 September 2008.
15. Onuch, *Mapping Mass Mobilization.*
16. Hale and Orttung, *Beyond the Euromaidan.*
17. Hale, "Formal Constitutions in Informal Politics."
18. Hale, *Patronal Politics*; Bálint Magyar and Bálint Madlovics, *The Anatomy of Post-Communist Regimes: A Conceptual Framework* (Budapest: Central European University Press, 2021). These works build on pioneering work on the relationship between a related phenomenon, neopatrimonialism, and democracy by Oleksandr Fisun. See: Aleksandr A. Fisun, *Demokratiya, neopatrimonializm i global'nyye transformatsii* (Kharkiv: Konstant, 2007).
19. Hale, "Democracy or Autocracy on the March?"
20. Bunce and Wolchik, *Defeating Authoritarian Leaders in Postcommunist Countries.*
21. Bret Barrowman, "The Reformer's Dilemmas: The Politics of Public Sector Reform in Clientelistic Political Systems," PhD dissertation in political science, George Washington University, Washington, DC, 2015.
22. Ibid.
23. Moses Shayo, "A Model of Social Identity with an Application to Political Economy: Nation, Class, and Redistribution," *American Political Science Review* 103, no. 2 (2009): 147–174; Jaroslav Tir and Michael Jasinski, "Domestic-Level Diversionary Theory of War Targeting Ethnic Minorities," *Journal of Conflict Resolution* 52, no. 5 (2008): 641–664.

24. Hale, *Patronal Politics*; Yuri Matsievski, "Change, Transition, or Cycle: The Dynamics of Ukraine's Political Regime in 2004–2010," *Russian Politics and Law* 49, no. 5 (2011): 8–33; Maria Popova, "Political Competition as an Obstacle to Judicial Independence: Evidence from Russia and Ukraine," *Comparative Political Studies* 43, no. 10 (2010): 1202–1229.
25. Kataryna Wolczuk, "Managing the Flows of Gas and Rules: Ukraine between the EU and Russia," *Eurasian Geography and Economics* 57, no. 1 (2016): 113–37; Thijs Van de Graaf and Jeff D. Colgan, "Russian Gas Games or Well-Oiled Conflict? Energy Security and the 2014 Ukraine Crisis," *Energy Research & Social Science* 24 (2017): 59–64; Adam N. Stulberg, "Out of Gas?: Russia, Ukraine, Europe, and the Changing Geopolitics of Natural Gas," *Problems of Post-Communism* 62, no. 2 (2015): 112–30; Alexander Motyl, "Ukraine vs. Russia: The Politics of an Energy Crisis," *Insight Turkey*, 2005, 26–31; Margarita Mercedes Balmaceda, "Gas, Oil and the Linkages between Domestic and Foreign Policies: The Case of Ukraine," *Europe-Asia Studies* 50, no. 2 (1998): 257–86.
26. Margarita M. Balmaceda, *Russian Energy Chains: The Remaking of Technopolitics from Siberia to Ukraine to the European Union* (New York: Columbia University Press, 2021).
27. Toru Nagashima, "Russia's Passportization Policy toward Unrecognized Republics: Abkhazia, South Ossetia, and Transnistria," *Problems of Post-Communism* 66, no. 3 (2019): 186–99; Nagashima.
28. Gerard Toal, *Near Abroad: Putin, the West, and the Contest over Ukraine and the Caucasus* (Oxford: Oxford University Press, 2017).
29. Steven Erlanger and Steven Lee Myers, "NATO Allies Oppose Bush on Georgia and Ukraine," *The New York Times*, 3 April 2008, https://www.nytimes.com/2008/04/03/world/europe/03nato.htm
30. Stephen Sestanovich, "The Less Said About NATO and Ukraine, the Better," 30 March 2022, https://www.foreignaffairs.com/articles/russia-fsu/2022-02-16/less-said-about-nato-and-ukraine-better
31. UNIAN, "Poll Says Ukraine's President Should Step Down Now," 17 February 2009, https://www.unian.info/society/191796-poll-says-ukraines-president-should-step-down-now.html
32. Razumkov Center, "The Opinion of the Citizens of Ukraine about the Results of 2008 (Survey)," archive.ph, 26 December 2008, https://archive.ph/07XO
33. Central Election Commission, "Presidential Election Reports, 1991–2014."
34. Freedom House, *Freedom in the World 2007* (Lanham, MD: Rowman & Littlefield, 2007), https://freedomhouse.org/sites/default/files/2020–02/Freedom_in_the_World_2007_complete_book.pdf, accessed August 21, 2022.
35. Oleksandr Sushko and Olena Prystayko, "Nations in Transit 2013: Ukraine," *Nations in Transit* (Freedom House, 2013); Freedom House, "Ukraine in 2011:

Freedom House Report," 2011, https://freedomhouse.org/report/freedom-world/2011/ukraine

36. Peter H. Solomon Jr, "Post-Soviet Criminal Justice: The Persistence of Distorted Neo-Inquisitorialism," *Theoretical Criminology* 19, no. 2 (2015): 159–78; Peter H. Solomon Jr, "Law in Public Administration: How Russia Differs," *Journal of Communist Studies and Transition Politics* 24, no. 1 (2008): 115–35; Maria Popova, *Politicized Justice in Emerging Democracies: A Study of Courts in Russia and Ukraine* (Cambridge University Press, 2012); Maria Popova, "Political Competition as an Obstacle to Judicial Independence: Evidence from Russia and Ukraine," *Comparative Political Studies* 43, no. 10 (2010): 1202–29.
37. Office of the President of Ukraine, Speech of the President of Ukraine Volodymyr Zelensky at the 16th annual meeting of the Yalta European Strategy (Authors' own translation).
38. Staffan I. Lindberg et al., "V-Dem: A New Way to Measure Democracy," *Journal of Democracy* 25, no. 3 (2014): 159–69; Michael Coppedge et al., "V-Dem Comparisons and Contrasts with Other Measurement Projects," V-Dem Working Paper 45 (2017); Michael Coppedge et al., "V-Dem Dataset V10," 2020.
39. Oleksandr Fisun, "Rethinking Post-Soviet Politics from a Neopatrimonial Perspective," *Demokratizatsiya: The Journal of Post-Soviet Democratization* 20, no. 2 (2002): 87–96.
40. Uri Gordon, "Israel's 'Tent Protests': The Chilling Effect of Nationalism," *Social Movement Studies* 11, no. 3–4 (2012): 349–55.
41. Office of the President of Ukraine, "Inaugural speech of the President of Ukraine Volodymyr Zelensky."
42. Onuch et al., "MOBILISE 2019: Ukrainian Nationally Representative Survey Wave One; Version 2 (with Oversample, N=2000)."
43. Albert Hirschman, *Exit, Voice and Loyalty: Responses to Decline in Firms, Organizations, and States* (Harvard University Press, 1970); Albert O. Hirschman, "Exit, Voice, and the Fate of the German Democratic Republic: An Essay in Conceptual History," *World Politics* 45, no. 02 (1993): 173–202.
44. Hale, "The Uses of Divided Power."
45. Megan Twohey and Scott Shane, "A Back-Channel Plan for Ukraine and Russia, Courtesy of Trump Associates," *The New York Times*, 19 February 2017, https://www.nytimes.com/2017/02/19/us/politics/donald-trump-ukraine-russia.html; Diana Pilipenko, "Yes, Paul Manafort Is on Trial for Crimes in the US But His Work in Ukraine Helped to Destroy a Country," *The Washington Post*, 17 August 2018, https://www.washingtonpost.com/news/democracy-post/wp/2018/08/17/yes-paul-manafort-is-on-trial-for-crimes-in-the-u-s-but-his-work-in-ukraine-helped-to-destroy-a-country/; Taras Kuzio, "Ukrainian Kleptocrats and America's Real-Life House of Cards: Corruption, Lobbyism

and the Rule of Law," *Communist and Post-Communist Studies* 50, no. 1 (2017): 29–40.

46. Central Election Commission, *Presidential Election Reports, 1991–2014*. OSCE/ODIHR, "Ukraine Presidential Election. 26 January 2010, OSCE/ODIHR Election Observation Mission Final Report" (Warsaw, 2010).
47. Central Election Commission, "Presidential Election Reports, 1991–2014"; Erik S. Herron, "How Viktor Yanukovych Won: Reassessing the Dominant Narratives of Ukraine's 2010 Presidential Election," *East European Politics and Societies* 25, no. 1 (2011): 47–67.
48. Central Election Commission, "Presidential Election Reports, 1991–2014."
49. Ordinary Citizens Focus Group Ukraine #4, 8/4/2009; Ordinary Citizens Focus Group Ukraine #1, 7/26/2009; Ordinary Citizens Focus Group Ukraine #3, 8/04/2009. EuroMaidan Focus Group Mixed SMO Activists, Kyiv, 08/28/2014; EuroMaidan Focus Group Ordinary 'Citizens', Kyiv, 08/26/2014; EuroMaidan Focus Group, Civic Sector Activists, Kyiv, 08/27/2014; EuroMaidan Focus Group Ordinary 'Citizens', Kyiv, 08/25/2014.
50. Hale, *The Foundations of Ethnic Politics*.
51. Hale, *Patronal Politics*.
52. Pop-Eleches and Tucker, *Communism's Shadow*; Neundorf, "Growing Up on Different Sides of the Wall: A Quasi-Experimental Test"; Olena Nikolayenko, *Youth Movements and Elections in Eastern Europe* (Cambridge: Cambridge University Press, 2017).
53. Nikolayenko, *Youth Movements and Elections in Eastern Europe*.
54. Hordon, "Zelens'kyy."
55. Ibid.
56. Ibid.
57. Office of The President of Ukraine, "Address by President Volodymyr Zelenskyy," Official website of the President of Ukraine, July 8, 2019, https://www.president.gov.ua/en/news/zvernennya-prezidenta-ukrayini-volodimira-zelenskogo-56257
58. Inter.ua, "Television Channel Inter Presents New Top Management," 2010, https://web.archive.org/web/20110213024949/https://inter.ua/uk/news/2010/12/24/4303
59. Hordon, "Zelens'kyy."
60. Ibid.
61. Ibid.
62. Ibid.
63. Ibid.
64. *Ukrayins'ka Pravda*, 4 December 2017, https://www.pravda.com.ua/news/2017/12/4/7164190; *Ukrayins'ka Pravda*, 17 January 2019, 22:15, https://www.

pravda.com.ua/news/2019/01/17/7204117/; "Volodymyr Zelens'kyy," *Ukrayins'ka Pravda*, 21 January 2019.

4. THE ART OF POLITICS

1. Office of the President of Ukraine, "The More Russia Uses Terror against Ukraine, the Worse the Consequences for It."
2. Office of the President of Ukraine, "We Continue to Fight, We Will Protect Our State and Liberate Our Land Thanks to Our Heroes," Official Website of the President of Ukraine, 4 March 2022, https://www.president.gov.ua/en/news/mi-prodovzhuyemo-borotisya-mi-zahistimo-nashu-derzhavu-i-zvi-73357
3. "Songs That Bring Tears to My Eyes Evening Quarter Best 2017," YouTube, 2018, https://www.youtube.com/watch?v=22e67ZWiDNc
4. Onuch, *Mapping Mass Mobilization*; Olga Onuch, "Who Were the Protesters?"
5. "Final Song 'They Beat Us, We Fly,' Evening Quarter 24.05.2014," YouTube, 2014, https://www.youtube.com/watch?v=3Gj_7n6pKGc
6. "'It Seems to Be ...,' Final Song, Evening Quarter 19.04.2014," YouTube, 2014, https://www.youtube.com/watch?v=p_z2qqFyb1g
7. Olga Onuch, "EuroMaidan Protest Participant Survey" (Ukrainian Protest Project, Funded by British Academy Newton Fellowship and John Fell Fund, 2014).
8. Olga Onuch, "EuroMaidan Protests in Ukraine: Social Media versus Social Networks," *Problems of Post-Communism* 62, no. 4 (July 2015): 217–35.
9. Ibid.
10. Onuch, "EuroMaidan Protest Participant Survey."
11. Emma Mateo, "'Together We Are Strong': Exploring Regional Protest during Moments of Mass Mobilisation in Ukraine and Belarus," University of Oxford, 2022, http://purl.org/dc/dcmitype/Text
12. TabloidID, "Zelens′kyy Viddav Mil′yon Hryven′ Na Potreby ATO," *TabloidID*, August 20, 2014, https://tabloid.pravda.com.ua/news/53f4940b31965/.]
13. "Songs That Bring Tears to My Eyes Evening Quarter Best 2017."
14. "Up to March 17, 120 People Died on the Maidan and across Ukraine," *Cenzor.net*, 18 March 2014, https://censor.net/ru/news/276347/na_17_marta_120_pogibshih_na_mayidane_i_po_ukraine_spisok; "From 67 to 100 People Killed in Clashes in Kyiv," *Ukrayins'ka Pravda*, 20 February 2014, https://www.pravda.com.ua/news/2014/02/20/7015249
15. Henry E. Hale and Volodymyr Kulyk, "Aspirational Identity Politics and Support for Radical Reform: The Case of Post-Maidan Ukraine," *Comparative Politics* 53, no. 4 (1 July 2021): 713–51.
16. Olga Onuch, "Maidans Past and Present: Comparing the Orange Revolution

and the EuroMaidan," in *Euromaidan*, ed. David Marples (London: Columbia University Press, 2015); Onuch, "'Maidans' and Movements: Legacies, Innovations, and Contention in Independent Ukraine," in *The Power of Populism and People: Resistance and Protest in the Modern World*, ed. Nathan Stoltzfus and Christopher Osmar (London: Bloomsbury Academic, 2021).

17. Samuel Greene, *Moscow in Movement: Power and Opposition in Putin's Russia* (Stanford: Stanford University Press, 2014); Graeme B. Robertson, *The Politics of Protest in Hybrid Regimes: Managing Dissent in Post-Communist Russia* (Cambridge: Cambridge University Press, 2010); Sam Greene and Graeme Robertson, "Explaining Putin's Popularity: Rallying Round the Russian Flag," *Washington Post*, 9 September 2014, http://www.washingtonpost.com/blogs/monkey-cage/wp/2014/09/09/explaining-putins-popularity-rallying-round-the-russian-flag; Regina Smyth, *Elections, Protest, and Authoritarian Regime Stability: Russia 2008–2020* (Cambridge: Cambridge University Press, 2020); Paul Chaisty and Stephen Whitefield, "Forward to Democracy or Back to Authoritarianism? The Attitudinal Bases of Mass Support for the Russian Election Protests of 2011–2012," *Post-Soviet Affairs* 29, no. 5 (2013): 387–403; Katerina Tertytchnaya, "Protests and Voter Defections in Electoral Autocracies: Evidence from Russia," *Comparative Political Studies* 53, no. 12 (2020): 1926–56; Greene and Robertson, *Putin v. the People: The Perilous Politics of a Divided Russia* (New Haven: Yale University Press, 2019).
18. Daniel S. Treisman, "Why Putin Took Crimea: The Gambler in the Kremlin," *Foreign Affairs* 95, no. 3 (2016): 47–54.
19. *Polit.ru*, 10 September 2013, http://www.polit.ru/news/2013/09/10/russkie
20. Adam Charles Lenton, "Why Didn't Ukraine Fight for Crimea? Evidence from Declassified National Security and Defense Council Proceedings," *Problems of Post-Communism* 69, no. 2 (2021): 1–10.
21. Joe Gould and Courtney Albon, "Amid Russia Crisis, Pentagon Nominee Criticizes Obama Response to Crimea," *Defense News*, 13 January 2022, https://www.defensenews.com/congress/2022/01/13/amid-border-crisis-pentagon-nominee-criticizes-obama-response-to-russias-ukraine-invasion
22. "Do Not Separate Loving Crimea", Evening Quarter, 2014, https://www.youtube.com/watch?v=HfoZdpPmGco.
23. *Segodnya*, 10 November 2014, http://www.segodnya.ua/regions/donetsk/iz-vremenno-okkupirovannyh-territoriy-oficialno-pereselilis-453-000-chelovek-minsocpolitiki-568087.html
24. "'It Seems to Be ...,' Final Song, Evening Quarter 19.04.2014."
25. Ibid.
26. "Search Ukraine in Google, the Final Song of the Evening Quarter at the Jurmaleto Concert from 24.09.2016," YouTube, 2016, https://www.youtube.com/watch?v=yKzEXCnjHPE

27. "Final Song 'They Beat Us, We Fly,' Evening Quarter 24.05.2014."
28. For example, Sunday, 14 December 2013 (Hale's field notes from Kyiv).
29. Ukrayins'ka *Pravda*, 14 October 2013, http://www.pravda.com.ua/news/2013/10/14/6999954; *Ukrayins'ka Pravda*, 21 October 2013, http://www.pravda.com.ua/news/2013/10/21/7000362; "Elektoral'ni namiry vybortsiv Ukrayiny," Kyiv International Institute of Sociology, press release, 6 March 2014, https://www.kiis.com.ua/?lang=ukr&cat=reports&id=240&page=1&y=2014&m=3
30. Hale, *Patronal Politics*.
31. Author interview with Gumenyuk.
32. Central Election Commission, "Presidential Election Reports, 1991–2014."
33. Hordon, "Zelens'kyy."
34. "'It Seems to Be ...,' Final Song, Evening Quarter 19.04.2014," YouTube.
35. Yuliya Mostova, "Prem"yernyy pokaz," *Dzerkalo Tyzhnya*, 28 November 2014, http://gazeta.dt.ua/internal/prem-yerniy-pokaz-_.html
36. *Ukrayins'ka Pravda*, 12 November 2014, http://www.pravda.com.ua/news/2014/11/12/7043958
37. *Ukrayins'ka Pravda*, 27 November 2014, http://www.pravda.com.ua/news/2014/11/27/7045650/, acc
38. For a comprehensive account of Poroshenko's successes, see Taras Kuzio, "Why the Euromaidan Revolution was a Success: Petro Poroshenko's Reform Record," *The Ukrainian Quarterly*, no. 3 (2020): 7–24.
39. Iryna Kyrychenko, "Krayina yedyna: Ale ne odnoridna," *Dzerkalo Tyzhnya*, 29 August 2014, http://gazeta.dt.ua/internal/krayina-yedina-ale-neodnoridna-_.html
40. *Segodnya*, 13 September 2014, http://www.segodnya.ua/politics/pnews/zachem-polevye-komandiry-idut-na-vybory-v-verhovnuyu-radu-551730.html
41. Mikhail Alexseev, "A Poisoned Chalice: How the Minsk Accords Destabilize Ukraine," PONARS Eurasia Policy Memo (Washington, DC: George Washington University, February 2017), https://www.ponarseurasia.org/wp-content/uploads/attachments/Pepm456_Alexseev_Feb2017–6.pdf; Samuel Charap and Timothy J. Colton, *Everyone Loses: The Ukraine Crisis and the Ruinous Contest for Post-Soviet Eurasia* (Abingdon: Routledge, 2017); Paul D'Anieri, *Ukraine and Russia: From Civilized Divorce to Uncivil War* (New York: Cambridge University Press, 2019).
42. Bryan Bender and Wesley Morgan, "How U.S. Military Aid Became a Lifeline for Ukraine," *Politico*, 30 September 2019, https://www.politico.com/news/2019/09/30/ukraine-united-states-military-aid-013792; Mariya Omelicheva, "Washington's Security Assistance to Kyiv: Improving Long-Term Returns on Military Investments in Ukraine," PONARS Eurasia Policy Memo (Washington, DC: George Washington University, September 2019), https://www.ponar-

seurasia.org/wp-content/uploads/attachments/Pepm614_Omelicheva_Sept2019–7.pdf

43. Yury Butusov, "Dobrovol'chi batal'yony: Struktura, strakhy, problemy boyovoho zastosuvannya," *Dzerkalo* Tyzhnya, 29 August 2014, http://gazeta.dt.ua/internal/dobrovolchi-batalyoni-struktura-strahi-problemi-boyovogo-zastosuvannya-_.html
44. Mariya Omelicheva, presentation on PONARS Eurasia's Ukrainathon, YouTube, https://www.youtube.com/watch?v=8ESSYwBiUnE&t=10748s
45. Henry E. Hale, Nadiya Kravets, and Olga Onuch, "Can Federalism Unite Ukraine in a Peace Deal?," PONARS Eurasia Policy Memo (Washington, DC: George Washington University, August 2015), http://www.ponarseurasia.org/sites/default/files/policy-memos-pdf/Pepm379_Hale-Kravets-Onuch_Aug2015.pdf
46. *Ukrayins'ka Pravda*, 28 December 2014, http://www.epravda.com.ua/news/2014/12/28/518866
47. Segodnya, 17 September 2014, http://www.segodnya.ua/politics/pnews/zakon-o-lyustracii-chinovnikov-rezhima-yanukovicha-obeshchayut-ne-puskat-vo-vlast-10-let-552900.html; *Ukrayins'ka Pravda*, 17 September 2014, http://www.pravda.com.ua/news/2014/09/17/7038036; *Ukrayins'ka Pravda*, 3 October 2014, http://www.pravda.com.ua/news/2014/10/3/7039705
48. "Poroshenko Restricts Access to Russian Websites, Social Networks," *RFE/RL*, 16 May 2017, https://www.rferl.org/a/ukraine-poroshenko-restricts-access-yandex-vkontakte/28490951.html
49. *Ekonomichna Pravda*, 25 September 2018, https://www.epravda.com.ua/news/2018/09/25/640926
50. "Ukrainian Lawmakers Approve Language Quotas for TV, Radio," *RFE/RL*, 23 May 2017, https://www.rferl.org/a/ukraine-language-quotas-tv-radio/28504751.html
51. Hale and Kulyk, "Aspirational Identity Politics and Support for Radical Reform."
52. "Kremlivs'ka dezinformatsiya," *Detektor Media*, 21 March 2019, https://detector.media/infospace/article/164308/2019-03-21-dzherela-informatsii-media-gramotnist-i-rosiyska-propaganda-rezultaty-vseukrainskogo-opytuvannya-gromadskoi-dumky
53. Joshua Zitser, "The Real Volodymyr Zelensky: His US Film Editor Reveals the Man behind the Scenes," *Business Insider*, 5 March 2022, https://www.businessinsider.com/zelensky-revealed-us-film-editor-on-his-friendship-ukraines-president-2022–3
54. Olga Surikova, "Zelensky Intends to Demand the Resignation of the Ministry of Culture of Ukraine," *Sevas.com*, 9 August 2022, http://news.sevas.com/world/zelenskij_o_zaprete_vezda_rossijskih_artistov_v_ukrainu

55. Marie Yovanovitch, *Lessons from the Edge: A Memoir* (Boston: Mariner Books, 2022).
56. "Ukraine's Reformist Central Bank Chief Resigns amid Pressure," *RFE/RL*, 10 April 2017, http://www.rferl.org/a/ukraine-reformist-central-bank-chief-resigns-amid-pressure/28420840.html
57. Andrew E. Kramer, "Questions Surround Ukraine's Bailouts as Banking Chief Steps Down," *New York Times*, 12 May 2017, https://www.nytimes.com/2017/05/12/world/europe/ukraine-central-bank-valeria-gontareva.html?module=inline
58. Ibid.
59. Ibid.
60. "Ukraine's Supreme Court Postpones PrivatBank Hearing Citing Media Pressure," *RFE/RL*, 27 April 2020, https://www.rferl.org/a/ukraine-s-supreme-court-postpones-privatbank-hearing-citing-media-pressure/30579282.html
61. "Ukraine's Reformist Central Bank Chief Resigns amid Pressure," *RFE/RL*, 10 April 2017.
62. Studio Kvartal 95 Online, "Kvartal 95: We Are So Different," 3 February 2016, YouTube, https://www.youtube.com/watch?v=BiJfaFvD_Bo
63. Yovanovitch, *Lessons from the Edge*, 218.
64. *Ukrayins'ka Pravda*, 4 October 2016, http://www.pravda.com.ua/news/2016/10/4/7122613
65. Yovanovitch, *Lessons from the Edge*, 219–27.
66. "Ukraine Arrests More Than 20 Former Tax Officials in 'Biggest-Ever' Corruption Crackdown," *RFE/RL*, 24 May 2017, https://www.rferl.org/a/ukraine-corruption-crackdown-tax-officials-arrested/28506910.html
67. *Ukrayins'ka Pravda*, 29 December 2014, http://www.pravda.com.ua/news/2014/12/29/7053682
68. *Ekonomichna Pravda*, 25 September 2018, https://www.epravda.com.ua/news/2018/09/25/6409262
69. *Ukrayins'ka Pravda*, 29 December 2014, http://www.pravda.com.ua/news/2014/12/29/7053682; *Ukrayins'ka Pravda*, 29 September 2018, https://www.pravda.com.ua/news/2018/09/29/7193585
70. "Preelection Dismissal at Ukraine's Public Broadcaster Sparks Outcry," *RFE/RL*, 1 February 2019, https://www.rferl.org/a/preelection-dismissal-at-ukraine-s-public-broadcaster-sparks-outcry/29746294.html
71. Serhiy Kudelia, "What Does the Murder of Pavel Sheremet Say about Contemporary Ukraine?," *OpenDemocracy*, 22 July 2016, https://www.opendemocracy.net/en/odr/what-does-murder-of-pavel-sheremet-say-about-contemporary-ukraine
72. UkrInform, "Zelensky: Sheremet's Assassination a Disgrace for Ukraine,"

UkrInform.net, 20 July 2020, https://www.ukrinform.net/rubric-polytics/3066209-zelensky-sheremets-assassination-a-disgrace-for-ukraine.html

73. Solomiia Kryvenko, "Symbols in the Ukrainian Public Discourse (Analysis of Presidential Speeches on the Occasion of Constitution Day)," *Kyiv-Mohyla Law and Politics Journal* 7 (29 December 2021): 109–27; Harris Mylonas and Scott Radnitz, eds, *Enemies Within: The Global Politics of Fifth Columns* (Oxford: Oxford University Press, 2022). Similar findings emerge from an analysis of other Poroshenko speeches: Pavao Jergović, "Zistavnyi Zistavnyy analiz promov presydentiv Petra Poroshenka ta Volodymyra Zelens'koho," master's degree thesis in East Slavic Languages and Literatures, University of Zagreb, Zagreb, 14 July 2021.
74. Ibid.
75. *Ukrayins'ka Pravda*, 3 September 2018, https://www.pravda.com.ua/news/2018/09/3/7190961
76. *Ukrayins'ka Pravda*, 4 September 2018, https://www.pravda.com.ua/news/2018/09/4/7191006
77. *Ukrayins'ka Pravda*, 4 October 2018, https://life.pravda.com.ua/society/2018/10/4/233438
78. Mikhail Alexseev, "Through Europe's Gate, Out of Russia's Net: How Ukrainians' Visa-Free EU Travel Offsets Moscow's Disinformation," PONARS Eurasia Policy Memo no. 627, George Washington University, Washington, DC, November 2019, https://www.ponarseurasia.org/wp-content/uploads/attachments/Pepm627_Alexseev_Nov2019-8.pdf]
79. Keith Darden and Lucan Ahmad Way, "Why Did Ukraine Impose Martial Law?," *Washington Post*, 29 November 2018, https://www.washingtonpost.com/news/monkey-cage/wp/2018/11/29/why-did-ukraine-impose-martial-law
80. Hordon, "Zelens'kyy Zelenskyy."
81. *Ukrayins'ka Pravda*, 20 September 2018, https://www.pravda.com.ua/news/2018/09/20/7192647
82. Author's Interview with unnamed well-known journalist.
83. Yulia Liubchenko, Pavlo Miroshnychenko, Katerina Sirinyok-Dolgaryova, and Olena Tupakhina, "Political Communication in the Post-Truth Era: Mind Mapping Values of Ukraine's Volodymyr Zelensky," *Communication Today* 12, no. 2 (November 2021): 146–167.
84. Natalya Ryabinska, "Politics as a Joke: The Case of Volodymyr Zelensky's Comedy Show in Ukraine," *Problems of Post-Communism* 69, no. 2 (2022): 179–191.]
85. Ibid.
86. "KrymNash," 18 October 2014, YouTube, https://www.youtube.com/watch?v=hD_QJ68zqfI
87. Volodymyr Zelensky, interviewed by Aleksei Sysoyev and Yuliya Katsun,

"Vladimir Zelenskii: Esli poidu v politiku, 'Kvartal' budet shutit' nado mnoy eshche pokhleshche," *KP v Ukraine*, 24 January 2018, https://kp.ua/culture/599107-vladymyr-zelenskyi-esly-poidu-v-polytyku-kvartal-budet-shutyt-nado-mnoi-esche-pokhlesche

88. "Volodymyr Zelensky" *Ukrayins'ka Pravda*, 21 January 2019, https://www.pravda.com.ua/articles/2019/01/21/7204341
89. Hordon, "Zelens'kyy."
90. Ibid.
91. *TSN*, 11 December 2015, https://tsn.ua/ru/glamur/serial-sluga-naroda-posmotrelo-20-mln-zriteley-542453.html
92. Hordon, "Zelens'kyy."
93. Ibid.
94. Hale, *Patronal Politics*.
95. *TSN*, 11 December 2015, https://tsn.ua/ru/glamur/serial-sluga-naroda-posmotrelo-20-mln-zriteley-542453.html
96. Dmytro Cheretun, "'Sluha narodu': Zelens'kyy ne vidpovidaye narodu, chy pide partiya na vybory," *Chesno.org*, 4 September 2018, https://www.chesno.org/post/721
97. Henry E. Hale, Oxana Shevel, and Olga Onuch, "Believing Facts in the Fog of War: Identity, Media and Hot Cognition in Ukraine's 2014 Odesa Tragedy," *Geopolitics* 23, no. 4 (2018): 851–81; Olga Onuch and Henry E. Hale, "Capturing Ethnicity: The Case of Ukraine."
98. Grigore Pop-Eleches and Graeme B. Robertson, "Identity and Political Preferences in Ukraine: Before and after the Euromaidan."
99. Kulyk, "Shedding Russianness."
100. Aaron Erlich and Calvin Garner, "Subgroup Differences in Implicit Associations and Explicit Attitudes during Wartime," *International Studies Quarterly* 65, no. 2 (2021): 528–41.
101. Hale and Kulyk, "Aspirational Identity Politics and Support for Radical Reform."
102. Democratic Initiatives Foundation, "Hromads'ka dumka, hruden'-2017: Vyborchi reytyngy i reytyngy doviry," 23 January 2018, https://dif.org.ua/article/reytingijfojseojoej8567547
103. Nataliya Sudakova, "Fenomen Vakarchuka i Zelens'koho," *Ukrayins'ka Pravda*, 6 April 2018, https://www.pravda.com.ua/articles/2018/04/6/7176901
104. Ibid.
105. Vijai Maheshwari, "The Comedian and the Oligarch," *Politico*, 17 April 2019, https://www.politico.eu/article/volodomyr-zelenskiy-ihor-kolomoisky-the-comedian-and-the-oligarch-ukraine-presidential-election
106. Sudakova, "Fenomen Vakarchuka i Zelens'koho."
107. Hordon, "Zelens'kyy."

108. *Tribuna*, 16 December 2021, https://tribune.com.ua/v-2014-godu-poroshenko-prosil-zelenskogo-vojti-v-spisok-ego-partii-na-vybory-v-radu-luczenko
109. *Ukrayins'ka Pravda*, 25 April 2019, https://www.pravda.com.ua/news/2019/04/25/7213606
110. Sysoev and Katsun, "Vladimir Zelenskii."
111. Ibid.
112. Ibid.
113. Article 24, "Law on Political Parties," Ukraine, https://kodeksy.com.ua/ka/o_politicheskih_partiyah_v_ukraine/statja-24.htm
114. Article 10, "Law on Parties," Ukraine, https://kodeksy.com.ua/ka/o_politicheskih_partiyah_v_ukraine/statja-10.htm
115. *Ukrayins'ka Pravda*, 4 December 2017, https://www.pravda.com.ua/news/2017/12/4/7164190
116. Ibid.; Cheretun, "'Sluha narodu'."
117. Cheretun, "'Sluha narodu.'"
118. Nataliya Patrikeyeva, "Yak narodylasya 'Sluha narodu' ta de vzyala ponad 200 mil'ioniv na vybory," *Chesno.org*, February 13, 2020, 09:30, https://www.chesno.org/post/3823
119. *Ukrayins'ka Pravda*, 4 December 2017, https://www.pravda.com.ua/news/2017/12/4/7164190
120. *Glavkom*, 27 January 2019, https://web.archive.org/web/20190127022553/https://glavcom.ua/publications/sluga-narodu-ozhiv-partiya-zelenskogo-otrimala-pershi-groshi-na-rahunok-559225.html
121. Cheretun, "'Sluha narodu.'"
122. Roman Kravets', "Mezha zhartu: Yak Zelens'kyy hotuyetsya do vyboriv," *Ukrayins'ka Pravda*, 25 October 2018, https://www.pravda.com.ua/articles/2018/10/25/7196270
123. Cheretun, "'Sluha narodu.'"
124. *Ukrayins'ka Pravda*, 7 May 2018, 15:15.
125. Volodymyr Zelensky is relatively trusted with such a rating of –11 percent, with Vakarchuk at –5 percent (Democratic Initiatives Foundation, "Hromads'ka dumka, hruden'-2017.)
126. *Ukrayins'ka Pravda*, 26 April 2018, https://www.pravda.com.ua/news/2018/04/26/7178828; *Ukrayins'ka Pravda*, 7 May 2018, https://www.pravda.com.ua/news/2018/05/7/7179666
127. *Glavkom*, 27 January 2019.
128. Patrikeyeva "Yak narodylasya 'Sluha narodu' ta de vzyala ponad 200 mil'yoniv na vybory."
129. "Volodymyr Zelens'kyy," *Ukrayins'ka Pravda*, 21 January 2019.
130. Kravets', "Mezha zhartu."

131. *Ukrayins'ka Pravda*, 4 September 2018, https://www.pravda.com.ua/news/2018/09/4/7191079
132. KIIS, Razumkov Center, and Sotsis, Press Release, "Sotsiyal'no politychna atsiya v Ukrayini," September 2018, https://razumkov.org.ua/uploads/socio/2018_Press_release_september.pdf
133. *Ukrayins'ka Pravda*, 4 September 2018, https://www.pravda.com.ua/news/2018/09/4/7191079
134. Tetyana Nikolayenko, "Spokusa Zelens'kym: Nervy shtabiv ta ihry Kolomoys'koho," *Ukrayins'ka Pravda*, 10 January 2019, https://www.pravda.com.ua/articles/2019/01/10/7203393
135. *Ukrayins'ka Pravda*, 4 September 2018, 14:01, https://www.pravda.com.ua/news/2018/09/4/7191062
136. *Ukrayins'ka Pravda*, 29 October 2018, https://www.pravda.com.ua/news/2018/10/29/7196572
137. These factors are statistically significant at the 95-percent level in an econometric analysis that regresses a binary variable capturing the intent to vote for Zelensky on age, sex, community size, education, nationality, language preference, macroregion, home internet, and mobile phone usage, with dummy controls for each survey except the first. Data from KIIS's May, September, October, and December 2018 omnibus surveys.

5. THE VIRTUAL INCUMBENT

1. Office of the President of Ukraine, "The More Russia Uses Terror against Ukraine, the Worse the Consequences for It."
2. Office of the President of Ukraine, "We Continue to Fight, We Will Protect Our State and Liberate Our Land Thanks to Our Heroes: Address by the President of Ukraine," Official Website of the President of Ukraine, 4 March 2022, https://www.president.gov.ua/en/news/mi-prodovzhuyemo-borotisya-mi-zahistimo-nashu-derzhavu-i-zvi-73357
3. "Volodymyr Zelenskyy: I Am Running for President of Ukraine!," YouTube, 2018, https://www.youtube.com/watch?v=Jjc4kcx8mlw
4. Volodymyr Zelensky, video of his declaration of candidacy for president, *Ukrayins'ka Pravda*, 1 January 2019, https://www.pravda.com.ua/news/2019/01/1/7202742
5. "Volodymyr Zelenskyy," *Ukrayins'ka Pravda*, 21 January 2019.
6. Adrian Karatnycky, "The World Just Witnessed the First Entirely Virtual Presidential Campaign," *Politico*, 24 April 2019, https://politi.co/2PsUg0Z
7. Markus Prior, "The Incumbent in the Living Room: The Rise of Television and the Incumbency Advantage in US House Elections," *Journal of Politics* 68, no. 3

(2006): 657–73; Thomas E. Mann and Raymond E. Wolfinger, "Candidates and Parties in Congressional Elections," *American Political Science Review* 74, no. 3 (1980): 617–32.

8. Gary King, "Constituency Service and Incumbency Advantage," *British Journal of Political Science* 21, no. 1 (1991): 119–28; Andrew Gelman and Gary King, "Estimating Incumbency Advantage without Bias," *American Journal of Political Science* 34, no. 4 (1990): 1142–64.
9. Cnaan Liphshiz, "Zelensky's Parents' Local Rabbi: They Don't Understand Why He Wanted to Be President," *Times of Israel*, 28 April 2022, https://www.timesofisrael.com/zelenskys-parents-local-rabbi-they-dont-understand-why-he-wanted-to-be-president
10. Al Franken, *Why Not Me? The Inside Story of the Making and Unmaking of the Franken Presidency* (New York: Delta, 2000); Ariel Levy, "Don't Laugh," *New York Magazine*, 2 November 2007, https://nymag.com/news/features/40294
11. "Volodymyr Zelens'kyy," *Ukrayins'ka Pravda*, 21 January 2019.
12. Office of the President of Ukraine, "Volodymyr Zelenskyy's Inaugural Address," Official Website of the President of Ukraine, 20 May 2020, https://www.president.gov.ua/en/news/inavguracijna-promova-prezidenta-ukrayini-volodimira-zelensk-55489
13. "Volodymyr Zelens'kyy," *Ukrayins'ka Pravda*, 21 January 2019.
14. *Ekonomichna Pravda*, 25 October 2018, https://www.epravda.com.ua/news/2018/10/25/641969
15. *Ukrayins'ka Pravda*, 9 October 2018, https://www.pravda.com.ua/news/2018/10/9/7194591
16. *Ekonomichna Pravda*, 12 October 2018, https://www.epravda.com.ua/news/2018/10/12/641571
17. *Glavkom*, 27 January 2019, https://web.archive.org/web/20190127022553/https://glavcom.ua/publications/sluga-narodu-ozhiv-partiya-zelenskogo-otrimala-pershi-groshi-na-rahunok-559225.html
18. *Ukrayins'ka Pravda*, 25 December 2018, https://www.pravda.com.ua/news/2018/12/25/7202288
19. Shaun Walker, "Ukraine's First Lady Olena Zelenska on Being Russia's Target No 2: 'When You See Their Crimes, Maybe They Really Are Capable of Anything,'" *The Guardian*, 18 June 2022, https://www.theguardian.com/world/2022/jun/18/olena-zelenska-ukraine-first-lady-rare-interview-family-under-threat
20. Office of the President of Ukraine, "Volodymyr Zelenskyy's Inaugural Address."
21. "Volodymyr Zelens'kyy," *Ukrayins'ka Pravda*, 21 January 2019.
22. *Glavkom*, 8 January 2019, https://web.archive.org/web/20190420160101/https://glavcom.ua/news/zekonomiv-na-polittehnologah-zelenskiy-zaproponuvav-ukrajincyam-napisati-yomu-peredviborchu-programu-559192.html

23. *Ukrayins'ka Pravda*, 8 April 2019, https://www.pravda.com.ua/news/2019/04/8/7211588
24. "Holovni debaty krayiny," video recording of the Poroshenko–Zelensky presidential debate, YouTube, 19 April 2021, https://youtu.be/OEZfEfQXSco
25. "Volodymyr Zelenskyy," *Ukrayins'ka Pravda*, 21 January 2019.
26. Kravets, "Mezha zhartu" *Ukrayins'ka Pravda*, 25 October 2018.
27. *Ukrayins'ka Pravda*, 3 October 2018, https://tabloid.pravda.com.ua/scandal/5bb4c0aa64cec
28. *Ukrayins'ka Pravda*, 15 April 2019, https://www.pravda.com.ua/news/2019/04/15/7212264
29. "Volodymyr Zelenskyy," *Ukrayins'ka Pravda*.
30. *Vechernyy Kvartal* concert dated 23 March 2019, Studio Kvartal 95 Online, YouTube, https://youtu.be/vov6IoovpVs
31. *Vechernyy Kvartal* concert dated 16 March 2019, Studio Kvartal 95 Online, YouTube, https://youtu.be/Gj472J5wY3I
32. *Vechernyy Kvartal* concert dated 23 March 2019.
33. *Vechernyy Kvartal* concert dated 16 March 2019.
34. Tamara Martsenyuk, *Hender dlya vsikh: Vyklyk stereotypam* (2017).
35. *Vechernyy Kvartal* concert dated 16 March 2019, https://youtu.be/Gj472J5wY3I
36. "Volodymyr Zelens'kyy," *Ukrayins'ka Pravda*, 21 January 2019.
37. Alexander J. Motyl, "Ukraine's TV President Is Dangerously Pro-Russian," *Foreign Policy*, 19 April 2019, https://foreignpolicy.com/2019/04/01/ukraines-tv-president-is-dangerously-pro-russian; *Ukrayins'ka Pravda*, 15 April 2019, https://www.pravda.com.ua/news/2019/04/15/7212265
38. Kravets, "Mezha zhartu," *Ukrayins'ka Pravda*, 25 October 2018.
39. Ibid.
40. Patryikeyeva, "Yak narodylasya 'Sluha narodu' ta de vzyala ponad 200 milyoniv na vybory."
41. Hordon, "Zelens'kyy."
42. Hale, *Patronal Politics*; Jessica Allina-Pisano, *The Post-Soviet Potemkin Village: Politics and Property Rights in the Black Earth* (New York: Cambridge University Press, 2008); Wilson, *Virtual Politics*.
43. Hordon, "Zelens'kyy."
44. Kravets, "Mezha zhartu," *Ukrayins'ka Pravda*, 25 October 2018.
45. "Volodymyr Zelens'kyy," *Ukrayins'ka Pravda*, 21 January 2019.
46. "Nashi Hroshi" program, no. 266, on BihusInfo YouTube Channel, 19 April 2019, https://www.youtube.com/watch?v=y5GQHVyF5kE&t=1256s; "Volodymyr Zelenskyy," *Ukrayins'ka Pravda*, 21 January 2019.
47. Maheshwari, "The Comedian and the Oligarch.
48. *Radio Svoboda*, 11 April 2019, https://www.radiosvoboda.org/a/news-schemes-zelenskyy-perelyoty/29875430.html

49. "100 Wealthiest Ukrainains 2021," *Forbes*, 6 May 2021, https://forbes.ua/ratings/100-bogateyshikh-ukraintsev-2021–06052021–1536
50. Maheshwari, "Comedian and the Oligarch."
51. "Kremlivs'ka dezinformatsiya," *Detektor Mediya*, 21 March 2019.
52. *Ukrayins'ka Pravda*, 16 April 2019, https://www.pravda.com.ua/news/2019/04/16/7212381; *Ukrayins'ka Pravda*, 17 April 2019, https://www.pravda.com.ua/news/2019/04/17/7212535
53. Ibid.
54. "Kremlivs'ka dezinformatsiya," *Detektor Media*, 21 March 2019.
55. *Ukrayins'ka Pravda*, 13 April 2019, https://www.pravda.com.ua/news/2019/04/13/7212145
56. *Ukrayins'ka Pravda*, 16 April 2019, https://www.pravda.com.ua/news/2019/04/16/7212381; *Ukrayins'ka Pravda*, 17 April 2019, https://www.pravda.com.ua/news/2019/04/17/7212535
57. *Ukrayins'ka Pravda*, 13 April 2019, https://www.pravda.com.ua/news/2019/04/13/7212145
58. "Nashi Hroshi," 19 April 2019.
59. "Volodymyr Zelenskyy," *Ukrayins'ka Pravda*, 21 January 2019.
60. *Radio Svoboda*, 11 April 2019, https://www.radiosvoboda.org/a/news-schemes-zelenskyy-perelyoty/29875430.html; *Radio Svoboda*, 12 April 2019, https://www.radiosvoboda.org/a/29877632.html
61. *Radio Svoboda*, 11 April 2019, https://www.radiosvoboda.org/a/news-schemes-zelenskyy-perelyoty/29875430.html
62. "Nashi Hroshi," 19 April 2019.
63. *Radio Svoboda*, 12 April 2019, https://www.radiosvoboda.org/a/29877632.html; Maheshwari, "Comedian and the Oligarch."
64. *Ukrayins'ka Pravda*, 27 April 2019, https://www.pravda.com.ua/news/2019/04/27/7213783
65. Hordon, "Zelens'kyy."
66. "Volodymyr Zelens'kyyy," *Ukrayins'ka Pravda*, 21 January 2019.
67. Ibid.
68. "Nashi Hroshi," 19 April 2019; *Ukrayins'ka Pravda*, 10 April 2019, https://www.pravda.com.ua/news/2019/04/10/7211835
69. Oleksandr Chornovalov, "Investigation Finds Suspicious Donations in Tymoshenko's Presidential Campaign," *RFE/RL* 1 March 2019, https://www.rferl.org/a/tymoshenko-s-presidential-campaign-reported-suspicious-donations-investigation-finds/29798380.html
70. Office of the President of Ukraine, "Volodymyr Zelenskyy's Inaugural Address."
71. Karatnycky, "The World Just Witnessed the First Entirely Virtual Presidential Campaign"; Motyl, "Ukraine's TV President Is Dangerously Pro-Russian."

72. "Volodymyr Zelensky's Inaugural Address," Official Website of the President of Ukraine.
73. "Holovni debaty krayiny," video recording of the Poroshenko–Zelensky presidential debate.
74. Office of the President of Ukraine, "Volodymyr Zelenskyy's Inaugural Address."
75. Hordon, "Zelens'kyy."
76. "Volodymyr Zelens'kyy," *Ukrayins'ka Pravda*, 21 January 2019.
77. Hordon, "Zelens'kyy."
78. Ibid.
79. *Ukrayins'ka Pravda*, 18 April 2019, https://www.pravda.com.ua/news/2019/04/18/7212583
80. Hordon, "Zelens'kyy."
81. Ibid.
82. Ibid.
83. *Ukrayins'ka Pravda*, 3 September 2018, https://www.pravda.com.ua/news/2018/09/3/7190961
84. Ibid.
85. *Ukrayins'ka Pravda*, 22 September 2018, https://www.pravda.com.ua/news/2018/09/22/7192901; 7 April 2019, https://www.pravda.com.ua/news/2019/04/7/7211508
86. *UNIAN*, 29 January 2019, https://www.unian.ua/politics/10426296-abo-poroshenko-abo-putin-na-forumi-prezidenta-ukrajini-glyadachiv-prigolomshili-divnim-gaslom-foto.html?fbclid=IwAR16eGgY4TPg7NAF2NqEJ5_T0AH0ziskF4vJTsTeI958ZMX-vOG30qrOyrQ
87. Mykola Ryabchuk, "Strashnyy son patriota," *Zbruch*, 22 April 2019, https://zbruc.eu/node/88723
88. *Ukrayins'ka Pravda*, 9 April 2019, https://www.pravda.com.ua/news/2019/04/9/7211701. The Ukrainian word used was *vyrishal'nyy*, which can mean both "crucial" and "final."
89. Nikolayenko, "Spokusa Zelens'kym."
90. "Volodymyr Zelens'kyy," *Ukrayins'ka Pravda*, 21 January 2019; Hordon, "Zelens'kyy."
91. *Ukrayins'ka Pravda*, 12 April 2019, https://www.pravda.com.ua/news/2019/04/12/7212053; *Ukrayins'ka Pravda*, 12 April 2019, https://www.pravda.com.ua/news/2019/04/12/7212080
92. *Ukrayins'ka Pravda*, 12 April 2019, https://www.pravda.com.ua/news/2019/04/12/7212068
93. *Ukrayins'ka Pravda*, 20 April 2019, https://www.pravda.com.ua/news/2019/04/20/7212922
94. *Ukrayins'ka Pravda*, 16 April 2019, https://www.pravda.com.ua/news/2019/

04/16/7212381; *Ukrayins'ka Pravda*, 17 April 2019, https://www.pravda.com.ua/news/2019/04/17/7212535

95. "Kremlivs'ka dezinformatsiya," *Detektor Media*, 21 March 2019.
96. "Ukraine Election Commission Receives 83 Filings for Presidential Candidates," *RFE/RL*, 4 February 2019, GMT, https://www.rferl.org/a/ukraine-presidential-election-poroshenko-tymoshenko-zelensky-boyko-russia-crimea/29749637.html
97. *Ukrayins'ka Pravda*, 7 April 2019, https://www.pravda.com.ua/news/2019/04/7/7211530
98. *Ukrayins'ka Pravda*, 11 April 2019, https://www.pravda.com.ua/news/2019/04/11/7211913
99. *Ukrayins'ka Pravda*, 30 April 2019, https://www.pravda.com.ua/news/2019/04/30/7213926
100. *Ukrayins'ka Pravda*, 11 April 2019, https://www.pravda.com.ua/news/2019/04/11/7211908
101. *Ukrayins'ka Pravda*, 21 April 2019, https://www.pravda.com.ua/news/2019/04/21/7213123
102. *Ukrayins'ka Pravda*, 22 April 2019, https://www.pravda.com.ua/news/2019/04/22/7213228

6. PRESIDENT "ZE!"

1. Office of the President of Ukraine, "The More Russia Uses Terror against Ukraine, the Worse the Consequences for It."
2. Office of the President of Ukraine, "Address by the President of Ukraine on the Evening of the Second Day of the Large-Scale War," Official Website of the President of Ukraine, 26 February 2022, https://www.president.gov.ua/en/news/zvernennya-prezidenta-ukrayini-vvecheri-drugogo-dnya-masshta-73189
3. Text caption accompanying photo from Zelensky's meeting with Merkel, Macron, and Putin in Paris on 20 December 2020, from Zelensky's official Instagram account: https://www.instagram.com/p/CIkP81LlaJS/
4. Shanto Iyengar et al., "The Origins and Consequences of Affective Polarization in the United States," *Annual Review of Political Science* 22, no. 1 (2019): 129–46; Magdalena Wojcieszak and R. Kelly Garrett, "Social Identity, Selective Exposure, and Affective Polarization: How Priming National Identity Shapes Attitudes toward Immigrants via News Selection," *Human Communication Research* 44, no. 3 (2018): 247–73, doi:10.1093/hcr/hqx010
5. Ryabchuk, "Strashnyy son patriota."
6. Office of the President of Ukraine, "Address by the President on the Day of Unity of Ukraine," Official Website of the President of Ukraine, 22 January 2022,

https://www.president.gov.ua/en/news/zvernennya-prezidenta-z-nagodi-dnya-sobornosti-ukrayini-59353

7. Hale, *Patronal Politics.*
8. Serhiy Rudenko, *Zelensky: A Biography*, trans. Michael M. Naydan and Alla Perminova (Medford: Polity, 2022).
9. *Ukrayins'ka Pravda*, 16 April 2019, https://www.pravda.com.ua/news/2019/04/16/7212334
10. *Ukrayins'ka Pravda*, 18 April 2019, https://www.pravda.com.ua/news/2019/04/18/7212661
11. Roman Romaniuk and Roman Kravets, "Anti-Bohdan: Who Is Andriy Yermak, the New Head of the OPU, and Where Did He Come From?," *Ukrayins'ka Pravda*, 12 February 2020, https://www.pravda.com.ua/articles/2020/02/12/7240284
12. "Ukrainian President Names Saakashvili to Head Reform Council," *RFE/RL*, 7 May 2020, https://www.rferl.org/a/ukraine-president-names-saakashvili-to-head-reform-council/30599789.html
13. "Ukrainian Lawmakers Vote to Remove Parliament Speaker Razumkov," *RFE/RL* 1 October 2021, https://www.rferl.org/a/ukraine-parliament-speaker-razumkov-fired/31497427.html
14. Kateryna Reshchuk and Yevhen Buderatsk'kyy, "Khto takyy Denys Shmyhal', yakyy zaminyv Honcharuk," *Ukrayins'ka Pravda*, 3 March 2020, https://www.pravda.com.ua/articles/2020/03/3/7242407
15. "Zelensky Shakes Up Ukraine Government and Proposes New Prime Minister," *Financial Times*, 3 March 2020, https://www.ft.com/content/17dd0122–5d8a-11ea-8033-fa40a0d65a98
16. "Ukraine President Gives Premier 'One More Chance' after Leaks," *Financial Times*, 17 January 2020, https://www.ft.com/content/175450ba-390a-11ea-a6d3-9a26f8c3cba4
17. *Ukrayins'ka Pravda*, 17 September 2020, https://www.pravda.com.ua/news/2020/09/17/7266739; *Ukrayins'ka Pravda*, 24 May 2021, https://www.pravda.com.ua/news/2021/05/24/7294601; *Ukrayins'ka Pravda*, 20 October 2021, https://www.pravda.com.ua/news/2021/10/20/7310998
18. *Ukrayins'ka Pravda*, 17 September 2020, https://www.pravda.com.ua/news/2020/09/17/7266739
19. "Hundreds Rally in Kyiv against Appointment of Acting Education Minister," *RFE/RL*, 30 June 2020, https://www.rferl.org/a/ukraine-protests-against-acting-education-minister/30699263.html
20. In the nationwide party-list voting, the party received a plurality of 43 percent, but this made up only half of the seats in parliament. The other half was decided in single-member district voting, in which Servant of the People nominees won a large majority of seats.

21. Gwendolyn Sasse, "Who Is Who in the Ukrainian Parliament?," Carnegie Europe, 24 September 2019, https://carnegieeurope.eu/strategiceurope/79905
22. *Ukrayins'ka Pravda*, 25 April 2019, https://www.pravda.com.ua/news/2019/04/25/7213553
23. "Council of Europe Blasts Ukraine's Investigations into Odesa Violence," *RFE/RL* 4 November 2015, https://www.rferl.org/a/ukraine-odesa-fire-council-europe-report/27345601.html
24. "Ukraine Bans Zelenskiy Film over Inclusion of Russian Co-Star," *RFE/RL*, 19 February 2020, https://www.rferl.org/a/ukraine-bans-zelenskiy-filmrussian-actress/30443431.html
25. *Ekonomichna Pravda*, 9 July 2020, https://www.epravda.com.ua/news/2020/07/9/662776
26. Omelicheva, in Ukrainathon.
27. *Ukrayins'ka Pravda*, 17 July 2020, https://www.pravda.com.ua/news/2020/07/17/7259715
28. *Ukrayins'ka Pravda*, 4 March 2021, https://www.pravda.com.ua/news/2021/03/4/7285551
29. Tymofii Brik and Jennifer Brick Murtazashvili, "The Source of Ukraine's Resilience," *Foreign Affairs*, 28 June 2022, https://www.foreignaffairs.com/articles/ukraine/2022–06–28/source-ukraines-resilience
30. *Ukrayins'ka Pravda*, 17 September 2020, https://www.pravda.com.ua/news/2020/09/17/7266743
31. "Plenary Session of St Petersburg International Economic Forum," President of Russia, 7 June 2019, http://en.kremlin.ru/events/president/transcripts/60707
32. Andrew Higgins, "In First Meeting with Putin, Zelensky Plays to a Draw Despite a Bad Hand," *New York Times*, 9 December 2019, https://www.nytimes.com/2019/12/09/world/europe/putin-zelensky-paris-ukraine.html
33. Justin Lynch, "Zelensky Flounders in Bid to End Ukraine's War," *Foreign Policy*, 11 October 2019, https://foreignpolicy.com/2019/10/11/zelensky-pushes-peace-deal-ukraine-war-russia-donbass-steinmeier-formula
34. Volodymyr Zelensky, video address to Ukrainians of 4 October 2019, transcript published in "Zelensky Addresses Ukrainians, Explains 'Steinmeier Formula,'" *Kyiv Post*, 4 October 2019, https://www.kyivpost.com/ukraine-politics/zelensky-addresses-ukrainians-explains-steinmeier-formula-full-transcript.html
35. Ibid.
36. *Ukrayins'ka Pravda*, 26 August 2020, https://www.pravda.com.ua/news/2020/08/26/7264187
37. *Ukrayins'ka Pravda*, 24 August 2020, https://www.pravda.com.ua/news/2020/08/24/7264006
38. Shane Harris et al., "Road to War: U.S. Struggled to Convince Allies, and

Zelensky, of Risk of Invasion," *Washington Post*, 16 August 2022, https://www.washingtonpost.com/national-security/interactive/2022/ukraine-road-to-war

39. "Ukrainian President Signs Decree Imposing Sanctions against Medvedchuk, Others with Ties to Kremlin," *RFE/RL*, 19 February 2021, https://www.rferl.org/a/ukraine-sanctions-putin-friendly-politician-and-tycoon-medvedchuk/31112119.html
40. Ibid.; "Ukrainian Secret Services Search House of Kremlin-Friendly Politician Medvedchuk," *RFE/RL*, 11 May 2021, https://www.rferl.org/a/ukrainian-secret-services-search-medvedchuk/31249748.html
41. *Ukrayins'ka Pravda*, 25 April 2019, https://www.pravda.com.ua/news/2019/04/25/7213542; also 26 April 2019, https://www.pravda.com.ua/news/2019/04/26/7213675
42. *Ukrayins'ka Pravda*, 25 April 2019, https://www.pravda.com.ua/news/2019/04/25/7213542; *Ukrayins'ka Pravda*, 26 April 2019, https://www.pravda.com.ua/news/2019/04/26/7213675
43. Yovanovitch, *Lessons from the Edge*.
44. Ivan Gomza, "The Political Consequences of Public Relations Miscalculations: Will Ukraine's Anti-Corruption Bureau Be Terminated?," PONARS Eurasia Policy Memo, no. 694 (Washington, DC: George Washington University, 12 March 2021), https://www.ponarseurasia.org/the-political-consequences-of-public-relations-miscalculations-will-ukraines-anti-corruption-bureau-be-terminated
45. *Ukrayins'ka Pravda*, 20 May 2020, https://www.pravda.com.ua/news/2020/05/20/7252470
46. Gomza, "Political Consequences of Public Relations Miscalculations."
47. "Ukrainian Lawmakers Approve Bill to Strengthen National Anti-Corruption Bureau's Independence," *RFE/RL*, 19 October 2021, https://www.rferl.org/a/ukraine-nabu-independence-vote-corruption/31519388.html; "Zelensky Asks Rada to Sack All Constitutional Court Judges following Controversial Ruling," *UNIAN*, 30 October 2020, https://www.unian.info/politics/zelensky-asks-rada-to-sack-all-constitutional-court-judges-following-controversial-ruling-11200502.html
48. Chesno, "Dubins'kyy Oleksandr Anatoliyevych," *PolitKhab*, https://www.chesno.org/politician/157017
49. Gomza, "Political Consequences of Public Relations Miscalculations."
50. *Ukrayins'ka Pravda*, 11 May 2021, https://www.pravda.com.ua/news/2021/05/11/7293080
51. "Ukrainian President Signs 'Anti-Oligarch Law,'" *RFE/RL*, 5 November 2021, https://www.rferl.org/a/ukraine-zelenskiy-anti-oligarch-law/31548053.html
52. *Ukrayins'ka Pravda*, 3 June 2021, https://www.pravda.com.ua/news/2021/06/3/7295879

53. *Ukrayins'ka Pravda*, 5 June 2021, https://www.pravda.com.ua/news/2021/06/5/7296162
54. *Ukrayins'ka Pravda*, 11 May 2021, https://www.pravda.com.ua/news/2021/05/11/7293080
55. "Ukrainian Lawmakers Vote to Remove Parliament Speaker Razumkov," *RFE/RL*, 7 October 2021, https://www.rferl.org/a/ukraine-parliament-speaker-razumkov-fired/31497427.html
56. Roman Romanyuk, Roman Kravets', and Mykola Topalov, "Probna bytva, abo Repetytsiya viyny Akhmetova i Zelens'koho," *Ukrayins'ka Pravda*, 11 November 2021, https://www.pravda.com.ua/articles/2021/11/11/7313562; "Ukrainian President Signs 'Anti-Oligarch Law,'" *RFE/RL*, 5 November 2021, https://www.rferl.org/a/ukraine-zelenskiy-anti-oligarch-law/31548053.html
57. "Ukraine Hits Oligarch Firtash, Dozens of Others with Sanctions," *RFE/RL*, 24 June 2021, https://www.rferl.org/a/ukraine-sanctions-firtash/31324797.html
58. Todd Prince, "Ukraine Slaps Sanctions on Oligarch Wanted by U.S. ahead of President's Trip to Washington," *RFE/RL*, 18 June 2021, https://www.rferl.org/a/ukraine-sanctions-firtash-zelenskiy-washington-trip/31315218.html
59. "Ukraine's Supreme Court Postpones PrivatBank Hearing Citing Media Pressure," *RFE/RL*, 27 April 2020, https://www.rferl.org/a/ukraine-s-supreme-court-postpones-privatbank-hearing-citing-media-pressure/30579282.html
60. Romanyuk, Kravets', and Topalov, "Probna bytva."
61. Volodymyr Zelens'kyy, "Minus Medvedchuk," *Fokus*, 14 April 2021, https://focus.ua/uk/opinions/482442-kolonka-zelenskogo-medvedchuk-v-chem-smysl-politiki-deoligarhizacii-v-ukraine
62. "U.S. Embassy Warns Ukraine about Its Justice System as Arrest of Poroshenko Mulled," *RFE/RL*, 18 June 2020, https://www.rferl.org/a/u-s-embassy-warns-ukraine-about-its-justice-system-as-arrest-of-poroshenko-being-mulled/30678095.html
63. *Ukrayins'ka Pravda*, 30 June 2020, https://www.pravda.com.ua/news/2020/06/30/7257612
64. "Ukrainian Prosecutors Widen Investigation of Kremlin-Allied Lawmaker Medvedchuk," *RFE/RL*, 9 October 2021, https://www.rferl.org/a/ukrainian-prosecutors-investigation-medvedchuk/31500762.html
65. *Ukrayins'ka Pravda*, 18 September 2020, https://www.pravda.com.ua/news/2020/09/18/7266836; "Ukraine's Ex-President Calls on President 'To Stop Persecuting Opposition,' before Questioning," *RFE/RL*, 28 February 2020, https://www.rferl.org/a/ukraine-ex-president-calls-on-president-to-stop-persecuting-opposition-before-questioning/30460238.html; *Ukrayins'ka Pravda*, 25 June 2021, https://www.pravda.com.ua/news/2021/06/25/7298380

66. Nineteen percent found it hard to say, *Ukrayins'ka Pravda*, 29 June 2020, https://www.pravda.com.ua/news/2020/06/29/7257532
67. "Ukraine's Former President Sells TV Channels following Passage of 'Oligarch' Bill," *RFE/RL*, 9 November 2021, https://www.rferl.org/a/ukraine-poroshenko-sells-tv-channels/31552756.html
68. *Ukrayins'ka Pravda*, 8 November 2021, https://www.pravda.com.ua/news/2021/11/8/7313266
69. Anton Troianovski, "A Ukrainian Billionaire Fought Russia: Now He's Ready to Embrace It," *New York Times*, 13 November 2019, https://www.nytimes.com/2019/11/13/world/europe/ukraine-ihor-kolomoisky-russia.html
70. Andrew E. Kramer, "Oligarch's Return Raises Alarm in Ukraine," *New York Times*, 16 May 2019, https://www.nytimes.com/2019/05/16/world/europe/ukraine-zelensky-kolomoisky.html
71. "Ukraine's Supreme Court Postpones PrivatBank Hearing Citing Media Pressure," *RFE/RL*, 27 April 2020, https://www.rferl.org/a/ukraine-s-supreme-court-postpones-privatbank-hearing-citing-media-pressure/30579282.html
72. "Ukrainian President Fires Chief of Staff, Appoints Aide Who Met With Giuliani," *RFE/RL*, 11 February 2020, https://www.rferl.org/a/ukrainian-president-fires-chief-of-staff-appoints-aide-who-met-with-giuliani/30428584.html
73. "Ukraine Arrests Ex-PrivatBank Official as U.S. Prioritizes Criminal Probe of Former Owners," *RFE/RL*, 22 February 2021, https://www.rferl.org/a/ukraine-oligarchs-kolomoyskiy-boholyubov-us-case-suspended-forfeiture-criminal-investagion/31115946.html; Oleg Sukhov, "Former Kolomoisky Executive Charged with Theft in PrivatBank Case," *Kyiv Post*, 22 February 2021, https://www.kyivpost.com/ukraine-politics/former-kolomoisky-executive-charged-with-theft-in-privatbank-case.html?cn-reloaded=1
74. *Ukrayins'ka Pravda*, 31 March 2021, https://www.pravda.com.ua/news/2021/03/31/7288452
75. Taras Kuzio, tweet, 20 December 2021, https://twitter.com/TarasKuzio/status/1472989028614127626
76. Cnaan Liphshiz, "Zelensky Said to Strip 3 Jewish Oligarchs of Citizenship; All Hold Israeli Passports," *The Times of Israel*, 28 July 2022, https://www.timesofisrael.com/zelensky-reportedly-strips-3-jewish-oligarchs-of-ukrainian-citizenship/
77. "Ukraine's Former President Sells TV Channels following Passage of 'Oligarch' Bill," *RFE/RL*, 9 November 2021, https://www.rferl.org/a/ukraine-poroshenko-sells-tv-channels/31552756.html; *Ukrayins'ka Pravda*, 3 June 2021, https://www.pravda.com.ua/news/2021/06/3/7295923; *Ukrayins'ka Pravda*, 8 November 2021, https://www.pravda.com.ua/news/2021/11/8/7313266
78. Romanyuk, Kravets', and Topalov, "Probna bytva"; "Ukrainian President Signs

'Anti-Oligarch Law,'" *RFE/RL*, 5 November 2021, https://www.rferl.org/a/ukraine-zelenskiy-anti-oligarch-law/31548053.html

79. Todd Prince, "Trump Prodded Zelenskiy to Look Into Biden, Called Dismissed Ukraine Prosecutor 'Very Good,'" *RFE/RL*, 25 September 2019.
80. Ibid.
81. Ibid.
82. Jo Becker et al., "Why Giuliani Singled Out 2 Ukrainian Oligarchs to Help Look for Dirt," *New York Times*, 25 November 2019, https://www.nytimes.com/2019/11/25/us/giuliani-ukraine-oligarchs.html
83. Natasha Bertrand, "Decoding the Explosive Ukraine Text Messages," *Politico*, 4 October 2019, https://www.politico.com/news/2019/10/04/how-to-read-the-explosive-ukraine-texts-028139
84. "Read the Transcript of Trump's Conversation with Volodymyr Zelensky," *CNN*, 26 September 2019, https://www.cnn.com/2019/09/25/politics/donald-trump-ukraine-transcript-call
85. Todd Prince, "Trump Prodded Zelenskiy to Look Into Biden, Called Dismissed Ukraine Prosecutor 'Very Good,'" *RFE/RL*, 25 September 2019.
86. Olga Onuch and Orysiya Lutsevych, "Iran Shot down a Ukrainian Plane: How Did Ukraine Respond?," *Washington Post*, 17 January 2020, https://www.washingtonpost.com/politics/2020/01/17/iran-shot-down-ukrainian-plane-how-did-ukraine-respond
87. Office of the President of Ukraine, "Address by the President of Ukraine on the situation with the UIA plane shot down in Tehran," Official Website of the President of Ukraine, 11 January 2020, https://www.president.gov.ua/news/zvernennya-prezidenta-ukrayini-shodo-situaciyi-zi-zbittyam-l-59253
88. Cynthia J. Buckley, Ralph S. Clem, and Erik. S. Herron, "The COVID-19 Pandemic and State Healthcare Capacity: Government Responses and Citizen Assessments in Estonia, Georgia, and Ukraine," *Problems of Post-Communism* 69, no. 1 (2022): 14–25.
89. Katya Gorchinskaya, "Some Citizens Chafe, Businesses Push Back as COVID-19 Lockdown Lengthens in Ukraine," *RFE/RL*, 30 April 2020, https://www.rferl.org/a/ukrainians-chafe-businesses-push-back-as-covid-19-lockdown-lengthens/30585399.html
90. "Ukraine's Zelenskiy Cancels Meetings after Wife Tests Positive for Coronavirus," *RFE/RL*, 12 June 2020, https://www.rferl.org/a/ukraine-zelenskiy-wife-coronavirus/30667991.html
91. Olga Onuch et al., "MOBILISE 2021: Ukrainian Nationally Representative Survey Wave Two; Version 2 (with Oversample, N=1640)," February 2021; Onuch et al., "MOBILISE 2022: Ukrainian Nationally Representative Survey Wave Three; Version 2 (with Oversample, N=1218)," 16 February 2022.
92. "No Sputnik Shot for Ukraine as Kyiv Bans Registration of COVID Vaccines

from 'Aggressor States,'" *RFE/RL*, 11 February 2021, https://www.rferl.org/a/ukraine-covid-sptnik-vaccine-banned-aggressor-states-zelenskiy/31097774.html

93. *Ukrayins'ka Pravda*, 2 March 2021, https://www.pravda.com.ua/news/2021/03/3/7285341
94. *Ukrayins'ka Pravda*, 29 June 2020, https://www.pravda.com.ua/news/2020/06/29/7257530. And directly from: "National Survey of Ukrainians OMNIBUS," KIIS, June 2020.
95. This analysis reflects an econometric analysis regressing a binary variable capturing the self-reported intention to vote for Zelensky on age, sex, community size, education, nationality, language preference, macroregion, and a series of control variables for time-related factors, using a standard 95-percent confidence threshold for determining statistical significance. The data include 21,957 respondents from 12 KIIS omnibus surveys from February 2020 through February 2022.

7. THE ZELENSKY EFFECT AT WAR

1. Office of President of Ukraine, "The More Russia Uses Terror against Ukraine, the Worse the Consequences Will Be for It: Address by President Volodymyr Zelenskyy."
2. Office of President of Ukraine, "Every Day of Resistance Creates Better Conditions for Ukraine in the Negotiations to Guarantee Our Future in Peace: Address by President Volodymyr Zelenskyy," Official Website of the President of Ukraine, 7 March 2022, https://www.president.gov.ua/en/news/kozhen-den-sprotivu-stvoryuye-dlya-ukrayini-krashi-umovi-na-73417
3. "'It Seems to Be ...,' Final Song, Evening Quarter, 19 April 2014, https://www.youtube.com/watch?v=p_z2qqFyb1g; "'I Love My Motherland,' Evening Quarter in Jurmala 2016," https://www.youtube.com/watch?v=1xnqHS9h_PM
4. Interview with Gumenyuk.
5. Roger B. Myerson and Robert J. Weber, "A Theory of Voting Equilibria," *American Political Science Review* 87, no. 1 (1993): 102–14; Thomas Romer and Howard Rosenthal, "The Elusive Median Voter," *Journal of Public Economics* 12, no. 2 (1979): 143–70; Randall G. Holcombe, "The Median Voter Model in Public Choice Theory," *Public Choice* 61, no. 2 (1989): 115–25.
6. Hale, *Patronal Politics*; Guillermo O'Donnell, "On the State, Democratization, and Some Conceptual Problems: A Latin American View with Some Glances at Postcommunist Countries," *World Development* 21, no. 8 (August 1993): 1355–69.
7. "The country of strong people—the final song. New Evening Quarter 2017,"

Studio Kvratal 95 Online, 28 October 2017, https://www.youtube.com/watch?v=tT1yJhCCSwM

8. Nick Reynolds and Jack Watling, "Ukraine through Russia's Eyes," *RUSI commentary*, 25 February 2022, https://rusi.org/explore-our-research/publications/commentary/ukraine-through-russias-eyes
9. Volodymyr Kulyk and Henry E Hale, "Imperfect Measures of Dynamic Identities: The Changing Impact of Ethnolinguistic Characteristics on Political Attitudes in Ukraine," *Nations and Nationalism* 28, no. 3 (2022): 841–60.
10. Oleksandra Keudel, *How Patronal Networks Shape Opportunities for Local Citizen Participation in a Hybrid Regime: A Comparative Analysis of Five Cities in Ukraine* (Stuttgart: ibidem Press, 2022).
11. Olga Onuch, "Rallying around Democracy in Times of Crisis: The Puzzling Case of Ukrainian Democrats on the Rise," *Journal of Democracy* (forthcoming).
12. Olga Onuch and Javier Pérez Sandoval, "A Majority of Ukrainians Support Joining NATO: Does This Matter?," *Washington Post*, 4 February 2022, https://www.washingtonpost.com/politics/2022/02/04/majority-ukrainians-support-joining-nato-does-this-matter
13. *24 Kanal*, 26 May 2022, 19:32, https://24tv.ua/ru/my-gotovilis-k-vojne-s-fevralja-2021-goda-danilov_n1989140
14. Vladimir Putin, "On the Historical Unity of Russians and Ukrainians," President of Russia, 12 July 2021, http://en.kremlin.ru/events/president/news/66181
15. James Marson, "Putin to the West: Hands off Ukraine," *Time*, 25 May 2009, http://content.time.com/time/world/article/0,8599,1900838,00.html
16. Mikhail A. Alexseev and Henry E. Hale, "Russians See Ukraine as an Illegitimate State," *Washington Post*, 20 May 2015, http://www.washingtonpost.com/blogs/monkey-cage/wp/2015/05/20/russians-see-ukraine-as-an-illegitimate-state
17. Putin, "On the Historical Unity of Russians and Ukrainians."
18. Dmitrii Medvedev, "Pochemu bessmysleny kontakty s nyneshnym Ukrainskym rukovodstvom," *Kommersant*, 11 October 2021, https://www.kommersant.ru/doc/5028300
19. "Ukraine–Russia Conflict: Zelensky Alleges Coup Plan Involving Russians," *BBC News*, 26 November 2021, https://www.bbc.co.uk/news/world-europe-59428712
20. David L. Stern and Robyn Dixon, "Ukraine's Zelensky's Message Is Don't Panic: That's Making the West Antsy," *Washington Post*, 30 January 2022, https://www.washingtonpost.com/world/2022/01/30/ukraine-zelensky-russia-biden
21. Shane Harris et al., "Road to War."
22. *24 Kanal*, 26 May 2022, https://24tv.ua/ru/my-gotovilis-k-vojne-s-fevralja-2021-goda-danilov_n1989140.
23. Stern and Dixon, "Ukraine's Zelensky's Message."

24. Ellen Nakashima et al., "U.S. Intelligence Shows Russia's Military Pullback Was a Ruse, Officials Say," *Washington Post*, 17 February 2022, https://www.washingtonpost.com/world/2022/02/17/ukraine-russia-putin-nato-munich; Ministry of Defence, "INTELLIGENCE UPDATE: Russia Retains a Significant Military Presence That Can Conduct an Invasion without Further Warning; Below Demonstrates President Putin's Possible Axis of Invasion; He Still Can Choose to Prevent Conflict and Preserve Peace," Twitter, @defencehq, 17 February 2022, https://twitter.com/defencehq/status/1494315294382297091; Ministry of Defence "INTELLIGENCE UPDATE: We Have Seen No Evidence That Russian Forces Are Withdrawing from Ukrainian Border Regions. Russia Retains a Significant Military Presence That Can Conduct an Invasion without Further Warning," Twitter, @defencehq, 17 February 2022, https://twitter.com/defencehq/status/1494344646864031758
25. Alexander Ward and Quint Forgey, "Putin Could Attack Ukraine on Feb. 16, Biden Told Allies," *Politico*, 11 February 2022, https://www.politico.com/newsletters/national-security-daily/2022/02/11/putin-could-attack-ukraine-on-feb-16-biden-told-allies-00008344
26. "Address of the President of Ukraine on the Unity of Ukrainian Society," Official Website of the President of Ukraine, 14 February 2022, https://www.president.gov.ua/en/news/zvernennya-prezidenta-ukrayini-shodo-yednosti-ukrayinskogo-s-72893
27. "Volodymyr Zelenskyi on Instagram: 'We Are Together; We're Home; We Are in Ukraine," Instagram, @Zelenskiy_official, 14 February 2022, https://www.instagram.com/p/CZ-D_xKghp8
28. Shaun Walker, "Putin's Absurd, Angry Spectacle Will Be a Turning Point in His Long Reign," *The Guardian*, 21 February 2022, https://www.theguardian.com/world/2022/feb/21/putin-angry-spectacle-amounts-to-declaration-war-ukraine
29. "Putin Comment on 'Taking Kiev in 2 Weeks' Twisted, Aide Says," *Moscow Times*, 2 September 2014, http://www.themoscowtimes.com/news/article/putin-comment-on-taking-kiev-in-2-weeks-misinterpreted-aide-says/506271.html
30. Office of the President of Ukraine, "Address by the President of Ukraine," Official website of the President of Ukraine, 24 February 2022, https://www.president.gov.ua/en/news/zvernennya-prezidenta-ukrayini-73137
31. Interview with Gumenyuk.
32. Kessler, "Zelensky's Famous Quote of 'Need Ammo, Not a Ride' Not Easily Confirmed."
33. See @Zelenskiy_official post: https://www.instagram.com/p/CaaFzibgLES/?hl=en
34. For an example, see this December 2020 post: https://www.instagram.com/p/

CI83iWUFvBw/?hl=en. Or this April 2020 post about the country's fight with COVID-19: https://www.instagram.com/p/B_fTqbsFJLo/?hl=en

35. For a particularly Hollywood-style production, see his New Year's video from 2020, @Zelenskiy_official post: https://www.instagram.com/p/CJeK0n9FNgH/?hl=en
36. See @Zelenskiy_official post: https://www.instagram.com/p/CaXKn-0AGpG/?hl=en
37. See @Zelenskiy_official post: https://www.instagram.com/p/Cdu2hTPF9KQ/?hl=en
38. See @Zelenskiy_official post: https://www.instagram.com/stories/zelenskiy_official/2892549492153713296/?hl=en
39. See @Zelenskiy_official post: https://www.instagram.com/p/Cgh4Kc4jXKS/?hl=en
40. See @Zelenskiy_official post: https://www.instagram.com/p/CfYMQsVllI6/?hl=en
41. See this series of @Zelenskiy_official posts on one such visit: https://www.instagram.com/p/CDi_zr7FOCB/?hl=en; https://www.instagram.com/p/CDjLxE0FDRp/?hl=en; and https://www.instagram.com/p/CDjlaptlscc/?hl=en
42. See @Zelenskiy_official post: https://www.instagram.com/p/CbdmZAugPSw/?hl=en
43. Rudenko, *Zelensky*, also makes a "new Zelensky" argument
44. See @Zelenskiy_official post: https://www.instagram.com/p/CaWbyZLATKY/?hl=en
45. One such example was: Stephen Collinson and Maeve Reston, "'I need you': Biden asks Americans to do their part to help country emerge from Covid crisis," *CNN.com*, 12 March 2021, https://www.cnn.com/2021/03/12/politics/joe-biden-primetime-speech-covid-vaccine-may/index.html
46. Tayisiya Chernyshova, "Politychnyy dyskurs presydenta Ukrayiny Volodymyra Zelens'koho: Stratehiyi & taktyky movlennyevoho vplyvu (na materiali vystupiv pershoho roku prezydentstva," *Problemy humanitarnykh nauk: Zbirnyk naukovykh prats': Seriya "Filolohiya"* 46 (2021), pp. 147–156.
47. "Address of the President of Ukraine on Strengthening the State's Defense Capability," Official Website of the President of Ukraine, 24 February 2022, https://www.president.gov.ua/videos/zvernennya-prezidenta-ukrayini-pro-posilennya-oboronozdatnos-2013
48. Lyubchenko et al., "Political Communication in the Post-Truth Era."
49. See @Zelenskiy_official post: https://www.instagram.com/p/CaY9xmVg20_
50. See @Zelenskiy_official post: https://www.instagram.com/tv/Caaowxeg8Sn
51. Cindy D. Kam and Jennifer M. Ramos, "Joining and Leaving the Rally: Understanding the Surge and Decline in Presidential Approval following 9/11," *Public Opinion Quarterly* 72, no. 4 (2008): 619–50.

52. Marc J. Hetherington and Michael Nelson, "Anatomy of a Rally Effect: George W. Bush and the War on Terrorism," *PS: Political Science and Politics* 36, no. 1 (2003): 37–42.
53. John E. Mueller, *War, Presidents and Public Opinion* (New York: John Wiley & Sons, 1973); Henri Tajfel, *Human Groups and Social Categories* (Cambridge: Cambridge University Press, 1981).
54. William D. Baker and John R. Oneal, "Patriotism or Opinion Leadership? The Nature and Origins of the 'Rally 'Round the Flag' Effect," *Journal of Conflict Resolution* 45, no. 5 (2001): 661–87; Adam J. Berinsky, *In Time of War: Understanding American Public Opinion from World War II to Iraq* (Chicago: University of Chicago Press, 2009); Richard A. Brody and Catherine R. Shapiro, "The Rally Phenomenon in Public Opinion," in *Assessing the President: The Media, Elite Opinion, and Public Support*, ed. Richard A. Brody (Stanford: Stanford University Press, 1991), 45–77.
55. See also Kulyk and Hale, "Imperfect Measures of Dynamic Identities"; Oxana Shevel, "Nationality in Ukraine: Some Rules of Engagement," *East European Politics and Societies* 16, no. 2 (1 May 2002): 386–413.
56. That is, they are statistically significant at the 95 percent level or more.
57. Hale and Kulyk, "Aspirational Identity Politics and Support for Radical Reform."
58. For one thing, most of the displaced abroad are not adults but minors. In addition, displacement is relatively even nationwide, not coming disproportionately from southeastern regions. In our July 2022 survey, the agency we worked with (KIIS) was unable to interview people living in temporarily occupied territories. For these and other figures presented in this book, we use weights KIIS constructed for us to standardize the data over time.
59. Henry E. Hale, "Authoritarian Rallying as Reputational Cascade? Evidence from Putin's Popularity Surge after Crimea," *American Political Science Review* 116, no. 2 (2021): 1–15.
60. Greene and Robertson, *Putin v. the People*; Gulnaz Sharafutdinova, *The Red Mirror: Putin's Leadership and Russia's Insecure Identity* (Oxford: Oxford University Press, 2020).
61. For readers interested in technical details, checks include considering the possibility of floor effects (minimal, since under 8 percent of respondents in the control group reported approving of 0 figures) and including a placebo experiment using the footballer Oleksandr Zinchenko in place of Zelensky.
62. Marta Dyczok and Yerin Chung, "Zelens′kyi uses his communication skills as a weapon of war," *Canadian Slavonic Papers* (2022): 1–16, https://www.tandfonline.com/doi/full/10.1080/00085006.2022.2106699
63. Using the Twitter API on 14 July 2022.
64. The maximum raw number of tweets issued on any given day during this period is 37.

65. The maximum average number of retweets per tweet was 18,298 and the maximum average number of likes per tweet was 159,722.
66. Google Trends: "Interest over time: Numbers represent search interest relative to the highest point on the chart for the given region and time. A value of 100 is the peak popularity for the term. A value of 50 means that the term is half as popular. A score of 0 means there was not enough data for this term." See https://trends.google.com/trends/explore?q=zelensky&geo=CA

8. UKRAINE'S FUTURE HISTORY

1. Office of President of Ukraine, "Address by the President: Ukrainians Are a Symbol of Invincibility," Official Website of the President of Ukraine, 2 March 2022, https://www.president.gov.ua/en/news/zvernennya-prezidenta-ukrayinci-simvol-nezlamnosti-73281
2. Office of President of Ukraine, "They Wanted to Destroy Ukraine so Many Times, but Failed: Address by President Volodymyr Zelenskyy," Official Website of the President of Ukraine, 3 March 2022, https://www.president.gov.ua/en/news/ukrayinu-stilki-raziv-hotili-znishiti-ale-ne-zmogli-zvernenn-73297
3. Office of President of Ukraine, "We Have Survived the Night That Could Have Stopped the History of Ukraine and Europe: Address by President Volodymyr Zelenskyy," Official Website of the President of Ukraine, March 2022, https://www.president.gov.ua/en/news/mi-perezhili-nich-yaka-mogla-zupiniti-istoriyu-ukrayini-ta-y-73337
4. Benedict Anderson, *Imagined Communities: Reflections on the Origin and Spread of Nationalism* (London: Verso, 1983); Hale, *The Foundations of Ethnic Politics*; Anthony D. Smith, *The Nation in History: Historiographical Debates about Ethnicity and Nationalism* (Hanover, NH: Brandeis/Historical Society of Israel, 2000).
5. Keith Darden, *Resisting Occupation: Mass Literacy and the Creation of Durable National Loyalties* (New York: Cambridge University Press, forthcoming); Darden and Grzymala-Busse, "The Great Divide"; Ernest Gellner, *Nations and Nationalism* (Ithaca, NY: Cornell University Press, 1983).
6. Anderson, *Imagined Communities.*
7. "'It seems like...', the final song, Evening Quarter 19. 04. 2014".
8. "Country of strong people, final song, New Evening Quarter 2017," Studio Kvartal 95 Online, YouTube, 2017, https://www.youtube.com/watch?v=tT1yJhCCSwM
9. Ibid.
10. Mikhail Alexseev and Serhiy Dembitskyi, "Ukrainians Believe They'll Win the War, a Survey Finds," *Washington Post*, 15 August 2022, https://www.washingtonpost.com/politics/2022/08/15/ukraine-survey-war-democracy-resilience

11. "'It seems like...', the final song, Evening Quarter 19. 04. 2014".
12. Olexiy Haran, presentation at PONARS Eurasia's Ukrainathon, 16–17 March 2022, video recording available at https://www.youtube.com/watch?v=e6knLvTnVsg&t=7825s
13. Liz Sly, "Zelensky faces outpouring of criticism over failure to warn of war," *Washington Post*, 19 August 2022, https://www.washingtonpost.com/world/2022/08/18/zelensky-ukraine-wapo-interview-warn-of-war/
14. The reference to "ethnocultural identity" here is to the 21 percent our July 2022 survey finds do not identify with the Ukrainian language as their native tongue, an identification that Kulyk has long shown reflects identity more than actual language use. Kulyk, "Language Identity, Linguistic Diversity and Political Cleavages." The conclusions reported here regarding subpopulations most critical of Zelensky come from an OLS econometric analysis regressing a binary variable capturing the intent to vote for Zelensky on variables for age, sex, region, Ukrainian nationality, Ukrainian-language preference, Ukrainian-language use in private life, higher education, rural residence, and poverty.
15. Hordon, "Zelens'kyy."
16. Fisun, *Demokratiya, neopatrimonializm i global'nye transformatsii*; Magyar and Madlovics, *The Anatomy of Post-Communist Regimes*; Way, *Pluralism by Default.*
17. Henry E. Hale, "Regime Cycles: Democracy, Autocracy, and Revolution in Post-Soviet Eurasia," *World Politics* 58, no. 1 (2005): 133–65; Hale, "Formal Constitutions in Informal Politics"; Hale, *Patronal Politics.*
18. Hordon, "Zelens'kyy."
19. Harris Mylonas, *The Politics of Nation-Building: Making Co-Nationals, Refugees, and Minorities* (Cambridge: Cambridge University Press, 2012).
20. Alexseev and Dembitskyi, "Ukrainians Believe They'll Win the War, a Survey Finds."
21. Barrowman, "The Reformer's Dilemmas."
22. Hale, *Patronal Politics.*

APPENDIX OF FIGURES

1. Onuch et al., "MOBILISE 2022: Ukrainian Nationally Representative Survey Wave Three; Version 2 (with Oversample, N=1218)"; Onuch et al., "MOBILISE 2019: Ukrainian Nationally Representative Survey Wave One; Version 2 (with Oversample, N=2000)," April 2019; Onuch et al., "MOBILISE 2020: Argentine Nationally Representative Survey Wave One: (Version 2 (with Oversample, N=2000))," 30 March 2020; IBIF Ukraine, "April 2020 Survey," Identity and Borders in Flux: The Case of Ukraine (blog), 30 April 2020, https://ibifukraine.com/2020/04/30/april-2020-survey

2. "Corruption Perceptions Index: 1998–2021," Transparency International, 2021, https://www.transparency.org/en/cpi/2021
3. Olga Onuch et al., "MOBILISE 2021: Ukrainian Nationally Representative Survey Wave Two; Version 2 (with Oversample, N=1640)," February 2021; Onuch et al., "MOBILISE 2022: Ukrainian Nationally Representative Survey Wave Three; Version 2 (with Oversample, N=1218)"; Onuch et al., "MOBILISE 2022: Ukrainian Nationally Representative Survey, KIIS OMNIBUS May; (N=2009)."
4. Onuch et al., "MOBILISE 2019: Ukrainian Nationally Representative Survey Wave One; Version 2 (with Oversample, N=2000)"; Onuch et al., "MOBILISE 2021: Ukrainian Nationally Representative Survey Wave Two; Version 2 (with Oversample, N=1640)"; Onuch et al., "MOBILISE 2022: Ukrainian Nationally Representative Survey Wave Three; Version 2 (with Oversample, N=1218)"; Onuch et al., "MOBILISE 2022: Ukrainian Nationally Representative Survey, KIIS OMNIBUS May; (N=2009)."
5. Leonid Kravchuk, "Speech of President Kravchuk during the Inauguration Ceremony," 5 December 1991, tinyurl.com/bdcrn4sc
6. "Inflation, Consumer Prices (Annual %)," World Bank, 2022, https://data.worldbank.org/indicator/FP.CPI.TOTL.ZG?locations=UA
7. "Adults (Ages 15–49) Newly Infected with HIV," World Bank, 2022, https://data.worldbank.org/indicator/SH.HIV.INCD
8. "Unemployment, Total (% of Total Labor Force) (Modeled ILO Estimate)," World Bank, 2022, https://data.worldbank.org/indicator/SL.UEM.TOTL.ZS?locations=UA
9. "Population, Total: Ukraine," World Bank.
10. "GDP per Capita (Current US$)," World Bank, 2022, https://data.worldbank.org/indicator/NY.GDP.PCAP.CD?end=2021&locations=UA&start=1987&view=chart
11. "Kryvyi Rih Population 2022 (Demographics, Maps, Graphs)," World Population Review.
12. Ibid.
13. "All-Ukrainian Population Census," State Statistics Committee of Ukraine, 2001, http://2001.ukrcensus.gov.ua/eng/results
14. "Presidential Election Reports, 1991–2014," Central Election Commission.
15. "All-Ukrainian Population Census," State Statistics Committee of Ukraine; "Presidential Election Reports, 1991–2014," Central Election Commission.
16. "Presidential Election Reports, 1991–2014," Central Election Commission.
17. Sushko and Prystayko, "Nations in Transit 2013: Ukraine"; Freedom House, "Ukraine in 2011: Freedom House Report."
18. Marshall, Gurr, and Jaggers, "Polity IV Project."
19. Coppedge et al., "V-Dem Dataset V10."

20. Transparency International, "Corruption Perceptions Index: 1998–2021."
21. World Bank, "GDP per Capita (Current US$): Ukraine."
22. World Bank, "Poverty Headcount Ratio at $1.90 a Day (2011 PPP) (% of Population)."
23. World Bank, "Unemployment, Total (% of Total Labor Force) (Modeled ILO Estimate)."
24. World Bank, "Inflation, Consumer Prices (Annual %)."
25. World Bank, "Population, Total: Ukraine."
26. World Bank, "Personal Remittances, Received (% of GDP)."
27. Central Election Commission, "Presidential Election Reports, 1991–2014."
28. Television Industry Committee (TIC), "CHASTKY TOP KANALIV: 2003–2013 (Television Audience Research)."
29. Central Election Commission, "Presidential Election Reports, 1991–2014," Kyiv, Ukraine, 2014, http://www.cvk.gov.ua
30. World Bank, "Unemployment, Total (% of Total Labor Force) (Modeled ILO Estimate): Ukraine," 2022, https://data.worldbank.org/indicator/SL.UEM.TOTL.ZS?locations=UA
31. World Bank, "Population, Total: Ukraine," 2022, https://data.worldbank.org/indicator/SP.POP.TOTL?locations=UA
32. World Bank, "Personal Remittances, Received (% of GDP): Ukraine," 2022, https://data.worldbank.org/indicator/BX.TRF.PWKR.DT.GD.ZS?locations=UA
33. World Bank, "Proportion of People Living below 50 Percent of Median Income (%): Ukraine," 2022, https://data.worldbank.org/indicator/SI.DST.50MD?locations=UA
34. Transparency International, "Corruption Perceptions Index. 1998–2021," Transparency.org, 2021, https://www.transparency.org/en/cpi/2021
35. Rating Group, "Political Opinion Poll of Ukrainian Voters: 2014–2018," 2018.
36. "Presidential Elections of Ukraine 2019," Central Election Commission of Ukraine, April 2019, https://www.cvk.gov.ua/vibory_category/vibori-prezidenta-ukraini-2.html
37. "Presidential Elections of Ukraine 2019," Central Election Commission of Ukraine, April 2019, https://www.cvk.gov.ua/vibory_category/vibori-prezidenta-ukraini-2.html
38. Henry Hale et al., "Ukrainian Crisis Election Panel Survey (UCEPS)," 2014; Olga Onuch et al., "MOBILISE 2019: Ukrainian Nationally Representative Survey Wave One; (Version 1 (without Oversample, N=1600))," April 2019; Onuch et al., "MOBILISE 2021: Ukrainian Nationally Representative Survey Wave Two; Version 2 (with Oversample, N=1640)," February 2021; Onuch et al., "MOBILISE 2022: Ukrainian Nationally Representative Survey Wave Three; Version 2 (with Oversample, N=1218)," 16 February 2022; Onuch et al.,

"MOBILISE 2022: Ukrainian Nationally Representative Survey, KIIS OMNIBUS May; (N=2009)," 24 May 2022; Onuch et al., "MOBILISE 2022: Ukrainian Nationally Representative Survey, KIIS OMNIBUS July (N=2000)," 6 July 2022; IBIF Ukraine, "April 2020 Survey," Identity and Borders in Flux: The Case of Ukraine, 30 April 2020, https://ibifukraine.com/2020/04/30/april-2020-survey

39. Onuch et al., "MOBILISE 2021: Ukrainian Nationally Representative Survey Wave Two; Version 2 (with Oversample, N=1640)"; Onuch et al., "MOBILISE 2022: Ukrainian Nationally Representative Survey Wave Three; Version 2 (with Oversample, N=1218)"; Onuch et al., "MOBILISE 2022: Ukrainian Nationally Representative Survey, KIIS OMNIBUS May: (N=2009)"; Onuch et al., "MOBILISE 2022: Ukrainian Nationally Representative Survey, KIIS OMNIBUS July (N=2000)."
40. Onuch et al., "MOBILISE 2022: Ukrainian Nationally Representative Survey, KIIS OMNIBUS May; (N=2009)"; Onuch et al., "MOBILISE 2022: Ukrainian Nationally Representative Survey, KIIS OMNIBUS July (N=2000)"; Onuch et al., "MOBILISE 2019: Ukrainian Nationally Representative Survey Wave One; (Version 1 (without Oversample, N=1600))"; Onuch et al., "MOBILISE 2021: Ukrainian Nationally Representative Survey Wave Two; Version 2 (with Oversample, N=1640)"; Onuch et al., "MOBILISE 2022: Ukrainian Nationally Representative Survey Wave Three; Version 2 (with Oversample, N=1218)."
41. Onuch et al., "MOBILISE 2019: Ukrainian Nationally Representative Survey Wave One; (Version 1 (without Oversample, N=1600))"; Onuch et al., "MOBILISE 2021: Ukrainian Nationally Representative Survey Wave Two; Version 2 (with Oversample, N=1640)"; Onuch et al., "MOBILISE 2022: Ukrainian Nationally Representative Survey Wave Three; Version 2 (with Oversample, N=1218)."
42. Ibid.
43. Vladimir Putin, "Address by the President of the Russian Federation," 21 February 2022, http://en.kremlin.ru/events/president/news/67828; Putin, "Transcript: Vladimir Putin's Televised Address on Ukraine," *Bloomberg*, 24 February 2022, https://www.bloomberg.com/news/articles/2022–02–24/full-transcript-vladimir-putin-s-televised-address-to-russia-on-ukraine-feb-24
44. Onuch et al., "MOBILISE 2022: Ukrainian Nationally Representative Survey, KIIS OMNIBUS July (N=2000)"; Onuch et al., "MOBILISE 2022: Ukrainian Nationally Representative Survey, KIIS OMNIBUS May; (N=2009)"; Onuch et al., "MOBILISE 2022: Ukrainian Nationally Representative Survey Wave Three; Version 2 (with Oversample, N=1218)."
45. Onuch et al., "MOBILISE 2019: Ukrainian Nationally Representative Survey Wave One; (Version 1 (without Oversample, N=1600))"; Onuch et al., "MOBILISE 2022: Ukrainian Nationally Representative Survey Wave Three.

Version 2 (with Oversample, N=1218)"; Onuch et al., "MOBILISE 2022: Ukrainian Nationally Representative Survey, KIIS OMNIBUS May; (N=2009)"; Onuch et al., "MOBILISE 2022: Ukrainian Nationally Representative Survey, KIIS OMNIBUS July (N=2000)"; Onuch et al., "MOBILISE 2021: Ukrainian Nationally Representative Survey Wave Two; Version 2 (with Oversample, N=1640)."

46. Olga Onuch and Henry E. Hale, "Capturing Ethnicity: The Case of Ukraine," *Post-Soviet Affairs* 34, no. 2–3 (2018).
47. Onuch et al., "MOBILISE 2022: Ukrainian Nationally Representative Survey, KIIS OMNIBUS July (N=2000)."
48. Onuch et al., "MOBILISE 2019: Ukrainian Nationally Representative Survey Wave One; (Version 1 (without Oversample, N=1600))"; Onuch et al., "MOBILISE 2022: Ukrainian Nationally Representative Survey Wave Three; Version 2 (with Oversample, N=1218)"; Onuch et al., "MOBILISE 2022: Ukrainian Nationally Representative Survey, KIIS OMNIBUS May; (N=2009)"; Onuch et al., "MOBILISE 2022: Ukrainian Nationally Representative Survey, KIIS OMNIBUS July (N=2000)"; Onuch et al., "MOBILISE 2021: Ukrainian Nationally Representative Survey Wave Two; Version 2 (with Oversample, N=1640)."
49. Onuch et al., "MOBILISE 2022: Ukrainian Nationally Representative Survey, KIIS OMNIBUS May; (N=2009)"; Onuch et al., "MOBILISE 2022: Ukrainian Nationally Representative Survey, KIIS OMNIBUS July (N=2000)."
50. Onuch et al., "MOBILISE 2022: Ukrainian Nationally Representative Survey, KIIS OMNIBUS May; (N=2009)."
51. Onuch et al., "MOBILISE 2022: Ukrainian Nationally Representative Survey, KIIS OMNIBUS July (N=2000)."
52. Onuch et al., "MOBILISE 2022: Ukrainian Nationally Representative Survey, KIIS OMNIBUS May; (N=2009)"; Onuch et al., "MOBILISE 2022: Ukrainian Nationally Representative Survey, KIIS OMNIBUS July (N=2000)."
53. Olga Onuch et al., "MOBILISE 2022: Ukrainian Nationally Representative Survey, KIIS OMNIBUS May. (N=2009)," 24 May 2022; Onuch et al., "MOBILISE 2022: Ukrainian Nationally Representative Survey, KIIS OMNIBUS July (N=2000)," 6 July 2022.
54. Onuch et al., "MOBILISE 2022: Ukrainian Nationally Representative Survey, KIIS OMNIBUS May; (N=2009)"; Onuch et al., "MOBILISE 2022: Ukrainian Nationally Representative Survey, KIIS OMNIBUS July (N=2000)."
55. Olga Onuch et al., "MOBILISE 2022: Ukrainian Nationally Representative Survey, KIIS OMNIBUS May; (N=2009)," 24 May 2022; Onuch et al., "MOBILISE 2022: Ukrainian Nationally Representative Survey, KIIS OMNIBUS July (N=2000)," 6 July 2022.
56. Olga Onuch et al., "MOBILISE 2022: Ukrainian Nationally Representative

Survey, KIIS OMNIBUS May; (N=2009)," 24 May 2022; Onuch et al., "MOBILISE 2022: Ukrainian Nationally Representative Survey, KIIS OMNIBUS July (N=2000)," 6 July 2022.

INDEX

INDEX

INDEX

INDEX

INDEX

INDEX

INDEX